RACE AND AMERICAN CULTURE
Arnold Rampersad and Shelley Fisher Fishkin
General Editors

The New Red Negro

The LITERARY LEFT *and*
AFRICAN AMERICAN POETRY, 1930–1946

James Edward Smethurst

NEW YORK   OXFORD

OXFORD UNIVERSITY PRESS

1999

Oxford University Press

Oxford   New York
Athens   Auckland   Bangkok   Bogotá   Buenos Aires   Calcutta
Cape Town   Chennai   Dar es Salaam   Delhi   Florence   Hong Kong   Istanbul
Karachi   Kuala Lumpur   Madrid   Melbourne   Mexico City   Mumbai
Nairobi   Paris   São Paulo   Singapore   Taipei   Tokyo   Toronto   Warsaw

and associated companies in
Berlin   Ibadan

Published by Oxford University Press, Inc.
198 Madison Avenue, New York, New York 10016

Oxford is a registered trademark of Oxford University Press

Library of Congress Cataloging-in-Publication Data
Smethurst, James Edward.
    The new red Negro : the literary left and African American poetry,
  1930–1946 / James Edward Smethurst.
        p. cm. — (Race and American culture)
    Includes bibliographical references and index.
    ISBN 0-19-512054-X
      1. American poetry—Afro-American authors—History and criticism.
  2. Communism and literature—United States—History—20th century.
  3. American poetry—20th century—History and criticism.
  4. Political poetry, American—History and criticism.   5. Left and
  right (Political science) in literature.   6. Afro-Americans—
  Intellectual life—20th century.   7. Afro-Americans—Politics and
  government.   8. Afro-Americans in literature.   9. Race relations in
  literature.   10. United States—Race relations.   I. Title.
  II. Series.
  PS310.N4S64 1998
  811'.5209896073—dc21   98-17128

9 8 7 6 5 4 3 2 1

Printed in the United States of America
on acid-free paper

Permissions

for Edward William Smethurst Jr.
and Ludlow Bixby Smethurst,
and in memory of
Edward William Smethurst Sr.,
who took me to see Shakespeare

Acknowledgments

Many people have supported, influenced, and generally made possible this project. As usual, all shortcomings are strictly my own and should not be attributed in any way to the people listed here.

I am grateful to those scholars at Harvard, visiting and resident, who gave me a broad view of American literature and culture and "ethnic studies," especially Dwight Andrews, Sacvan Bercovitch, Juan Bruce-Novoa, King-Kok Cheung, Laurence de Looze, Henry Louis Gates Jr., Maryemma Graham, Phillip Brian Harper, the late Nathan Huggins, Walter Jackson, Meredith McGill, and Jeffrey Melnick.

I am also indebted to many scholars outside Harvard who have encouraged me, read drafts of my work, shared panels with me, commented on conference papers, shared their own work, and provided invaluable material and / or advice for my project. I am most grateful to Kenneth Rosen of the University of Southern Maine and James De Jongh of CUNY who in various ways inspired the direction my work has taken. Among the many other scholars to whom I owe thanks are Byrne Fone, John Gennari, Cheryl Greenberg, Leo Hamalian, Matthew Jacobson, Robin Kelley, Diana Linden, Bill Maxwell, William McFeeley, Jim Miller, Bill Mullen, Richard Newman, Susan Pennybacker, Paula Rabinowitz, Mark Solomon, Patricia Sullivan, Michael Thurston, and Alan Wald (whose knowledge of literary radicalism is only surpassed by his generosity in sharing that knowledge).

Much gratitude is due to those friends with whom I have shared (and argued about) poetry, politics, food, music, and all the other things that make life worth living. Among those whose arguments I have particularly valued are the late Harold Buchman, Druanne Dillon, the late Edward Fielding, David Gilbert, Leon Jackson, Geoffrey Jacques, Elizabeth Nicklus, Scott Penney, Ann Rebeck, Pedro Rodriguez, the late Nancy Rubin, John Rummel, Carolyn Rummel, Scott Stevens, Douglas Stewart, Sam Webb, Sue Webb, and Cindy Weisbart.

Since so much of the work of this project was spent reading crumbling documents (or microform copies of crumbling documents), I would like to thank the staffs of the following libraries for making those documents available to me: the Boston Public Library; the Mugar Memorial Library at Boston University; the John Hay Library at Brown University; Hilles, Houghton, Lamont, Loeb Music, and Widener Libraries at Harvard University; the Moorland-Springarn Library at Howard University; the Main Research Division and the Schomburg Center for the Research of Black Culture of the New York Public Library; the Tamiment Institute at New York University; Schlesinger Library at Radcliffe College; the Reference Center for Marxist Studies; and Beineke, Mudd, Music, and Sterling Libraries at Yale University.

I also wish to thank T. Susan Chang and Susan Barba of Oxford University Press as well as the general editors of the Oxford Race and American Culture series, Shelley Fisher Fishkin and Arnold Rampersad. In addition, the two anonymous readers of my manuscript for Oxford made many useful and generous comments on my project.

As with many things in my life, this project would not have been possible without the help of Rachel Lee Rubin, most astute reader, critic, colleague, co-parent, friend (and possessor of an amazing collection of recorded music).

Since I have paid tribute to my friends whose support and arguments have sustained me for years, I also have to acknowledge my incredibly supportive and argumentative family: Andrew Smethurst, Alejandra Ramirez, Katherine Smethurst, Anthony Schlein, and my parents to whom this project is (in part) dedicated. I also wish to make special mention of Richard Smethurst and Mae Smethurst who have educated and encouraged me my whole life and who have provided me academic role models whose standards I can only hope to approach. And last, and most, I wish to thank my son and fellow nature enthusiast Jacob Rubin who has more than anyone kept me going through this project.

My debt of gratitude to Werner Sollors is impossible to detail. Suffice it to say that for me he has been the perfect mentor: informed, engaged, encouraging, and constructively critical—but willing to let me pursue my own course.

Finally, I have to thank Carol Forney for her practical, moral, and emotional support, including her amazing willingness and ability to constructively criticize many flawed drafts, that allowed me to finish this project.

Contents

The New Red Negro

Introduction

Of the Coming of the New Red Negro

Mob Voices: (snarling)
  Quick! Quick! Death there!
  The chair! The electric chair!

8th Boy:
  No chair!
  Too long have my hands been idle.
  Too long have my brains been dumb.
  Now out of the darkness
  The new Red Negro will come:
  That's me!

—LANGSTON HUGHES,
"SCOTTSBORO LIMITED"

The 1930s and 1940s saw the publication of significant works by such African-American poets as Gwendolyn Brooks, Sterling Brown, Countee Cullen, Waring Cuney, Frank Marshall Davis, Owen Dodson, Robert Hayden, Langston Hughes, Melvin Tolson, Margaret Walker, and Richard Wright. While some of these writers retain a relatively "minor" status within current assessments of African-American poetry, others, especially Brooks, Brown, Cullen, Hayden, and Hughes (and Wright for his fiction), figure prominently in virtually any survey of twentieth-century African-American literature. With the exception of Cullen, and to a certain extent Hughes, the poets listed above developed their mature style during the 1930s and 1940s. Even Hughes, who was certainly an accomplished artist before the 1930s, developed more fully the poetic stance rooted in popular urban African-American culture with which he is most frequently associated by both "popular" and "literary" audiences.

Yet African-American poetry of the 1930s and 1940s has received little serious and focused scholarly consideration as a whole. The few studies that do treat poetry by black authors during those decades do so only as part of a larger survey (as in the case of Eugene Redmond's *Drumvoices*) or as a coda to the study of an earlier period of literary production (as in Jean Wagner's *Black Poets of the United States*). There has been a comparative groundswell of autobiography, biography, and bio-criticism examining the life and/or work of individual poets from that era.[1] But with a few exceptions, such as Joanne Gabbin's *Sterling A. Brown: Building the Black Aesthetic Tradition*, these works are basically historical rather than critical. Those studies that focus on the works rather than the lives of the poets, such as Onwuchekwa Jemie's *Langston Hughes: An Introduction to the Poetry*, generally treat poets whose careers stretch before or beyond the 1930s and 1940s and give the 1930s scant attention. This lack of scholarship is even more striking when compared to the scholarly outpouring concerning African-American narrative—though it should be added that there is not even a provisionally satisfying general study of African-American fiction in the 1930s and 1940s. More important, as far as the study of poetry is concerned, the amount of criticism devoted to poetry written by black authors during the two decades preceding the 1930s is far greater than that considering the period from the onset of the Great Depression to the beginning of the cold war following World War II. However, as this study will attempt to demonstrate, this severe critical asymmetry, on the basis of either aesthetic worth or importance in terms of the development of later black literature (and American literature generally), is extremely problematic.

While African-American poetry of the 1930s and 1940s has been generally neglected by African Americanists, it has not fared any better in other accounts of various aspects of the literary culture of the United States during those decades. For example, Langston Hughes was, among other things, the belletristic author and translator published most frequently by *New Masses* during the first half of the 1930s. He was also president of a major Communist "mass" organization—The League of Struggle for Negro Rights—and a supporter of a huge number of Communist Party initiatives. Yet Hughes receives only two brief mentions in Daniel Aaron's groundbreaking *Writers on the Left*, which after thirty years remains the standard work on the subject of literature and the Left in the United States during the first half of the twentieth century. None of the other poets mentioned above fares even as well as Hughes in Aaron's book, although they too were connected to the political Left to one degree or another during the period. African-American poets are better represented in such recent literary histories as David Perkins's *A History of Modern Poetry*. But even there they tend be discussed in a single chapter that surveys several decades of African-American literary production without much reference to what other American poets were doing, even if, as in the case of the 1930s, such connections are important.

In fact, African-American writers of the 1930s and 1940s have generally been considered more systematically by such intellectual histories as Harold Cruse's *The Crisis of the Negro Intellectual* or such political and/or cultural histories as Mark Naison's *The Communist Party in Harlem during the Great Depression* than by literary criticism or history. The limitations of such "nonliterary" scholarship for the study of the period's poetry are clear. The most obvious problem is that the subject of such histories is not poetry. When these studies examine the work of important writers of the period, they consider the texts that are most amenable to their purposes. Such texts are rarely fiction and almost never poetry. (When Harold Cruse, for example, discusses Richard

Wright, he essentially ignores Wright's poetry and fiction, preferring to concentrate on Wright's essay "Blueprint for Negro Writing.")

Another weakness of much of this "nonliterary" scholarship for the study of literature is an undue focus on New York City when Chicago is at least as important a center of black literary production during the period—not to mention a large number of significant "secondary" centers and scattered institutions and individuals of importance outside of New York and Chicago. Other problems of these histories include ideological blind spots, such as unexamined anti-Communist dogmas and, less commonly, romantic valorizations of the different periods of the Communist movement (the Third Period, the Popular Front, etc.), as well as various essentialist genealogies that trace pure literary bloodlines during a time when the drawing of such a lineage was possibly more untenable than at any other period of American literary production.

Perhaps the most disputed aspect about African-American literature in the 1930s and 1940s is that of periodization. Some accounts stretch the New Negro Renaissance well into the 1930s and some even as far as the Harlem riot of 1943.[2] While this periodization recognizes important links between the 1920s and 1930s, it also has the effect of obliterating the 1930s as a period of black literary production distinct from that of the New Negro Renaissance, a distinction that many writers and readers of the era certainly felt.[3]

Other accounts separate the 1930s from the New Negro Renaissance in ways that basically deny any continuity from the earlier period. This approach is closely related to the general formulation of the disjunction between modernism and "proletarian" (and Popular Front) literature, of which the 1934 edition of Malcolm Cowley's *Exile's Return* is perhaps the earliest and certainly the most influential articulation. This approach tends to be filled with a conversionary rhetoric—something along the lines of "the writers are struck by the stock market crash in 1929 and turn left." The way this basic paradigm of conversion is expressed in African-American literary history, most notably by Nathan Huggins in his pioneering study of the New Negro Renaissance, is that the optimism of the New Negro Renaissance foundered on the realities of the Great Depression and the most important writers of the 1920s moved to the left or fell silent.[4] Essential to this rendering of the 1930s is the counter-conversion—both recorded and re-enacted in the 1951 edition of Cowley's book—which takes place after the Hitler-Stalin pact in 1939.

Generally speaking this conversion to radicalism is seen as affecting the heart rather than the head. As a result, there is virtually no consideration of the possibility that the writers of the period could have been seriously engaged with the ideology of the Left, particularly the theoretical stands of the Communist Party of the United States (CPUSA) on the "national question." In fact, most accounts speak of the appeal of the CPUSA as being *in spite of* its theoretical stands. The attraction of many black writers and intellectuals to the CPUSA is usually portrayed as relatively superficial and based on the work of the party on specific issues such as the Scottsboro Case, and on the CPUSA's reputation as the predominantly white national organization most fanatically opposed to racism and the Jim Crow system. Other commentators, such as Harold Cruse and Claude McKay, attribute the influence of the Communist Left on black writers and intellectuals to a sort of left-wing patronage system. Certainly the concrete actions of the Communists were crucial in building the CPUSA's credibility (and membership) in the black community. But these historiographic formulations vastly underestimate the ideological impact of the Left.

Whatever the individual scholar's intent, this anti-ideological approach tends to reinforce the notion of black writers, and indeed all writers associated with the Left to one degree or another, as dupes or opportunistic cynics. It also works within a larger discourse that poses "modernism" (read "serious" or "universal" literature) against "proletarian" or "social realist" (read "hack" or "provincial") writing, to which only a deluded, naive, or dishonest artist could subscribe. However, the term "proletarian literature" was much debated during the 1930s and no authoritative "line" developed even within the pages of *New Masses*, which was more or less a publication of the CPUSA, much less in the many small left-wing cultural journals with fewer formal connections to the Communist Party. As James Murphy, Michael Denning, and Barbara Foley have persuasively argued, the rejection of modernism did not exist as an official literary policy of the Communist movement outside of the Soviet Union, and certainly not in the United States. However, this alleged opposition to modernism would be taken up by *The Partisan Review* in its reincarnation as a journal of the "anti-Stalinist Left," and by many later critics and scholars, as an anti-Communist characterization of both "proletarian" and Popular Front literary production during the 1930s. One goal of this study is to reexamine the question of "what was modernism" with respect to African-American writing during the 1930s and 1940s and to reconsider this opposition of modernism and social realism. Ralph Ellison, certainly no friend of the CPUSA after the mid-1940s, raises the complexity of this issue when he claims that he initially recognized the importance of Richard Wright after reading a poem of Wright's in *New Masses* that seemed to him "modern" in a way that the works of Pound and Eliot were modern.[5] At the same time, I want to avoid the familiar reclamation project that attempts to prove the value of some neglected body of work by demonstrating its modernism—a move that may reveal the lingering influence of the culture wars of the 1940s and 1950s.

Those relatively few scholarly works that deal at all with black literary or cultural history in the 1930s and 1940s, even such valuable studies as Naison's *Communists in Harlem* and William J. Maxwell's "Dialectical Engagements," follow the standard periodization in ending the "Red Decade" with the Hitler-Stalin pact in 1939. However convenient the pact is as an end marker for a period of American literature generally, it is clearly inadequate for African-American literature, since a number of the most important works of African-American literary engagement with the Communist-influenced Left, including Wright's *Native Son*, Walker's *For My People*, Hayden's *Heart-Shape in the Dust*, Dodson's *Powerful Long Ladder*, Tolson's *Rendezvous with America*, Ann Petry's *The Street*, and Gwendolyn Brooks's *A Street in Bronzeville*, as well as the early works of Ralph Ellison, come after the pact. In fact, Richard Wright wrote in support of the pact.

Both the account of African-American literature that describes the 1930s as essentially an extension of the New Negro Renaissance and that which sees the decade as absolutely disjunct from the 1920s have the effect of making the 1940s a sort of non-period, effectively excluding the 1940s from a discussion of the 1930s. Those poets who publish books for the first time in the 1940s and who now are considered "important" black writers—Margaret Walker, Robert Hayden, Melvin Tolson, Gwendolyn Brooks—are variously attached to earlier or later periods. Those accounts that do speak, however briefly, of black poetry, and of African-American literature generally, of the 1940s tend to link it with the 1950s and a growing use of "high modernist" or "cosmopolitan" styles, signaling a retreat from vernacular-influenced forms, if not actually a withdrawal from "racial" or "protest" literature.

All of these arguments as to periodization have their particular power. However, I am convinced that, as far as African-American poetry is concerned, the decades of the 1930s and 1940s can be most profitably studied as a single period distinct from the New Negro Renaissance and from the era of the "high" cold war that began in the late 1940s. This is not to say that the conditions of black literary production were identical in 1932, 1939, and 1946. Nonetheless, poetic texts by African-American writers share a number of important formal strategies and thematic concerns that distinguish these works from most texts of the preceding periods of black writing, most notably in the representation and recreation of the folk, and later "the people," and the folk voice. While Hughes's poetry, for instance, does go through various changes during this period, there is a continuity of theme and form between *Scottsboro Limited* in 1932 and *Shakespeare in Harlem* in 1942 that does not exist to the same extent between these works and Hughes's poetry in the 1920s and the later 1950s. This is to not posit an absolute disjunction between the New Negro Renaissance and the 1930s and 1940s, or even between the 1930s and 1940s and the era of the cold war: the themes and strategies that dominated the 1930s and 1940s obviously had antecedents and continued to be important even when the institutions that had been important in producing them—the CPUSA, for example—diminished in immediate influence or virtually disappeared altogether as a significant cultural force.

I pay considerable attention to the role of the ideology and the organizations and institutions of the Left, particularly the CPUSA and those cultural institutions it led or influenced in shaping black poetry during the 1930s and 1940s. Or perhaps rather than shaping, it might be more accurate to say the approach of the CPUSA to the "national question" provided a paradigm that African-American writers found congenial. I am not so much concerned about the specific paraphrasable ideological message that the individual poem—say, Countee Cullen's "Scottsboro, Too, Deserves Its Song" or Hughes's "Ballad of Lenin"—contains as in the formal influence of ideology and institutions on the period's poetry.

This is not to say that the "messages" of these poems are unimportant for this study, since at the very least they indicate that it might be necessary to look at the work of an author who is not generally associated with "social realism" or "proletarian literature" in a different way. For example, the fact that Cullen wrote a poem on the Scottsboro case and first published it in the *Daily Worker* would seem to indicate that it is worth considering Cullen's body of work in the 1930s within the framework of the literary Left. Though this may seem to be a simple observation, Cullen's work has yet to be considered seriously in this way. In fact, some critics, such as James O. Young and Blyden Jackson, go so far as to argue that Cullen remained outside the political and cultural concerns of the period despite the existence of poems such as "Scottsboro, Too, Deserves Its Song" and "Fear Not the Red" (which argued for opening a second front in Europe during the Second World War and which was published in *New Masses*) and despite the fact that Cullen publicly endorsed the Communist Party candidates for president and vice president in 1932. One could look at the body of Cullen's work in 1930s and decide that it was essentially at odds with the dominant spirit of the time (which in fact I do), but to do so one must seriously consider Cullen's engagement with the Left.

A discussion of a new approach by African-American authors to vernacular-oriented poetry during the 1930s and 1940s, and the reception of that poetry, has to be situated within a general discussion of vernacular culture and American literature during the period. Many non-African-American writers also mixed "high" and "low" art forms. It would be far too essentialist to discuss, for example, the collaboration of the poet Waring Cuney with the blues singer Josh White on the record *Southern Exposure* as a peculiarly "black" production without recognizing that Woody Guthrie, also a serious writer, was engaged in a similar enterprise when he compressed John Steinbeck's *The Grapes of Wrath* into a six-minute song using the tune of the folk song "John Hardy." Perhaps more important than the identification of those non-African-American writers who may have been engaged in similar projects as black writers is the recognition that what made the engagement of poetry, vernacular language, and popular culture possible was the creation of a new audience, black and white, who would support such writing and for whom, under the influence of the Left, this support was a duty.

Finally, what marked this literary period was an internationalism on the part of African-American writers that was unprecedented in its scope, even by the Garvey movement and by those promoters of the New Negro Renaissance who proclaimed Harlem "the Capital of the Negro World." This was in no small part due to the Comintern's connection of African Americans with the colonial populations of the world, as well as with the working classes of the metropoles. In addition to the theoretical connection of all colonial peoples, including African Americans, the Comintern and its member parties and their various cultural institutions made possible a practical literary connection of "oppressed peoples" that had never existed before on such a large scale. The effects of these connections outlasted the Comintern itself. As a result, one could find in the pages of various left-wing American journals and the productions of left-wing presses Langston Hughes's translations of Roumain, Pederoso, and Guillén, as well as of Mayakovsky and Lorca. And one could find the work of Hughes and Wright in the pages of *International Literature*, "Central Organ of the International Union of Revolutionary Writers," as well as critical articles discussing the importance of Hughes and Sterling Brown.

My project is not to vindicate the CPUSA's theory and practice concerning the "national question" during the 1930s and 1940s. Neither is it primarily an attempt to reveal more fully an aspect of the history of the Left and left-wing cultural expression in the United States that has been obscured or even suppressed—though I welcome any new light shed on this subject as a by-product of this work (and perhaps it is impossible to separate this sort of "recovery" from my real project). Instead, I conceive of this study more simply as an effort to understand how and why the poetry written by African Americans took the formal directions that it did, and to place this development within the larger discourse(s) of American poetry and American culture. These directions had significant consequences for African-American poetry in the following decades and, I would argue, though I dislike such rankings, made the period at least as important in determining the shape of contemporary African-American writing than the far more discussed New Negro Renaissance, if one limits the New Negro Renaissance to the 1920s. Of course, with the current problematics of literary history in mind, it is worth remembering Sterling Brown's caveat in his 1937 *Negro Poetry and Drama* that, despite his own predilection for what he called "social realist" poetry, the poetry written by African Americans of the 1930s was too diverse to be subsumed under any single rubric. (In this regard, one question that must be addressed is the "gender gap" of "proletarian literature." African-American women poets are noticeably absent from the various groups of writers associated with the Left until, at least, the establishment of the Federal Writers Project in 1935. This stands in contrast to the New Negro Renaissance, where black women, though suffering from various sorts of discrimination, were clearly important as writers and organizers, and were recognized as such.)

The current reservations about the narrativization of literary history not withstanding, it seems to me that such a narrative always exists at least in outline. For example, despite the recent work of such scholars as Paula Rabinowitz, Cary Nelson, Michael Denning, Walter Kalaidjian, Barbara Foley, and Alan Wald, most scholars "know" what the literature of the 1930s is like because they have internalized the narrative of the failure of "proletarian literature." And while Truth may be problematic, some narratives are truer than others—or our daily lives are premised at least implicitly on such a conviction. The question is not whether narrativization is possible without distorting the subject under question, but which narratives will be heard. Simply to problematize already existing narratives, whether implicit or explicit, without offering some other admittedly provisional narrative leaves the older narratives in place.

My first chapter will examine the relations between African-American poetry and the institutions and ideology of the Left during the 1930s and 1940s. This engagement with the Left was crucial to the particular manner in which the folk subject and the folk voice were represented and recreated in the poetry of the period. To this end, I delineate the relationship between the CPUSA and African-American intellectuals and artists in some detail. Rather than opposing integrationism to nationalism or nationalism to internationalism, the Communists argued that African Americans constituted an oppressed nation in the South and a national minority in the North. This position produced a cultural model that attempted to accommodate a revolutionary black nationalism with a sort of working-class integrationism within an internationalist framework. In practice the CPUSA tended to favor one side or another of the nationalist-integrationist equation depending on the political moment. Like many of the formulations of the folk by earlier African-American intellectuals (for example, Du Bois's *The Souls of Black Folk*), the "Black Belt Thesis," as the Communist position became known, was plagued also by a romantic assessment of African-American rural culture based in no small part on European valorizations of peasants, soil, and blood. Nonetheless this approach, which saw African Americans as an integral part of the United States and yet culturally distinct, had a huge impact on black poetry and its audience.

What this unstable yoking of cultural nationalism, integrationism, and internationalism within a construct of class struggle helped shape was a new relationship of African-American poetry to "vernacular" African-American culture, a relationship that persisted even during the muting of the nationalist aspect of the "national question" during the Popular Front and the Second World War. This new relationship included the representation of African-American working-class and "peasant" life and its cultural products ostensibly from the "mass" or "popular" perspective. (This is quite different from New Negro Renaissance portraiture of the folk or popular subject by, say, Claude McKay or Rudolph Fisher, which tended to be framed by an "intellectual" perspective, whether of Ray in McKay's *Banjo* and *Home to Harlem*, an unnamed and exiled poet-narrator in McKay's *Harlem Shadows*, or Fred Merrit in Fisher's *The Walls of Jericho*.) It also included the dissemination of urban forms of African-American popular culture—music, rhetoric, and so on—as well as rural "folk" forms as the paradigms for poetry. In part, this was due to the efforts of amateur and professional folklorists and musicologists, including John and Alan Lomax, B. A. Botkin, John Hammond, Zora Neale Hurston, Sterling Brown, and Lawrence Gellert, which made such forms more readily available to black and white intellectuals and artists. The work of the more radical of these folklorists also argued for an already existing tradition of overt expressions of social struggle in southern African-American folk culture that could be utilized by black (and white) writers.

Of course, some poets—most notably Langston Hughes, Sterling Brown, Waring Cuney, and, to a certain extent, Helene Johnson—had been doing this during the New Negro Renaissance. But these poets were a small minority of the black poets of the 1920s. Even the Garveyites adhered to "standard" or "high" Euro-American diction and forms in their poetic efforts. Hughes himself was assaulted ferociously in the African-American press for his "low-rate" representations of black Americans in *Fine Clothes to the Jew*, a 1927 collection filled with poetry that drew on the music of "classic" female blues singers such as Bessie Smith and the urban blues of such musicians as Leroy Carr and Scrapper Blackwell, as well as other forms of African-American sacred and secular vernacular expression.

This new relationship between "high" and "vernacular" art in the 1930s and 1940s also resulted in the production of many interesting hybrids of "high" and "popular" media. For example, the poet Waring Cuney wrote a series of "protest" lyrics set to music by the blues musician Josh White. These songs were recorded by White, a familiar figure of the Left cultural circuit, on the album *Southern Exposure*, a record that had liner notes by Richard Wright. Another instance of such a hybrid involving Wright is the song "King Joe" (about the boxer Joe Louis). Wright composed the lyrics to the song and Count Basie the music. "King Joe" was recorded by Paul Robeson with the Count Basie Orchestra backing him. Langston Hughes similarly took part in many such "high"–"low" productions. In the aftermath of the 1943 Detroit riot,

Hughes and composer Earl Robinson (who wrote such Left favorites as "Joe Hill" and "Ballad for Americans" and who put Melvin Tolson's poem "Dark Symphony" to music) combined to write a song "We'll Hammer It Out Together," which was sung by Paul Robeson on the radio show of the Michigan Congress of Industrial Organizations. Hughes's 1938 agitational play "Don't You Want to Be Free," performed first in Harlem under the auspices of the International Workers Order, combined poetry with sections of blues and spirituals. Of course, serious African-American poets, most notably James Weldon Johnson and Paul Laurence Dunbar, had written popular drama, musicals, and songs earlier, but never before were the different levels of "high" and "low" art so overtly mixed and aimed at an ideal audience substantially of the "black masses."

After the initial chapter, the plan of this book is roughly chronological, uneasily dividing into two sections, the first dealing with the 1930s, the second with the 1940s. I say uneasily because, as I have argued earlier, this division replicates a periodization that I find troublesome. Besides the obvious convenience of such a division, I nonetheless divide the sections in this way so as to confront the question of periodization head-on, demonstrating the continuity between writing in the two decades as well as the new features of African-American writing after the official end of the Popular Front and the onset of World War II. The first two chapters look closely at the work of Sterling Brown and Langston Hughes in the 1930s. Hughes and Brown merit separate chapters not only because of their importance today in the African-American canon but also because they represent two poles of Left-influenced African-American poetry in the 1930s. These chapters examine strategies of representing the folk and recreating the folk voice within the work of Hughes and Brown. These strategies of documentation and "authenticity" in their different ways seek, without complete success, to escape the long shadow cast by Paul Laurence Dunbar with his opposition of "high" and "low" art, as well the heritage of minstrelsy and other mass-culture representations of the folk and the folk voice. The crucial relationship of the narratorial consciousness to the recreated folk voice is also considered. Hughes creates an urban, internationalist, and popular culture aesthetic while Brown's is essentially rural, local, and folkloric. My takes on Hughes and Brown are not remarkable in and of themselves, but what I hope will be new is my consideration of how these poetic practices were related to ideological models on the Left.

Chapter 4 focuses particularly on work by Lucy Mae Turner, Ida Gerding Athens, Frank Marshall Davis, Waring Cuney, Richard Wright, and Countee Cullen, considering them roughly within the parameters established by the work of Hughes and Brown. Again, special attention is paid to the location of the narratorial consciousness to the recreated folk voice, arguing that one of the main distinctions among the black poets of the 1930s is not whether they attempt to directly recreate the African-American folk or popular voice, but where they locate the narratorial consciousness with respect to that voice: as insider, as outsider, or as both insider and outsider at the same time. The relation of the recreated folk voice to popular culture (and the increasing use of popular culture forms in a way that interrogates the categories of the "literary," the "modern," the "folk," and the "real" without either fully accepting or rejecting them) also receives considerable attention.

Chapter 2 traces the rise of "neomodernist" styles in African-American poetry during the late 1930s and early to middle 1940s. Rather than breaking with 1930s aesthetic and thematic concerns, as is often claimed, these styles maintain considerable continuity with the work of the "red decade," particularly of the Popular Front era. In this respect, I take issue with those critics and cultural commentators from the 1940s to the present who see the Popular Front as the font of "middlebrow" art as opposed to "modernist" or "avant-garde" art. At the same time, I do consider the obvious links between African-American neomodernism and the practices of reading and writing promoted by the New Critics and the New York Intellectuals for whom a self-conscious "modernism" was a weapon against the Popular Front.

These neomodernist styles are divided roughly into two categories: high neomodernism and popular neomodernism. Chapters 5 and 6 are devoted to the two authors whom I see as the exemplars of the different neomodernists styles: Langston Hughes as the creator of a popular neomodernism; Gwendolyn Brooks as the leading exponent of high neomodernism. Once again, it is important to reiterate that I use the term "neomodernism," not because I am trying to prove the worth of particular bodies of work by demonstrating their modernism, but because what I term "high" neomodernism and "popular" neomodernism featured a heightened conscious engagement with earlier literary and artistic modernism, albeit with different emphases. As in the first section of this study, the often blurry line of demarcation between the two types of neomodernism is seen as residing in differing stances toward popular culture and the location of the narratorial consciousness with respect to the African-American folk or popular subject. These two chapters are followed by a chapter that considers the issues raised in the previous two chapters through the work of a number of African-American poets, primarily Margaret Walker, Robert Hayden, Melvin Tolson, and Owen Dodson. Also traced is the intertextual relationship between these authors and earlier African-American literary production, particularly that of the early 1930s, of the New Negro Renaissance, and, again, of Paul Laurence Dunbar.

This study closes with a short conclusion that considers the enduring influences of 1930s and 1940s African-American poetry on the following generations of African-American poets, particularly those of the 1950s and 1960s. The conclusion also summarizes my specific arguments made in earlier chapters, which locate the work of black poets within a larger Left cultural matrix, a matrix that is significantly shaped by the work of these poets. Finally, a general claim is made for the importance of black poetry of the 1930s and 1940s for the development of postwar American poetry, particularly that poetry known as the New American Poetry and its various poetic offspring.

A few of the key terms that I use in this study may need some clarification. In speaking of the "re-creation" of the folk or popular voice, I use the term "re-creation" to indicate the notion commonly held by the poets of this study, or a fiction they promoted, that they are not so much representing the folk voice as allowing the actual folk or popular voice to oracularly emerge. By "narratorial consciousness" I mean the implicit or explicit consciousness that supervises a particular poem or collection of poems, a consciousness that is at least potentially different from that of author, the poem's speaker, or the implied poet. For example, in Sterling Brown's *Southern Road*, there is clearly a general supervisory consciousness of the collection that is different from that of the folk speakers of individual poems. By "documentation" or "documentary" I refer not only to those forms and practices typically associated with the category of the "documentary" but also with all other forms of cultural documents, whether film, reportage, work songs, "classic" blues, vaudeville, or "folk" rhetoric, used to attest to the "authenticity" of folk or popular representation and re-creation within a poem. When I use the term "neomodernist," I allude to the increasing engagement by poets in the late 1930s and early 1940s with various strains of pre-Depression "modernist" art in ways that foregrounded that engagement as one of the preeminent marks of its neomodernism.

The terms "popular culture" and "mass culture" appear somewhat interchangeably in this study, in both cases to refer to commodity or commercial culture.[6] However, while I have no desire to enter into any of the old debates signaled by the preference of one term over another, the terms do have slightly different casts—at least in my usage. "Mass culture" here is taken to comprehend those forms and expressions of commodity culture that are transmitted through media that reach, or potentially reach, a mass audience. This would include, though is not limited to, the products of the film, broadcast, recording, popular theater, magazine, and popular publishing industries. "Popular culture" comprehends "mass culture," but also includes other forms of commercial culture that are not distributed in a "mass" form. I would include in this category, for example, the street performances of blues artists in Chicago's Maxwell Street Market. I realize that this division is somewhat problematic. For one thing, those blues artists, like rock bands who only play in band members' basements or at local school dances, often, if not always, modeled themselves after successful "mass" artists whose path they would like to follow, commercially as well as artistically. For another, the local "popular" artist might also be in some senses a "mass" artist (e.g., Blind Willie McTell might cut a commercially released record one day and be singing on a street corner in Atlanta for change the next.) Ironically, it is precisely because the "local" artist and the "mass" artist are so closely related—if not one and the same in many instances—that it seems worth making a distinction of emphasis that allows both types of cultural production to be closely linked without flattening out the obvious difference in playing a country dance at a cabin in rural Mississippi from broadcasting nationwide on the CBS radio network. But if "mass culture" or "popular culture" refers to commercial or commodity culture, then what is "high culture," since what is commonly thought of as "high culture" was, by the 1930s, transmitted largely in various mass-circulated commercial forms? I am inclined to agree with Michael Denning's notion that "mass culture has won; there is nothing else."[7] However, I continue to use terms such as "high culture" and "high literature" to indicate a certain construct, or constructs, of traditional or modernist European and American literariness or artfulness that the writers, critics, and audiences of the period posed against "nonliterary" and popular genres, such as journalism, advertising, popular music, and pulp fiction, as well as against constructs of "folk culture" that are outside of commercial culture and of "high" culture.[8] These distinctions, clearly untenable if a rigorous definition is attempted and yet deeply ingrained (in me at least), are useful precisely because so many African-American writers of the 1930s and 1940s explored their persuasive power while questioning the validity and result of being so persuaded.

Finally, when referring to the period of African-American literary production immediately preceding the Depression, I employ the term "New Negro Renaissance" rather than "Harlem Renaissance." I do so with a certain amount of trepidation owing to what I feel is a subrosa homophobia that lies beneath various polemics against the use of "Harlem Renaissance," beginning with those of Sterling Brown.[9] Nonetheless, despite these overtones, I find compelling the arguments of Brown and others that "New Negro Renaissance" is geographically and ideologically more apt than "Harlem Renaissance."[10]

My reasons for focusing on particular poets and particular works are various, but not wholly arbitrary. In the course of my research, I read every collection of poetry by an African-American author and every anthology of African-American literature during the 1930s and 1940s that I was able to discover. I also looked at many of the periodical publications by black poets during this period, though copies of a number of journals and broadsides associated with the literary Left of the 1930s appear not to have survived, or barely survived, the auto-da-fé of the McCarthy era—not to mention the usual mortality rate for issues of small press literary journals. In addition to the actual periodical publications by African-American poets, I examined the full run of a considerable number of journals in which these poets published or that formed a significant part of the cultural milieu of the 1930s and 1940s in order to get a better sense of the era than simply reading selectively in, say, *New Masses*, *The Crisis*, *Opportunity*, and *Poetry* would give. Finally, I read unpublished work by important poets of the 1920s, 1930s, and 1940s.

In general, I tended to concentrate on poetry that was published in book form, particularly collections by individual poets. This, of course, is a questionable tack for a period in which periodicals played such a crucial role and in which important poets, such as Waring Cuney and Richard Wright, never published a book of poetry. Also, while I make an argument for the importance of anthologies in defining particular moments of African-American literary production, nowhere do I examine at any length specific anthologies such as Sterling Brown, Arthur P. Davis, and Ulysses Lee's important *The Negro Caravan* (1941). However, I chose to focus on collections of poems because I believe they offer the best opportunity to see the strategies of the individual poets played out. And, despite my focus on published collections, I do spend a reasonable amount of space considering poems that only appeared in anthologies, periodicals, or in some other media, such as the Waring Cuney–Josh White collaborations that were recorded and released on vinyl. I tend to consider unpublished work by poets only when it was clearly important to the development of a poet who published significant work in the 1930s and 1940s, as was the case with Melvin Tolson's unpublished (until 1979) manuscript *A Gallery of Harlem Portraits*, or when it reveals some significant aspect of the work of a poet covered by this study, as was the case with Sterling Brown's unpublished (until 1980) collection *No Hidin' Place*. As a result, I spend relatively little time looking at unpublished, but often interesting poetry written during the 1930s and 1940s by such writers as Claude McKay, Helene Johnson, and Gwendolyn Bennett, who were important literary figures in their own ways during the 1930s and 1940s, but whose poetry written during the period was not, so far as I can tell, a significant part of African-American poetry's discursive space.

As far as the selection of which work to investigate closely is concerned, my methodology is guided by my own sense of which poets were most significant in defining the literary moment. In considering these poets, I often look at material that might be viewed as at the boundaries of the genre of poetry, but that was important to the development of the work of individual poets, as in the case of the verse plays and "mass chants" of Langston Hughes and the development of his lyric poetry. Additionally, I examine the work of certain poets—Lucy May Turner and Ida Gerding Athens, for example—whom no one would accuse of any overarching significance, but who are interesting to me precisely because they were, as far as I could tell, removed from the centers and organizations of Left African-American literary production and yet manifested important thematic and formal concerns in their work that I argue marks 1930s and 1940s African-American poetry. Nonetheless, there were a number of poets whom I consider interesting (if minor in various ways) and germane to my arguments, such as David Cannon and Mae Cowdery, to whom I devote little space. In the spirit of a Steven Wright joke ("You can't have everything. But that's good. Where would you put it?"), I have had to let much interesting material go.

Similarly, I am tempted to extend the limits of my periodization until the early 1950s. As I argue in my conclusion, the influence of the 1930s and 1940s extends far beyond that of the immediate postwar era. (I am now convinced that what was sometimes referred to as the Black Arts Movement or the New Black Poetry during the 1960s and 1970s was in no small part an Old Left–New Black alliance.) And, as I also point out, there is a murky period from the end of World War II to the early 1950s in which earlier literary alignments and institutions were clearly coming to an end, or were becoming increasingly isolated, but in which the literary Left that blossomed in the 1930s and early 1940s among African-American writers retains considerable influence. My greatest regrets, however, are not due to an uneasiness about the validity of my periodization, since I consider such uneasiness to be an appropriate by-product of any scholarly endeavor, but that I would be able to write about some of my favorite texts, notably *Annie Allen* and *Montage of a Dream Deferred*, in only a cursory fashion. Nonetheless, I remain of the opinion that the increasingly hot climate of the domestic cold war fundamentally altered the African-American literary landscape in a way that even World War II failed to do.

I point out the limitations of my methodology not simply as a means of defusing potential objections to my work but also as a way of suggesting other work that might be done in this area. I do not consider my work in any sense definitive. It is my hope that this study will help initiate further scholarly efforts in a grossly underexamined area. Not only will such efforts help us place the many canonical and semi-canonical figures of the period within a historicized and broadly conceived discursive field, but they will be significant additions to the burgeoning subfield of literary radicalism and 1930s American culture. They will also be an invaluable part of the reevaluation of the development of American poetry in the twentieth century.

I

African-American Poetry, Ideology, and the Left during the 1930s and 1940s from Third Period to the Popular Front and Beyond

> But I must warn you it's a nasty job you're stepping into,
> not in line with your pink teas and your coming out parties.
> It's going to mean contact with people you've only read about.
> So if there's anyone afraid of realism, this is the time to back out.
>
> —MOON OVER HARLEM (1939 FILM)

The New Type of Party and the New Negro

The Communist Party of the United States of America (CPUSA) and the New Negro Renaissance originated at roughly the same time. The precise birth dates of both are impossible to fix exactly. Even the start of the CPUSA as an organization is variously put at the foundings of the Communist Party and the Communist Labor Party after a split within the Socialist Party of America (SP) in 1919 and at the unification of the two Communist organizations in 1921.[1] Nonetheless, both the CPUSA and the New Negro Renaissance were products of the post–World War I, post–October Revolution moment that produced an ideological crisis in the capitalist world order, as well as what might be thought of as the prewar world of the Left.

In the years immediately following World War I, an antiradical, xenophobic, racist, antilabor atmosphere reigned in the United States. The postwar years saw the Red Scare and Palmer Raids of 1919–20 that drove the new Communist organizations underground, a largely successful open-shop drive against organized labor, severe legal restrictions on immigration, a resurgence of lynching, a wave of racist riots that swept the United States in 1919 from Chicago to Longview, Texas, and the growth of the Ku Klux Klan into a mass organization with tremendous political power in the North and the South. At the same time a relative prosperity, albeit one that bypassed a significant section of workers and farmers, engendered an optimism with respect to the power of the American economy that affected the leadership of organized labor in the American Federation of Labor (AFL) and the independent Railroad

Brotherhoods. This optimism reached even a segment of the leadership of the CPUSA, led by Jay Lovestone, that argued that as a young capitalist power the United States was an "exception" to the decay of capitalism taking place in the older capitalist nations of Europe. (Though in the case of Lovestone and his circle, the optimism might be seen more accurately as a pessimism as to the amenability of the United States to a Marxist model of the revolutionary process.) This spirit of optimism also informed many of the leading African-American intellectuals of the period, as is evidenced by much of the rhetoric of the New Negro Renaissance that posited Harlem as the center of a potentially great intellectual and cultural expansion—a rhetoric that some black intellectuals, such as James Weldon Johnson in *Black Manhattan* (1930), maintained even in the early days of the Depression. Nonetheless, the concept of the New Negro, particularly in the more radical African-American journals such as *The Messenger* and *The Crusader*, arose largely as a figuration of a new type of response to the upsurge of racist violence and racist organizations at the end of World War I and so was at least in part a product of an era of racist and nativist (and antiradical) paranoia rather than simply of optimistic expansion.[2]

The history of the CPUSA in the early and middle 1920s, also marked by this social paranoia in a time of economic optimism, was characterized largely by an increasing isolation caused by political repression, intense internal strife, and fierce sectarian struggles with the SP and the AFL, particularly in the CPUSA strongholds among needle-trades workers in New York City and other garment industry centers. The vast majority of the CPUSA's rank and file—like the majority of industrial workers in the United States—were foreign-born workers (Finns, Russians, South Slavs, Hungarians, Eastern European Jews, and so on) and their children. These members had come to the Communist movement en masse from the old SP Foreign Language Federations in 1919. Many of the original members that the Communists inherited from the Foreign Language Federations ultimately left the CPUSA as a result of factionalism and attempts to limit the autonomy of the federations and integrate them into a centralized, "Bolshevized" party organization. Other factors that diminished the original membership of those who left the SP to join the Communist organizations in 1919 were ferocious and persistent battles for control of the CPUSA by shifting circles of party leaders throughout the decade, as well as a clandestine style of organization during the first half of the 1920s, owing to actual repression as well as, perhaps, the influence of an "underground" European model of party structure.

A "dual union" trade union policy initiated by the Communist International (Comintern), largely as a result of the theory of the Third Period that emerged from the Sixth Comintern Congress in 1928, as well as the mass expulsion of CPUSA members and sympathizers from American Federation of Labor unions in the early and middle 1920s, led to the establishment of separate Left-led industrial unions under the auspices of the Trade Union Unity League (TUUL), a Communist-led trade union center that grew out of the agitational Trade Union Educational League (TUEL).[3] The CPUSA and the TUUL became the standard-bearers of industrial unionism (the organization of workers on an industry-wide basis as opposed to a craft basis) and of the organization of the mass-production industries in the 1920s, leading bitter and often bloody strikes in such industries as coal, auto, and textile. However, despite the

TUUL's role in leading strikes and serving as a center for left-wing labor militants, its dual union policy in opposition to the AFL left it relatively small and isolated from the main body of organized workers in the United States. In short, while the CPUSA won a reputation for militancy and radical integrity, it remained small and relatively isolated until the early 1930s and was at the end of the 1920s only one among a number of Left organizations, albeit still the largest group to the left of the SP.[4]

Until the Sixth World Congress of the Comintern in 1928, which took the stand that African-Americans constituted an "oppressed nation" in the South and a "national minority" in the urban centers of the North, the position of the CPUSA with respect to African Americans was essentially that of the left wing of the old SP and other radical groups, such as the Industrial Workers of the World (IWW).[5] These older radical groups, when they took up the issue of race at all, argued against racism as destructive to class consciousness, but did not see any special considerations necessary beyond those of class unity. The "Negro Problem," declared a 1923 article by Otto Huiswood, a leading African-American Communist, in the CPUSA (then Workers Party) paper The Worker, was "fundamentally an economic question intensified by racial antagonism."[6] Similarly, Mike Gold, though hardly an official spokesperson for the CPUSA at the time, claimed that "the only real division is that of economic classes."[7] In short, the outlook of the CPUSA, particularly at the beginning of the decade, was not dissimilar to that of George Schuyler's 1926 article "Negro-Art Hokum," in which Schuyler claimed that the African American "is merely a lamp-blacked Anglo Saxon."[8] Probably the clearest articulation of this attitude with respect to literature by a critic of the Communist Left was Kenneth Fearing's condescendingly mixed review of Langston Hughes's Fine Clothes to the Jew in the September 1927 issue of New Masses. In that review, Fearing grants that Hughes "uses Negro dialect and jazz rhythms, in this particular volume, with as much success as anyone has achieved using those limiting devices. But with the American language, to which Hughes will have to turn, he is not familiar."

At the same time, New Masses was still influenced by the images of African-American primitivism and exoticism that had been so influential in the 1920s. A striking example of this attitude—one that would be almost unthinkable in New Masses a few years later—is a February 1928 ad for the New Masses "Artists and Writers Spring Frolic" benefit dance. The visual in the ad, drawn in a "modern" style, features what the accompanying "Explanation" describes as an "artist and writer from the New Masses staff interviewing Spring in order to get inspiration for the SPRING FROLIC." In fact, the white male pair, pads of paper in their hands, leer at Spring, personified by a naked white woman, who dances while male African-American jazz musicians holding oversized instruments play in the background, staring off into space rather than at the dancer. The "Explantion" adds, "It is fitting for this modern age that Spring should be wakened from her long slumber, not by the old-fashioned nightingale, but by Vernon Andrade's Dusky Jazzbirds. Nothing like syncopation to shake off the winter's chill."[9] This triangulation of the white male gaze, the "natural" white female body, and the male African-American modern primitive, who is both essential and peripheral, captures a spirit of early-twentieth-century bohemia that retains a strong presence in the literary Left well into the Depression even after the overt expression of that spirit in such a graphic and accompanying text would no longer be possible.

As noted above, the CPUSA largely held to the old SP position on the "Negro question" until 1928. Nonetheless, by the middle of the decade, particularly after the Fifth Congress of the Comintern in 1924 where the United States "Negro question" was specifically addressed, the CPUSA made unprecedented efforts, for what might be thought of as a historically white left-wing organization, to reach the African-American community, especially in the urban North. A number of initiatives were made, with the 1925 establishment of the American Negro Labor Congress (ANLC), an organization designed both to further the organization of African American workers into trade unions, including all-black unions where necessary, and to break down existing barriers in the trade union movement to African-American workers, as perhaps the most important. However, the same infighting and sectarianism that dogged other areas of party work also characterized much of the CPUSA's work in the ANLC and other efforts aimed at African Americans. As a result of this infighting and sectarianism, the CPUSA failed to recruit significant numbers of African Americans and remained largely peripheral in most African-American communities, though the CPUSA and the ANLC did provide a focus for the expression of militant socialism and anticolonialism by African American radicals in much the same way that the TUUL served as a center for labor militants.[10]

It was in the area of the arts, particularly literature, that the CPUSA was perhaps least isolated through most of the 1920s. As with the ANLC for African-American radical socialists and the TUUL for radical labor militants, the CPUSA-influenced *New Masses*, founded in May 1926 and drawing progressively closer to the CPUSA during the rest of the decade, became a focal point for radical writers and artists. Initially, *New Masses* drew on the old constituency of the bohemian-radical *Masses* magazine (which ceased publication under the pressure of the wartime repression by federal authorities of the IWW, anarchists, Left socialists, and other radicals opposed to World War I) and the pro-Bolshevik *Liberator* that replaced it. Some of the same sectarian conflict and vitriol that shaped the CPUSA's relations with radical non-Communists, progressives, and liberals in other areas also emerged in the party's hostile attitude toward various writers who had been often quite sympathetic initially to the Bolsheviks and the CPUSA. Nonetheless, these conflicts tended to be with individuals, such as Floyd Dell, V. F. Calverton, and Max Eastman, variously castigated as bohemians, bourgeois, and, later, Trotskyists and Lovestoneites, rather than with organizations. Perhaps this was because, unlike the cases of the labor movement and the African-American community, there were no organizations that had the authority and / or the mass followings to push the CPUSA to the margins or preempt the CPUSA's appeal as did the AFL in the labor movement or, in different ways, the NAACP and the Garveyites in the African-American community. The mass support among liberal writers and intellectuals in defense of Sacco and Vanzetti in the middle 1920s, and the subsequent radicalization of many of these writers and intellectuals after the two were executed in 1927, brought them into various sorts of working relationships with the Communists. As a result, while the Left writers of the 1920s were perhaps (as critics since at least Alfred Kazin's *On Native Ground* [1942] have suggested) on the margins of the "mainstream" of American literature during the 1920s, as were the "modernists" of *Broom* and *transition* for that matter, nonetheless an important Left literary subculture with links to the CPUSA emerged, forming much of the core to which younger, and older, radicalized writers would be attracted during the Depression. Thus, not only is it possible to trace, somewhat problematically, a radical genealogy from *Masses* to *The Liberator* to *New Masses*, but also to draw, as Cary Nelson and Walter Kalaidjian have suggested in a more limited way, a similar line of descent from the radical anthologies of the 1920s (such as *May Days* [1925], *Poems for Workers* [1927], *America Arraigned!* [1928], and *An Anthology of Revolutionary Poetry* [1929] through the *Unrest* anthologies of 1929, 1930, and 1931, *Proletarian Literature of the United States* [1935], *This Generation* [1939], and *Seven Poets in Search of an Answer* [1944].[11]

Focusing more narrowly on African-American writers and intellectuals in the 1920s, the Communist Left was far less peripheral for those writers than was the case in the African-American community as a whole.[12] Many of the leading younger writers of the New Negro Renaissance had some connection to the CPUSA-influenced literary Left, though these links remain for the most part less studied than the connection of the New Negro Renaissance to the SP through A. Philip Randolph's *The Messenger*. Claude McKay's relationship to the Communist movement in the United States, Soviet Union, and Britain is well known. Both Jean Toomer and Eric Walrond—in addition to McKay—were listed in the masthead of *New Masses* at different times in the 1920s. Toomer had also been active with *The Liberator*. Walrond would continue to support initiatives of the Communist Left in the 1930s, such as the campaign of the Anti-Imperialist League of the United States against the Japanese invasion of China and the National Committee for the Defense of Political Prisoners.[13] Hughes published in the CPUSA (then Workers Party) journal *The Workers Monthly*—which had absorbed *The Liberator* and eventually became the CPUSA theoretical journal *The Communist* in 1927—and published poems in *New Masses* for the first time in the December 1926 issue when that magazine was only in its sixth month. Hughes participated as a reader at the third annual "Red Poet's Nite Dance Bacchanal" sponsored by the *Daily Worker*.[14] Hughes was also a member of the Rebel Poets group organized by Jack Conroy and Ralph Cheney, which published a newsletter, *The Rebel Poet*, as well as the *Unrest* anthologies. (Sterling Brown also became involved with the Rebel Poets in the early 1930s.) Countee Cullen (who, like Hughes and Conroy, would endorse the CPUSA candidates William Z. Foster and James W. Ford for president and vice president in 1932) joined the campaign to defend Sacco and Vanzetti. (Cullen wrote the poem "Not Sacco and Vanzetti," which was included in *Justice Arraigned!*, Ralph Cheney and Lucia Trent's radical 1928 anthology memorializing Sacco and Vanzetti, as well as in Cullen's own 1929 collection, *The Black Christ and Other Poems*.) He also participated in the Red Poets' Nites. George Schuyler, before his journey to the right, was sympathetic to the Left and a sometime contributor to *New Masses*. It is also worth noting, though New Negro Renaissance writing sometimes received mixed reviews from Left cultural critics, Wallace Thurman's ill-fated 1926 modernist journal *Fire!!* featured a full-page ad from *New Masses* inside its cover. Similarly, an ad for *Fire!!* appeared in the December 1926 issue of *New Masses*. (Beyond the mutual financial support this exchange of ads provided, their appearance suggests that the two journals saw their audience as at least potentially overlapping.)

Even a number of those older African-American intellectuals and writers who have been seen as "midwives" of the New Negro Renaissance had some involvement with Left institutions in the 1920s. Walter White, later an ardent anti-Communist, was one of the original contributing editors of *New Masses* and would publish an article on African Americans and the southern great floods of 1927 in the July 1927 issue of the journal, even though his name was removed from the masthead at the beginning of the year. Alain Locke, who would be associated with the Communist Left in the 1930s and 1940s, first contributed to *New Masses* in the August 1928 issue with a book review. Locke, W. E. B. Du Bois, and Charles S. Johnson published in V. F. Calverton's *Modern Quarterly* during the 1920s, when it was an independent radical journal that still had good relations with the CPUSA and its cultural institutions. Locke, Johnson, and White, as well as Hughes and Schuyler, participated in the liberal-left cultural circle centered in Calverton's home in Baltimore.[15] Calverton's engagement with African-American literature and intellectual currents would form the basis of his important *Anthology of American Negro Literature*. Interestingly, in what is perhaps a foreshadowing of the masculinist, and masculine, character of Left-influenced African-American poetic production in the 1930s, none of the important female writers of the 1920s appears to have any obvious ties to the organized Left, though some, notably Gwendolyn Bennett, would develop such ties in the 1930s.

It would be grossly overstating the matter to say that the Communist Left was the secret, and hitherto unmentioned, motor running the New Negro Renaissance. Neither was the general mood of the older generation of writers and intellectuals, at least, of the New Negro Renaissance that of a revolutionary rejection of American prosperity rather than a liberal optimism. For that matter, to call the Rebel Poets or *America Arraigned!* Communist would be equally erroneous—both involved a wide range of radicals of diverse ideological sympathies ranging from anarchist to pacifist to Communist, though a general sympathy for the October Revolution was common to nearly all of them.[16] But it is safe to say that the move closer to the CPUSA for many African-American writers in the 1930s was a far shorter and easier trip than has generally been allowed, particularly after the new Communist emphasis on the "national question" after the Sixth Congress of the Comintern in 1928. It is obvious also that the considerations of radical literature of the 1920s that implicitly, through exclusion, or explicitly pose that literature as absolutely disjunct from African-American literature are as problematic as those that do the same for the 1930s and 1940s.[17]

The Holler Men: The Black Belt Republic and the Republic of Letters

After the onset of the Depression in 1929, the CPUSA became, fairly rapidly, the predominant force on the Left in the United States. Whether the influence of the Left on American culture in the 1930s has been overestimated, as Warren Sussman argues, or whether it has been underestimated, as claimed by many of the so-called revisionist scholars of the Communist Left, such as Michael Denning and Cary Nelson, the CPUSA broke out of its isolation and became a significant force in American culture. Again scholars differ as to the relative effectiveness of the CPUSA during different moments of the 1930s: some historians and cultural critics such as Mark

Naison, Fraser Ottanelli, and Walter Kalaidjian point to the Popular Front as the period of greatest Communist influence; others such as the historian Robin Kelley and the literary scholar Lawrence Schwartz—and Richard Wright, for that matter—see the Third Period as the high point of the CPUSA as a truly oppositional force. Once again, it is worth noting that while some of these differences point to the scholar's particular political sympathies, others are a reminder that the Communist experience in the United States during the 1930s and 1940s was very diverse. Thus it is possible, for example, that both Kelley and Naison are correct because the focuses of their studies are quite different. That is to say, while the Popular Front notion of public Communists working openly together with white and black liberals might have functioned effectively in New York City, it might have been much less feasible in 1930s Alabama—hence, as Kelley argues, producing a sharp decline in CPUSA membership in Alabama after the beginning of the Popular Front.[18]

Whatever the exact nature and extent of Communist influence and activity during the 1930s, the question arises as to why the CPUSA emerged as the dominant organization on the Left around which, or against which, other Left groups defined themselves when it had been relatively small and isolated in the 1920s. Many possible reasons could be advanced: the perceived militancy of the CPUSA in the face of the economic crisis, the material and ideological benefits of the connection of the party to an international revolutionary movement and a socialist nation in which the economy seemed to be growing rather than shrinking, its focus on the organization of unskilled and semiskilled workers (many of them foreign-born) in the mass-production industries when other groups seemed to have little practical interest in these workers, and a more effective grassroots style of work. However, what could be said to distinguish the CPUSA most sharply from other Left organizations was the degree to which it elevated the struggle against racism and what it called "Negro liberation" to the center of its work, particularly after the Comintern's Sixth Congress, which linked "Negro liberation" to anticolonial struggles around the world.

As nearly all historians of the Communist Left have commented, the battle against "white chauvinism" and the "national oppression" of African Americans became a virtual religion for Communists, black and white.[19] This approach to the "national question" might seem to be a liability in the efforts of the CPUSA to influence American culture, given the degree to which concepts of race and racial hierarchies have defined that culture. Unquestionably, it did place certain limits on the mass appeal of the party. For example, despite somewhat relaxed standards as to the expression of what might be considered racist sentiments, the CPUSA had great difficulty attracting and retaining white members in the Deep South, particularly before the Popular Front. This phenomenon was not limited to the South, but also narrowed the appeal of the CPUSA in the North.[20] However, the elevation of the question of race to the center of its work allowed the CPUSA to approach practical problems of organizing across racial lines, among workers in various industries, among the unemployed, among tenants, and so on, in a new and productive manner. It also was a recognition of what most Americans know: race is a crucial constitutive principle of American culture. Thus, it followed for many Americans that the radical reorganization of American society seen as necessary under the impact of the Great Depression required a redefinition of the role of race in America. The CPUSA's position on the "national question" (and the practical activity stemming from that position) demonstrated its militance, its seriousness with respect to fundamental change in the United States, and its willingness to take on the thorniest, and most profound, aspects of American culture. As a result, it attracted black and white Americans radicalized by the Depression.

This approach has been said by many commentators to represent a use of African Americans by the CPUSA to further its image of militancy and distinguish itself from its competitors on the Left, a charge that no doubt contained an element of truth. However, this elevation of "Negro Liberation" under the directives of the Comintern provided a useful tool for African-American Communist leaders, such as Cyril Briggs and Harry Haywood, to influence party policy and allowed African-American writers and intellectuals in and around the CPUSA more ideological latitude than they might have had otherwise.[21] This ability to have an impact on CPUSA policy, within limits, can be contrasted to the earlier failure of African-American Socialists, such as A. Philip Randolph and others associated with *The Messenger*, to have any serious effect on the policies of the Socialist Party in the 1910s and 1920s.

Much of the power of the CPUSA's placement of the "national question" at the center of the agenda of the Left lay in the Communists' willingness to take into account, if sometimes erroneously, the specific cultural results of the function of race as a basic organizing principle of American society. Even the most militant and egalitarian of earlier radical organizations, such as the IWW, had attempted to redefine American society by essentially ignoring the cultural consequences of race and using a concept of class unity in which racial or national identification simply represented a sort of false consciousness. The CPUSA position claiming that African Americans constituted a "nation" was a cultural argument that denied any biologically determined essentialism as to the African-American character. Harry Haywood, who was involved in the original formulation of the Black Belt Thesis by the Comintern, and who became the chief CPUSA theoretician of the "national question" in the early 1930s, wrote in the August 1930 issue of CPUSA theoretical journal *The Communist*:

> It is therefore quite evident, that race as an ideology plays a big role in the national oppression of the Negroes in the U.S. Regarded in this sense it must be said that race becomes a factor in the national question.
>
> But it would be absolutely erroneous, on the basis of this, to ascribe to what is in fact an ideology the importance of a social question in itself. To do so would be equivalent to reducing the national question to one of its factors. Concretely it would be tantamount to reducing the Negro question, a social question, to a question of race-ideology, i.e., to blur over the economic and social roots of this question, and finally to a capitulation before bourgeois race theories. (Foner and Shapiro, 25)

Instead of opposing integrationism to nationalism or nationalism to internationalism, the CPUSA argued that African Americans constituted an oppressed nation with the right to political and economic control, including the right to form a separate political state, in the so-called Black Belt region of the rural South where African Americans formed the majority of the population. The Communists also held that African Americans in the ghettos of the urban North and West that resulted from the "great migration" of the 1910s, 1920s, and 1930s were members of a "national minority" that needed to be integrated into society on the basis of full equality. An important corollary of the Black Belt Thesis, as the Communist position became known, was that African Americans had a distinct national culture that was rooted among the black farmers, sharecroppers, and farm laborers in the South and that needed to be defended and encouraged in its development, particularly in its opposition to national oppression and capitalist exploitation.

Most historians, even scholars relatively sympathetic to rank-and-file Communist activity, such as Mark Solomon and Mark Naison, let alone anti-Communists, such as Theodore Draper and Harvey Klehr, consider the Black Belt Thesis to be something forced on the CPUSA by the Comintern. This position is often held up as an example of how a slavish American party blindly followed the Comintern's—read Stalin's—dictates no matter how unsuited to practical conditions in the United States. The general consensus is that the Black Belt Thesis had no basis in the realities of black Americans North and South and was alien to African-American cultural and intellectual traditions. In the view of such disparate historians as Klehr and Naison, the party only made real progress among African Americans after it downplayed and practically abandoned its program of self-determination.[22]

The Black Belt Thesis was, in fact, severely flawed so far as its conception of African-American culture was concerned. Its most serious problem was a sentimental valorization of black "peasant" culture in the South at the expense of African-American culture in the urban centers of the North. This valorization had much in common with various forms of nineteenth-century European nationalism, particularly those inspired by Johann Gottfried von Herder, in which an idealized peasant culture (often opposed to a degenerate mass culture) is apotheosized as the base of the "authentic" national culture.[23] It also recalled many nineteenth-century English novels of the industrial revolution, such as Benjamin Disraeli's *Sybil* and Charlotte Elizabeth Tonna's *Helen Fleetwood*, wherein sturdy English farm families exemplifying true Anglo-Saxon values and culture are tried and even ruined by the new culture of the industrial north. As I will examine at greater length later in this chapter, this opposition of the "authentic" folk culture of the rural South to the urban black culture of the northern ghettos (often associated by the party with mass culture) has a particular significance with respect to the gendering of the folk voice.

However flawed the Communist position may have been, it is not true that it had no precedent in African-American intellectual and artistic tradition. What distinguishes the poetry of African-American modernists of the New Negro Renaissance from that of white American "high" modernists during the 1920s is a relative identification with the black folk subject, or a desire to identify with the folk subject, by the narratorial consciousness that frames the poem in the work of African-American poets. Even the white poets most concerned with the creation of an American literary language rooted in the vernacular, notably William Carlos Williams, maintain a rigid distance between the literary consciousness and the vernacular subject. In Williams's *Spring and All* (1923), the narratorial consciousness, whether observing a patient (as in section XVI), a maid (as in section XVIII), or a crowd at a baseball stadium (as in section XXVI), is represented as that of a somewhat horrified voyeur observing an un-knowing, potentially unwilling, and often eroticized other. There is sometimes a sim-ilar gap in the works of black poets, as in many of the poems of Claude McKay's *Harlem Shadows* (1922). But the gap in McKay's poetry generally stems from the poet-speaker's estrangement from what he sees as his symbolic, if not actual, folk roots. As a result, the folk becomes something to be returned to or re-approached rather than approached or simply observed.

In the work of black poets during the 1920s, there is almost always either a frame of what might be called bourgeois individualistic uplift placed around the folk sub-ject that attempts to bridge the gap by raising the subject or else a frame of primi-tivism, as in much of McKay's work, through which the gap is narrowed by an imag-inative return to the "naturalness" of the folk. Thus it is not surprising that the white poets most influential as literary models for those African-American poets, such as Brown and Hughes, whose work during the New Negro Renaissance was largely ver-nacular based are not the "high" modernists, despite the similarity of, say, the lin-guistic projects of Hughes and Williams. Much more important are the proto-modern E. A. Robinson and Robert Frost and such "popular" modernists as Edgar Masters, Vachel Lindsay, and Carl Sandburg in whose work the narratorial con-sciousness identifies more closely with the vernacular subject than was the case in the work of the "high" modernists.

The New Negro Renaissance, like the Comintern's view of the "national ques-tion," was also heavily influenced by nineteenth- and early-twentieth-century Euro-pean nationalism. Perhaps the most famous articulation of this influence was Alain Locke's introduction to *The New Negro*, where he speaks of Harlem as the capital of the Negro world in the same way that Dublin is the capital of the "New Ireland." Like the Communists' position, Locke's conception of African-American culture has somewhat conflicting integrationist and nationalist elements. Locke, as well as James Weldon Johnson (whose 1922 and 1931 editions of *The Book of American Negro Poetry* were defining landmarks of the literary moment of the New Negro Renaissance), Du Bois and many of the so-called mid-wives of the New Negro Renaissance, also share with the Communists the notion that the base of black culture arises from the farmers and farm laborers of the rural South.

Of course, Locke and Johnson differ considerably from the Communists. One of the basic contradictions of the CPUSA construction of African-American identity was between the nationalist implications of the Black Belt Thesis and the assimila-tionist implications of the proletarianization of African Americans caused by the "great migration," which the CPUSA also viewed favorably. Where Locke and John-son see Harlem as the focal point for the development of the ur-folk culture into a "higher" form and the prototype for other such centers, the Communists claim dur-ing the Third Period that the goal of nearly all black Americans in the North is as-similation into their respective class identities, not racial or national expression. Even here, the views of Locke and Johnson and of the CPUSA are not so far apart since they both posit and praise an essential black culture in the South and yet valorize African-American urbanization in North. As a result, it is not surprising that during the Popular Front period—and after—the CPUSA adopted a de facto position that is close to that of Locke, with a new emphasis on the African-American communities of the urban North—though the Black Belt Thesis would remain its official policy until the 1950s. Nor is it surprising that Locke became associated with the Communist Left, an association he would retain through the rest of the 1930s and the 1940s.[24]

The view of African-American culture underlying Sterling Brown's 1932 collection of poems *Southern Road* even more closely resembles the CPUSA position than did that of Locke. Brown's book explicitly proposes the culture of African Americans in the rural South as the "authentic" black culture while deriding the culture of ghettos in the cities of the North, particularly Harlem, as shallow and false. Though the CPUSA lacked Brown's animus toward African-American migrants from the South to the North, cultural critics of the Communist Left before the Popular Front also tended to reject the forms of vernacular expression linked with African Americans in the North because of the connection of such forms to mass culture and, perhaps, to discourage African-American cultural separatism in the urban North. Like the Communists, at least before the Popular Front, Brown clearly values various male-identified secular vernacular forms associated with the rural South (work songs, early "folk" blues, "badman" stories, and so on) over others popularly associated with the urban North, particularly the types of jazz played in such northern urban centers as Chicago and New York. Brown draws on these vernacular forms, infusing many of his poems, perhaps most notably "Strong Men," with an overt message of protest (rendered in a masculine voice) where traditionally such a message would have been more covert in those forms. (In fact, Brown's "Strong Men" involves an unusual transformation of the rhetoric of the New Negro in that it renders African-American stoicism and endurance as a masculine act of resistance rather than the more usual feminine act of accommodation.) The one notable exception to this is Brown's famous poem "Ma Rainey," though even here it is worth noting that the voice of the poem is that of a male folk subject who briefly, and in truncated form, quotes Ma Rainey singing "Backwater Blues." *Southern Road* indicates that Brown's ideological position with respect to the essential nature of black culture was not very far from that of the Black Belt Thesis even before Brown became formally associated with the Left—though the "protest" aspect of Brown's poetry becomes more pronounced by the time he finished his second (unpublished) collection, *No Hiding Place*. No doubt it was this similarity that facilitated his move left as well as making him the black poet most acclaimed by the Communist-influenced Left, despite the fact that Hughes was far more directly connected to the CPUSA than was Brown.[25]

Works at least as far back as Dunbar's 1902 novel *Sport of the Gods* (not to mention Toomer's *Cane* and Johnson's *God's Trombones*) could be cited to argue that there are precedents for the Communist position valorizing African-American culture in the rural South (often at the expense of black urban culture) within African-American letters. Certainly, non-Communist black writers (or even anti-Communist writers, such as Zora Neale Hurston) in the 1930s posited an essential African-American culture in the rural South that was to be distinguished from ideologically assimilationist black communities in the North. In short, while it may be true that these notions of an ur-African-American culture in the South were quite questionable and were, in fact, derived largely from European national romances of the folk, it was a romance that the Communists substantially shared with non-Communist black intellectuals and writers—many writing in advance of the 1928 Comintern congress.

However, despite the significant antecedents for the CPUSA position on the "national question" among earlier African-American intellectuals and artists, the yoking of cultural nationalism, integrationism, and internationalism by the CPUSA that largely emerged from the Sixth Congress (with a further push from the Comintern in 1930) helped shape a new relationship of African-American poetry to black popular culture. Or perhaps it is more accurate to say that the Communist position on the "national question" did not shape black poetry so much as it provided a paradigm that African-American writers found congenial.[26] Langston Hughes, the early Sterling Brown, Waring Cuney, and, to a certain extent, Helene Johnson had been more or less unique, and sometimes reviled, for their vernacular "low-rate" representations of African Americans in the late 1920s. But the use of such vernacular language, forms, and subjects relatively unmediated by the distancing frames of primitivism and uplift became commonplace in the 1930s and 1940s—even by poets heavily influenced by "high modernism," such as Robert Hayden and Gwendolyn Brooks. One mark of this change in the literary environment is the difference between the reception of Hughes's *Fine Clothes to the Jew* in 1927 and that of Wright's *Native Son* in 1940. Bigger Thomas is much more sociopathic, and misogynist, than any figure in *Fine Clothes to the Jew*. Yet Wright's book was on the whole far better received by the African-American press than had been Hughes's book, which many reviewers had attacked for its portrayals of poor "lecherous and lust-seeking characters."[27] In short, what might be thought of as the previously powerful strictures of "bourgeois" uplift were extremely attenuated by the end of 1930s, replaced to a large extent by an aesthetic for African-American literature that privileged both the representation and formal recreation of a largely male-identified vernacular culture, as well as the social experience that was alleged to produce that culture. This change is not simply the rise of African-American "naturalism," "social realism," or the "Wright School." After all, with respect to poetry, it is hard to see why the "badman" poems of Sterling Brown, such as the Slim Greer cycle in the 1932 *Southern Road*, are more "realistic" than Claude McKay's 1922 *Harlem Shadows*. What distinguishes Brown's poems from most African-American poetic production during the 1920s is not their verisimilitude but their reliance on the diction, form, and subject of rural African-American vernacular song and storytelling traditions.

The Communists proposed that African-American farmers and farm laborers (and semiproletarians of southern railroad section crews, turpentine camps, and sawmills) were engaged in struggle, however unequal, with the southern agricultural oligarchy and that their culture was naturally opposed to that of the planter class and, by extension, the capitalist class that stood behind the planters. Thus, the culture that most expressed the battle against national oppression and capitalist exploitation was that of the lowest and the largest section of southern black society. As a result, the CPUSA began to emphasize rural southern African-American traditions of overt struggle for freedom. During the early 1930s the CPUSA first spoke of the "revolutionary tradition" of the slave revolts, a claim that the Communist historian Herbert Aptheker would support in a more academic fashion in the late 1930s.[28] Given the

Communists' constant representation of the working class and "authentic" working-class cultural expressions of class consciousness and class struggle as male, a gendering that found an echo in nationalist and modernist conceptions of a masculine and active black vanguard that would redeem the folk from feminine accommodationism, it is not surprising that the elements of active resistance found in, or read into, southern black folk culture were coded as male and held up as the truly authentic and progressive.

In short, folk humor, storytelling, music, dance, and religious rhetoric (to name a few prominent "folk" forms) were not something to be elevated to "higher" art forms or more "standard" language, as James Weldon Johnson did with his "folk" sermons in *God's Trombones* (1927). They were already the most appropriate forms for the national expression of black people. Hence, a slogan of the Communist-organized League of Struggle for Negro Rights—of which Langston Hughes was the president—was "Promote Negro Culture in Its Original Form with Proletarian Content." What was necessary was not the transmuting of the folk culture into high art, but rather the infusing of old forms with a new consciousness of class and national self-interest. This new consciousness linked the planters with the northern capitalists and provided the sense that the political organization of sharecroppers and farm laborers was part of a larger battle of black and white industrial workers against the capitalist class, as well as part of a worldwide struggle against colonial and economic exploitation.[29]

There was even a certain valuation by the Communist Left of expressions of black vernacular culture that were not overt protests, but were nonetheless held up as examples of a vibrant "people's" culture that allegedly stood outside bourgeois culture. For example, the sixth anniversary celebration of the founding of the *Daily Worker* in New York on January 11, 1930, featured the African-American baritone Taylor Gordon singing work songs on the same program with various "high" art presentations, such as symphonic music and interpretative dance.[30] Thus, it is not surprising that, as Henry Louis Gates Jr. has noted, the first anthology of African-American literature to include vernacular literature under the rubrics of "spirituals," "blues" and "labor songs" and to posit African-American literature as a formally discrete and integral body was *An Anthology of American Negro Literature* (1929) edited by a Communist Party supporter, V. F. Calverton—though Calverton and the CPUSA would split rancorously shortly after the publication of the anthology and its favorable review in *New Masses*.[31]

As a general model for aesthetic excellence and for social liberation, this valorization of various African-American vernacular forms as vehicles for "serious" artistic work (as opposed to the perceived ephemerality or inherent minor status of earlier "dialect" poems seen within Paul Laurence Dunbar's hugely influential opposition of "high" and "low" within his own poetry) was something new for African-American poetry. While there were certainly "protest" poems in the 1920s, these poems, such as McKay's famous protest sonnets, were generally "standard" and "high" in form and diction.[32] During the 1920s even the literary Garveyites published in *The Negro World* and other U.N.I.A journals and broadsides almost never used African-American vernacular language or music in their poetry, writing instead in decidedly "high" diction and poetic forms.[33] Outside of the work of Hughes, Brown (nearly all of whose vernacular poems were published after 1929), Cuney, and Helene Johnson, those relatively few poems of the New Negro Renaissance that were more colloquial in language usually employed a sort of Sandburgian "standard American" vernacular.

As indicated in the title of this study, *The New Red Negro*, which is taken from a line in Langston Hughes's verse play "Scottsboro Limited," radical African-American writers in the 1930s saw a certain continuity in their construction of African-American identity with that of the New Negro of the 1920s. But they also clearly signaled their discontinuity with the earlier period. For example, Hughes's "Red Negro" is not an intellectual or professional, but an ideologically transformed farm laborer. African-American writers such as Hughes, Frank Marshall Davis, and Richard Wright significantly urbanized and proletarianized the Communist-influenced concept of the vernacular. Still an attachment to an essential African-American culture of the rural South remained influential in the CPUSA and its cultural institutions, as demonstrated theoretically in the form of the Black Belt Thesis, which was officially retained, though deemphasized after the rejection of the Third Period policies, and more practically in the lionization of more "traditional" "folk" performers such as Huddie Ledbetter and Sonny Terry during the Popular Front period.

There were practical reasons for a heightened concern with the concrete conditions of black men and women as a result of the economic crisis of the Great Depression, which struck African Americans particularly hard. And as noted earlier, the idea that the folk culture of African Americans provided valuable raw material to be exploited was a common, if not dominant, notion in the 1920s. But if there was a certain precedent for the use of vernacular culture by black poets in "its original form," there was also a tremendous resistance—for example, in the well-known statements of Countee Cullen and James Weldon Johnson on the limitations of "dialect." The most obvious problem was that African-American artists and intellectuals were not the only ones to draw on the raw material of African-American folk culture. The appropriation of African-American vernacular culture by minstrelsy and "plantation literature" in their various permutations was clearly disturbing to most of the artists and intellectuals of the New Negro Renaissance.

To no small extent, the project of many African-American poets in the 1930s was to recapture the folk from minstrelsy. These poets were also engaged in a polemic against those black writers who did more or less adhere to the conventions of "dialect" literature and who used "dialect" as a means of marking and reinforcing intraracial distinctions that lionized a "better class" of African-American "strivers."[34] In order to reclaim the folk without some sort of "high" culture transmutation, it was necessary to create an "authentic" construction of the folk that could be posed against mass-culture appropriations of vernacular culture.[35] Thus, a reciprocal relationship was established: folk culture served to validate or document Left constructions of oppositional culture; Left oppositions of bourgeois culture, including mass culture, to working-class and peasant cultures, however fragmentary or skeletal, could be used to reappropriate vernacular expressive forms, including "dialect," without the contamination of minstrelsy, popular "dialect" literature (such as that of Octavus Roy Cohen), and other forms of popular "misappropriation" of vernacular black culture. Of course, the resulting construct of a pure folk culture was quite problematic since these created "folk" forms generally existed only on the printed page— or the phonograph record—and since lines between the new "folk" works, much less the actual culture of African Americans in the rural South, and mass culture were quite blurry.

One somewhat anxious aspect of this recovery of the folk from minstrelsy can be seen in the "tributary poems" written by radical white authors during the 1930s. These poems dealt with ostensibly African-American topics, often in a "black" voice. They appeared frequently in the journals and newspapers of the Communist Left— including *The Liberator*, which was aimed at an African-American audience. Sometimes these tributary works dealt with specific events, such as the Scottsboro Case (as in Mike Quin's "They Shall Not Die") or the Angelo Herndon case (as in Don West's "Angelo Herndon's Dream"), and at other times with more general, or at least more chronic, manifestations of racism (as in V. J. Jerome's "A Negro Mother to her Child"). These poems differ, at least in the minds of their creators, from earlier humorous "dialect" poems or primitivist representations of the African-American subject (such as Vachel Lindsay's "The Congo") in their adoption of a point of view that assumes the full humanity of the African-American subject even as they admit a cultural and historical particularity. While these poems might seem problematically close to mimicry of the "blacked-up" white minstrel show performer, especially in the poems that speak in a "black" voice, nonetheless they helped create a space in which works by African-American poets dealing with the same subjects could be written and received. For example, without the body of poems written by white radicals about Scottsboro, African-American poets such as Sterling Brown, Countee Cullen, Frank Marshall Davis, Robert Hayden, and Langston Hughes (who all wrote Scottsboro poems) might not have found the case such an attractive subject. This is not to say that there was a unidirectional influence from white poets writing about Scottsboro to African-American poets. African-American poets clearly influenced white poets in this regard. (In fact, if one had to point to a single writer as the most important literary progenitor of the subgenre of Scottsboro poetry, it would have to be Langston Hughes. Hughes wrote a one-act verse play, "Scottsboro Limited," and numerous shorter poems about Scottsboro, many of the them, including the play, first published in *New Masses*.) Rather, the poetry about Scottsboro is a good example of how the frequent interaction in Left journals between the "tributary poems" of white authors and poems by African-American authors helped shape an audience for an African-American poetry of militant protest in a folk voice as well as influencing the thematic concerns of African-American poets.

In the construction of an "authentic" oppositional folk voice, the virtual explosion of folkloric "collecting" done in the late 1920s and in the 1930s by amateur and professional folklorists, anthropologists, and musicologists such as John and Alan Lomax, Mary Elizabeth Barnicle, B. A. Botkin, John Hammond, Melville Herskovits, Zora Neale Hurston, Sterling Brown, and Lawrence Gellert is crucial. Many of these "collectors" were connected to the Left, though the anti-Communist Hurston and John Lomax are obvious exceptions. These scholars made folk material readily available to black and white intellectuals and artists. This was a crucial service at a time when even folk materials with some commercial value, such as the "folk" or "country" blues that formed an important part of the "race" record catalogues of commercial recording companies, were often inaccessible outside of the rural South and the Midwestern cities where black migrants from the Deep South tended to go.[36] The work of the more radical of these folklorists not only argued for an already existing tradition of overt expressions of social struggle in southern African-American folk culture that could be utilized by black (and white) writers but also provided models for writers and their audiences by which a certain vernacular "authenticity" could be measured.

For example, an important, if now overlooked, work was Lawrence Gellert's *Negro Songs of Protest*. These songs, which began to appear in *New Masses* in 1930, were "work reels" with "protest" themes, collected by Gellert in the South from African-American laborers and farmers. The subjects of these songs range from generalized complaints about racism and exploitation to the specifically topical, including the Scottsboro trial. Gellert claimed in his Preface to a 1936 selection of the songs printed by the CPUSA-influenced American Music League:

> [T]hese songs, reflecting as they do the contemporary environment—the daily round of life in the Black Belt—aside from their musical and literary worth, are human documents. They embody the living voice of the otherwise inarticulated resentment against injustice—a part of the unrest that is now stirring in the South. They speak, now mildly, now sarcastically, now angrily—but always in a firm and earnest manner. (7)

There was debate on the Left for decades about the authenticity of the songs.[37] But whether or not the songs were a sort of African-American Ossian cycle, Gellert's "discovery" of songs that validated the cultural premises of the Black Belt Thesis had a significant impact. Gellert's work was a justification of an ideological position that legitimized black writers (and white writers) working with vernacular forms and encouraged others to do so by helping to create an audience that was ready, in fact felt obligated, to receive such work.[38]

For the first time the aesthetic, the political, and vernacular cultures were linked together in a widely accepted construct. This linkage was crucial in developing a new audience and opening new avenues of institutional support for African-American writers. The development was of obvious importance to African-American writers; "mainstream" publishers and journals that were not influenced by the Left showed markedly less interest in publishing works by black authors during the financially difficult years of the Depression than they had been when, to quote Langston Hughes, "the Negro was in vogue" during the 1920s.[39] In addition, many of the African-American journals that published belletristic literature cut back severely on the amount of poetry they published, as in the cases of *Opportunity* and *The Crisis*. Other journals ceased publishing altogether, as in the cases of the "popular" magazines *Abbott's Monthly* and *The Bronzeman*, which both folded in 1933, and the more "literary" *Saturday Evening Quill*.[40]

Such a linkage of the political and "folk" or "popular" African-American culture was not limited to black writers and intellectuals, but rather penetrated deeply into African-American culture. During the 1930s and 1940s, African-American vernacular songs were commonly refashioned into vehicles for explicit social protest on a large scale for the first time since Reconstruction. The most famous example of this process is undoubtedly the transformation of the hymn "I Shall Overcome" by striking members of the Left-led Food, Tobacco and Agricultural Workers Union into the secular standard of political struggle "We Shall Overcome."[41] Of course, this process was not the sole property of the Communist Left, as activities of the SP-led Southern Tenant Farmers Union (STFU) in the 1930s and 1940s indicate. John Handcox, an African-American Socialist and organizer for the STFU, was one of the most prolific radical "rewriters" of vernacular hymns and folk songs. (His reworking of the hymn "Roll the Chariot On" into "Roll the Union On" with the aid, apparently, of CPUSA member or sympathizer Lee Hays at the Commonwealth Labor School in Arkansas remains a trade union standard.) Yet the politics and political style of the movement culture associated with such Socialist activists in the South as Handcox and Myles Horton, the director of the Highlander School in Tennessee, had more in common with the Communists, with whom they often worked closely during the 1930s and 1940s, than with either the uncompromising "Leftism" of Norman Thomas or the economism of "right" SP leaders based in the bureaucracy of the needle trades unions.

This period, particularly after the official inauguration of the Popular Front policy of the CPUSA in 1935, also saw the emergence of new hybrids of "high" and popular media. For example, Waring Cuney wrote a series of "protest" lyrics in a blues or blues-inflected mode. These songs were set to music and recorded by Josh White, a familiar figure of the Left cultural circuit, on the record *Southern Exposure*, a record which also had liner notes by Richard Wright.[42] Wright himself wrote the lyrics to the blues song "King Joe" (about boxer Joe Louis), which was recorded by Paul Robeson and the Count Basie Orchestra. (Count Basie was credited with the authorship of the music.) One could also mention Langston Hughes's agitational play "Don't You Want to Be Free," performed first in Harlem under the auspices of the International Workers Order, which combined Hughes's poetry with sections of blues and spirituals. This type of "high" culture–mass culture hybrid continued into the 1940s, as demonstrated by the musical collaboration of Langston Hughes and the left-wing composer Earl Robinson, "We'll Hammer It Out Together," written in response to the Detroit riot of 1943, which was sung by Paul Robeson on a CIO radio show in November 1943. Of course, "serious" African-American poets, most notably James Weldon Johnson, had written songs for the popular stage earlier, but never before were the different levels of "high" and "low" art so mixed.[43] (And again it is important to note that this mixing of "high" and "low" was not restricted to black artists, as Woody Guthrie's six-minute condensation of *The Grapes of Wrath* to the tune of the folk song "John Hardy" attests.)[44]

The Infrastructure of Feeling: Left Institutions and African-American Writing in the 1930s and 1940s

The importance of the CPUSA and the cultural institutions it led or influenced for African-American poetry was practical as well as ideological. Of course, since the ideological positions on the "national question" that resulted from the Sixth Congress of the Comintern caused "Negro liberation" to be put at the center of the CPUSA agenda, the practical promotion of African-American literature flowed from the ideological. The emphasis on "Negro liberation" that resulted from the Sixth Congress made the promotion of African-American writers a prime imperative for the cultural institutions of the Communist Left. For example, one of the directives to *New Masses* from the Kharkov conference of writers and artists organized by the International Union of Revolutionary Writers (IURW) in November 1930 was to promote the "development of Negro writers and artists."[45] This directive was clearly a part of the Comintern's 1930 drive to take much more seriously the positions on the "question" adopted at the Sixth Congress in 1928.

This practical promotion of black writers by the Left during the 1930s and 1940s falls into three basic categories, which will be listed here in brief and then described in more detail later in the chapter. First, the Left facilitated the access of African-American authors to institutions, both Left and "mainstream," outside of the African-American community, providing these authors with financial support and an expanded audience. Second, the Left encouraged the development of specifically African-American institutions aimed at developing African-American literature as a distinctive body of literature and at creating new African-American audiences for that literature. Finally, the Left made possible a new level of international contact with writers abroad, in Asia, Africa, the Caribbean, Latin America, and Europe, allowing African-American writers to reach a larger international audience than ever before.

In order to understand more clearly how this promotion of African-American writers was carried out by Left and Left-influenced institutions, it is necessary to sketch out these institutions and make some basic distinctions between them with respect to their organizational and ideological relationship to the CPUSA. There are, of course, some problems with what is essentially a "center-periphery" model outlined below. The distinctions between the various types of institutions often seem somewhat arbitrary. Also, placing the CPUSA at the center can play into various anti-Communist distortions. Nonetheless, such distinctions are helpful in tracking institutional behavior with respect to African-American writing in the 1930s and 1940s.

Prominent among Left cultural institutions of the early 1930s were journals and newspapers openly affiliated with the CPUSA or CPUSA-led organizations, such as the John Reed Clubs (JRC).[46] These would include official CPUSA organs such as the *Daily Worker*, the *Southern Worker*, and the *Western Worker* (followed by the *People's World*), as well as the quasi-official CPUSA journal *New Masses*. Poems by Langston Hughes as well as a large number of Hughes's translations of poetry and prose were printed in virtually every journal or organ connected with the CPUSA. Sterling Brown's poetry appeared in the pages of *New Masses* as well as *Partisan Review* (while it was still affiliated with the CPUSA) when his second collection of poetry was rejected by mainstream publishers, possibly for being too radical.[47] Countee Cullen published "Scottsboro, Too, Deserves Its Song" in the *Daily Worker* in 1932; other poems by Cullen were printed in *New Masses* in the 1940s. Gwendolyn Bennett's poetry also appeared in the *Daily Worker* as well as *New Masses*. The local organizations and journals of the JRC, such as *Partisan Review* in New York City, *Left Review* in Philadelphia, *Left Front* in Chicago, *Midland Left* in Indianapolis, and *New Force* in

Detroit, played a crucial role in developing young African-American intellectuals and writers, including Richard Wright, Eugene Gordon (the former editor of a Boston literary journal the *Saturday Evening Quill*), Eugene Clay Holmes (under the name Eugene Clay), Frank Ankenbrand, and Robert Hayden, and in bringing them close to the CPUSA.[48]

Beyond the actual publication of African-American poets, these journals and newspapers frequently reviewed books by African-American authors—and often the reviews were by African-American authors and intellectuals such as Sterling Brown, Ralph Bunche, Ralph Ellison, Eugene Gordon, Eugene Clay Holmes, Alain Locke, Loren Miller, and Richard Wright. In addition to reviewing, these journals of the Communist Left frequently promoted books by black authors in other ways—*New Masses*, for example, often had books by African Americans in its list of books that one could get with a subscription to the magazine. Of course, African-American writers had appeared in *New Masses* and other CPUSA and CPUSA-influenced journals before the Sixth Comintern Congress. But, despite articles, reviews, and poems by African-Americans, and, less frequently, articles about African-Americans, and, despite the appearance of well-known African-American writers and intellectuals on the masthead as contributing editors, *New Masses*, for example, published far more pieces by African Americans and about African Americans after 1930, when the Comintern directives with respect to the "national question" were seriously undertaken by the CPUSA.[49]

A group of closely related CPUSA institutions were the network of Workers Bookstores that were run by the various districts and sections of the CPUSA, the Central Distribution Agency (CDA) that distributed Left literature to newsstands as well as to various bookstores, including the Workers Bookstores, and Left publishers affiliated with the CPUSA. While these bookstores and the CDA dealt mainly in affordable editions of Marxist and Marxist-Leninist classics and contemporary CPUSA newspapers, books, and pamphlets, they also sold a considerable amount of "imaginative" literature. The sales volume of these bookstores was apparently enormous, particularly by the early 1930s. Though reliable sales figures are not available, one sign of the importance of these bookstores to the literary Left is Jack Conroy's claim that the CPUSA was able to compel his journal *The Anvil* to merge with *Partisan Review* in 1936 against his wishes with a threat by CPUSA cultural "commissar" V. J. Jerome that CPUSA bookstores and the CDA would stop selling *The Anvil*.[50] While Conroy may have been exaggerating Jerome's threat, the threat's apparent effectiveness is still a testimony to the success of the CPUSA bookstores. Though it is hard to say definitively, it seems safe to assume that some sigificant part of the sales of Hughes's *Scottsboro Limited* and *A New Song*, both heavily promoted by the Communist Left, was through the Workers Bookstores and the CDA.

The CPUSA publishing house International Publishers was condemned with some justification by Mike Gold in the early 1930s as being "stodgy and unenterprising" with respect to the fiction and poetry it published. But it did occasionally issue the work of African-American poets. For example, the work of Sterling Brown was included in *Get Organized*, a 1940 collection of three authors, at a time when Brown could not find a "mainstream" publisher. The poetry of Hughes and Wright (as well as a couple of Gellert's *Negro Songs of Protest*) appeared in the well-known International Publishers' collection *Proletarian Literature in the United States* (1935). To the work issued by International Publishers needs to added that put out by organizations closely affiliated with the CPUSA, such as the International Workers Order (IWO), which issued Langston Hughes's collection *A New Song* in 1938 in a run of 10,000—Hughes's largest initial run to that date.

Other cultural institutions directly connected with the CPUSA were part of what might be thought of as an educational and recreational network: the many schools, reading tours, forums, classes, lectures, choruses, exhibits, study circles, and summer camps organized by the JRC; CPUSA Districts, Sections, and Units; Left Fraternal [sic] Organizations, such as the IWO; and "Cultural Clubs" (often offshoots of the old Foreign Language Federations). Events sponsored by these institutions often featured the poetry of African-American authors. Langston Hughes, for example, traveled to twelve cities in the Northeast and the Midwest on a reading tour sponsored by the IWO in 1938. Hughes's close friend Louise Thompson generated considerable pre-publication excitement about Hughes's 1938 *A New Song* by reading poems from the collection at various functions in her capacity as an organizer for the IWO.[51] African-American poets, including Gwendolyn Bennett, Arna Bontemps, Sterling Brown, Waring Cuney, Frank Marshall Davis, Jessie Fauset, Langston Hughes, and Richard Wright, read, taught, or guest-lectured at the various educational forums and schools, such as the Jefferson School for Social Research in New York, the George Washington Carver School in Harlem (headed by Gwendolyn Bennett), and the Abraham Lincoln School in Chicago, sponsored by the CPUSA or organized by CPUSA members and sympathizers.[52] Somewhat more distant from the CPUSA were radical educational institutions, such as the Highlander School in Tennessee and Commonwealth School in Arkansas, which were organizationally independent of the CPUSA. In fact, Highlander and Commonwealth were largely run by Socialists. But Communists and their supporters were often among the student body, faculty, and guest lecturers. (There was an active John Reed Club branch at Commonwealth in the early 1930s.)

This network was not simply restricted to the formal educational and recreational institutions of the Left but also included an entire subcultural social life: parties; picnics; informal meetings at cafeterias, apartments, bars, restaurants, and social centers; and so on. Such unofficial social events gave a further density to the support provided by institutions.[53] As Margaret Walker and Frank Marshall Davis point out, this official and unofficial subcultural network provided many African-American writers with what was often their first positive experience of American culture outside the ghetto.[54]

Beyond the journals and other institutions organizationally connected with the CPUSA is the network of Left or Left-influenced journals and other institutions that were not organizationally linked with the CPUSA, but which were sympathetic to the party.[55] These would include journals such as *Dynamo* in New York City; *The Anvil* in Moberly, Missouri; and *Contempo* in Chapel Hill, North Carolina. Though they were not official JRC or CPUSA journals, these periodicals were edited by members of the JRC and / or the CPUSA. *The Anvil* in particular was open to radical African-American poets such as Hughes and Wright. *Contempo*, which for a time combined modernist aesthetics and radical politics, also devoted considerable space to writing by and about African Americans, especially during the first two years of its three-year existence. During this period, Langston Hughes was listed as a contributing editor and Countee Cullen as a contributor on *Contempo*'s masthead.

Close in spirit to these journals, and those of the JRC, were the many other little magazines of the proletarian literature movement in the early 1930s, such as *The Windsor Quarterly* in Vermont and *Blast* in New York. These magazines were unabashedly pro-Communist and enthusiastic about proletarian literature (even if no one could quite decide what it was). Nonetheless, these journals (and their editors) generally lacked a direct organizational connection to the CPUSA—except perhaps through a loose affiliation with the JRC. Subvariants of this sort of journal were the largely Midwest-based Left regionalist magazines, such as *Hub* in Cedar Rapids, Iowa, and *Hinterland* in Cedar Rapids and later Des Moines, which simultaneously promoted regional literature and proletarian or radical literature.[56]

On the fringes of the early 1930s "proletarian" literary network were journals such as *Morada* in New Mexico and *The Magazine* in Beverly Hills that were in many ways closer in spirit to 1920s small, formally "experimental" magazines such as *transition* and *Broom*, but that became politically radicalized to some significant degree and were open to the burgeoning Left literary movement. Even *Poetry* in Chicago, a product of pre–World War I American modernism, published much poetry by Left-influenced writers, including Sterling Brown, Langston Hughes, and Margaret Walker, until the onset of the "high" cold-war period.[57] A similar case was that of *Fantasy*, which began in 1931 as a journal of genteel and formally conservative poetry. Over the next few years, *Fantasy* became progressively more engaged with modernism and with the radical Left, publishing poems by white radicals on lynching and the Scottsboro case as well as poems by Left African-American writers such as Frank Ankenbrand Jr. and Frank Marshall Davis.

Other significant institutions that were organizationally outside the CPUSA and yet within the circle of the literary Left included publishers, such as Vanguard, the Negro Publication Society of America, Dryden Press, Covici-Friede, and Dynamo. These presses were not directly run by the CPUSA (as was International Publishers), but were Left influenced. However, other than the Negro Publication Society of America (probably closest organizationally and ideologically to the CPUSA) and Dryden Press, these publishers were not particularly interested in African-American literature or, with the exception of Dynamo, poetry in general, preferring fiction instead.[58]

Beyond those officially Left journals, but within the circle of Left literary culture, were "mainstream" journals opened to radical African-American writers through the political sympathies of Left editors. Well-known examples of this influence by the Communist Left, at least for a time in the 1930s, were The *New Republic* (where Langston Hughes's pro-Third Period "Ballad of Roosevelt" appeared in 1934) and *The American Spectator* (where Hughes's "Broadcast on Ethiopia" was first published in 1936). For that matter, "liberal" publications such as *The Nation* and *Common Ground*, while lacking a well-known connection to the Communist Left in the manner of Edmund Wilson and Malcolm Cowley at *The New Republic*, were influenced by the Communist Left's interest in African-American cultural production. *Common Ground*, with its commitment to multiculturalism, was particularly open to the work of African-American writers as well as non-African-American left-wing writers whose connection to the CPUSA was quite open, such as Woody Guthrie, Meridel Le Sueur, Carlos Bulosan, and Eve Merriam. During its existence from 1940 to 1949, *Common Ground* published poems by such African-American writers as Gwendolyn Brooks, Owen Dodson, Langston Hughes (who was an editorial adviser to the journal), and Melvin Tolson.[59] Another "mainstream" institution in which there was a discernible Left bent after the beginning of the Popular Front was the Yale Series of Younger Poets, largely through the office of the series editor Stephen Vincent Benét. Left-wing writers in the 1930s and 1940s, including James Agee, Muriel Rukeyser, Joy Davidman, Eve Merriam, and Norman Rosten, were frequently given the Yale Younger Poet award. Margaret Walker's manuscript of *For My People* won the award in 1942.

Another institution that was certainly not controlled by the CPUSA, but in which the influence of the Communists was decisive so far as African Americans were concerned, was the WPA Federal Writers Project. A definitive history of the Federal Writers Project (FWP) has yet to be written. Likewise, comprehensive studies of either the influence of the Left on the FWP or of the role of African-Americans within the FWP have not been completed. However, the role of the CPUSA in fighting for jobs for African Americans on the WPA is well documented.[60] Certainly, African-American poets, novelists, and essayists who were members of the FWP, including William Attaway, Arna Bontemps, Waring Cuney, Robert Hayden, Fenton Johnson, Claude McKay, Willard Motley, Margaret Walker, and Richard Wright, were overwhelmingly concentrated in state FWP organizations, particularly New York and Illinois, where the CPUSA had much influence. As Jerre Mangione notes, the financial support of the FWP was crucial to these writers during the period. The FWP also allowed black writers to network with other writers inside and outside the African-American community, resulting in publishing opportunities that would have been otherwise unavailable, especially to the younger artists. (For example, Robert Hayden's exposure to a national audience took place for the first time in the 1937 anthology of writing from the FWP, *American Stuff.*)[61] In addition to the Left connections of African-American workers at the individual state projects, the national editor for "Negro affairs" was Sterling Brown, whose Left sympathies were well known during the 1930s and 1940s. One of Brown's chief assistants at the FWP, Eugene Clay Holmes, a member of the Howard University philosophy department, was closely associated with the CPUSA in the middle and late 1930s, writing frequently on African-American culture for CPUSA newspapers and journals (often under the name Eugene Clay).[62]

Beyond providing an entree into many journals and institutions not specifically oriented toward African Americans, the CPUSA emphasis on "Negro liberation" and the fight against racism often supported the development of specifically African-American journals and institutions that promoted African-American poets. This is a somewhat controversial claim. Literary scholars, cultural critics, and historians as diverse as Claude McKay, Zora Neale Hurston, Harold Cruse, Mark Naison, and Walter

Kalaidjian have argued in varying degrees that the CPUSA inhibited, and even sabotaged, the development of organic African-American-led political and cultural institutions. They assert that the CPUSA insisted instead on a sort of "integration from above" in which African Americans would never have any real power.

One problem with these arguments is that they tend to focus on the Harlem Section of the CPUSA as the model of the typical relationship of the CPUSA to African Americans. While the precise demographics of the CPUSA during the 1930s and 1940s are difficult to determine, the black membership of the Harlem Section of the CPUSA was probably less than 10 percent of the total African-American membership of the CPUSA for most of the 1930s and 1940s.[63] The Harlem Section thus never represented more than a small percentage of black Communists in the United States. Neither was the CPUSA organization in central Harlem notably "typical."

In fact, the organizational culture of the CPUSA varied considerably from region to region (and even from locale to locale in a specific region), particularly with respect to African Americans. For example, as Robin Kelley has pointed out, the CPUSA in Alabama had a considerably larger African-American membership than the Harlem Section for much of the 1930s before the Popular Front. While the Alabama Communist Party was not formally a "black" organization, it had few white members so that the bulk of the work of the Alabama Communist Party was led and carried out by and among African Americans. Kelley notes that in Alabama much of the culture of rank-and-file black Communists was rooted in African-American religious expression. Unlike the case in New York and Chicago before the Popular Front, this use of black Christianity was not opposed by local CPUSA leadership.[64] Similar scholarship about the work of the CPUSA in other southern centers of significant Left activity, such as Chattanooga (where the *Southern Worker* was edited), Nashville, Winston-Salem, Charlotte, Greenville, New Orleans (home of a branch of the Southern Negro Youth Congress's People's Theater), Richmond (in which another branch of the SNYC People's Theater was located), Norfolk, Houston, Atlanta (site of the famous Angelo Herndon case as well as one of the first United Auto Worker's sit-down strikes), Miami, and Tampa remains scanty, if not nonexistent. But the work of Robin Kelley, that of historian Michael Honey, and a number of other studies that touch on the work of the Communist Left in the South, suggest that the African-American experience in the CPUSA in the South was in itself quite varied.

Similarly, the experience of African-American Communists in the Midwestern industrial centers differed considerably from that of their counterparts in Harlem. Generally speaking, the proportion of African-American membership to the total number of CPUSA members in these cities was much higher than in New York.[65] Richard Wright's portrait of his life in the CPUSA in Chicago is instructive in this regard. Wright's account in the portion of *Black Boy* first published as *American Hunger* is frequently taken as the canonical example of the cynical mistreatment of the artist and the African-American by the CPUSA. Leaving aside the historical accuracy of Wright's chronology of events (which is at the very least temporally compressed and misleadingly framed since Wright did not leave the CPUSA at the point the book ends in 1937, but moved to New York in the same year, where he remained in the CPUSA until 1942), a number of interesting things can be gleaned from Wright's account about the CPUSA organization among African-Americans in Chicago.[66] Wright describes the party "unit" that he joins on the South Side as entirely African-American. It is also clear from Wright's description that a certain subcultural style (of dress, speech, cultural interests, and so on) had developed among African-American Communists, a style with which Wright is not entirely comfortable.

Robert Stepto suggests that Wright's problem is that he is uncomfortable with vernacular working-class African-American culture in general.[67] However, it is not the general culture with which Wright has problems but the particular subculture of black South Side Communists. Wright actually describes his conflict with the party not in terms of conflict with a particular party policy or with the top leadership. Rather his problem is with the anti-intellectual rank-and-file "Negro Communists" who "did not know anything and did not want to learn anything."[68] In short, whether or not Wright is accurate in his assessment, his portrait of the CPUSA in the "black belt" of the South Side is of an all-black local organization with a cultural and intellectual life that he negatively counterposed to the party organization outside of the South Side.

The situation in the far West was still another story. When CPUSA membership among AfricanAmericans was declining in New York—and many other regions—after World War II, there was apparently a sharp increase in the black membership in southern California. According to Dorothy Healey, a former district organizer for the Southern California District of the CPUSA, the African-American membership of the CPUSA in Los Angeles numbered several hundred in the late 1940s and was much larger relatively and, perhaps, absolutely, than in the Harlem Section.[69] Jessica Mitford, a leader of the Communist-led Civil Rights Congress (CRC) in northern California during the late 1940s and the early 1950s, made a similar point about the growth of the East Bay CRC in the post-World War II era.[70]

Even in New York there was considerable space for institutions run largely by African Americans for African Americans (and perceived by African Americans as African American) despite the connection of those institutions to the CPUSA. For example, as Robin Kelley has pointed out, the New York–based CPUSA journal that was known variously as *The Negro Champion*, *The Liberator*, *The Negro Liberator*, and *The Harlem Liberator* during the 1920s and 1930s was taken by a largely African-American audience as a "Negro" journal. (*The Negro Liberator* contained many poems that were quite nationalist in content and were hardly distinguishable formally and thematically from poems published in the Garveyite *The Negro World*.)[71] Similarly, the initial 1938 run of Langston Hughes's "poetry-play" "Don't You Want to Be Free" was produced in Harlem under the auspices of the CPUSA-led International Workers Order using an African-American cast and crew for a primarily African-American audience that received it enthusiastically.[72]

In short, despite some claims to the contrary, the development of specifically African-American cultural institutions and practices within the context of the Left was quite possible (and sometimes encouraged by the CPUSA leadership), even in Harlem. In fact, the CPUSA position that "African Americans" were a nationality or national minority, a position held throughout the 1930s and 1940s with varying degrees of intensity, virtually dictated the necessity of such institutions. (Though, as noted above, the actual practice of CPUSA varied considerably according to historical period and locale.) As with the cultural institutions of the Left generally, the range of these African-American institutions included those affiliated with the CPUSA, others sympathetic or open to the Left in some degree, but not directly linked to the CPUSA, and "mainstream" institutions not normally thought of as "Left," but which the Left was able to influence.

Among the African-American institutions and journals directly affiliated with the CPUSA and the organizations it led during the 1930s and 1940s would be the *Negro Liberator* in its various incarnations. (The *Negro Liberator* published poetry ranging from "spirituals" and "blues" rewritten (allegedly by workers and farmers) with a "struggle" message, to quasi-nationalist poems using the lofty diction and rhymed couplets typical of many poems published earlier in the Garveyite *Negro World*, to the work of well-known poets, particularly Langston Hughes.) This category also includes the 1940s journals *Negro Quarterly*, edited by Ralph Ellison and 1930s Communist hero Angelo Herndon, and *Cavalcade*, the magazine of the Southern Negro Youth Congress (SNYC), which during its short career was a significant African-American literary voice in the South. In addition to the various journals are the readings, publishing ventures such as the Negro Publication Society of America (which published Langston Hughes's 1943 collection of poetry *Jim Crow's Last Stand* as well as the journal *Negro Quarterly*), study groups, schools, literary groups, theater groups, news services (notably the Crusader News Agency which served 250 African-American newspapers), and so on organized by African-American organizations such as the League of Struggle for Negro Rights, SNYC, and the National Negro Congress, which were led or strongly influenced by the CPUSA.[73]

A closely related category is that of African-American journals and institutions run, or significantly influenced, by people who were members of the CPUSA even if the institution itself was not attached to the CPUSA as such. This category includes such journals and newspapers as *New Challenge* (after Dorothy West had abandoned the editorship to Richard Wright) in the 1930s, *Harlem Quarterly* in the late 1940s, Paul Robeson's *Freedom* (which first appeared in 1951), and the Harlem newspaper *People's Voice* during the period in the 1940s when it was edited by the well-known African-American Communist Doxey Wilkerson.[74] Under this rubric would also be placed the South Side Writers Group in Chicago. (Largely organized by Richard Wright in 1936 as a spin-off of the National Negro Congress, the South Side Writers Group included among its participants the poets Frank Marshall Davis and Margaret Walker and, on occasion, Arna Bontemps and Fenton Johnson.)[75] A somewhat similar grouping of African-American artists and intellectuals in which publically identified Leftists played key roles was that associated with the Vanguard Arts Center and the "306 Group" in Harlem.[76]

Again, somewhat farther from the CPUSA are those black journals and institutions that were influenced by the Left, though their connection (and that of their editors, organizers, chairs, and so on) to the CPUSA was generally indirect. In this group can be placed such journals and institutions as *Challenge* under the editorship of Dorothy West in the 1930s, the South Side Community Art Center in Chicago (site of Inez Cunningham Stark's influential poetry workshop which Gwendolyn Brooks and Margaret Danner attended) whose director Fern Gayden was an active member of the South Side Writers Group as well as a co-editor of the journal *Negro Story*, and *Negro Story* itself. (*Negro Story*, despite its name, was one of the most significant outlets for African-American poetry in the 1940s, publishing poems by Langston Hughes [including his famous "Madam" series], Owen Dodson, Frank Marshall Davis, Margaret Walker, and Gwendolyn Brooks.)[77]

Finally, there were those "mainstream" African-American institutions, such as the newspapers the *Baltimore Afro-American*, the *Chicago Defender*, and the *Michigan Chronicle* (which published Robert Hayden's first and politically radical collection *Heart-Shape in the Dust*), in which publishers (as in the case of George Murphy of the *Afro-American*), editors (as in the cases of Louis Martin of the *Michigan Chronicle*, Charlotta Bass of the *California Eagle*, Ben Burns of the *Chicago Defender*, and William Harrison of the *Boston Chronicle*), and/or reporters and columnists (such as Earl Conrad of the *Chicago Defender*, Marvel Cooke of the *Amsterdam News* [and later the *People's Voice*], and Loren Miller of the *California Eagle*) were extremely sympathetic to the Communist Left—if not actually party members. These columns and stories of African-American writers, often literary or cultural criticism, were a crucial, and still generally unconsidered, aspect of the Popular Front reaching hundreds of thousands of readers. Next to the Federal Writers Project, the African-American press, particularly the more Left-influenced newspapers, was probably the most important institution promoting and sustaining belletristic African-American writers during the 1930s and 1940s. Among the poets and fiction writers of the era who worked in the black press as editors, reporters, and columnists are Robert Hayden (*Michigan Chronicle*), Langston Hughes (*Baltimore Afro-American* and *Chicago Defender*), Ann Petry (*People's Voice*), Melvin Tolson (*Washington Tribune*), and Frank Marshall Davis (Associated Negro Press).[78]

The impact of the CPUSA on African-American writers had a worldwide scope. Earlier moments of African-American culture had reached beyond the boundaries of the United States, as in Locke's claim of Harlem as "the capital of the Negro world" during the 1920s and in the Pan-African claims of the Garvey movement. But this reach was more rhetorical than actual with respect to literary production. However, because of the global connections of the CPUSA through the Comintern and the internationalist ideology it espoused, the Communist Left encouraged an ideological and practical internationalism among African-American writers to a greater extent than ever before. The *Daily Worker* in the early 1930s was filled with news and editorials about the anticolonial—and antineocolonial—struggles in Asia, Africa, and the Americas, drawing connections between the conditions of African-Americans in the South and the oppression of workers and peasants in Haiti, Cuba, Brazil, Liberia, the Congo, South Africa, and so on.

The cultural apparatus of the Comintern, principally the International Union of Revolutionary Writers (IURW) and its journal *International Literature*, brought the work of Langston Hughes, Sterling Brown, and Richard Wright to a large new foreign audience during the 1930s. The resulting international reputation of various African-American writers in turn facilitated the ability of these writers to expand their audience through the efforts of Left organizations and individuals throughout the 1930s and 1940s. Hughes's first public reading in Britain, for instance, was organized by the Readers and Writers Group of the Popular Front Left Book Club in 1938.[79]

In addition to providing new potential audiences for African-American writers, this apparatus promoted new associations of African-American writers with other writers on the Left, particularly those from the nonanglophone colonies and semi-colonies of the European and North American colonial powers. Thus, for example, an important aspect of Hughes's work in the 1930s and 1940s as a result of his engagement with the Communist Left is the translation of such radical "colonial" or "neocolonial" writers as Nicolás Guillén, Jacques Roumain, and Regine Pederoso, as well as Europeans such as Federico Garcia Lorca (the martyr of Spanish Republicanism) and Soviet modernist-Bolshevik icon Vladimir Mayakovsky. Many of these translations appeared in *International Literature*, *New Masses*, *Partisan Review*, and other Left journals. In all these cases, the translations were not simply acts of artistic interest or even sympathy but also declarations of ideological kinship. Another interesting product of this internationalism was Nancy Cunard's 1934 anthology *Negro*, which combined an enormous amount of belletristic, sociological, anthropological, and historiographical material about Africa and the African diaspora collected over several years within a frame that mixed an evident enthusiasm for the New Negro Renaissance and African-American cultural expression in the 1920s with an equally apparent sympathy for the Communist movement. While various practical problems prevented *Negro* from reaching more than a handful of people, it remains an important transitional document between the 1920s and 1930s and had the effect of making a number of African-American writers see themselves in a new intercontinental context.

Interestingly, one impact of this internationalism that distanced itself from Garveyite metonymies of Africa as the "race" and primitivist constructs of African naturalness is that there was less focus on Africa as a spiritual home of African Americans. There remained a special interest in Africa, particularly in the Italian invasion of Ethiopia in 1935 (as attested by Hughes's "Ballad of Ethiopia" and "Broadcast on Ethiopia"). However, this interest was placed within a general anticolonialism and anticapitalism posing a certain commonalty of colonial oppression (often related to "color") and class oppression without the same metonymic relationship between Africa and "Negroes" that characterized the rhetoric of the Garveyites (who also had a general anticolonialist outlook).[80] For example, Richard Wright's "I Am a Red Slogan" can be said to have an internationalist (and antiracist) stance, but not one which is particularly concerned with Africa.[81] The spiritual African-American homeland is much more commonly located in the South, and when extended beyond the South, tends to be American in the hemispheric sense, as in Margaret Walker's "Sorrow Song"—though Walker is one poet who often alludes to some, generally distant African connection in her first collection, *For My People* (1942).

A Dream Referred: Continuities from the Crash to the Cold War

Of course, the problem with the above consideration of the ideological and institutional impact of the Communist Left on African-American poetry is that it is overly synchronic and, despite various caveats, tends to flatten the distinctions between the various cultural moments of the 1930s and 1940s. For example, the Left literary landscape looked quite different in 1932, when a huge number of journals affiliated with the "proletarian literature" movement began to appear, than after the official abandonment of that movement and the John Reed Clubs themselves by the Communist Left in 1934, marking a sharp decline in what Michael Denning calls the "mushroom mags" of the "proletarian avant-garde."[82] Other literary journals influenced by the Communist Left emerged during and after the Popular Front, including *The Clipper*, *Negro Quarterly*, *Direction*, and *The Span* (of which Langston Hughes was an "editor at large")—but far fewer than during the "proletarian" era. The League of American Writers that replaced the JRC was, at least in its inception, more oriented to well-established writers and less interested in finding new "proletarian" voices. (Though, as I will note later, this break between Third Period proletarianism and the Popular Front is much less clear than is often assumed by commentators on the literary Left of the 1930s.)[83]

Other disruptions of any easy notion of a unified period can be cited. The CPUSA advocacy of the Black Belt Thesis varied considerably in its intensity during the 1930s and 1940s, though it would remain the official position of the CPUSA throughout the period. The 1939 Nonaggression Pact between Germany and the Soviet Union was an intense shock to many writers and intellectuals, particularly in New York. And so on. One explanation of these disjunctions of CPUSA ideology and practice that presents the organizational behavior of the CPUSA as a coherent whole is that the CPUSA (and Popular Front) as a tool of the Soviet Union was an expression of Stalin's domestic and foreign policy needs. This attitude remains the dominant historiographical explanation of "elite" Communist behavior not only in the "orthodox" histories, such as those of Draper and Klehr, but also in most of the "revisionist" histories. While the influence that Stalin exerted on the CPUSA was no doubt crucial, these views tend to see the CPUSA leadership after the 1920s as essentially unified except in periods of crisis. (Ironically, both Communists and extreme anti-Communists tend to promote this view of party unity, if for quite different reasons.) The fact is, as Harry Haywood points out in his autobiography *Black Bolshevik*, that serious political differences, arising largely from domestic concerns existed from the rank-and-file level up to the top leadership throughout the history of the CPUSA. While these differences were often relatively subterranean, during the period covered by this study they broke out into the open in 1945 and 1946 over the dissolution of the CPUSA and the formation of the Communist Political Association in 1944 at the behest of CPUSA General Secretary Earl Browder and the subsequent reconstitution of the CPUSA under the apparent prodding of Stalin through the agency of French Communist Party leader Jacques Duclos in 1945.

However, a considerable institutional and ideological continuity can be traced through the whole period—at least as far as African-American writers are concerned. With the partial exception of the period from the German invasion of the Soviet Union to the end of the Second World War, the CPUSA placed the issue of race and the fight against Jim Crow near the center of all its work, whether or not it was actually agitating for a Black Belt republic. The most extended discussion of the literary applications of the Black Belt Thesis, and the burning necessity of such applications, by a leading writer connected to the Communist Left, Richard Wright's

"Blueprint for Negro Writing," appeared at the height of the Popular Front period.[84] James W. Ford, the executive secretary of the Harlem Division of the CPUSA and the leading African-American Communist during the Popular Front era, declared in a speech on the relation of African Americans to the "Democratic Front" at the Tenth National Convention of the CPUSA in 1938:

> It is the life, the work, the struggles of the Negro masses—in the cottonfields, on the wharves, on the railroads, in the factories—which constitute the essence of the authentic culture of the American Negro. More and more the younger writers, artists and musicians among the Negro people are coming to recognize this fact. The revolutionary tradition, the true folk experiences of the race, are being newly appraised and utilized in all the arts. Langston Hughes and Sterling Brown have done outstanding work in reinterpreting this folk experience in poetry. Richard Wright, Frank Davis and others make up a group of younger writers who are keenly aware of the Negro's past and present position in American history. (92)

Ford's speech represents a break with Third Period conceptions of the African-American folk in that industrial workers and rural laborers are considered as a cultural whole. However, in his insistence that there is a distinctive African-American oppositional culture rooted in the folk and that this culture presents formal and thematic models for contemporary "high" African-American artists, Ford has much in common with the earlier CPUSA formulation of the "national question."[85] For that matter, the lionization of Abraham Lincoln by the Communist Left during the Popular Front from "Lenin-Lincoln Memorial Meetings" to the Abraham Lincoln Brigade marked a continuation of this overwhelming concern with racial and "national" oppression as much as it did an effort to more broadly "Americanize" and "popularize" the CPUSA.[86]

As late into the World War II period as July 1942, Samuel Sillen, a leading reviewer for *New Masses*, criticized Sterling Brown, Arthur P. Davis, and Ulysses Lee's anthology *The Negro Caravan* (1942) on the basis that the anthology insufficiently considered the "national question."[87] During the various factional fights of the 1940s, the ideological issue of "Negro liberation" was used by the anti-Browder forces as a tool to defeat "Browderism." Thus it was not accidental that what might be thought of as the "de-Browderization" campaign of the late 1940s involved a renewed commitment to the Black Belt Thesis and the (temporary) rehabilitation of Harry Haywood as a Communist theoretician (as signaled by the publication of his 1948 book *Negro Liberation*).

With respect to literature, this persistent concern with the "national question," however it was posed, meant that the cultural institutions of the CPUSA sought to promote relatively unknown African-American writers who were not "names" even after the end of the John Reed Clubs and the adoption of the Popular Front.[88] Of course, whatever the new attitude toward "bourgeois" "name" writers and artists after the beginning of the Popular Front, most of Left cultural activists associated with the CPUSA, particularly those whose association with the Left antedated the Popular Front, such as Mike Gold, Jack Conroy, Langston Hughes, Richard Wright, and Meridel Le Sueur, remained committed to nurturing "authentic" voices of the working class and the racially and/or nationally oppressed, whether Huddie Ledbetter, Owen Dodson, Bunk Johnson, or Woody Guthrie.[89] Thus, in theory one could argue that the integrationist implications of the construction of a polyvocal, but relatively unified "people" during the Popular Front and the World War II period tended to (in theory) discourage the notion of "African-American" identity as distinct from an "American" identity. But, in practice Leftist African-American artists continued to represent and recreate the African-American folk voice and folk subject, sometimes while engaging with Popular Front rhetoric of "the People."[90] As I will discuss in the next section of this chapter, the change in the gendering of the folk and the folk voice during the Popular Front was a change of greater significance to poetry by African Americans than the abolishment of the John Reed Clubs and the formation of the League of American Writers (in which African-American poets, including Langston Hughes, Richard Wright, Sterling Brown, and Frank Marshall Davis, continued to have important roles).[91]

Similarly, the 1939 non-aggression pact caused few major ruptures between Left African-American writers and intellectuals and the CPUSA. It is true that the pact had a significant impact on the work of the CPUSA in Harlem, especially among the intelligentsia. This impact was seen not so much in the loss of actual party members and supporters as in the limiting of the ability of the CPUSA to work with non-Communist liberals and progressives. But no major Left African-American literary figure broke with the CPUSA over the pact in the manner of Granville Hicks or Malcolm Cowley—though some, such as Frank Marshall Davis and Langston Hughes, would later claim that they were deeply troubled by the pact.[92] But even Hughes, who would testify before the Senate Committee on Government Operations in March 1953 that the signing of the pact marked the end of his active engagement with the Left, continued to support many CPUSA-initiated organizations, such as the League of American Writers and the School for Democracy (where he lectured in 1942). Hughes also published frequently in Left journals such as *New Masses* and *Mainstream* until the late 1940s. Richard Wright actually wrote in defense of the pact.[93] Other African-American writers publishing poetry in *New Masses, Negro Quarterly, Cavalcade, Mainstream, Masses and Mainstream,* and other CPUSA or CPUSA-initiated publications after the signing of the pact include Countee Cullen, Waring Cuney, Sterling Brown, Owen Dodson, Frank Marshall Davis, and James Baldwin. During the same period these periodicals also featured stories, articles, reviews, comments, and plays by Sterling Brown, Richard Wright, Ralph Ellison, Alain Locke, Frank Marshall Davis, Gwendolyn Bennett, Carl Offord, Theodore Ward, J. Saunders Redding, L. D. Reddick, and Lloyd Brown.

The downplaying of race in the interests of "national unity" by the CPUSA during the Second World War was of far greater consequence to most African-American writers than was the Hitler-Stalin pact. It was this issue that in no small part caused a number of the CPUSA's leading African-American writers, most notably Wright, Ellison, and Chester Himes, to become disaffected from the party—and made many of the other African-American writers associated with the party very uncomfortable. However, what appears to have influenced Wright and Ellison the most was a shift in CPUSA ideology regarding the "Negro nation" rather than a practical shift in its policy regarding African Americans. To a much greater extent than during the Popular Front of the 1930s, the concept of the "Negro question" as a national question was downplayed. Thus, it seems quite likely that it was the retreat from the hybrid ideological position combining international class solidarity and revolutionary nationalism (and the quasi-nationalist aesthetic that grew out of that position) that characterized the earlier Comintern theory of the national question that alienated Ellison and Wright, however much Ellison himself might retreat from revolutionary nationalism himself by the end of the decade.

On a practical level, as historians such as Roger Keeran and Maurice Isserman have argued, and what even a casual glance at its press will indicate, the CPUSA continued to work actively against Jim Crow and for racial equality—particularly on the local level.[94] The CPUSA was ambivalent (at best) about A. Philip Randolph's 1941 March on Washington Movement (MOWM) demanding "National Defense" jobs for African Americans and an end to segregation in the armed forces and was opposed to the slogan of the "Double V" (victory over Hitler, victory over Jim Crow), first proposed by the *Pittsburgh Courier*. In both cases, the CPUSA argued against putting the fight against Jim Crow on the same level of priority as the victory over fascism. At the same time, the war effort against a country so publicly identified with extreme and highly organized racism gave the CPUSA a powerful rhetorical weapon with which to attack Jim Crow. For example, hardly an issue of *New Masses* passed without an article, editorial, editorial note, or letter connecting segregation in the Armed Forces abroad with segregation at home and commenting on the irony of such segregation in the war against Nazism.[95] This does not mean the CPUSA did not backpedal at times on the practical battle against racism, as some Communists, such as Herbert Aptheker, would later admit. (The most eggregious retreat before racism happened with respect to Asian Americans when the CPUSA supported the internment of Japanese Americans, including some of its own members.) But it is important not to overstate the impact of the CPUSA opposition to the "Double V" in terms of day-to-day work by its local organizations.

Despite the problems the CPUSA World War II policy created for African-American writers, of the writers listed above only Ellison and Wright completely severed their ties to the cultural institutions of the Communist Left during World War II. In fact, a casual glance at the mastheads of *Masses and Mainstream* (formed in 1947 from a merger of *New Masses* and *Mainstream*) and the *Harlem Quarterly*, revealing names such as Theodore Ward, Lorraine Hansberry, Langston Hughes, W. E. B. Du Bois, Alain Locke, Shirley Graham, Owen Dodson, Jacob Lawrence, and Charles White, suggest that the Communist Left remained influential among a significant sector of African-American artists, writers, and intellectuals while it was becoming increasingly marginal in the republic of letters as a whole. Of course, during the cold war the influence of the Communist Left, which faced extreme political repression as well as severe internal shocks and dissension following the invasion of Hungary, Krushchev's 1956 speech about Stalin's crimes, and debates about how to handle the hostile political climate within the United States, greatly diminished in the African-American community, including among artists and intellectuals. Even so, despite the losses and relative isolation of the Communist Left, African-American intellectuals still associated with the old Harlem and South Side Lefts retained enough cohesiveness and influence once the domestic cold war receded a bit to start the journal *Freedomways* in 1963, a journal which remained a significant institution until its demise in 1987.[96]

It is also important to point out that not all white writers and intellectuals who were alienated from the CPUSA in the years after the Moscow Show Trials and the Hitler-Stalin pact followed the trajectory of those associated with the *Partisan Review*. Many retained aesthetic enthusiasms that they developed in the Communist Left even as they moved away from the CPUSA organizationally. For example, Edwin Seaver, who had been closely associated with *New Masses* in the 1930s, remained far more interested in African-American writing than the editors and writers of the *Partisan Review*. (Seaver included poems by Gwendolyn Brooks, Robert Hayden, and Langston Hughes, as well as prose by Ralph Ellison, Carl Offord, and Richard Wright in his important *Cross Section* anthologies of the mid- and late-1940s.)

Thus, while it is possible to distinguish among different cultural moments during the 1930s and 1940s, which I will attempt to delineate in my discussion of the individual poets in subsequent chapters, a huge proportion of African-American poets (and writers and intellectuals generally) remain engaged with the Communist Left and cultural institutions from at least the early 1930s until at least the early 1950s. Even the work of those no longer actively connected organizationally with the Communist Left often remains thematically and formally marked by their earlier organizational engagement. Older journals that were often indifferent or hostile to the Communist Left, such as the NAACP's *The Crisis* and the Urban League's *Opportunity*, continued important, if diminished, roles as did newer non-Left journals, such as the academic journal *Phylon* (founded in 1940). But these journals were at least occasionally influenced by the concerns of the Left as evidenced by the editorial against the jailing of Haitian writer and Communist activist Jacques Roumain in the May 1935 issue of *Opportunity* and Communist Benjamin Davis's article "Why I Am a Communist" in the Second Quarter 1947 issue of *Phylon*.

Of course, there were other Left influences on African-American poets during the 1930s and 1940s besides that of the CPUSA. However, these influences tended to be individual rather than organizational. Those African-American poets who could be classed among the "anti-Stalinist" Left rarely became identified with specific Left groups. For example, Claude McKay, who met Trotsky at the Fourth Comintern Congress in 1922, was sympathetic to Trotskyism after his break from the Communist movement in the early 1930s, but did not become connected to organized American Trotskyism (though he did write on occasion for the rabidly anti-Communist Socialist journal *The New Leader*, as did James Baldwin). Similarly, after leaving the CPUSA, Richard Wright had a close relationship with C. L. R. James, one of the leading intellectuals of the Trotskyist Workers Party and Socialist Workers Party during the 1930s and 1940s, but never was associated directly with any Trotskyist organization. Melvin Tolson was a close friend of V. F. Calverton after Calverton's break with the CPUSA in the early 1930s. (Calverton was briefly a member of the American Workers Party, an uneasy alliance of the main body of American Trotskyists and the followers of A. J. Muste.) Tolson published several poems and reviews in Calverton's *Modern*

Quarterly from 1937 to 1940, and yet remained ideologically sympathetic to the Popular Front.[97] Frank Marshall Davis wrote poetry attacking Stalin by name, which appeared in his collections *I Am the American Negro* (1937) and *47th Street Poems* (1948). Yet Davis worked closely with the Communist Left both as a journalist and as a poet through virtually the entire period—and was almost certainly a CPUSA member for at least part of those years.

Nonetheless, while one can discern the influence of the non-Communist Left on various African-American writers, only the Communist Left had any significant institutional impact on African-American writing during the 1930s and 1940s. The complex network of cultural institutions of the Communist Left outlined above gave support to African-American writers on many levels: promoted the development of a new and enthusiastic audience, both in the United States and abroad; provided outlets for their work; increased their access to "mainstream" journals and institutions; organized various sorts of spaces in which they could develop their art and the theoretical underpinning of their art; offered an ideological framework in which to place their work; facilitated their contacts with other writers, in the United States and around the world. This support was crucial as the institutions that had maintained the New Negro Renaissance faded. And for better or for worse, the leading CPUSA functionaries involved in "Negro work" took a direct interest in African-American cultural production in a manner that was unusual, if not unique. For example, one of the most important discussions of Richard Wright's *Native Son*, at least as far as the position of the CPUSA was concerned, was the long article by Benjamin Davis in the April 14, 1940, *Sunday Worker*.[98] Earl Browder's speeches to the American Writers Congresses notwithstanding, this sort of sustained public interest in literature by a leading CPUSA functionary, whose assignment was outside of "cultural work," was quite rare (even when the writer under examination was a Communist), indicating the seriousness with which the CPUSA, or at least African-American Communists, took "cultural work" by African Americans.

This is not to say that the impact of the Communist Left on African-American writers in the 1930s and 1940s flowed from some absolute unity of ideology and practical application of that ideology. As mentioned before, the CPUSA itself, despite the claims of both the party leadership and its most ardent detractors, contained various, often conflicting tendencies. These conflicts appeared within top leadership, where Earl Browder and William Z. Foster and their supporters were frequently at odds. They also surfaced in the regional leadership of important districts that were occasionally, and in the case of southern California frequently, in opposition to the national leadership. Finally, at the rank-and-file level, when leadership debates broke out into the open (as they did in 1929, 1945–1946, and 1956), they were replayed in almost every CPUSA unit, often serving as the vehicle for the expression of a wide range of "unorthodox" political beliefs (ranging from social democratic to anarcho-syndicalist). With respect to literary politics, for example, some writers, including Richard Wright, never really accepted the policy of the Popular Front and the abandonment of the "proletarian literature" movement and the downplaying of the nationalist side of the Comintern view of the "national question." Others, such as Meridel Le Sueur, Jack Conroy, and Don West, retained a regionalist suspicion of

New York and the Left political and literary institutions there.[99] Nonetheless all remained affiliated with the Communist Left through the 1930s and into the 1940s—and beyond in the cases of Le Sueur and West.

Left African-American poets were no less divided than other radical American poets during the 1930s. There were broadly speaking two major tendencies into which these Left-influenced writers fell. One, of which the preeminent example is Sterling Brown, is the previously noted folkloric alternative approach that was related to the Third Period agitation around the Black Belt Nation. "Authentic" folk expression associated with a rural, southern oppositional culture relatively unpenetrated by commercialism was drawn on by the folkloric poet who provided the "folk" form with a new, more actively struggle-oriented content in an attempt to create *the* voice of the folk. The other tendency, of which the chief example is Langston Hughes, is an approach much more engaged with mass commercial culture, drawing on "popular" forms such as jazz, advertising, popular journalism, the newsreel, pulp literature, Tin Pan Alley, the "classic blues," radio, movies, and vaudeville. This approach was associated with an urban African-American culture that is a hybrid or "miscegenated" culture through its "dialogic" relationship with mass culture and other cultural communities. One hallmark of this approach is the foregrounding of the problems of documenting and communicating the "authentic" folk or popular experience to an "authentic" popular or folk audience. This is in contrast to the folkloric alternative approach in which the possibility of such "authenticity" uncontaminated by mass culture is more or less a given. (As I will note in the next chapter, the real question in the folkloric alternative approach is more often whether the narratorial consciousness of the poet-narrator will be able to successfully negotiate a return to the "authentic" folk culture.)

Of course, the dualism between the folkloric alternative literary model and the "popular" model was not peculiar to African-American writers on the Left, but was part of a division within the Left as a whole. Thus, the work of the radical white Appalachian poet Don West, the folk song movement that had its origin in the Third Period and began to flourish during the Popular Front continuing through the Peoples Song movement of the late 1940s and early 1950s, and the promotion of early "primitive" jazz (as opposed to swing and bebop) by white jazz critic and one-time *Daily Worker* writer Charles Edward Smith can be seen as part of larger folkloric alternative discourse into which the poetry of Brown, and others can fit.[100] In fact, *Proletarian Literature in the United States* included African-American folk songs collected by Lawrence Gellert as well as songs written by white southern protest balladeers Ella Mae Wiggins and Aunt Molly Jackson in its poetry section.

At the same time, the work of Hughes and Frank Marshall Davis, particularly by the late 1930s, can be productively paired with the work of white poets such as Kenneth Fearing, in which there is a similar mixing of "high" and "low" diction, "high" culture and "mass" culture. The major distinction between black and white radical writers of the 1930s viewed broadly is that there was no group of Left African-American writers that directly drew on the work of the "high modernists" to the same degree as such white Left writers as Sol Funaroff and Joy Davidman (heavily marked by Eliot), Muriel Rukeyser (much influenced by Hart Crane in her first book

Theory of Flight), and Stanley Burnshaw (an admirer of Wallace Stevens).[101] For those African-American writers such as Brown, Cullen, and McKay who did write "high" verse during the 1930s, the romantics and their Pre-Raphaelite descendants remained more important formal models than Eliot—though the paradigm of modern culture proposed by Eliot was influential, particularly on Sterling Brown.

This is not to say that there were not considerable overlaps between the broader tendencies of African-American poetry or that the two poets whom I have taken as exemplars of these tendencies did not transgress these categories: Brown did write polyphonic urban poems that engaged mass culture; Hughes did write essentially monologic poems of the southern folk. But I would suggest that these poets in general do represent two poles in the range of responses of poets engaged in the unstable hybrid of nationalism, internationalism, and integrationism in the Communist Left's ideological stance toward African Americans. Of course, as I will discuss in chapter 4, there were those poets, notably Countee Cullen, who, despite sympathies with the Communist Left during the 1930s and 1940s, fell outside this range of formal poetic responses. But these poets, as in the case of Cullen, did not flourish (as poets) during the 1930s, either through an alienation from the formal concerns of the period or from a lack of institutional support or both.

As I will discuss at some length in the last three chapters, the greatest shift between African-American poetry of the 1930s and that of the 1940s is not a shift away from social engagement or from the organized Left so much as the increasing ascendancy of the urban landscape and urban African-American culture over the rural landscape and the culture of the rural folk as well as a much greater and overt engagement with "high" American literary modernism. The landscape and folkloric forms associated with the rural South would continue to have an impact, as is attested in the first collection of Margaret Walker, *For My People* (1942), and Owen Dodson's first book, *Powerful Long Ladder* (1946). Nonetheless, the urban—in fiction as well as poetry—would begin to dominate African-American poetry considerably before the isolation of the Communist Left in the postwar period. The work of most younger black poets in the 1940s, such as Gwendolyn Brooks and Robert Hayden, as well as that of the older poets, such as Langston Hughes, Frank Marshall Davis, and Melvin Tolson, was almost entirely urban in setting.

Instead, African-American poetry in the 1940s can be broadly divided into two tendencies, both of which are what might be termed neomodernist in form. By "neomodernist" I mean poetry that utilizes more directly, and self-consciously, the formal resources of various currents of 'teens and twenties modernist art than had generally been the case in the 1930s. One of these tendencies draws on certain "high" modernists, particularly Eliot and Stevens, and is sympathetic in form, if not in spirit, to the strictures of the New Critics. The other is more closely related to the work of William Carlos Williams and to the more formally "radical" Left art and literature of the 1920s and 1930s, whether the photomontage of Heartfield, the film montage of Eisenstein, or the polyphonic poems of Rukeyser, Hughes, or Fearing. Not surprisingly, the chief exemplar of the latter tendency is Langston Hughes, whose work in the 1940s flowed quite logically out of his work of the late 1930s. Gwendolyn Brooks is the purest example of the former.

In both cases, the use of neomodernist forms actually allows the writers to main-tain a continuity with the radical past. The formal difficulty and greater thematic am-biguity that characterized the later writing allowed the neomodernist writers to ex-press radical politics without drawing the attention of antisubversive governmental investigators, such as the Committee on Un-American Activities and, later the House Un-American Activities Committee and Joseph McCarthy's Senate Permanent Sub-Committee on Investigations.[102] Certainly these writers, particularly Hughes (who by the late 1940s had already had considerable experience with governmental and quasi-governmental anti-Communism), were quite uneasy about the increasing at-tacks on the Left in the United States.[103] In addition to the pragmatic benefits of adopting more ambiguous styles, the neomodernist styles represented formally, as well as thematically, what the poets saw as a relatively inchoate postwar African-American anger and dissent that coexisted with postwar anxiety about domestic po-litical repression. This anger was predicted to erupt violently in a manner that was a sort of return to Third Period millenarian predictions by the Communist Left about the inevitability of social revolution—again linking the "social realism" of the 1930s to the neo-modernism of the middle and late 1940s.

The Roles of Black Folk: Gender, Left Ideology, and the Construction of the Folk

Modernism and the New Negro Renaissance

One of the most striking aspects of the representation and recreation of the folk voice in African-American poetry during the first two-thirds of the 1930s is how this voice, and the figure of the folk itself, is relentlessly gendered as male. Or perhaps it is more accurate to say that the folk voice is split into a conservative or even reactionary voice that is generally represented as female (or effeminate) and a progressive, militant voice that is male and stereotypically virile. While there are some antecedents for such a gendering in African-American literature, the masculinization of the folk in the 1930s stands in contradistinction to the tendency of earlier African-American lit-erature to render the folk voice as female. The construction of the folk in the 1930s is significantly informed by interrelated masculinist discourses of modernism, African-American nationalism, and the Third Period ideology of the Comintern and the CPUSA, particularly with regard to what were referred to as "culture" and the "na-tional question." These discourses combine to create a hyper-masculinism that only begins to fade with the latter part of the Popular Front period.

The construction of the folk in African-American literature before the New Negro Renaissance is mixed with respect to gender. On one hand, the Negro Mother was probably the most common figuration of the folk (and continued to be so through the New Negro Renaissance).[104] Similarly, the use of Mother Africa as fig-uring an ur-state of natural blackness (with the rape of Africa as a narrative of the black fall into civilization) remains an important trope from the nineteenth century to the present. Along these lines, one sees the common use of the figure of an elderly black woman as the transmitter of folk culture, particularly that derived from Africa as in, for example, the African song of Du Bois's great-great grandmother in *The Souls of Black Folk*.[105]

On the other hand, the speaking black folk subject, such as Charles Chesnutt's Uncle Julius, and the narrators of the majority of the "dialect" poems of Paul Laurence Dunbar and James Edwin Campbell, were somewhat more likely to be male than female. But this was far from a hard-and-fast rule—as the male and female speaking "folk" characters of the poetry of Fenton Johnson and Frances Harper's *Iola Leroy* and W. E. B. Du Bois's *The Souls of Black Folk* attest. (For that matter, the representatives and caretakers of folk tradition within the narration of Chesnutt's Julius are almost always female.)

This mixed gendering of the folk continued during the New Negro Renaissance among the "younger generation" of black poets, most notably Langston Hughes, Gwendolyn Bennett, and Helene Johnson. For example, the ur-folk voice is female in Hughes's "Aunt Sue's Stories" from the 1926 *The Weary Blues*. But in "Proem," the poetic prologue to the same collection, the voice of the essential "Negro" is implicitly male.[106]

However, among cultural nationalist and nationalist-influenced writers one sees the beginning of a concerted attempt to recode the folk as univocally male. To the degree that the folk is somehow feminine, this femininity is associated with passivity, accommodationism, and racial self-hatred. Therefore the task becomes one in which "the race" is rhetorically rendered male, maleness being associated with action, resistance, and racial self-worth, reclaiming an original African "manhood," visions of Mother Africa notwithstanding.

While this masculinist rhetoric is most pronounced among the now almost entirely unknown poets associated with the Garveyite journal *The Negro World*, it is far from restricted to such writers. As Hazel Carby has pointed out, this narrative of a sort of folk sex change is found as early as Du Bois's *The Souls of Black Folk*. When the narrator descends south in Chapter 4, "On the Meaning of Progress," the first and most powerful figure of the southern folk he meets is the dynamic farm girl Josie. Josie is dead by the end of the chapter, leaving the narrator to muse on the meaning of progress for the folk in the face of her death.[107] Yet after a chapter meditating on the spiritual sickness of modern capitalism in the South—a soulless materialism that is implicitly female through its association with the Greek myth of Atalanta—Du Bois's subsequent chapters seem to render Josie forgotten as well as dead in their persistent naming of the modern folk as essentially male: "Of the Training of Black Men"; "Of the Sons of Master and Man"; "Of the Faith of the Fathers"; "Of the Passing of the First-Born"; "Of the Coming of John." In the final chapter "Of the Sorrow Songs," Du Bois returns to a female figure of the folk, his African great-great grandmother, in a personal genealogy of the folk inheritance. Yet in brief we see the gender transformation that the book enacts elsewhere at more length. In this family history, the great-great grandmother is the American point of origin for an African song handed down from generation to generation. But after the initial transmission the song is passed along by subjects named male by Du Bois so that he can end his chapter on the sorrow songs speaking of the "songs of my fathers."[108]

The key New Negro Renaissance theorizing of the "New Negro" as opposed to the submissive "Old Negro" is largely couched in such a gendered rhetoric. While the notion of a "New Negro Woman" existed, the New Negro was almost always represented as male; the men, often soldiers returned from the First World War, who violently resisted the many racist attacks on black communities in 1919, became perhaps the most widespread symbol of the New Negro. The most famous literary representation of the New Negro, one which was seen as largely defining a new moment of black literature, was Claude McKay's 1919 "If We Must Die," which ends with the couplet:

Like men we'll face the murderous, cowardly pack,
Pressed to the wall, dying, but fighting back.

(*Harlem Shadows,* 53)

Generally speaking, the New Negro is envisioned not only as more bold, and more masculine, than the Old Negro but also more educated, more traveled, and more urbanized. Thus the New Negro can be thought of as a figure opposed to the black folk culture of the rural South, a culture associated with slavery. However, the New Negro should not be seen as a negation of the folk so much as a transformation of the folk into something that is both more modern and yet also a return to the cultural wholeness (and virility) of Africa before the fall into slavery. In this regard, it is worth noting that the figures of the fall into cultural decay are most frequently female, as is the case in McKay's "Harlem Shadows" and "The Harlem Dancer"— though occasionally they are male as in Helene Johnson's "Bottled."

As Sandra Gilbert and Susan Gubar have argued convincingly, many of the male writers associated with "high" modernism—Eliot, Pound, Stevens, Williams, Joyce— conceived their literary projects as virile, masculine, and heterosexual in opposition to a popular literary culture and readership that they figured as female or effete. Gilbert and Gubar suggest that the motivation behind modernist masculinism was in large part an effort by male writers to eliminate their female competitors in much the same spirit that Hawthorne's famous comment about "scribbling women" was aimed at the female writers of sentimental fiction who dominated the mid-nineteenth-century literary market.[109]

A similarly gendered paradigm of African-American literature is proposed by African-American intellectuals and writers in the early and mid-1920s, in which the old is associated with formal conservatism, sentimentality, and uplift and the new with formal experimentation. This opposition of old and new called for a rejection of what Alain Locke called "cautious moralism and guarded idealizations" and a willingness to engage African-American folk culture on something like its own terms (though often with the goal of elevating that folk culture into a unique African-American contribution to "high" culture with the "Irish Renaissance" of the early twentieth century frequently invoked as a model). Locke remarked in his introduction to "The Youth Speaks" section of the seminal 1925 anthology *The New Negro:*

The newer motive, then, in being racial is to be so purely for the sake of art. Nowhere is this more apparent, or more justified than in the increasing tendency to evolve from the racial substance something technically distinctive, something that as an idiom of style may become a contribution to the general resources of art. (51)

Here Locke does not explicitly assign specific gender to his division of formal conservatism and formal innovation as did many white modernists. Nonetheless, in the same essay he lists the "older generation" of poets, including Anne Spencer, Georgia Douglas Johnson, and Angelina Weld Grimké. Yet Claude McKay is included in a catalogue of younger poets even though he was only three years younger than Georgia Douglas Johnson (and actually published his first books of Jamaican "dialect" poetry several years before Johnson's first book, *The Heart of a Woman*, appeared in 1918). This would suggest that Locke's distinction between literary generations was as much about form as it was about literary or biographical chronology. However, Locke's list of the younger generation lacks any mention of a female writer despite the fact that *The New Negro* included works by two young female poets, Gwendolyn Bennett and Helene Johnson. (Both Bennett and Johnson are more self-consciously "modern" than either McKay or Countee Cullen—another of Locke's "younger" poets.)[110] The question then arises as to whether these inclusions and exclusions implicitly reveal the familiar modernist model of the feminine "old" and the masculine "new."

Similarly, in his famous 1926 essay "The Negro Artist and the Racial Mountain," Langston Hughes codes genteel culture as female in much the same way as that of white male modernists:

> Yet the Philadelphia clubwoman is ashamed to say that her race created it [jazz] and she does not like me to write about it. The old sub-conscious "white is best" runs through her mind. Years of study under white teachers, a lifetime of white books, pictures and papers, and white manners, morals and Puritan standards made her dislike the spirituals. And now she turns up her nose at jazz and all its manifestations— likewise almost everything else coded racial. . . . She wants the artist to flatter her, to make the white world believe that all Negroes are as smug and as near white in soul as she wants to be. (308)

It would be simplistic to assert that there was a radical opposition of old and new, or genteel and modernist, within black literary culture of the 1920s. Also, it would be overstating the case to say that the modern was always coded as male and heterosexual and the Victorian as genteel or as female (or effeminate). Despite the previously quoted passage, Hughes frequently represented black speaking subjects as female during the 1920s. More formally conservative writers and more formally radical writers, male and female, coexisted in journals such as *The Crisis*, *The Messenger*, and *Opportunity*, at various parties, clubs, lectures and salons, and in anthologies without the degree of antagonism that marked the relations of say, T. S. Eliot and William Carlos Williams, or, after the initial stages of American imagism, Ezra Pound and Amy Lowell.[111] Of course, the presence of female writers does not preclude the gendering of "modern" African-American literature as essentially male. It was also no doubt true, as Gloria Hull argues, that practical opportunities for male writers were far greater than those for female writers.[112] But the inclusion of female writers—and gay writers—in African-American journals, anthologies, literary prizes, and so on created a sense that the "new" literature was not absolutely identified as male and heterosexual. It was also a period in which black gay writers, and to a lesser extent lesbian writers, were at least able to thematize and figure homosexuality in various positive and relatively open ways—as seen in the poetry of Cullen, Angelina Grimké, and Gladys May Casely Hayford and the fiction of Wallace Thurman and Nella Larsen.

Nonetheless, as a theoretical or critical paradigm, the gendered discourse of modernism opposing a female, conservative Victorianism to a masculine new wave dominated the New Negro Renaissance. Interestingly, this paradigm was also seized in a negative manner by more "traditional" African-American writers who also linked gender and poetic tradition. The relatively "conservative" 1927 anthology edited by Countee Cullen, *Caroling Dusk*, emphasized African-American literature that was formally "conservative" and "high" in a manner strongly identified with such twentieth-century American women writers as Edna St. Vincent Millay and Eleanor Wylie. Again, while the presence of women writers does not preclude a gendered modernist dichotomy of old and new, it is telling that Cullen's anthology included far more women writers in its representation of the New Negro Renaissance than did the other anthologies of the era.[113] (Writing by women made up about a third of the poetry in *Caroling Dusk* whereas the work of female writers constituted only about a sixth of the poetry contained in the more "modern" *The New Negro*.) While it is hard to untangle the reasons for the rejection of "high" modernism by these writers, many of whom were female or gay, it may be that it was occasioned as much by a repulsion from the aggressive masculinity of "high" modernism as by any conservative Eurocentricism, demonstration of literacy, or rejection of what they saw as racial parochialism.

The CPUSA, Masculinity, the Working Class, and the Folk

When imagining the African-American folk, the CPUSA (and the cultural institutions it influenced) inherited the gendered rhetoric of modernism and African-American nationalism. This inheritance has been obscured by the CPUSA's opposition to what it called the "bourgeois nationalism" of the Garveyites and the neo-Garveyites and by the often bitter argument within Communist-influenced journals and cultural organizations as to the value of literary modernism.[114] But while there was far less consensus among critics and intellectuals associated with the CPUSA than most current scholarship still allows, an extremely influential construct resembling that of nationalism and "high" modernism was created in which an actual or potential masculine proletarian (or folk) culture was opposed to a feminine or effete bourgeois culture. Exactly what constituted bourgeois culture was of considerable debate. This question of definition was further compounded by the Marxist notion that industrial capitalism had been in its origin progressive and democratic insofar as it replaced earlier modes of production and social organization (feudalism in Europe and the plantation system of the South in the United States) with a more dynamic economic system that at first employed a rhetoric of democracy. But, according to this view, as capitalism developed, it grew into the world system that Lenin termed "imperialism" and became progressively reactionary and decadent.[115]

This narrative of growth and decay was seen also to hold for culture generally through the "base and superstructure" model accepted by the CPUSA. Thus, the problem for Left cultural critics was not merely one of distinguishing working-class or peasant culture from that of the bourgeoisie, but, particularly in the field of literature, telling the "good" bourgeois from the "bad." This problem could not be resolved by chronologically distinguishing the writing of early "progressive" capitalism from that of late capitalism. Rather, it was a matter of determining whether a particular work (regardless of its date of composition) was in the humanist and, by extension, democratic bourgeois tradition of, say, Shakespeare and Whitman or the elitist poetic tradition, whether decadent or genteel, of the late Victorian period. This notion of a potent and vigorous bourgeois tradition as opposed to an exhausted and essentially sterile tradition often was posed in terms of masculinity and femininity— or masculinity and effeminacy.[116]

Thus the Left critics' stereotypical construct of nineteenth-century Euro-American genteel culture, which again was close to that of both Pound and Hughes in the 1920s, is always bourgeois and female or effeminate, as is mass commercial culture (at least during the Third Period leftism before the Popular Front). However, modernism is a matter of considerable contestation among these critics. A significant section of Left critics attacked what they saw as obscurantist and pessimistic "high" modernist writing. But even Michael Gold, who attacked many of best known modernist figures—Gold called Proust "the master-masturbator of the middle class"— frequently used a favorite European modernist form, the manifesto, and held up modernists William Carlos Williams and Sergei Eisenstein as models of artistic excellence. Gold's well-known attack on Thornton Wilder rejects Wilder's work not as modernist but as the "synthesis of all the chambermaid literature, Sunday-school tracts and boulevard piety there ever were." In short, according to Gold, it is genteel; it is mass culture; it is feminine.[117]

Thus what defined reactionary bourgeois literature for most Left critics connected to the CPUSA was not its connection to modernism as such but bourgeois literature's essentially feminine (or effeminate) nature—as opposed to the male and virile working class. In this regard it is instructive to examine the cartoons and illustrations of *New Masses* and other CPUSA publications where the working class is almost always figured as a large muscular man and where the bourgeoisie, especially with respect to its relation to the arts and intellectual discourse, is often figured as an overweight woman in a drawing room. While this "Old Left androcentrism," as Walter Kalaidjian terms it, was largely inherited from even older Left movements, particularly the IWW, it became emphasized to an almost hysterical extent during the Third Period.[118] Another favorite trope was to render the bourgeois male as effete, physically weak, and/or, in drag. Thus even those Left critics who rejected modernism to one degree or another largely (and often quite consciously, as in the case of Jack Conroy and Malcolm Cowley) adopted the notion of the masculine and virile avant-garde from the "high" modernists (while often including the "high" modernists as part of that feminized or effete bourgeois culture), a notion which also closely resembled black nationalist gendering of the folk.[119] Many European and American Left cultural critics before the Popular Front also took from these modernists a hostility to a similarly feminized mass culture, though where the high modernists saw an invasion of art by the masses, many of the critics and artists of the Communist Left viewed mass culture as a bourgeois tool of ideological control or as a sign of the decadence of late capitalism.[120] Interestingly, as Paula Rabinowitz points out, while this gendering takes place, gender as an ideological category for these critics, and, to a significant extent, for the CPUSA itself, is largely invisible.[121]

This masculinist rhetoric of a largely otherwise inchoate proletarian literature movement, and of the CPUSA itself, was consonant with ideological and critical notions of literature and the folk of black authors influenced by modernism and African-American nationalism. At the same time the concepts of black folk culture that derived from the Black Belt Thesis gendered the folk, and "authentic" literary representations and recreations of the folk, as male to an extent never seen before even in black nationalism and modernism before the 1930s. The opposition of the "authentic" folk culture of the rural South to the urban black culture of the northern ghettos (often associated by the party with mass culture) has a particular significance with respect to the gendering of the folk voice. The cultural forms that the CPUSA generally emphasized—the work song, the "badman story," the folk blues—were chosen in part because they were relatively easy to transmit in the medium of print and in part because of their secular nature. (The party and its institutions before the Popular Front tended to condemn spirituals as accommodationist and illusionary, and even effeminate.)[122] These forms were for the most part male-identified insofar as they were predominantly performed by men and spoke in the voice of the male subject. Thus where Langston Hughes and other writers had frequently used the "classic" blues of female singers such as Bessie Smith and Clara Smith as the model of the folk utterance, such urban forms were now seen in this scheme as no longer authentically representative of the folk, if not actually condemned as part of mass commercial culture.[123] Interestingly enough, where the culture of the southern rural folk had been essentially coded female in African-American modernist, nationalist, and New Negro rhetorics, it was now rendered as male in the Left-influenced paradigm of the 1930s, particularly in CPUSA accounts of the "revolutionary tradition" of African-American culture. Or at least the folk culture was divided into two parts: a male-identified tradition of resistance and protest and a female-identified tradition of accommodationism and stoic deference.

As Robin Kelley has noted, much of the poetry by black authors published in the journals and newspapers of the Communist Left, particularly those addressed to African Americans, such as the *Negro Liberator,* closely resembled the nationalist poetry published in the Garveyite *Negro World* through a common use of a masculinist rhetoric of black pride in which the manhood of the race is redeemed.[124] Even Langston Hughes, who often used female subjects to figure the black folk in the 1920s and in the 1940s, published few poems in the 1930s using such subjects. This is especially true of the Hughes poems printed in Left journals and under Left imprints, such as his 1938 collection, *A New Song,* published by the IWO. Instead, Hughes's poems of the 1930s are almost always explicitly or implicitly in a male voice and often addressed directly to a male listener.

The Popular Front, Gender, and the People

With the official arrival of the Comintern and CPUSA policy of the Popular Front in 1936, the gendering of African-American folk by black writers associated with the Left began to change. While the working class still tended to be coded as masculine, the downplaying of social class in the 1936–1939 period of the Popular Front and in the 1940–1944 period following the Nazi invasion of the Soviet Union placed an emphasis on "the people," a construct which was far more neutral as to gender than the CPUSA notion of "the proletariat" had been. Also during this period, the Black Belt Thesis was much diminished in Communist literature and agitation, though it would be somewhat revived in the second half of the 1940s. This, of course, does not mean that the use of a masculinist Third Period rhetoric of the African-American folk disappeared, particularly among black male writers. As previously noted, the poems in Hughes's *A New Song* were not significantly different from his poems from the early and middle 1930s. (In fact, many were produced before the Popular Front policy was fully developed, including the famous "Let America Be America Again" written in 1935.) Similarly, Frank Marshall Davis in the title poem of his 1937 collection *I Am the American Negro* embodies the African-American people as a male giant.[125] Likewise, the representative voice of the folk is male in the blues poetry of Waring Cuney published in such Left journals as the Southern Negro Youth Congress's *Cavalcade* during the 1940s.[126]

However, it was during the extended Popular Front era that African-American women poets engaged productively with the Left. During this period Margaret Walker and, later, Gwendolyn Brooks became associated with a network of black left-wing intellectuals and writers in Chicago linked through a complex of organizations including the South Side Writers Group, the FWP, the National Negro Congress, the Congress of Industrial Organizations (CIO), and the League of American Writers, as well as the CPUSA itself.[127] By the 1940s, Walker and Brooks published their first books. These early works of Walker and Brooks contained representations of the female figure of the folk as something other than the type of the Negro Mother, practically for the first time in poetry since the 1920s. They rendered female the voice of vernacular poems, such as Brooks's "Ballad of Pearlie May Lee" from her 1945 collection *A Street in Bronzeville*. The speakers of most of Walker's vernacular poems in her 1942 *For My People* are males and focus on male figures of the folk as in "Yalluh Hammuh" and "Stagolee." However, one important transformation takes place in Walker's "bad woman" poem "Kissie Lee." Some of the "classic" blues singers (such as Bessie Smith) had already essentially created a significant "bad woman" tradition; nevertheless Walker is the first to recast the "badman" song and story into written verse with a female protagonist.

In addition to the emergence of black women poets as recognized authors, there is a change by the 1940s in the gendering of the vernacular voice by a number of black male poets. Starting with *Shakespeare in Harlem* (1942), Langston Hughes includes poems in his collections recreating the voices of female subjects after a hiatus in using such voices during the 1930s. The first section of Owen Dodson's *Powerful Long Ladder* (1947) employs the figure of the black mother and familiar gendering of the Old as feminine and New as largely masculine in poems such as "Black Mother Praying." But Dodson, who published in CPUSA journals such as *New Masses* and *Negro Quarterly*, portrays the mother as far more active and with far more agency than such representations of the Negro Mother in the 1930s as Brown's "Maumee Ruth" or Frank Marshall Davis's "Old Woman Praying." The hypermasculinity of the African-American vernacular subject is also undermined by Robert Hayden's attempt in *Heart-Shape in the Dust* to combine political radicalism and overt male homoerotic elements for the first time in African-American poetry since Cullen's last significant publications of poetry in the early 1930s. (Though it is not until much later in his career that Hayden, in such poems as "Elegies for Paradise Valley," would as successfully integrate homoeroticism with a sense of social outrage as did Cullen.)

Thus if one is going to track the relationship of the continuities and discontinuities of African-American poetry from the 1920s to the early 1950s, a crucial marker is how the folk is represented and how the folk voice is recreated. And the key to how this process of representation and re-creation works is found in the gendering of the representation of the folk and the folk voice. When viewed in this way, the disjuncture between the New Negro Renaissance and the "proletarian" period is far less than sometimes represented, and the differences between the works of the 1930s and those of the 1940s, while quite real, are actually signs of the continuity between the two decades since they result from a continuing engagement with Left ideology and Left cultural institutions.

2

"The Strong Men Gittin' Stronger"

Sterling Brown and the Representation and Re-creation of the Southern Folk Voice

"Awake Negro Poets": Sterling Brown, the New Negro, and the New Red Negro

In the December 25, 1945, *New Masses*, an ad appeared for an awards dinner sponsored by the magazine and chaired by Howard Fast "Honoring Negro and White Americans for Their Contributions Toward a Democratic America."[1] Sterling Brown was to be given an award for his poetry at the dinner despite the fact that he had published virtually no poetry in the 1940s.[2] For that matter, except for a handful published in African-American and Left journals and anthologies, relatively few of the poems Brown wrote in the middle and late 1930s saw the light of literary day until *The Collected Poems of Sterling Brown* appeared in 1980.[3] On the other hand, Langston Hughes had published many poems during the first half of the 1940s (including five in *New Masses*). While not as closely associated with the CPUSA as he had been during the 1930s, Hughes had remained a high-profile supporter of many organizations and activities initiated by the Communist Left—for example, he was a sponsor of the *New Masses* dinner. Brown, while sympathetic to the Left (as were all the recipients of the *New Masses* awards), had a far lower political profile at the time of the awards dinner.[4] Yet Brown was to receive an award and Hughes was not. In essence, *New Masses* honored Brown in 1945 for his work in the 1930s and ignored Hughes, who was among the most productive African-American poets of the 1940s.

This seeming anomaly indicates the continuing attachment on the part of many critics of the Communist Left to the aesthetics generated by earlier CPUSA conceptions of "Negro liberation" and the Black Belt Thesis. This attachment persisted despite the changes in the Communist approach to the "national question." An example of these changes can be seen in the explicitly integrationist rhetoric of the ad framing the *New Masses* event that was clearly organized around the issue of race in terms of a generalized "Democratic America" rather than in the quasi-nationalist terms that characterized the CPUSA construction of African-American identity during the early 1930s. By looking at the work of Brown—and Langston Hughes—in the 1930s, one can see most clearly the contradictions in the discursive space that Brown, Hughes, and other African-American poets had to negotiate as well as in the stances of the critics and general audience who received the poetry. In this respect, perhaps the chief contradiction as far as Brown is concerned is the process by which Brown became the most admired contemporary African-American poet by the critics associated with the Communist Left, retaining this admiration into the 1940s and beyond, at the same time he ceased to publish poetry after 1940.[5]

Even before the end of the New Negro Renaissance, Brown's implicit stance concerning the African-American literary scene of the late 1920s contained in his 1932 collection *Southern Road* was strikingly consonant with the earliest serious discussion of African-American literature by CPUSA critics and intellectuals. The African-American Communist William L. Patterson in "Awake Negro Poets," an article which appeared in the October 1928 issue of *New Masses* while Patterson was attending the Sixth Comintern Congress, notes the boom of poetic production by African-American writers during the 1920s including "Stirling [*sic*] Brown." After expressing some enthusiasm for McKay, Hughes, and Helene Johnson, Patterson largely dismisses the work of the New Negro Renaissance poets for much the same reasons that Brown would, calling instead for revolutionary African-American poets who could give voice to the "toiling masses" of African-American workers and farmers, particularly those in the Black Belt:

> There is little in recent Negro poetry that would lead one to believe that the poets are conscious of the existence of the Negro masses. There is no challenge in their poetry, no revolt. They do not echo the lamentations of the downtrodden masses. Millions of blacks are suffering from poverty and cruelty, and black poets shut their eyes! There is no race more desperate in this country than the black race, Negro poets play with pale emotions!
>
> We can be frank. Our Negro poets voice the aspirations of the rising petty bourgeoisie. Occasionally they express the viciousness of black decadents. And that is all. They are sensationalists, flirting with popularity and huge royalties. They are cowards. Instead of leading heroically in the march of the world's workers, they are whimpering in the parlours of white and black idlers and decadents. (10)

Patterson was not an early supporter of the notion of a "Negro nation" in the Black Belt. At the Sixth Congress, he co-authored a "discussion article" with James W. Ford that opposed the support of African-American nationalism by the CPUSA. However, the discussion article also rejected the concept that the "Negro question" was simply a function of economic class oppression. Calling African Americans "an oppressed racial minority," the Ford and Patterson article advocated the establishment of a "mass race organization for Negro workers" that would include farm laborers, farmers, professionals, and small-business people in addition to industrial and service workers. This organization would serve as a vehicle to overcome the distrust and discomfort the average African American felt with respect to working with white people, a distrust that was particularly acute in the South.[6] Patterson's call in *New Masses* for African-American revolutionary poets who could articulate the conditions and concerns of the "Negro Masses" from a racial stance that was realistic, heroic, and sympathetic in ways that would be familiar to African Americans, and that would constitute a break from the earlier New Negro movement, was one that was answered by Brown with *Southern Road*. Whether or not Brown read Patterson's call—though it is quite likely he did—and was directly influenced by it, Patterson's article was one of the first critical statements by a member of the Communist Left that helped create the discursive space in which *Southern Road* was created and favorably received.

Sterling Brown's own critical distinction between the term "Harlem Renaissance," dismissed as strictly box office, and the term "New Negro Renaissance," describing a literary moment with which Brown identifies, is not just a question of semantics or geographical accuracy, but is in fact a distinction between the values derived from a nationalism embodied in *Southern Road* similar to that of late-nineteenth-century and early-twentieth-century European nationalism and those of the allegedly transnational values of "high" modernism.[7] Or perhaps it is more accurate to say that Brown accepts the Eliotic premise—and the Comintern premise for that matter, at least as far as life under modern capitalism was concerned—that modern urban life is afflicted by a sickness of the spirit caused to a large extent by rampant individualism and the breakup of social and moral consensus. In fact, this spiritual malaise is in Brown's view perhaps more intense for African Americans in the northern urban centers than for other Americans. But Brown rejects the notion that such a sickness was universal in "the West" and instead posits, like Jean Toomer in *Cane*, an essential African-American culture in the South that is able to resist the sickness of modern society if only black Americans are willing to hold on to their history and the cultural forms of expression and resistance that developed in the intense racial oppression of the South. Unlike Toomer, who believes that the rural culture, and the perceived closeness of that culture to the land and nature which he chronicles in *Cane*, is fading, Brown argues that the culture of the Black Belt is alive and vital, though threatened by the inroads of mass culture and migration. And where black intellectuals such as Alain Locke in *The New Negro* and James Weldon Johnson in *Black Manhattan* locate the future of African-American social and artistic development in Harlem and, to a lesser extent, in the other urban black communities of the North and West, Brown seeks a return to the future in culture produced by black farmers, tenant farmers, farm laborers, and common workers in the rural (and urban) South.

North and South: Regionalism, Mass Culture, and Oppositional Culture in *Southern Road*

Southern Road has often been described by critics as articulating an opposition of the country and the city. But Brown, a product of the city himself, did not so much oppose the urban to the rural as the North to the South. The black population of the urban South and border states, while sharing a certain sense of dislocation and alienation with northern African-American urban dwellers, is represented by Brown in much the same voice and with much the same sympathy as African Americans on the land in the Black Belt. On the other hand, the African-American communities of the North, and the assimilationist ideology Brown associates with those communities, are treated with sarcasm and undisguised scorn.[8] In this respect, Brown differs from William L. Patterson (and the later Comintern and CPUSA theorists of the Black Belt Thesis) in that he does not simply associate this false consciousness primarily with the African-American intelligentsia but also claims this delusionary individualistic "striver" mentality infects all strata of the migrants who went north. Nonetheless, though African-American writers and intellectuals in the North do not directly figure in *Southern Road*, the book, like Patterson's article, is a direct challenge to the Harlem Renaissance. (Ironically, Brown comes closer to this early CPUSA position in the "Harlem Stopover" section of his second collection *No Hidin' Place* where the African-American urban intelligentsia is mercilessly lampooned. Northern African-American workers are treated more sympathetically than in *Southern Road*, where the targets in the "Tin Roof Blues" section are basically workers and certainly not members of the intelligentsia. I say ironically because, as I note later, the second collection is a product of the Popular Front period when the CPUSA courted the African-American "middle class.")[9]

The title of *Southern Road* is a declaration of independence from the Harlem Renaissance specifically set in opposition to the poem "Bound No'th Blues" of Langston Hughes, a writer who is often connected with Brown because of Hughes's exploration of African-American vernacular English and various "folk" forms as the basis of literature that went beyond the humor and sentimentality of nineteenth-century "dialect" and regional poetry.[10] In "Bound No'th Blues" from the 1927 collection *Fine Clothes to the Jew*, Hughes creates a black narrator who rejects his former life in the South and surrenders himself to the uncertainty and cultural dislocation of the immigrant on the "Northern road":

> Road's in front o' me,
> Nothin' to do but walk.
> Road's in front o' me,
> Walk . . . and walk . . . and walk.
> I'd like to meet a good friend
> To come along an' talk.
>
> (*Fine Clothes to the Jew*, 87)

Here is a rendering of the most common type of "folk blues," wherein the first line of a stanza is repeated in the second line, sometimes with a slight variation or "worrying," setting a scene and / or identifying a conflict, followed by a third rhyming line that is generally a resolution of and conclusion to the first two lines. Hughes splits each of the usual three lines in this type of blues stanza (also known as the *aab* type stanza) to create six-line stanzas with the break between Hughes's lines corresponding to the caesura characteristic of lines as they are actually performed in the "folk blues."[11]

In what Hughes himself saw as a traditional southern rural blues form, the narrator clearly articulates a rejection of the South and the narrator's past life there:[12]

Road, road, road, O!
Road, road . . . road . . . road, road!
Road, road, road, O!
On de No'thern road.
These Mississippi towns ain't
Fit fer a hoppin' toad.

(87)

The narrator is not rejecting simply southern racism and poverty but also the black communities of the rural and small-town South in which a single sympathetic or supportive person cannot be found. (It can be assumed from the poem that the narrator is a refugee from the rural South since, with the exception of Jackson, there were virtually no urban areas in Mississippi in the 1920s.)

This alienation stands in contrast to *Southern Road*. In *Southern Road*, even Brown's road poems and poems of individual portraiture set in the South emphasize the protagonists' generally positive connections to other members of the southern African-American community. If the sympathetic folk narrators and characters move around, it is not the linear and unidirectional movement of the emigrant but rather a circular movement implicitly or explicitly linked with the itinerant blues musician that generally terminates back home in the South—often after trial in the North, as in the poems "Tin Roof Blues" and "Odyssey of Big Boy." These sympathetic characters, such as Calvin "Big Boy" Davis in "Odyssey of Big Boy," remain, like Odysseus, more or less unchanged during their travels. Thus their returns differ from the sort of prodigal return of a formerly alienated protagonist common in African-American literature from, at least, the late nineteenth century (and in Brown's own figure of the poet-narratorial consciousness in *Southern Road*) in that they never spiritually leave the folk. There are, of course, genuine emigrants in *Southern Road*, but, as we shall see, they are the subject of derision and condemnation.

Ironically, Hughes's use of a folk blues form and rhetoric as the vehicle for this declaration of alienation from the South and of a search for a new community ("to find somebody / To help me carry this load") by a southern emigrant suggests a certain continuity of African-American culture between North and South—a continuity that Brown would basically deny in *Southern Road*. Thus the emigrant narrator of "Bound No'th Blues," who has detached himself practically and psychologically from his former community in the South, seeks another more nurturing community in the North while remaining emphatically, and even traditionally, "Negro" in culture.[13]

Brown's choice of *Southern Road*, as opposed to Hughes's "Northern Road," as a title indicates that he is following a different cultural model. Instead of focusing on a vision of liberation through progess (which in Hughes's case admittedly retains a decided sense of continuity with a folk tradition), Brown emphasizes an endurance that occasionally flashes into anger and heroic (and fatal) self-defense, as well as a relatively indirect cultural resistance by African Americans in the rural South. The opposition to Hughes's work suggested by the naming of the collection is further emphasized in the form of Brown's title poem—the first published instance of Brown's use of the blues form. "Southern Road" is unusual in that it, as Joan Gabbin and Henry Louis Gates Jr. point out, is a chain-gang work song with its stanzas cast in the form of a blues in which, as in much of Hughes's blues poetry, the lines of the basic three-line blues stanza are split to create six-line stanzas:[14]

> Swing dat hammer—hunh—
> Steady, bo';
> Swing dat hammer—hunh—
> Steady, bo';
> Ain't no rush, bebby,
> Long ways to go.

> *(Southern Road, 46)*

Though the form of Brown's stanzas resembles that of Hughes's, the implications of the work song–blues hybrid are far different. The "hunh" that punctuates the first and third lines of each stanza is a reminder that the narrator is a member of a community engaged in a common effort, albeit against its will. (The focus on the coercive power of the state operating on a group of people as opposed to individual acts of racism or "unofficial" social attitudes also distinguishes this poem from most of the poetry of the New Negro Renaissance concerning racism and racist violence, say Cullen's "The Black Christ" or Hughes's "Song for a Black Gal," while linking it to other poetry of the 1930s, such as Hughes's verse play "Scottsboro Limited.") The "hunh" marks the moment when all the men on the chain gang swing their hammers together. The injunction "Steady bo'" of the first stanza (and the following "Ain't no rush, bebby, / Long ways to go") is not directed by the narrator to himself, but to the rest of the crew that he is presumably leading. This injunction is a call to communal self-preservation, endurance, and a type of resistance that attempts to negotiate the terms of the community's exploitation by setting a limit to the work pace. The voice of the narrator is speaking a communal story in which the narrator's individual story, or what might be considered the blues aspect of the poem, is inextricably bound up with common experience and activity signified by the elements drawn from the work song.[15] While the dominant sentiment of the poem seems to be that of personal despair, the hybrid of blues and work song, individual and community, emphasizes communal resistance and survival in the face of crushing oppression from which there is no immediate escape.[16]

However, that there is no immediate escape does not imply, as Jean Wagner and Alain Locke have suggested, that there is no hope or that resistance is futile.[17] There is not what Wagner calls a "stoic acceptance" by the narrator of his situation; the narrator declares that his condition weighs "on my min.'" Rather, when read with the other poems of the "Road So Rocky" section of *Southern Road* with the epigraph from an old spiritual "Road may be rocky / Won't be rocky long," "Southern Road" suggests that the survival of community and a communal expression that authorizes and frames the individual narrative, even on the chain gang, is a form of resistance. (In this section, many types of resistance are clearly represented. In some, such as "Sam Smiley," the representation of direct resistance as essentially futile in any practical sense does not prevent the protagonists from rebelling violently at the cost of their lives. In others, Brown depicts more successful and more indirect rebellion as in "Ruminations of Luke Johnson" where the character Mandy Jane steals from the plantation owner's kitchen as a partial restitution for the enslavement of her grandfather and for her own exploitation.)

In Hughes's poem cited above, the narrator denies the possibility of community in the South and leaves for the North with a new, if unarticulated, type of community in mind. Brown's speaker in "Southern Road" recounts in much more detail than Hughes's the disruption of community through the loss of family and freedom while at the same time affirming his relationship to other black men in the South, a relationship which he could not break even if he wished to do so. In this way there is a masculinist reconstruction of the African-American family in which the folk becomes totally male. While this situation may seem to be represented as abnormal, such a recasting of the folk as male appears again and again in Brown's poetry from "Strong Men" in *Southern Road* to "Side by Side" in his later unpublished collection *No Hidin' Place*.

This notion of the survival of African Americans as a community being the main form of resistance to racial oppression becomes more obvious when "Southern Road" is seen in conjunction with "Strong Men," which ends the first section of Brown's collection:

> *What, from the slums*
> *Where they have hemmed you,*
> *What, from the tiny huts*
> *They could not keep from you—*
> *What reaches them*
> *Making them ill at ease, fearful?*
> *Today they shout prohibition at you*
> *"Thou shalt not this"*
> *"Thou shalt not that"*
> *"Reserved for whites only"*
> *You laugh.*

> (53)

Interestingly, the rhetorical opposition in "Strong Men" is not between "They" and "We," but "They" and "You." There is a certain distance not only between black and white but also between the folk and the sympathetic narrator, who is presumably the persona of the black poet-intellectual coming to grips with the folk. This distinction between the poet's persona and the folk is seen in many of the poems in *Southern Road* where an unnamed narrator observes the folk. This narrator speaks in essentially "standard" English (whether "literary" or generically "colloquial" with a slight "hard-boiled" cast), though at certain moments this narrator adopts a "folk" voice, usually to indirectly render the speech or thoughts of "folk" characters. As in "Strong Men," the relationship between the observer and the observed is often uneasy, if sympathetic. In "When De Saints Go Ma'ching Home," the speaker's statement about the singer "Big Boy" Davis, "he'd go where we / could never follow him

/ to Sophie probably / or his dances in old Tinbridge Flat" (18), does not indicate the alienation of the singer from the folk community, but rather the distance between his immediate audience of black intellectuals and the blues culture from which the singer comes.[18] Thus the project of *Southern Road* is not simply a portraiture of southern black folk, and a northern falling away from the folk but also is a representation of the difficult process of an at least partially alienated urban intellectual attempting to reconnect with the folk community. At the same time the poet-intellectual brings a new perspective and a higher self-consciousness to the folk culture that had been previously lacking.

Probably the clearest expression of the distinction between the narratorial consciousness of *Southern Road* and the folk that is represented and recreated is the frequent anticlericalism and discomfort with religion despite the invocation of various forms of African-American culture and speech associated with religion. The disapproval of religion is particularly noticeable when the speaker is clearly the persona of the poet-intellectual. This anticlericalism is quite close to that of the Third Period Communist Left regarding African-American religious practice.[19] Perhaps the sharpest demonstration of the narratorial antireligious attitude takes place in "Maumee Ruth":

> Preach her the lies about
> Jordan, and then
>
> Might as well drop her
> Deep in the ground,
> Might as well pray for her,
> That she sleep sound. . . .

> (11)

This antireligious sentiment can also be found in Brown's parodies of spirituals. In the second section of "The Memphis Blues," the traditional "Sinner man, where you gonna run to" is transformed into a series of humorous stanzas involving such figures as "Mistah Lovin' Man" and "Mistah Gamblin' Man" ("Gonna pick up my dice fo' one las' pass"). While there are some nonparodic invocations of the spirituals, notably "Sister Lou" and "New Steps," these always occur in the first-person vernacular of a sympathetic folk persona rather than in the voice of the more detached narrator of, say, "Maumee Ruth." (And even the protagonist of "New Steps" has a certain pathos about her.) When Brown does draw on African-American sacred music, he uses the spirituals rather than the more contemporary, urban, and commercial gospel music, possibly because of the same antagonism toward mass culture that causes him to avoid or criticize the more commercialized and urbanized forms of blues and jazz. This antireligious sentiment is perhaps less overtly antagonistic to African-American Christianity than the militant denunciations of organized religion in Hughes's "Good Bye Christ" or "God to a Hungry Child," relying more on irony. But the ironic criticism of popular African-American religous belief and practice clearly marks a distinction not only of voice but also of attitude and certain social values between the narratorial consciousness of the collection and the folk embodied.

This distinction between the folk and the persona of the poet-intellectual points toward what a positive role the poet-intellectual might play. If it is true that, as Jean Wagner suggests, the black folk characters of *Southern Road* inhabit what they see as a tragic universe without hope, this is not the view of the persona of the poet-intellectual, who recognizes in the African-American folk characters the ability to endure, to insist on their own humanity, whether directly or indirectly, comically or tragically, and ultimately to triumph over their oppressors. The poet-intellectual's contribution is a consciousness of this struggle, and of the weaknesses of the folk, that will allow the southern folk values of endurance and cultural opposition to racial oppression to better resist the challenge posed by the great migration to the North and the potential penetration of mass culture (as embodied by the North) into the authentic culture of the South.[20] In this *Southern Road* is a sort of transposition from the tropics into the South of much of the work of Claude McKay, where a similar split and ultimate rapprochement between the black intellectual and the folk is represented. Brown's poetry differs from McKay's poetry (and novels) in that Brown posits a vanguard role for the poet-intellectual that is missing, or much less emphasized, in McKay's work.[21] (It is not hard to see how this implicit intellectual vanguardism would be appealing to critics of the Communist Left to which such a move would be consonant with their general sense of the CPUSA's own political mission.) At the same time the relatively unified voice of *Southern Road* is quite different from the work of Hughes in the 1930s where, as will be argued in the next chapter at some length, the narrative consciousness is dialogic and the poet's voice is, sometimes quite explicitly, just another voice among many—as in the 1936 "Air Raid Over Harlem."

"Dudes and Dicties": Migration and Mass Culture

> "Good-bye, folks."
> —BRUTUS JONES IN THE FILM *THE EMPEROR JONES* (1933)

In the "Tin Roof Blues" section of *Southern Road*, Brown characterizes life in the cities of the North, especially New York City, as fraudulent, pretentious, and downright delusionary and the black immigrants there as similarly pretentious and deluded, if not immoral. This combination of delusion, pretension, and criminality is seen vividly in "Mecca":

> Tom bought him a derby and pearl gray spats,
>   When his first week's work was done,
> Mag bought herself a sealskin coat,
>   Hot in more ways than one.

(109)

The narrative voice of the poem speaks in the sing-song of the comic song's 4/3/4/3 ballad meter, using what might thought of as a "standard" colloquial diction in which such slang words as "stomp," "hot," and "steadies" are employed idiomatically without being particularly identifiable as African American. Brown's use of the word "hot" pointedly invokes a complicity, at least, with crime and a shallow mass-consumer culture.

The final stanza of "Mecca" turns up the level of the migrants' pretensions and Brown's heavy sarcasm, emphasized by a pseudo-British "poetic" rhyme (again-cane) matching the faux aristocratic pretension of Maggie ("Lady Margaret") and Tom ("Lord Thomas"). As the poem's title and a sarcastic invocation of Caanan suggest, these migrants worship the popular culture associated with the urban North. If the new black city-dwellers in the North are tragic, they are tragic only in their pettiness and self-deceit and their integration into mass commercial culture, at least on the level of induced consumer desires if not in terms of social equality. Here the sympathetic tone of the poems in the "Road So Rocky" and "On Restless River" sections, which are set in the South and often narrated in a first-person vernacular voice, is missing. Instead, the tone is distant and contemptuously satiric without any sympathy for the poem's protagonists—again, a sympathy that had been accorded to murderers, thieves, and prostitutes in the first two sections of *Southern Road*. As with his portrayal of sexual infidelity in other poems in the "Tin Roof Blues" section, Brown here links mass culture, criminality, and northern migration, infusing the poem with a sense of immorality that is missing in the poems of the "Road So Rocky" and "On Restless River" sections that contain poems, such as "Georgie Grimes" and "Johnny Thomas," describing what would appear to be far greater social transgressions than those of Maggie and Tom. Interestingly, Brown ignores, or dismisses, the participation of Maggie and Tom in a communal and distinctly African-American vernacular culture as signified by the institution of the "house-rent stomp," possibly because the "house rent stomp" is, as its name suggests, essentially a commercial venture. Thus the "stomp" is part of the contaminating consumer culture, since it exists only, in Brown's account, as a financial relationship, emphasizing the couple's discarding of old "authentic" racial and ethnic identities while literally assuming the "bargain" costume of a ludicrous consumer fantasy.

This dichotomy of the real and the unreal, or of the "authentic" folk culture and the embodiment of mass culture, is not simply an opposition of town and country. There are two sorts of cities in *Southern Road*. One sort is the cities of the South and the border states—Atlanta, New Orleans, St. Louis, Memphis, even Washington, D.C. (though Washington is somewhat liminal between North and South). In Brown's poetry, these cities have a schizoid character for their black residents. As centers of the "sporting life," they are home to brothels, gut bucket saloons, gambling houses, and a whole gamut of institutionalized vices. African Americans in these cities are also exposed to much the same raw oppression as they are in the rural South. Brown's poems argue a longstanding relationship between the southern and border cities and the mass of African Americans still living on the land. In these poems there is a cultural and social continuity between the black community in the country and the city in the South that is absent between North and South. Musicians, for example, particularly rural male blues singers and guitarists, such as Calvin "Big Boy" Davis, move from the country to the city and back again.

Thus even the most degraded African-American residents of the urban South are presented with a sympathetic seriousness that acknowledges these subjects as members of an authentic African-American community. For example, in the "Market Street Woman" portion of "New St. Louis Blues," an aging prostitute is compassionately described:

> Market Street woman have her hard times, oh my Lawd,
> Market Street woman have her hard times, oh my Lawd,
> Let her git what she can git, 'fo dey lays her on de coolin' board.

(70)

This portrait of the Market Street woman is directly opposed to the ironic elegy for a northern ghetto "easy" woman "Effie" in the "Tin Roof Blues" section:

> She who would veer with any passing wind
> Like a rusty vane with rickety ways,
> She is aloof now, and seems—oh, so determined;
> And that is the Paradise crowning her days.

(106)

The satiric and detached tone, the "standard" diction, the "standard" quatrains filled with alliteration and assonance skillfully create a ponderous and decorous formal permanence that mirrors Effie in death and contrasts with Effie's lack of identity in life. Each line that begins with the construction "She who" functions as an indictment of Effie. In fact, the poem resembles an ironic and idealized courtroom speech in which the reader's condemnation of Effie is asked by the prosecuting attorney of the speaker. And what Effie is indicted for is an absence of an authentic self.

This ironic and condescending indictment contained within an overemphatically standard form is sharply at odds with the sympathetic voice, "black" diction, and blues structure of "Market Street Woman," where assonance and alliteration are also important but subsumed in the blues structure of the poem. A telling moment of comparison is the "oh" of "oh my Lord" in "Market Street Woman" as seen against the "oh" of "oh, so determined" in "Effie." The former is an apostrophe that conveys an overflow of empathic sympathy, linking the poem's speaker and the Market Street woman emotionally and within an African-American rhetorical tradition; the latter, tellingly separated from "so determined" by a comma, archly emphasizes with this caesura the distance between the speaker and Effie, undermining any sense of communal sympathy for Effie. The reader could ask why it was all right for the Market Street woman to "git what she can git" while Effie was condemned because she was "easy with any chance lover" and veered "with any wind." But this would to be to miss the point suggested by the formal aspects of the poem as well as by the denotative sense of both the poems. The Market Street woman is sympathetic, despite the fact that she literally makes her body a commodity, because she is connected to the African-American culture of the South and makes no attempt to shed that connection—at least in the mind of the implicit narratorial consciousness ventriloquizing the speaking folk subject who insists on the connection. Effie has abandoned that culture, or so judges the speaker now speaking in an openly "high" authorial (and authoritative) voice, and has no true identity, only a series of disposable poses that are the emotional and spiritual analogues of the northern consumer culture.

At times the conditions of the southern urban black poor are presented in a deceptively light-hearted manner drawing on the trickster tall tale and the "badman" story. The Slim Greer poems, for example, lampoon Jim Crow in rollicking short lines with two stresses each in a sort of literary two-step, recreating and thematizing African-American folk dance as well as music and oratory:

> An' he started a-tinklin'
> Some mo'nful blues,
> An' a-pattin' the time
> With No. Fourteen shoes.

The cracker listened
An' then he spat
An' said, "No white man
Could play like that. . . ."

(84)

Once again this differs from similarly humorous poems set in the North, such as "Mecca" and "Sporting Beasley," in that the Slim Greer poems satirize the institution of Jim Crow whereas in "Mecca" and "Sporting Beasley" it is the black emigrants to the North who are lampooned. As Joanne Gabbin notes, while the Slim Greer poems draw on the popular humor tradition of minstrelsy and vaudeville, they turn these racist jokes back on themselves, critiquing popular culture's use and misuse of African Americans. In contrast, poems such as "Mecca" and "Sporting Beasley" represent the northern migrants as essentially reducing themselves to a sort of vaudeville or minstrel show without even an ironic self-knowledge of their acts.

The other sort of city in *Southern Road* besides the southern/border city is the northern city to which African Americans were moving in larger and larger numbers by the beginning of the twentieth century. There are a dozen poems in *Southern Road* that are set in, or mention, northern cities. The bulk of these poems are found in the "Tin Roof Blues" section of the collection. Of the dozen, four are explicitly set in or refer to New York City and Harlem. In fact, Harlem is the only black community mentioned in the poems dealing with African-American life in the northern cities, even though some of the ghettos growing in other cities of the North at the same time as Harlem's transformation into a black neighborhood were as old or older and, in the case of Chicago's South Side, nearly as large. One of the poems, "Cabaret," is set in Chicago, though Chicago never appears by name in the body of the poem. The other poems in the dozen mention no particular city or neighborhood, but are located in generic northern urban settings. This singling out of Harlem again suggests that it is not merely the life of the immigrant to the North, who could live in any number of ghettos from Omaha to Boston, that is under satiric scrutiny, but also the northern African-American intellectuals and artists who were linked almost exclusively, if inaccurately, with Harlem. Or perhaps it is more accurate to say that Harlem is singled out because Brown, and others, associate it with a system of patronage in which the artists and writers who participate in the system are essentially a form of exotic entertainment purchased by the rich patrons.

The sarcastic tone of the "Tin Roof Blues" section is in sharp distinction to

"Vestiges," the other section of *Southern Road* rendered primarily in some variety of "standard" literary English. In "Vestiges," the narrator's restrained and gloomy diction, derived largely from Frost and Robinson, seldom mocks, except where the narrator mocks himself, and is nearly always sympathetic. Thus there is greater distance between the narratorial consciousness and the represented subjects of the poems in the "Tin Roof Blues" section than in any other section of the book. This distance underscores the satire on the subjects of the poems in the section without the sympathy for and emotional identification with the subjects that characterize the narratorial consciousness in the other sections of *Southern Road*.

With the exception of the title poem, formally a standard blues lyric, where the speaker is about to leave the North to return to the South, none of speakers in the poems in the "Tin Roof Blues" section of *Southern Road* uses any version of African-American vernacular speech except for ironic effect. In fact, other than in the title poem, there is virtually no direct speech from any speaker besides the poet-intellectual-narrator besides a few fragments. All the speakers, fragmentary and otherwise (again, with the exception of the narrator of the section's title poem), talk in a sardonic "standard" English, generally employing a "literary" diction with an occasional colloquial touch. African-American vernacular diction and forms are invoked, though not exactly recreated, as in "Chillen Get Shoes," which draws on the spiritual "All God's Chillen Got Wings" and the lullaby "All the Pretty Little Horses," and in the rhetorical forms of "Sporting Beasley":

> Good Glory, give a look at Sporting Beasley
> Strutting, oh my Lord.
>
> > Tophat cocked one side of his bulldog head
> > Striped four-in-hand, and in his buttonhole
> > A red carnation; Prince Albert coat
> > Form-fitting, corset like; vest snugly filled
> > Gray mourning trousers, spotless and full-flowing,
> > White spats and a cane.
>
> Step it, Mr. Beasley, oh step it till the sun goes down.

> (113)

Here, as in "Chillen Get Shoes," the vernacular is invoked in a parody of African-American religious and secular song and anaphoric rhetoric that makes the black subject of the poem the butt of the parody rather than the vernacular itself. The parodic nature is emphasized by the fact that the speaker of the poem is someone who makes frequent hyperbolic vernacular interjections for the purpose of mocking Beasley, but whose natural speech appears to be a rather high "standard" English. Rather than connecting Beasley to a larger community, this parodic use of the vernacular emphasizes his distance from authentic community.

Instead of using the minstrel tradition against itself, as does Slim Greer, Beasley has essentially transformed himself into a version of the stock minstrel character "Zip Coon," who makes himself ridiculous through his inept aping of upper class whites.[22] As in "Effie" and "Mecca," the poem's protagonist is engaged in a willful delusion and self-forgetting. This self-forgetting is emphasized by the anaphoric "forget":

> Forget the snippy clerks you wait upon,
> Tread clouds of glory above the heads of pointing children,
> Oh, Mr. Peacock, before the drab barnfowl of the world.
>
> Forget the laughter when at the concert
> You paced down the aisle, your majesty,
> Down to Row A, where you pulled out your opera glasses.
>
> (113)

Unlike the people on the African-American circuit between city and country in the South, few of these migrants to the North in *Southern Road* are coming back. In Brown's view, they are radically separated from the folk and are engaged in self-delusion on a massive scale. Perhaps the most succinct exposition of this is in "Tin Roof Blues," where the folk speaker prepares to return to the rural South:

> Gang of dicties here, an' de rest wants to git dat way,
> Dudes an' dicties, others strive to git dat way,
> Put pennies on de numbers from now unto de jedgement day.
>
> (105)

Like the speaker of Hughes's "Bound No'th Blues," the isolated and alienated speaker here is emigrating in search of community, only for Brown's speaker it is a return to the rural South rather than a flight to the urban North. Significantly, this poem of return to the South is the single first-person poem in the section and the only poem that recreates the vernacular in an allegedly unmediated form. It also the only poem that draws on a form of vernacular expressive culture, the blues, without parody or irony.

This practical and ideological separation of African Americans in the North from the folk is seen as particularly true for many of the African-American artists and intellectuals associated with the New Negro Renaissance. Brown engages in this poetic polemic with poets such as Hughes, Cullen, and McKay, who write about the South on occasion in the early and middle 1920s, but poetically locate the central drama of African-American culture in the urban North, particularly Harlem. For example, Brown mocks the pretensions of those writers who endow the Harlem landscape with an overwrought literariness in his "Harlem Street Walkers". The diction of this brief poem combines the "literary" ("grateful grave"), the pseudo-archaic ("tragical"), and the colloquial ("Oh, never mind") to undermine the notion of such a landscape as the scene for anything as profound as tragedy. In addition to its general mockery of northern social and intellectual pretension, "Harlem Street Walkers" appears particularly to satirize Claude McKay's "Harlem Shadows," where a black female prostitute figures the speaker's "fallen race." "Harlem Shadows" is the title poem of a 1922 collection that was held by many to mark a new moment of African-American letters.[23]

"Show Your Tricks to the Gentleman":
Jazz and the Commodification of the Folk

Unlike the poetry of Langston Hughes in the 1920s and early 1930s, and unlike many of the novels of the New Negro Renaissance, *Southern Road* contains few mentions of jazz. In fact, Brown goes out of his way to avoid any positive mention of jazz. For example, in "Ma Rainey," Brown represents Rainey as the organic voice of the folk. During the 1920s Rainey was frequently accompanied by the Wildcats Jazz Band led by pianist Thomas Dorsey. (Dorsey later became known as the "father" of gospel music—another form of popular music absent from *Southern Road*.) Rainey's touring band once included the great jazz saxophonist Coleman Hawkins; her recording sessions featured Hawkins, Louis Armstrong, Fletcher Henderson, and other members of the Henderson band during the 1920s. However, Brown only mentions a single accompanist, a pianist named "Long Boy." Thus, Brown here is eliding Rainey's connection to jazz and emphasizing her link to the "down-home" blues of itinerant guitarists and pianists.

Brown's single direct treatment of jazz (except for a mention in passing in "New Steps") occurs in the poem "Cabaret." Here jazz is a sign of commercialized cultural degradation rather than African-American folk or popular expression. "Cabaret" contains the most extreme example of the cultural co-optation and hucksterism, the fraudulent exhibitionism and primitivism that Brown associates with the northern cities:

> The jazzband unleashes its frenzy.
>
> *Now, now*
> *To it, Roger; that's a nice doggie,*
> *Show your tricks to the gentleman.*
>
> The trombone belches, and the saxophone
> Wails curdlingly, the cymbals clash,
> The drummer twitches in an epileptic fit
>
> (115)

This empty and degrading show of supposedly joyous and carefree black life, where African Americans have been reduced again to commodities as they were during slavery, is contrasted with the real drama and tragedy of African Americans in the South:

> *Oh you too,*
> *Proud high-stepping beauties,*
> *Show your paces to the gentlemen.*
> *A prime filly, seh.*
> *What am I offered, gentlemen, gentlemen. . . .*
>
> I've been away a year today
> To wander and roam
> I don't care if it's muddy there

(Now that the floods recede,
What is there left the miserable folk?
Oh time in abundance to count their losses,
There is so little else left to count.)

(116–117)

As Jean Wagner points out, the formal arrangement of the poem presents a counterpoint of three psychological levels: that of the white customers in a Chicago jazz club, that of the performers in the club, and that of the common black people of the rural South. Perhaps it is more accurate to say that the counterpoint is not between what Wagner calls "the customers, the performers and the people" as it is between the supply-and-demand economy of the club where black performers transform African-American vernacular music—and themselves—into a product both exotic and reassuring to rich white audiences and the actual conditions of "the people" in the South as seen through the mediating consciousness of the poem's speaker.[24] The three levels of the poem are not so much the three psychological levels of audience, performers, and people as they are the narrator's differing attitudes toward those three groups. Thus the nonitalicized sections set in the club are descriptive and bitterly satiric while the bracketed and italicized sections set in the South are descriptive and sympathetic and on one occasion ventriloquize the voice of the folk:

(In Mississippi
The black folk huddle, mute, uncomprehending,
Wondering "how the good Lord
Could treat them this a way")

(117)

There are also two unbracketed italicized stanzas that seem to be the speaker's direct comments to the band and the dancers. Here the speaker compares the performers to domesticated animals, suggesting that they are participating in a double erasure: erasing their own identity as human beings as well as the true identity of the black communities of the rural South. Again Brown's concern here is the abandonment of a true identity to a commercialized delusion and the destruction of authentic communal expression. Brown not only critiques the studied "primitivism" of the shows at such whites-only clubs, so far as the audience is concerned, but also what he sees as the patronage system of the New Negro Renaissance in which artists and intellectuals willingly become performing animals for their patrons.

What links the different sections of the poem together is the jazz band's music, represented by song lyrics and onomatopoeic imitations of instrumental riffs. For the speaker the music represents the greatest crime since it is appropriated from the folk and is transformed into a vehicle for the erasure of both the musicians as full humans and the southern black communities from which the music is ultimately drawn. As noted earlier, Brown's attitude toward jazz and African-American participation in

mass culture is remarkably like that of many Third Period Communist cultural critics in Europe and the United States, for whom jazz is at best a plaything of the bourgeoisie and at worst a means of disseminating a false consciousness in the working
class and the "nationally oppressed"—especially in the North. Thus this poem could
be seen in opposition to Langston Hughes's "Negro Dancers" from *The Weary Blues*,
which uses a similar onomatopoeic representation of jazz to proclaim a sort of
African-American difference and resistance to white appropriation by remaining literally one step (or two steps) ahead of white dancers in trickster fashion.[25]

Brown also uses popular music, especially jazz, in *Southern Road*, not only to critique a commodified exoticism designed to retail black "primitivism" and "natural"
joy to the prurient tastes of jaded white people but also to figure a corrupting commercialization of African-American culture. This commercialization causes African
Americans in the urban North to lose touch with the folk to such an extent that they
no longer know what they are missing. Though jazz is not specifically identified,
"Children's Children" extols the blues, hollers, work songs, and spirituals of the rural
South at the expense of what appears to be jazz or "Tin Pan Alley" sentimentality.
Popular music ("Saccharine melodies of loving and its fevers") becomes the cultural
embodiment of the foolish and self-destructive forgetting of the southern past and
present of African Americans by the intellectuals and "strivers" associated with
Harlem:

> They have forgotten, they have never known,
> Long days beneath the torrid Dixie sun
> In miasma'd riceswamps;
> The chopping of dried grass, on the third go round
> In strangling cotton;
> Wintry nights in mud-daubed makeshift huts,
> With these songs, sole comfort.

(107)

The rhymes here, when they do occur, are almost never exact. The anaphoric phrases
"When they hear" and "They have forgotten" beginning the poem's stanzas give the
poem a certain regularity. But even this regularity breaks down after the twenty-first
line—a regularity that was none too regular in the first place given the varying length
of the poem's lines and stanzas. As a result, there is a sense of slackness, particularly
in stanzas that describe the "children's children," where the alliteration of liquids and
sibilants dominate. This slackness corresponds to the self-willed forgetfulness that
again erases both the southern folk as well as the African-American subjects themselves as African Americans ("With their paled faces, coppered lips, / And sleek hair
cajoled to Caucasian straightness").

The African-American musical forms Brown draws upon in *Southern Road* as positive artistic models have a slightly archival feel to them (though they were certainly
still living, if declining, traditions in 1932). The tall tales, the "badman" stories, the work
songs, spirituals, and the blues of the itinerant male country blues singer that Brown
invokes, as well his aforementioned exclusion or deprecation of jazz, stand in contrast
to the more contemporary "classic" blues of female singers, such as Ida Cox and Bessie

Smith, and the urban blues of musicians, such as Leroy Carr and Scrapper Blackwell, that form the basis of many of Langston Hughes's blues poems in the 1920s, particularly in his 1927 collection *Fine Clothes to the Jew.* Conversely, Brown had reservations about newer and more "commercial" recorded blues.[26] Brown's tribute to Ma Rainey praises the most countrified of the "classic" blues singers (rather than the more urban "classic" blues singers such as Ida Cox, Bessie Smith, and Clara Smith) from the perspective of a rural tent show audience. Even here, as noted earlier, Brown found it necessary to underplay Rainey's considerable connection to jazz.[27] In short, the discriminating, and often opposed, uses of African-American vernacular music not only proposed "authentic" and "inauthentic" models of recreating the folk voice but also entered in an intertextual and often bitingly critical relationship with earlier African-American poetic production and with the institutional support for that earlier work.

The Return of the Depressed: The Narratorial Consciousness and the Folk

The "Vestiges" section of *Southern Road* shares with the other sections of the book a sense of orality in which a narrative voice actually speaking is strongly present in every poem. However, even more than in the "Tin Roof Blues" section, the voice heard here is the naked voice of the poet's persona without the ventriloquisms or re-creation of the folk that mark the earlier sections. In many respects, "Vestiges" is the most crucial to Brown's vision of African-American progress in *Southern Road*, even if the poems in the section are also the most "conventional." "Vestiges" represents an intellectual-artist's return to the folk in which its values and endurance are wedded to his vision of the future and an understanding of the present.

"Vestiges" is prefaced by the graphic of the well-known African-American cartoonist E. Simms Campbell. This graphic shows the homecoming of a well-dressed male, presumably the returning African-American intellectual or artist, to a cabin with an older couple in homespun clothes, presumably his parents, waiting outside. Campbell's illustration serves as a visual gloss on Brown's poetry, providing a coherence to the section that might otherwise escape the reader. (The progression of Campbell's graphics throughout *Southern Road*, from images of forced labor preceding the first section to scenes of disaster and displacement before the second section to figures of commercialism, ostentation, and northern Jim Crow before the third to the scene described above, summarizes the movement of the collection and gives a sense of narrative unity between the sections.)

This intellectual prodigal's return is most clearly seen in the sonnet "Salutamus," which begins the section:

> And yet we know relief will come some day
> For these seared breasts; and lads as brave again
> Will plant and find a fairer crop than ours.
> It must be due our hearts, our minds, our powers;
> These are the beacons to blaze out the way.
> *We must plunge onward; onward, gentleman. . . .*

The poem is more or less an Italian sonnet with a slightly variant sestet (*cdeecd* instead of *cdecde* or *cdcdcd*) in a fairly uniform iambic pentameter using equally "high" and formal "poetic" diction. While Joanne Gabbin is correct in pointing out the resemblance of this poem to "high" works by James Weldon Johnson and Countee Cullen, as well as to the spirituals, it also recreates the images of agriculture and journey found in many of the vernacular poems of the first two sections within the framework of a very "high" and "conventional" literary practice.[28] It is also a counternarrative of the Cain and Abel story, which was of tremendous importance in the justification of slavery during the antebellum period. (Africans were seen as the children of Ham, whose lineage was traced to the tiller Cain). In Brown's clearly masculinist version, the tiller of the soil will escape the irrational curse of racism placed upon him through the tilling of his intellectual capacities.[29] Thus the formal aspects of "Salutamus" can be seen to embody the hybrid consciousness of the returning (male) intellectual and his revision of the folk.

However, the section itself is not as neat or schematic as "Salutamus" and Campbell's graphic would seem to indicate. In practice, the section appears to be a catch-all for a number of Brown's "high" lyrics—sonnets, elegies, praise poems, and so on—so that the section would seem to be at odds with the rest of the collection. Of course, the notion of a "high" culture tour de force to demonstrate that the African-American artist who employs a distinctly African-American lexicon does so because he or she chooses to speak that way has a long tradition in African-American expressive culture.[30] Such a tour de force becomes a mark of the artfulness of the artist's vernacular achievement rather than of his or her intellectual or artistic limitations. While Brown may be drawing on this tradition, it is telling that he chooses to end his book with this section so that it is the "high" poems that leave the final impression on the reader rather than the vernacular poems.

The question of why Brown chooses to do this is further compounded by the enigmatic title of the section itself. Vestiges of what? the reader asks. African-American rural culture? (After all, two of Brown's most important predecessors, Jean Toomer with *Cane* and James Weldon Johnson with *God's Trombones*, were convinced that the southern rural African-American expressive culture they were representing and recreating was vanishing.) "High" Euro-American culture? Bourgeois individualism? Romanticism? Given the dominant thematic concerns (loss, decay, death, uncertainty, romantic disappointment) that can be characterized as those of an individual experiencing or imagining extreme isolation, it is the consciousness of the poet-intellectual whose subjectivity is embodied in a "high," bourgeois individualistic, romantic voice that the reader is left with at the end of the section. While, as "Salutamus" suggests, the poet-intellectual may be necessary to the folk in order to envision a future beyond one of simple endurance, he also needs the folk to end his isolation. Even connections of family and romantic love are not enough to overcome this isolation because such individual connections are mortal while the folk is not. However, though *Southern Road* formally and thematically projects a guarded optimism, it does not suggest that the synthesis of a new type of intellectual and the folk will be an easy one. Rather, it implies that vestiges of individualism and romanticism will not be so easily left behind insofar as they exert an often morbid appeal that is as strong as, perhaps even a part of, the lure of consumer culture.

In some important respects, the figure associated with the New Negro Renaissance that Brown is most closely related to in sensibility is his colleague at Howard, Alain Locke. Locke's praise of *Southern Road* as marking the advent of the folk-poet laureate was not merely a dig at Langston Hughes caused by various personal disputes of the New Negro Renaissance but also the recognition of a kindred artistic spirit. Locke quite explicitly linked the surge of African-American writing under the rubric of the "New Negro" as a parallel endeavor to the cultural activity associated with nationalist movements of the oppressed, or recently oppressed, nationalities of Europe, specifically the Irish and the Czechs who had only recently gained their full or partial independence from the old imperial powers of Europe:

> That is why our comparison is taken with those nascent centers of folk-expression and self- determination which are playing a creative part in the world today. Without pretense to their political significance, Harlem has the same rôle to play for the New Negro as Dublin has had for the New Ireland or Prague for the New Czechoslovakia. (Locke, *The New Negro*, 7)

While he did not explicitly reject a modernist and transnational (or at least anational, if Eurocentric) model of literature and art of the early twentieth century, Locke, as well as James Weldon Johnson, viewed the black culture of the rural South as the raw material from which a "high" art could be created in much the same way that European nationalists in the internal colonies of the old European empires of the late nineteenth and early twentieth centuries worked to create new national cultures based on the peasant cultures of those peoples. In the way that various European composers, such as Dvorak and Janacek, used peasant folk songs to create a specifically national "high" music, Locke saw a possible use for the spirituals:

> We cannot accept the attitude that would merely preserve this music, but must cultivate that which would also develop it. Equally with treasuring and appreciating it as music of the past, we must nurture and welcome its contribution to the music of tomorrow. (210)

There are some obvious differences between the Sterling Brown of *Southern Road* and the Alain Locke of *The New Negro*. Brown clearly puts no stock in the notion of Harlem as the new cultural capital that will synthesize the various folk strains of Afro-America into new "high" art forms. In general, Brown is far more dubious about the effect of the new urban concentrations of black people in the North on African-American culture. It is also unclear to what degree Brown is interested in "elevating" the folk utterance or whether in fact he thinks it already as "high" as it needs to be. What Brown seems to be interested in is closer to the slogan of the CPUSA-led League of Struggle for Negro Rights, "Promote Negro Culture in Its Original Form with Proletarian Content." In other words, rather than attempting to transmogrify the form of the folk expression into something "higher," Brown proposed to approach this expression on something like its own formal terms, but with a different, and presumably higher, consciousness. Again, this approach can be compared to that of Hughes in *Fine Clothes to the Jew*, where Hughes for the most part attempts to recreate and document the folk voice without comment or any sense that the narratorial consciousness is significantly different from that of the folk. In this way Brown makes the problem of representing and recreating the folk subject and the folk utterance overt, whereas in Hughes it is covert.

But Brown does share Locke's notion of a tradition of African-American rural culture as the basis of modern African-American art and literature rather than the self-consciously modernist notions that influence most of the black writers associated with New York and/or Harlem (Hughes, Toomer, McKay, Walrond, Fauset, Larsen, and even Fisher). While Brown rejected the idea of a "Harlem Renaissance," he did subscribe to the notion of a "New Negro Renaissance," which implies that he shared Locke's sense of a movement, or at least a wish for that sort of movement, similar to that of a "New Ireland" or "New Czechoslovakia." Brown and Locke, like many European nationalists of the nineteenth and early twentieth centuries, saw a true national identity arising from somewhat static peasant culture whose essence was basically ahistorical. Or perhaps it is more accurate to say that Brown was not so much antimodernist as against any sort of African-American modernism that abandoned the experience and culture of the southern folk. Thus even such writers as Toomer and James Weldon Johnson, who invoked and represented the vernacular in their works, become problematic for Brown in that they saw the culture represented in *Cane* and *God's Trombones* as fading and their works as in part elegies for that culture. As discussed below, there is certainly a preservationist aspect to Brown's work, but it more closely resembles the utopian cultural nationalism that proposed a fading Irish as a national language with the notion that such an imagined linguistic revival would promote a genuine national culture than the cultural elegies of Toomer and Johnson.

There is an academic feel, a curatorial sense, to the work of both Locke and Brown. Locke proposes rural African-American folk culture as a basis for "high" culture, which would place the African-American artist and intellectual within the arena of international art and scholarship but would not change that scholarship much, only add to it in a manner that is not unlike T. S. Eliot's notion that literary tradition is something that is increased incrementally and changed slowly and nearly imperceptibly.[31] Brown, on the other hand proposed a whole new type of academy. The poems of *Southern Road*, written near the beginning of Brown's literary and academic career, are consonant with his lifelong work as a poet, anthologist, critic, teacher, promoter, and preserver of African-American literature, music—including jazz—and folklore. *Southern Road* is a radical redefinition of what has come to be known as the canon to include a far wider variety of cultural forms, specifically African-American folk forms, than had been accepted before. His project in *Southern Road* was not, however, to academize the folk, but rather to represent a process where an urban intellectual is able to rejoin the folk without glossing over the difficulties of such a process. At the same time, this process is not simply a sentimental return to the folk, or a new primitivism on the part of the intellectual, but also involves the intellectual-poet's giving a new consciousness to the folk that allows it to see its power and destiny more clearly while recognizing its weaknesses. As Kimberly Benston notes:

> Indeed, the 'tradition,' reconstructed anew with every Brown poem, is very much the poet's subject—but, as Brown incessantly examines it, tradition must be understood in its etymologically contradictory aspects of "betrayal" and "inheritance."

How, Brown's poems ask, can the transaction between individual and communal voice preserve the *continuous* integrity of each and thereby enlarge rather than merely reify a vital image of the Afro-American self? (34)

Thus Brown is authorized to create new "folk" forms such as the blues work song in the poem "Southern Road" and feels free to ridicule black folk religion and even black sacred rhetoric and music while recognizing a secular value in the religion and its rhetoric and music. In this sense, Alain Locke is certainly correct that Brown does establish "a sort of common denominator between the old and new Negro," however critical Brown may have been of those aspects of the New Negro movement associated with Harlem by such black intellectuals as Locke and James Weldon Johnson.[32] If it can be said that Brown's work is in a sense curatorial in that it privileges older rural "folk" cultural forms while rejecting newer, more urban and commercial forms, Brown does not have the feel of the "moldy fig" about him. He is not claiming that there has not been a good song since 1898. Rather than memorialize a residual culture after the manner of Toomer and Johnson, Brown attempts to promote what he sees as a vital oppositional culture largely, though not entirely, outside the orbit of the supply-and-demand commercial culture. For Brown, the commercialized blues and jazz are both alienating and a mark of the alienation of the black individual from community and from history, while folk forms are signs of communal resistance and in fact perhaps the most important community-building activity.[33]

This positing of rural southern African-American folk culture as the mythic foundation of African-American identity stands in contradistinction to Marcus Garvey's use of a mythic Africa for a similar purpose. As Jean Wagner points out, Africa never appears directly or indirectly in *Southern Road*, an absence that also distinguished Brown's work from even those black writers of the period, such as Hughes, Waring Cuney, Helene Johnson, and Zora Neale Hurston, who did do significant work in the vernacular.[34] The intellectual nineteenth-century European nationalism that influenced Locke and Brown was quite different from the distinctly twentieth-century mixture of utopian nationalism and black capitalism of Garvey, whose literary followers in the United States almost always employed an extremely "high" poetic diction.

What Brown did share with the literary Garveyites of the *Negro World*, and with the Communist Left (which was influenced by the rhetoric of Garveyism), was a masculinist rhetoric in which the voice of folk resistance was definitely male.[35] Women often appear in *Southern Road* as subjects of tragic or pathetic portraits. But even the sympathetically tragic women are never tragic in the classic sense of tragedy arising from a subject's actions. The tragedy of these women results from what was done to them rather than from what they did. Only the women of the pathetic portraits are allowed to be active, however foolishly or meanly. For example, Brown transforms the most famous African-American ballad of tragic African-American female revenge, "Frankie and Johnny," into a story where a hard-working African-American male is entrapped and destroyed by a half-witted white woman.[36]

One of the few exceptions to this pattern of the female as passive victim or foolish actor is in "The Ruminations of Luke Johnson," where a black woman, Mandy Jane, steals from a plantation owner as an act of restitution for slavery and exploitation. However, even here it takes a male folk speaker to interpret and articulate Mandy Jane's act of resistance. In fact, just one of the many first-person poems of *Southern Road*, "Sister Lou," is in the voice of a woman. In the one poem in which expressiveness of a female subject is portrayed, "Ma Rainey," the actual voice of the singer Ma Rainey appears only briefly in the fourth section of the poem and even there is represented filtered through the voice of a secondary male narrator rendered in turn by the poem's primary narrator who is, given the gendered nature of so many of the book's poems, almost certainly male.

Southern Road is also a rejection of what Brown perceived as the cosmopolitanism of the "Harlem Renaissance." Brown's collection contains criticism and commentary on specific African-American writers, as well as on the general values of the scene associated with Harlem. Brown examined Harlem and the writers around it in view of his newly defined canon and found it, and them, wanting. However, unlike Wallace Thurman and the critical descendants of his views on the period expressed in *Infants of the Spring*—Nathan Huggins, for example, in his seminal work on the New Negro Renaissance—who judged the New Negro writers as too parochial in their material and their standards, Brown considered them insufficiently grounded in the struggles, traditions, and aesthetics of the masses of their own people in the rural South and far too pretentious.[37] From this perspective, Brown in *Southern Road* could be said to have much in common with eighteenth-century English neoclassical satire in that his bitter attacks on various sorts of economic and intellectual "strivers" are measured against an idealized past, though in Brown's case it is not a neoclassical idealization of Greece and Rome but a model of the rural folk that is the measuring stick. Thus, again, Brown's enterprise can be said to be both deeply radical and deeply conservative.

The Road Further Left: Brown's *No Hidin' Place* and the Popular Front

Southern Road indicates that Brown's ideological position with respect to the essential nature of black culture was not very far from that of the CPUSA's Black Belt Thesis even before Brown became publicly associated with the Left. No doubt this similarity facilitated his move left. Brown's approach to poetic form and diction has to be seen within the previously noted Left discourse of regional "residual" cultures that are set in opposition to "mainstream" capitalist mass culture and are represented in literature largely through linguistic "difference." Thus, Brown's use of southern African-American rural culture was consonant with other work by non-African-American writers connected to the Communist Left, such as Missouri poet H. H. Lewis; Missouri editor, novelist, and short story writer Jack Conroy; Minnesota poet and fiction writer Meridel Le Sueur; and Appalachian poet Don West (a frequent contributor to the *Negro Liberator*). It was also closely related to the common Left editorial practice of reprinting the lyrics of songs by "authentically" regional or "national" folksingers, such as Woody Guthrie, Huddie Ledbetter, Aunt Molly Jackson, and Jim Garland, as literary productions. These writers and editors, like Brown, clearly valued various vernacular forms associated with the rural South, or other rural areas, over others popularly associated with the commercial culture of the urban North. And like Brown they infused much of their "folk" poetry and prose with an overt message of protest that would have been more covert, for the most part, in the tradition upon which they drew. For example, in Don West's "Dark Winds," one sees not only the use of a vernacular diction but also a stance toward the North, and the economic system associated with it, that is not unlike Brown's "Tin Roof Blues." Here West, like Brown, describes a migration, either to the North or to one of the factory towns, such as Birmingham or Bessemer, located at the southern end of the Appalachians:

> Smoke winds,
> Fouled with dirt frum th' sutty stacks
> Of a fac'try,
> A-scroungin' fer room
> An' blackin' me.
>
> Sad winds,
> They've blowed sorrow and sufferin'
> Frum northern mills,
> An' drug my people
> Down from th' hills.

> (Hicks et al., 198)

While the mills may or may not be physically located in the North (the "sad winds" from the northern mills may refer to the industrialization of the South rather than an exodus to the North), the North in West's poem, as in Brown's work, is clearly marked as the spiritual home of the economic system that has destroyed the community that West recreates linguistically. There are some obvious differences between West's poem and those of *Southern Road*. For instance, the migrants in Brown's work may be deluded by a false consciousness, but they leave the South willingly. Still, the work of both West and Brown posits a regional pre-proletarian culture, be it "Negro" or "Mountaineer," which lingers into the industrial era. This residual culture can be drawn on as an alternative to the mass commercial culture by those who have not lost contact with the pre-industrial traditions despite being caught up in crises and conflicts that are decidedly of the capitalist era, whether in the "dust bowl" of the Southwest, the coal fields of eastern Kentucky, the steel towns of northern Alabama, or the tenant farms of Georgia.

Interestingly enough, Brown's second unpublished collection of poems, *No Hidin' Place*, which was submitted for publication in 1936 or 1937, draws back a bit from the model of "authentic" African-American expressive culture proposed in *Southern Road* even though the later collection is more explicitly engaged with the organized Left and Left ideology than the earlier one. While Brown in *No Hidin' Place* still presents a linguistically based model of the African-American folk, there is less direct adaptation of vernacular expressive forms, particularly music. For example, there is only one poem, "Choices," that is formally a blues poem in *No Hidin' Place*—though others, notably "Long Track Blues," which ends the collection, draw on a blues form and sensibility even if the typical aab blues stanza is implied rather than fully present.[38]

The dominant type of poem in *No Hidin' Place* is the narrative poem of description and prescription that reveals and instructs. The main modes of *Southern Road*, the lyric and the vernacular monologue, that recreate the folk voice as an artifact in and of itself are far less common in *No Hidin' Place* —though the lyric voice does appear in its final two sections. As in *Southern Road*, there are a number of regularly rhymed poems. Unlike the earlier collection, the use of rhyme in *No Hidin' Place* is almost exclusively connected with an ironic or sarcastic tone, as in "Negro Improvement League" or "Transfer," so that the appearance of a regular rhyme scheme signals that the reader needs to be wary about accepting any statement uncritically—though in practice Brown's sarcasm is hard to mistake with or without the presence of rhyme. The relatively straightforward narrative poems, such as "An Old Woman Remembers" and "Remembering Nat Turner," tend to be rendered in prosy long lines that are irregular in length and stresses. In these poems, line breaks seem to be organized around a sense of the "natural" breaks of colloquial speech, whether that of the poet's persona or that of an elderly African-American woman, rather than according to conventional meter. Even "Sharecroppers," a narrative poem that does utilize rhyme, follows no regular rhyme scheme and, like the other narrative poems, varies quite a bit in line length.

The vanguard role of the artist-intellectual embodied—or at least envoiced—in the narratorial consciousness is even more pronounced here than in *Southern Road*. The vanguard poet here is also clearly identified with the "vanguard party" of the Left, the CPUSA. This identification with the Communist Left is particularly evident in the section "Road to the Left," which can be largely summed up by the Left slogan ubiquitous to the trade union and unemployed struggles of the 1930s: "Black and White Unite and Fight." The speaker can at times listen to the lessons of the folk experience, as in "Old Lem," or take on the voice of the folk either in part, as in "Transfer," or in whole, as in "Colloquy" (where he adopts the voices of a "black worker" and a "white worker"). However, the final note of the "Road to the Left" section is the narratorial consciousness instructing both the black rural laborer and white rural laborer:

> Listen, John Cracker; hear me, Joe Nigg.
> You on one side of the railroad, you on the other.
> This railroad track is no final separation.
> This eighteen foot cut isn't a canyon.
>
> Your shanty is shaky, John, the roof is leaky,
> The same wind whistles through yours and Joe's.
> And grits, and molasses like grease for belts,
> And chicory coffee and collards like jimson
> Are the same on both sides of the track.
> And the side meat comes from the same place on the hog.

> *(Collected, 218)*

What distinguishes Brown's vision in *No Hidin' Place* from that in *Southern Road* is an interracial Popular Front vision of the South that focuses primarily on the African-American subject and yet projects a "front" of poor whites, African Americans, and, implicitly, the radical intellectual, against the southern oligarchy rather than focusing on what might be thought of as the literary equivalent of the Black Belt Thesis. The negative portrait of the "Arkansaw" "Hill Billy" of the poem "Slim Greer" in *Southern Road* is replaced by the potentially positive "John Cracker" of "Side By Side"—though the speaker of the poem is still not entirely convinced that John will listen to him:

> Listen, John:
> But you will probably never listen,
> Your ears have been deafened by the roar so long,
> You have told yourself there is nothing Joe can say
> But "Yassuh," and "Be right there, Mister John"
>
> You have never got around to it, John,
> Either to listening or thinking.

> (222)

As noted earlier, the narratorial consciousness of Brown's poems in *Southern Road* frequently adopts the voice of the folk subject, either for the length of an entire poem or for as little as a single word or phrase. However, the ending of "Side By Side" signals a new sort of relationship between the narratorial consciousness and the black folk subject and white folk subject. The bulk of the poem draws a line between the instructing speaker of the poem and the folk(s) (as represented by his potential pupils) more clearly than any other poem of Brown's. The voice of the narratorial consciousness of the intellectual-poet employs a knowing, hard-boiled, and slightly slangy diction—a very common stance among male (and a few female) poets of the literary Left in the 1930s and 1940s, which was nonetheless clearly distinct from that of either of his addressees. But in the final two lines of the poem ("Listen, John Cracker, / Joe Nigg, I've an earful for yo"), the speaker adopts a folk voice that seems relatively free of irony. The narratorial voice merges with those of "Joe Nigg" and "John Cracker" into a single popular voice, albeit one in which the instructional mode of the narratorial consciousness still dominates.

Brown's vision then resembles the Popular Front concept of the unity of "the people"—a multiclass concept—against fascism and extreme reaction. Brown's self-consciously "Left" poems during the 1930s, such as "Colloquy," "Side By Side," and "Sharecroppers," differs from that of Hughes in "Scottsboro Limited," "Advertisement for the Waldorf-Astoria," and even the Popular Front–era "poetry-play" "Don't You Want to Be Free" in that Brown's poems imagine black-white unity, but with the goal of a hazily defined social justice rather than proletarian revolution. This move on Brown's part also dovetails with the Popular Front ideology that saw socialism as a relatively distant goal rather than as the imminent state found in the apocalyptic rhetoric of the CPUSA Third Period analysis.[39]

However, despite the aspects of *No Hidin' Place* that are consonant with the Popular Front, there are certain elements of the collection that make it strangely anachronistic within a Left ideological framework. Perhaps the most notable is the continuing hostility to the social and intellectual image of a "Harlem Renaissance" as figured in the landscape of Harlem of the collection's opening section "Harlem

Stopover." This landscape, filled with pretentious strivers ("Negro Improvement League"), Garveyites ("The Temple"), white Jazz Age slummers ("Roberta Lee"), and race "misleaders" ("The New Congo"), seems oddly out of sync with the mid-Depression Harlem of rent strikes, relief demonstrations, marches against the Italian invasion of Ethiopia, marches to save the Scottsboro defendants, the Harlem boycott movement, and the National Negro Congress—not to mention the Harlem Riot of 1935. There were, of course, still strivers, slummers, and Garveyites in Harlem in the 1930s. (The CPUSA fought pitched street battles with the Garveyites in Harlem during the early 1930s—and had serious conflicts with neo-Garveyites, such as Arthur Reid and Ira Kemp, during the Popular Front era.) Nonetheless, these figures, which had been so large a part of the symbolic landscape of Harlem in the 1920s, were much diminished by the middle 1930s. Brown's use of Harlem assaulted a cultural moment that had clearly passed without an acknowledgment that anything had changed in Harlem or in the nation's view of Harlem.

Even within the context of the Left, a number of aspects of Brown's work clashed with the dominant positions of the Popular Front. Much of the poetry of *No Hidin' Place* is closely akin to Hughes's "revolutionary" pre–Popular Front poems of the early 1930s, particularly such poems of Brown's as "The New Congo" and "Memo: For the Race Orators," which attack middle-class "misleaders" of the African-American community in the same way as Hughes's "Elderly Race Leaders." In both cases, the rhetoric of the poems mirrors Third Period Communist attacks on such "reformist" organizations as the NAACP and the African-American churches. Similarly, while work in the South was not disregarded by the CPUSA during the Popular Front, there was a new emphasis put on activities in urban African-American communities in the North and West. The CPUSA emphasis on urban industrial centers became especially pronounced with the rise of the Committee for Industrial Organization (CIO), later the Congress of Industrial Organizations. As a result there was a general revaluation of African-American urban vernacular culture by the Communist Left with which Brown's second collection was out of tune.[40] It is telling in this regard that of the thirteen poems in *No Hidin' Place* that were published in the 1930s and early 1940s, eleven of which appeared in Left-influenced journals and anthologies, none came from the "Harlem Stopover" section.

Once again in the "Harlem Stopover" section, as in the "Tin Roof Blues" section of *Southern Road*, Harlem is associated with mass culture and the degradation of the folk culture. For example, "Roberta Lee" is a rewriting of "Cabaret" set in a Harlem nightclub with the possessing white consumer female instead of male. The action of the poem moves from the white male gaze of Texas Henry, which discomforts his companion Roberta Lee even as it consumes the sight of the light-skinned dancers "Now in neat bandanas and blue ginghams / Quickly pulled above their shapely knees, / Now in silk shorts and jeweled brassieres" (170), and ends with Roberta Lee's own consuming gaze focused on a black male offered as mass culture product:

> Upon his head a crazy hat, his face
> A black mask, except for large white circles
> About his eyes, and thickly painted lips.
> He danced.

She drank some more to wake her to attention.
He shuffled his flat feet, swing back and fro,
Grotesque, ridiculous; he could not keep his balance,
His lips got in the way, he fell to the slippery floor,
While the drummer struck *zip, boom,* to time his falling.
He arched over backwards, fell upon his head,

(170)

Without belaboring the obvious link of the represented performance to minstrelsy even down to the onomatopoetic connection of the drummer's beats to the stock minstrel character "Zip Coon," Harlem here is the topos of the most extreme symbolic commodification of the black body. However, in this case the taste of the white consumers is not simply that of a nineteenth-century vision of the "Old South," as embodied in the heavy-handedly named Roberta Lee, or of a "modernist" sexualized primitivism, as embodied in Texas Henry, but both. Once again, while such a critique would not be invalid in the middle 1930s, its location in a Harlem Club (rather than, say, a movie) seems much more of the Jazz Age than the Great Depression. A similar point can be made about the next poem in the section, "Real Mammy Song" ("*With proudful apologies to Irving Berlin* et al. *and all the Tin Pan Alley Manipulators*") which describes a black man resisting a lynch mob in the South using the cliched phrases of various popular songs. The fact that such an assault on Tin Pan Alley as a commercial "manipulation" and obfuscation of the authentic African-American experience in the South is placed in the "Harlem Stopover" section further associates Harlem with such manipulations.[41]

Even more than in *Southern Road*, which contained "Ma Rainey" and a mention of boxer Jack Johnson in "Strange Legacy," positive references to mass commercial culture are missing in *No Hidin' Place*. Instead, the "authentic" folk characters, black and white, are shown as being virtually uncontaminated by mass culture whatever their other weaknesses. Thus in the "Music" section of the poem "Side by Side," Joe Nigg and John Cracker are shown to be related culturally in an archaic "folk" manner as seen in their spirituals, folk blues, and transplanted border ballads:

You on your side, on your harmonica,
Mix mournful blues with hill-billy tunes;
Joe sings Barbara Allen with some Tom-Tom swing.
John sings of a knight coming riding, riding
With rings and gold and gear;
Joe sings to a guitar of a sweet chariot
Swinging low for to carry him home.

(221–222)

The picture he draws of the two, who are not supposed to be unusually isolated individuals, but representative types of working-class black and white male southerners, is extreme in its folk purity. Apparently, neither of the two has been exposed to commercial "hillbilly" music, "race" music, Tin Pan Alley, or such popular traveling shows as Brown himself represented in "Ma Rainey."

However, as the Popular Front emerged in the middle 1930s, the dominant Third Period CPUSA notion of promoting oppositional or alternative culture and cultural institutions outside mass culture gave way to a much greater engagement with mass culture as a site of contestation for political power. Thus jazz (which had long been present at CPUSA benefit dances and other functions as entertainment) now became a topic for serious and approving discussion.[42] In the same spirit, the CPUSA and the Young Communist League started a campaign for the integration of professional sports, particularly Major League Baseball—and generally paid far more attention to professional sports rather than to the concept of alternative "Workers Leagues" that dominated CPUSA thinking about sports during the Third Period. Also, noted in the previous chapter, many mixtures of "high" and "popular" culture took place. Left composers and playwrights produced musicals, such as Hughes's "Don't You Want to Be Free." Richard Wright wrote positively of the effect of the victory of Joe Louis over Max Schmeling on African Americans in Harlem in *New Masses*. Wright also contributed the lyrics of the song "King Joe," which was recorded by Paul Robeson and the Count Basie Orchestra in 1941 and placed in barroom jukeboxes.[43] Thus, despite Brown's publicly announced move Left, his critique was out of sync with the direction of the cultural Left.

In fact, the anachronisms of the "Harlem Stopover" and "Road to the Left" sections raise one of the most striking contradictions of *No Hidin' Place* as "social realism": while there are mentions of various contemporary events, such as the Scottsboro case and attempts to organize a sharecroppers union, the Depression is strangely absent even though it struck African Americans much harder than white Americans. The problems of the African Americans in the South are represented as relatively timeless, or cyclical, as was the case in *Southern Road*. The new possibilities of black-white unity are not linked to the imperatives of the nation's economic collapse so much as to an enduring legacy of racism and southern poverty.

What is present in *No Hidin' Place* that was not present in *Southern Road* is a generational rhetoric in which the African-American folk culture is divided into a culture of accommodationism represented by the father and a culture of revolt represented by the son. This opposition is most clearly seen in "Legend," which ends:

> The young black man faced his old black father.
> The young black man faced the old white man.
> He straightened his shoulders, and threw back his head,
> "I wish you both in hell,"
> Said the young black man.
>
> The young black man broke the whipstock to pieces,
> The young black man cut the lash into bits.
> Then chained the old men together with the traces,
> "Your fine day is over,"
> Said the young black man.

(199)

This opposition is grounded in the masculinist rhetoric of the more militant aspect of the New Negro Movement, African-American nationalism, and Third Period communism discussed at some length in the previous chapter. It is a striking reversal of the generational rhetoric of *Southern Road* where a decadent and deracinated younger generation was posed against the "Strong Men" of an older generation—or at least an unbroken line of "authentic" cultural transmission.

In *No Hidin' Place* this folk transmission is called into question. For example, in "Remembering Nat Turner," the African-American folk are unable to recall Turner though the local white people do. As noted above with respect to religion and class consciousness, the southern folk culture is viewed far more critically than in *Southern Road*, having much in common with pre–Popular Front Communist visions of African-American culture that, using the masculinist opposition of virility and femininity or effeminacy, sought to identify the accommodationist or reactionary aspects of the folk culture as well as the "revolutionary tradition" from Nat Turner to the 1906 Atlanta Riot. Once again, this critique of the folk consciousness emphasizes the need for the returning radical intellectual such as the speaker of "Remembering Nat Turner." This speaker "returns" to the site of Turner's rebellion, knowing, like the local white people, the fact of Turner's rebellion, but also knowing, unlike the white people (and the African-American folk), of the need of the local African-American tenant farmers to remember Turner.[44] This generational model of folk accommodationism and rebellion has much in common with other Left African-American articulations of the folk—notably in the poetry of Hughes in the early and middle 1930s and the opposition of Bigger Thomas and his mother in *Native Son*. Of course, at other times, notably in "Old Lem" and "An Old Woman Remembers," an older generation is the source of historical knowledge of African-American struggle in the South, though it may be significant that in both cases, the older "informant" is recalling something they actually witnessed rather than passing down the folk memory.

Despite notable changes of stance from *Southern Road*, *No Hidin' Place* ends in much the same way as the earlier collection. The title of the final section of *No Hidin' Place*, "Remembrances," recalls that of the concluding "Vestiges" section of *Southern Road*. Like "Vestiges," "Remembrances" is a series of personal lyrics meditating on love, loss, and death. Given the explicit radicalism and social engagement of the rest of *No Hidin' Place*, the apparent disjunction of this section from the rest of the collection is even more striking than that of the "Vestiges" section from the rest of *Southern Road*. However, "Remembrances" differs importantly from "Vestiges" in that three of the ten poems in the former are rendered in a "folk" voice—and a fourth interpolates vernacular song into a "high" frame—whereas all poems in the latter are formally "high." In a sense, this section, and the preceding "Washington, D.C." section, are a sort of tribute to Brown's earlier representation of the folk, and, perhaps, a rebuke or corrective to the criticism of the folk by the narrating persona of the intellectual-poet:

> We who have fretted our tired brains with fears
> That time shall frustrate all our chosen dreams
> We are rebuked by Banjo Sam's gay strains.
> Oh Time may be less vicious than he seems;
> And Troubles may grow weaker through the years—
> Nearly as weak as those Sam told us of.—

Sam, strumming melodies to his honey love;
Sam, flouting Trouble in his inky lane.
Oh, I doan mess wid trouble . . .

(246)

The speaker is reminded of his limitations by the folk voice and folk artistic expression. His individualism threatens to result in an extreme and isolating vanguardism that can be reined in only by the communal perspective the folk culture brings. However, as in *Southern Road*, the narratorial consciousness is reminded, and reminds the reader that such a union, or reunion, is a difficult process.

One Way of Taking Leave: Brown and the Ideological
Contradictions of the Popular Front

Seen within the dominant rhetorics of the 1930s, *No Hidin' Place* is a deeply conflicted work. Brown's work both engages specific events of the 1930s and evades the largest single event—the Depression. It continues to attack the image of a "Harlem Renaissance" as figured in the Harlem landscape as if it were still 1928 and yet often draws heavily on a generational construction of the African-American folk that has important antecedents in the New Negro movement. At other points, as in the poems "Old Lem" and "An Old Woman Remembers," Brown returns to what might be thought of as the "Old Negro" generational model of cultural authenticity that had marked *Southern Road*. The collection embodies elements of the ideology of Third Period communism (e.g., the opposition of folk culture to mass culture) as well as of the Popular Front, (e.g., the generalized vision of social justice as opposed to a more millenarian vision of social revolution).[45] It foregrounds the difficult relation of the intellectual to the folk without resolving the contradictions of that relation. While less optimistic than *Southern Road* about the inherently progressive nature of the folk utterance and the folk memory, the book ends with the apparently unmediated folk expression of "Long Track Blues."

These contradictions are reflected in the text itself. Taken together the poems in *No Hidin' Place* form less of a coherent whole than those of *Southern Road* despite the fact that the second collection wears its political heart on its sleeve in a way that might lead a reader to believe that the author is seeking a greater unity in the second collection than he did in the first. In a way this relative lack of coherence is ironic because the range of formal choices for which the author opts in *No Hidin' Place* is narrower than that of *Southern Road*. The tone of *No Hidin' Place* is more consistent; the approach to rhyme, line, syntax, and rhythm more limited—at least in the first five sections. Perhaps the sense of a relative diffuseness is due in part to the greater number of sections in the second collection—seven as opposed to four in *Southern Road*. Or it may be that the final three sections of the book, which differ so radically in subject and attitude from the overtly radical politics of the earlier sections, finally overwhelm the sense of the book's thematic unity despite the best efforts of the reader to devise a scheme that encompasses them all. And yet the book is organized in such a way as to demand that it be read as more than a simple collection of poems written over a certain period; a number of poems Brown published in periodicals during this period, such as "The Ballad of Joe Meek," were not included in *No Hidin' Place*, suggesting that he had a sense of the book's structure in which certain poems would fit while others would not.

While all of these factors contribute to the relative lack of coherence in *No Hidin' Place*, the most serious obstacle to such a coherence is the collision of the conflicting discourses that informed the production and the reception of the collection. The vision of the folk promoted in *Southern Road*, while consonant with earlier Comintern notions of the "Negro Nation" in the South, became problematic during the Popular Front. The attachment to earlier constructions of the rural folk as the authentic representatives of oppositional African-American culture uncontaminated by mass culture remained, and even flourished, during the Popular Front, notably in a growing Leftist folk music and folklore boom. Third Period notions of the folk still had currency with respect to the reception of African-American authors. One example of the continuing power of this vision during the Popular Front was Brown's own participation in the December 24, 1939, "Spirituals to Swing" concert at Carnegie Hall, where he lectured on the blues.

Nonetheless, the more dynamic political and artistic activities of the Communist Left with respect to African Americans concentrated on the urban and the industrial. It was the jazz of the Count Basie orchestra, boogie-woogie piano, the urban blues, and gospel, not the singing of work songs, that were the focus of the famous 1938 and 1939 concerts organized in New York by John Hammond under the auspices of various CPUSA-led organizations.[46] Even those Left African-American writers, notably Richard Wright, who remained engaged with the pre–Popular Front Comintern analysis of the "national question," were increasingly concerned with the African-American urban experience—and urban vernacular culture—and the migration to the North in a way that Brown seemed unwilling, or unable, to consider.

There may well have been personal reasons for Brown's poetic silence after the late 1930s that have little to do with changes in the literary moment. Disclosure of those reasons, if they exist, will have to await a serious biography of Brown. However, it seems not unreasonable to surmise from the evidence of his second collection that Brown felt keenly the ideological contradictions of the transition from the New Negro Renaissance to the Third Period to the Popular Front, but was unable to resolve them within the oppositions of North and South, authentic folk culture and mass culture, peasant and migrant that he set up in *Southern Road* and held onto in *No Hidin' Place*. While his poetry of the 1930s continued to be valued by the Left in the late 1930s and the 1940s, as evidenced by the 1946 *New Masses* awards dinner, the ideological context of the era was not nearly so supportive of Brown as that of the early 1930s had been as shown by the populist—as opposed to radical—and integrationist rhetoric of the dinner itself. *No Hidin' Place* is notable because it so obviously tries to address the new moment of the Popular Front while maintaining much of the ideological content of *Southern Road*. This results in the peculiar contradictions and anachronistic character of much of the second collection that prevent it from completely cohering and give it an unfinished feeling despite the presence of a number of very strong poems. Even the lack of coherence is moving in that it lays out the conflicts that the persona of the poet-speaker is trying painfully to resolve. However, given the overwhelming move on the part of the narratorial conscious of the collection to unify the folk voice with that of the intellectual while excluding the northern urban culture, except as a negative example of the breakdown of authentic communal values, these contradictory rhetorics are particularly frustrating to the reader. The collection attempts to deliver something that it ultimately cannot—as is recognized in the final two sections to some extent—within the parameters it has set for itself. Thus perhaps Brown falls silent in the 1930s because of the contradictions between his construction of the folk and the ideological context which has changed, making his vision increasingly anachronistic, an anachronism that Brown keenly feels.[47]

Whatever prevented Brown from writing much poetry in the late 1930s and 1940s, his two collections—or at least *Southern Road* and those individual later poems that were published in African-American and / or Left journals—presented a construction of the African-American folk voice and an approach to representing the folk that would be influential through the entire period under study here and beyond. His location of authentic African-American culture in the South, his emphasis on authenticity itself, his opposition to mass culture that he set against a residual folk culture, his radical yet curatorial approach to folklore, and his notion of the vanguard intellectual who rejoins the folk attracted African-American writers of the 1940s, whose "neomodernist" poetics would seem as far from the spirit of *Southern Road* as one could imagine.

3

"Adventures of a Social Poet"
Langston Hughes in the 1930s

> Social forces pull backwards or forwards, right or left, and social poems get caught in the pulling and hauling. Sometimes the poet himself gets pulled and hauled—even hauled off to jail.
>
> —LANGSTON HUGHES, "MY ADVENTURES AS A SOCIAL POET" (1947)

The difficulty in authoritatively reading Hughes's "true" personality and "true" artistic enterprise—which are often conflated—has been much remarked, directly by critics and indirectly in the belletristic works of such writers as Wallace Thurman and Melvin Tolson.[1] Since the late 1920s, Hughes's use of a wide variety of tones, voices, styles, and subjects in many literary or quasi-literary genres has often been seen as a flaw, betraying a facility that, though possessing a certain charm, is at least a little shallow without any real distinctiveness. In many of these accounts, Hughes both evades the rigors of "high" literature while insufficiently mastering African-American "folk" utterance.[2]

No portion of Hughes's literary career has been more commonly dismissed than that of the 1930s. Even many of Hughes's admirers compare unfavorably his writings of the 1930s to his work in other decades. In this view, Hughes's 1930s efforts in many different genres—including short and long fiction, poetry, drama, reportage, song writing—largely sounded over and over the same ham-fisted didactic note, lacking the lyric humanism and folk wit of his work in the 1920s, 1940s, and 1950s. This asserted nadir of Hughes's literary efforts is almost always related to his engagement with the CPUSA.

That Hughes was, with the exception of Richard Wright, the black writer most identified with the Communist Left during the 1930s is undeniable. Hughes's frequent publication of "revolutionary" poetry in the journals and press of the CPUSA, his activity in Communist-initiated campaigns such as the drive to free the Scottsboro defendants and on behalf of the Spanish Republic, his willingness to lend his name to Communist-led or Communist-influenced organizations (e.g., the John Reed Clubs, the League of Struggle for Negro Rights, the National Negro Congress, the League of Professional Groups for Foster and Ford, the League of American Writers), and his public support of the Soviet Union (including his signing of a statement in 1938 supporting the purges of the Old Bolsheviks and others by Stalin) all marked him as an open member of the Communist Left—whether or not he formally joined the CPUSA.[3] As noted in chapter 1, Hughes's Left sympathies antedated the Great Depression. But it is unquestionably true that Hughes's participation in the Left increased astronomically during the 1930s and had a marked impact on the form and content (to use a favorite phrase of Left cultural critics of that time) of Hughes's poetry.

But, in fact, what is formally most interesting about Hughes's poetry in the 1930s is that the wide variety of voices, styles, and themes employed by Hughes in the late 1920s and early 1930s and addressed to equally disparate audiences become largely unified by the end of the decade in a manner that is crucial to the development of his later work.[4] This process of unification results in *Shakespeare in Harlem* (1942) and, ultimately, *Montage of a Dream Deferred* (1951), in which formerly distinct addresses and addressees are combined to imagine a single audience and a single subject. Or, to draw on Bahktin's discussion of the novel, if a diversity of speakers and auditors could be said to be retained by Hughes, this diversity is contained within a single volume in a dialogic relation rather than in different volumes and journals speaking to different audiences. The poetic voice that Hughes creates, unlike the voice established in most of the work of Sterling Brown, is not that of the individual narratorial consciousness, but of a simultaneously unitary and multiple urban community. While the persona of the poet-narrator may appear in a poem, as it does in "Air Raid Over Harlem," the poet-speaker is a liminal figure, who is both inside and outside the community, and whose only authority is that arrogated by the community. This relatively unified poetic voice, or collection of voices, bespeaks the existence of a new kind of audience, one which Hughes had a major part in creating, particularly through his work in the cultural institutions of the Communist Left. Ironically, despite Hughes's activity within the cultural (as well as more strictly "political") organizations and institutions affiliated with the CPUSA, his poetry frequently received mixed or poor reviews from left-wing American critics.[5]

The range of addresses and addressees in Hughes's poetry reached its zenith in the early 1930s. During this period Hughes largely abandoned the types of poems that had made his 1927 *Fine Clothes to the Jew* so notorious in the black press: poems formally rooted in the secular and sacred musical forms of the blues and gospel music, as well as in black rhetoric and representing as speaking subjects such "low-life" characters as prostitutes, gamblers, murderers, drunks, and suicides.[6] Instead Hughes's published poems fell into three general categories aimed at three relatively discrete audiences: "uplift" and comic poems aimed largely at an African-American audience that was outside the cultural orbit of the CPUSA, and outside the groups of black intellectuals associated with relatively elite institutions and journals such as *The Crisis* and *Opportunity* in such urban centers as New York, Boston, Philadelphia, and Washington; "literary" poems (as exemplified by those in the privately printed collection *Dear Lovely Death*, which if not "high" modernist were aimed at an audience that was consciously "literary" and "modern"); and Hughes's "revolutionary" or militant poems aimed at an audience defined largely by the cultural institutions of the CPUSA and the Comintern. As we shall see, the distinctions between these categories and their intended audiences are quite real. However, on closer examination Hughes's general formal strategies, and his sense of the work of the different types of poems, are not as far apart as they appear.

Lift High My Banner Out of the Dust: *The Negro Mother*
and Other Dramatic Recitations

It was during the early 1930s that Hughes began his extensive tours of poetry readings in the South, appearing for the most part at African-American churches and educational institutions. As Arnold Rampersad notes, this audience preferred a poetry that was uplifting, sentimental, and formally conservative.[7] However, using, to paraphrase Hans Robert Jauss, the horizon of this audience's expectations, Hughes drew on a variety of "high" and "popular" African-American discourses to create a poetry that strained at the boundaries of those conservative uplifting and sentimental discourses.

The volume best exemplifying this sort of poetry is *The Negro Mother and Other Dramatic Recitations* (1931), a book that Hughes self-published largely for the purpose of selling on his reading tours. The stage instructions of the anthemic title poem "The Negro Mother" read "A poem to be done by a woman in the bandana and apron of the Old South—but with great dignity and strength and beauty in her face as she speaks. The music of the spirituals may be played by a piano or an orchestra as the aged mother talks to her modern sons and daughters" (16). The poem is written in rhymed couplets using a "high" literary diction, despite the fact that the poem's speaker is explicitly the ur-mother of the African-American folk whom one would expect to speak in some representation of African-American vernacular after the fashion of the speaker in Hughes's earlier "Mother to Son." The poem utilizes a loose tetrameter where anapestic phrases and alliteration impel the poem along in a sort of march:

> But march ever forward, breaking down bars.
> Look ever upward at the sun and the stars.
> Oh, my dark children, may my dreams and my prayers
> Impel you forever up the great stairs—
> For I will be with you till no white brother
> Dares keep down the children of the NEGRO MOTHER.

(18)

"The Negro Mother" links earlier popular figurations of the southern folk, particularly Dunbar's, with a new militancy.[8] One would have to go back to the Reconstruction era, particularly in the work of Frances W. Harper, to find the popular figure of the Negro Mother so clearly associated with both the rural South and with an activist (as opposed to a stoic) resistance to racism.[9] Thus Hughes attempts to address a southern black audience by very largely assuming the formal and thematic literary stances that marked the last era of large-scale African-American political assertion in the

South as a model for political poetry. Interestingly, Hughes here avoids the masculinism of those "protest" poems of the New Negro Renaissance that would seem to have the most in common with "The Negro Mother," such as McKay's "If We Must Die," where a "conservative" formal structure and diction is used to express militant and even radical sentiments.

In other instances, Hughes does invoke the masculinist rhetoric of the New Negro and of the militant nationalism of the Garveyites, most notably in "The Black Clown," which concludes:

> Suffer and struggle.
> Work, pray and fight.
> Smash my way through
> to Manhood's true right.
> Say to all foemen:
> You can't keep me down!
> Tear off the garments
> That make me a clown!
>
> (*The Negro Mother,* 10–11)[10]

Here, like much Garveyite and New Negro poetry, the old folk culture (and Dunbar's figure of "the mask") is linked to an accommodationist and an effeminate minstrelsy past and the New Negro to an explicitly masculine, and surprisingly European, culture of rebellion. Accordingly, the stage instructions mark the movement from accommodationism to rebellion in the accompanying music as a shift from "a mournful tom-tom in the dark" to "a hymn of faith [which] echoes the fighting 'Marseillaise.'" Of course, the poem, particularly its diction, is formally more tricky than much of the Garveyite poetry in that Hughes's poem is frequently double-voiced as "high" and "low." For instance, the word "yonder" is both "poetically" archaic in the context of "standard" English and colloquial in African-American vernacular English, especially in the South. (In fact, "yonder" appears in the vernacular poem "Broke" of the same collection.)

Those poems that do speak in a representation of vernacular speech are either exaggeratedly comic, as in "Broke," or pathetic, as in "The Big Timer" (where the dramatic instructions accompanying the poem provide the reader with a gloss on how to read the text so that the sentiments of the self-described "moral poem" cannot be misunderstood and its protagonist, a "good time" "rounder," cannot be seen as a hero). The voice of these poems is somewhere between Dunbar's comic dialect poems and African-American vaudeville, particularly in "Broke":

> Aw-oo! Yonder comes a woman I used to know way down South.
> (Ain't seen her in six years! Used to go with her, too!)
> She would be alright if she wasn't so bow-legged, and cross-eyed,
> And didn't have such a big mouth.
> Howdy-do, daughter! Caledonia, how are you?
> Yes, indeedy, I sho have missed *you,* too!
> All these years you say you been *workin'* here?
> You got a good job? Yes! Well, I sho am glad to see *you,* dear!

> (6)

This poem is obviously a forerunner of Hughes's later comic vernacular writing, such as the "Simple" stories and the "Madam" poems. While "Broke" clearly owes a debt to Dunbar, like Hughes's later humorous vernacular works, its social criticism is much more overt than that of Dunbar. Much the same can be said of "The Big-Timer" with respect to Dunbar. Thus, Hughes maintains a sense of Dunbar's split between apparently humorous "dialect" poems and more straightforwardly "serious" (and "literary") poems. At the same time, Hughes infuses the "dialect" poetry with a considerable spirit of overt rebellion and the "uplift" poetry with a double-voiced confusion of "high" and "low," drawing on and yet undermining Dunbar's rhetoric of the vernacular mass culture "mask" and the "authentic" African-American self.

In short, Hughes synthesized a wide range of "high" and "popular" African-American discourses and styles from Reconstruction to contemporary vaudeville to create a genre of protest poetry that successfully appealed to a southern African-American audience.[11] This poetry was received by an audience consisting primarily of college students, faculty, and African-American professionals, at least initially. But its double-voiced aspect at least implicitly included the southern folk as part of the audience. Though Hughes wrote these poems before the era of his most active engagement with the Communist Left, they take up the problem of a usable past of African-American expressive culture, as well as the problem of a usable present of African-American popular culture within the limitations of a mass African-American audience. These investigations parallel similar discussions and debates within the literary Left as to uses of folk culture, popular culture, modernist art, and the nineteenth-century "high" art inheritance. As would be the case with much of Hughes's most successful later poetry, Hughes here drew on a complex of discourses that often contradicted each other, allowing many of the contradictions to remain within the poems.

Dear Lovely Death: Hughes and Modernist Exhaustion

Hughes's "literary" poems in *Dear Lovely Death* (1931) form a narrative describing the exhaustion of 1920s literary avant-gardism. In the first half of the collection is a series of apparently raceless meditations on death that literally ascend to a spiritual note in the four-line poem "Tower" in which Death is described as a tower where the soul is locked in eternal rumination.

"Tower" is followed by what appears to be an invocation of God, or some sort of personal cosmic destiny, in the poem "Two Things," which appears about halfway through the book:

> Two things possess the power,
> Two things deserve the name,
> Two things can reawaken
> Perpetually the flame,
> Two things are full of wonder,
> Two things cast off all shame.

(5)

In a multivalent move typical of Hughes, by not naming the second thing (the first is Death), the poem's speaker leaves all options open so that the anaphoric verses resembling an Old Testament psalm could as easily refer to love or sexual orgasm as to a supreme deity.

After ascending to whatever is not quite named at the end of "Two Things," the tone and voice of the collection changes drastically in the following poem "Flight":

> Plant your toes in the cool swamp mud.
> Step and leave no track.
> Hurry, sweating runner!
> The hounds are at your back.
>
> (6)

Gone is the calmly contemplative speaker who talks authoritatively and welcomingly of death. Instead the poem's narration is breathless, filled with fear and dissonant voices. The primary speaker of the poem appears to be a partisan observer of lynch violence, urging the fleeing victim onward. However, the voice of the pursued man interrupts the speaker ("No, I didn't touch her / While flesh ain't for me."), as African-American vernacular speech appears directly in the collection for the first time. There is a blurring between the speaker and the subject of the poem, particularly in the last two lines of the poem where the primary speaker's voice changes into a somewhat more colloquial voice ("Hurry! Black Boy, hurry! / They'll swing you from a tree!"). This blurring differs from earlier claims of the commonalty of all humanity in the face of death, asserting instead a common racial identity between the speaker and the southern African-American folk subject when pursued by a very specific form of death.

The narratorial voice shifts again in the collection's next poem, "Afro-American Fragment," assuming a sustained first-person voice for the first time. (Three out of the last five poems are also in the first person.) The halting short lines sandwiching longer, heavily alliterated lines and the irregularly rhyming lines of the first stanza formally mirror the notion of a link between Africans and African-Americans that has been disrupted or transformed to the point that it can no longer be clearly defined and yet remains as an African deep structure in African-American expressive culture:

> Not even memories alive
> Save those that history books create,
> Save those that songs beat back into the blood—
> Beat out of blood with words sad sung
> In strange un-Negro tongue—
>
> (7)

The lines between the repeated phrase "So long, so far away, is Africa" gradually lengthen and then shorten with the longest line occurring in the middle of the stanza in a sort of crescendo heightened by a concentration of anaphora, repeated words, and alliteration in the middle lines, presumably mirroring the music to which the speaker refers.

As with the CPUSA's Black Belt Thesis, the speaker here tries to balance a sense of a distinct identity with a hard appraisal of the origins of that identity that is transmitted culturally and not biogenetically. As in Harry Haywood's "Against Bourgeois-Liberal Distortions of Leninism on the Negro Question in the United States," the speaker argues against race as a "scientific" biological category, but instead uses race in the second stanza as a metaphorical displacement of nationality:

> Subdued and time lost are the drums—
> And yet, through some vast mist of race
> There comes this song
> I do not understand,
>
> (7)

Within this assertion of a connection between Africa and Afro-America, which as the title points out can only be received fragmentarily, is the implication that the African-American folk has remade this African heritage into something distinctly American to the extent that the original meaning of the African heritage has been lost or transformed beyond easy recognition. The poet-speaker of the poem is conscious of this loss of meaning, which he knows is the heritage of slavery. As a result, the second stanza takes on a much more melancholy cast than the first, filled with liquids and fricatives without the alliteration of stops in the first that mimic the drum the second claims is lost. Any attempt to recreate a musical effect after the manner of the first stanza is difficult to discern. A symbiosis between the African-American intellectual and the African-American folk is created that resembles that of much of Sterling Brown's work. On one hand, it is through the folk culture that any deep connection with Africa is maintained—and through which the deepest protest against the experience of slavery is made. Yet on the other, the intellectual is required to begin to uncover the outlines of that relationship (even as the intellectual claims to be unable to understand the song). Yet the intellectual speaker trails off into a melancholy hopelessness at the end that suggests that the process is not over—or is hardly begun.

The rest of the collection details this contradiction between an individual identity of the modern intellectual associated with death and exhaustion and a racial identity associated with life. Again, the tone of the poems concerned with death and the fate of the individual is far from the contemplative and accepting voice of the speaker in the first half of the collection. Rather, the voice is anxious, desperate, and filled with longing for something different:

> Listen!
> Dear dream of utter aliveness—
> Touching my body of utter death—
> Tell me, O quickly! dream of aliveness,
> The flaming source of your bright breath.
>
> (8)

The voice of this poem ("Demand") is clearly that of an alienated consciousness who can no longer speak calmly of "Dear Lovely Death," but instead demands that the "Dear dream of utter aliveness" speak to him or her.

The speaker receives no immediate answer. Instead, the voices of the next couple of poems go through some rapid shifts. In "Sailor," a relatively remote and ostensibly objective speaker describes a scene of isolation and, possibly, alienation, as a lone sailor sits on deck smoking a cigarette, displaying distorted emblems of home and family ("He had a mermaid on his arm, An anchor on his breast, / And tattooed on his back he had / A blue bird in a nest") on his body. In the following poem, "Florida Road Workers," the speaker of the poem is an African-American laborer who is absolutely tied to the land. Here a sort of reverse minstrelsy occurs where the speaker parodically interpolates phrases that one can imagine some local politician speaking at the highway's official opening into the blues-inflected structure of the poem. Thus in the first stanza, the speaker begins by a simple description of his labor, followed by the Chamber of Commerce description of the building of the road:

> Makin' a road
> Through the palmetto thicket
> For light and civilization
> To travel on.
>
> (10)

The second stanza concludes the series of restatements of the speaker's labor with the speaker's ironic view of the true nature of "light and civilization":

> Makin' a road
> For the rich old white men
> To sweep over in their big cars
> And leave me standin' here.
>
> (10)

These two stanzas taken together basically follow an AAB blues pattern of statement, unresolved restatement, and concluding statement—though the third statement is connected semantically to the other two through anaphora rather than through the end rhyme typical of the blues. A similar pattern occurs in the third stanza where another parodic fragment of an inaugural speech ("A road helps all of us!") is followed by a short variant of the AAB form keyed on the word "ride":

> White folks ride—
> And I get to see 'em ride.
> I ain't never seen nobody
> Ride so fine before.
>
> (10)

However, the poem changes dramatically at this point when the speaker demands that the listener, or the potential listener, pay attention to him ("Hey buddy! / Look at me!").

The road worker's final exhortation recalls Hughes's "Proem" in *The Weary Blues*, as well as a long line of radical and labor songs and poems (particularly those of the IWW) that seek to inscribe the common worker, or in this case the African-American worker, into a historical narrative that had denied him or her entry.[12] It can also be seen as an answer to the isolated intellectual who wants to know where to find utter aliveness. The worker's demand echoes of that of the speaker in

"Demand," with the difference that the worker's command to the listener is grounded in a group identity that he insists be acknowledged. In this respect, the plural of the poem's title is significant suggesting, despite the singular voice of the poem, that it is a sort of forerunner of the "mass chant" technique that Hughes would adapt shortly from the Left theater in "Scottsboro Limited." While it is unclear, intentionally so, precisely whom the speaker is addressing (whether the reader, the white drivers, the poet, and so on), this poem also resembles later Hughes works in the 1930s, particularly "Air Raid Over Harlem," in which the poet, through a sort of apostrophe, becomes simply a voice in the poetic text rather than an absolute authority, emphasizing the polyvocal effect of the text.

Following the colloquial voice of "Florida Road Workers," the collection swings back to the voice of the alienated intellectual who, contra Whitman, contemplates a natural scene in "Poem" without finding the secret of "utter aliveness" there. Instead, nature is described as a nightmare with each image of grass, trees, and flowers begun by the anaphoric "strange, distorted."

This brief anti-pastoral is immediately echoed by the "strange" that begins "Aesthete in Harlem," the final poem in the collection:

> Strange,
> That in this nigger place,
> I should meet Life face to face
>
> (12)

While no final synthesis of the folk and the intellectual occurs here, in the end the intellectual African-American speaker discovers Life in the chaotic, aggressive, loud-voiced "near-street" of Depression Harlem. *Dear Lovely Death* is double-voiced in that the poems in it, particularly those of the first half, can be read, and indeed are still read, as "high" lyric poetry with, as Onwuchekwa Jemie suggests, "no immediate social or political content."[13] No doubt Hughes was pleased to have people read the poems that way if they were not going to read them any other way. However, when read as a whole, a narrative emerges in the collection describing a solution to the modernist crisis of romantic individualism. This solution involved a polyphonic process of dialogue and rapprochement between the individual intellectual-poet and the folk. As I will discuss in the next section of this chapter, like the previously mentioned poems aimed at an African-American audience outside the black intellectual circles of the Northeast, these "literary" poems directed at a more "literary" audience shared far more with Hughes's "revolutionary poetry" of the 1930s than has generally been allowed.

A Red Movie to Mr. Hearst: Hughes's "Revolutionary Poetry"

The largest part of Hughes's poetic production during the 1930s was his "revolutionary poetry," often seen as his weakest or strongest work according to the political bent of the critic.[14] Given the anticommunism that has dominated American intellectual life since the 1940s, the predominant critical view has been that these poems are among Hughes's slightest. (As we shall see, critics associated with the Communist

Left in the 1930s often did not value Hughes's work much more than the anti-Communist critics.) Few of these scholars who dismiss Hughes's work of the 1930s consider the poetry formally in any specific way. (For that matter, the proponents of Hughes's revolutionary poems rarely consider formal questions, either.)[15] Ironically, these critics seem to accept the assumption that has been frequently attributed to intellectuals and artists most closely connected with the CPUSA: that the form of the revolutionary poem is, or should be, transparent, allowing the clear viewing of the message or "line." This poetry is seen as beyond form, but somehow filled with an unmediated, and generally false, meaning—to read one of these poems is to read them all. In short, such poetry is sloganeering, and a slogan, as everyone knows, is inherently uninteresting except perhaps sociologically.[16]

Such undervaluation of Hughes's revolutionary poetry misses the sly voice inhabiting the poems. This voice usually means what it says, but never quite says all that it means in a straightforward way. Instead it remains elusive through a skillful use of syntactic manipulation, rhythm, and other formal devices, conveying multiple meanings to multiple audiences. In this regard, it is ironic that with the plethora of critical discussions of the trope of the trickster and his or her linguistic polysemy, virtually none examine the work of Hughes, and certainly none consider his revolutionary poetry in this manner. Perhaps another way to say this is that there is a lyrical music to much of the 1930s poetry that requires the same sensitivity to tone and nuance as has been brought to bear on Hughes's blues poetry, most notably by Steven Tracy. What has also been generally missed in Hughes's revolutionary poetry is the continued connection with modernism formally and thematically as Hughes, like nearly all other radical poets of the 1930s, writes quite consciously with the legacy of earlier modernist art and literature in mind.

One characteristic of Hughes's poetry from his earliest work is his representation of a wide range of speaking folk subjects. In *The Weary Blues* (1926), most of the poems are in an overtly authorial voice that, if not exactly high, is clearly distinct from the African-American folk subject. But even in *The Weary Blues* there are poems, such as "Negro Dancers" and "The Cat and The Saxophone (2 A.M.)," spoken in "folk" or "popular" African-American voices clearly distinguished from that of the poet. In "Negro Dancers" and "The Cat and The Saxophone (2 A.M.)," two vernacular voices, that of each poem's speaker (or speakers) and that of jazz, emerge simultaneously in a manner not unlike the dadaist "simultaneous poems" of Tristan Tzara and Richard Huelsenbeck, as well as the notions of montage in the work of early Soviet filmmakers, particularly Sergei Eisenstein and Dziga Vertov:

EVERYBODY
Half-pint,—
Gin?
No, make it
LOVES MY BABY
corn. You like
liquor,
don't you honey?

   (*Weary Blues*, 27)

It is perhaps a little banal pointing out all the ways in which this poem is formally "modernist"—simultaneous voices, fragmented syntax, irregular line length (including one-word [and even one exclamation point] lines), un-"poetic" diction, lines beginning with lowercase words that emphasize the "natural" spoken aspect of the lines, lines entirely in uppercase, and so on. The particular aspect of this poem that is crucial in terms of the development of Hughes's vernacular poetry in the 1930s and 1940s, and that would distinguish this writing from that of Sterling Brown's vernacular poetry in the 1930s, is Hughes's attempt to represent a number of simultaneous voices within a single work. In short, Hughes's work here is a perfect example of Robert Pinsky's notion of "formal heteroglossia" that Pinsky claims is the distinguishing mark of American modernism.[17] However, since Hughes is rarely read against the work of the more linguistically oriented modernists, it is worth noting that what Hughes seems to be doing here is not all that different from sections of William Carlos Williams's 1923 *Spring and All*.[18]

Similarly, Hughes's 1927 *Fine Clothes to the Jew* can be seen as a collection of vernacular voices that form a chorus of the lower strata, the overwhelming majority, of the African-American community. This African-American chorus is in turn often in dialogue with white voices to which they are inextricably linked, sometimes by blood (as in "Mulatto") and sometimes by economics (as in "Brass Spittoons"). Of course, Edgar Lee Masters—and Sherwood Anderson—had done something like this previously, but where the voices of *The Spoon River Anthology* and *The New Spoon River Anthology* are nearly identical in diction, Hughes's poems are quite individual in linguistic differences, indicating what might be thought of as the social register of their voices. Not only do the poems form a sort of chorus, but within the individual poems, such as "Brass Spittoons," two or more voices often speak simultaneously. The words in "Brass Spittoons" are bonded by such devices as alliteration ("A bright bowl of brass is beautiful to the Lord"), assonance (spittoon-Chicago-Atlantic City-in-kitchens-spittoon), parallel constructions ("The steam in hotel kitchens / And the smoke in hotel lobbies / And the slime in hotel spittoons"), repeated phrases ("A nickel / A dime / A dollar / Two dollars") often somewhat altered, or "worried" (to use a blues term), in the repetition, and irregular end rhyme ("House rent to pay / Gin on Saturday / Church on Sunday"). However, the poem is held together most tightly by the repeated interruptions of the meditation of the black speaking subject by what the reader presumes is his white boss. (This bonding interruption is most obviously the anaphoric "Hey, boy!".) What takes place is not precisely a dialogue, but rather a linguistic representation of the interdependence and separation of the black and white speaking subjects of the poem. The representation reveals both the hierarchical position of the black subject and the independence and integrity, however accommodationist, within the consciousness of the black subject—an integrity which the white subject ignores or seeks to conceal, but which is uncovered by the poem.

In many respects, the revolutionary poetry of Hughes in the 1930s, including dramatic monologues, "mass chants," and verse plays, as well as shorter lyrics, is a logical development of Hughes's polyvocal work of the 1920s. In the 1932 one-act verse play "Scottsboro Limited," Hughes adapted the "mass chant" form of the Workers Theater movement.[19] The mass chant form allowed for the representation of a simultaneous collectivity and individuality that was missing in previous literary models, such Masters and Anderson.[20] In "Scottsboro Limited," a collectivity of voices speak to and against each other much as in *Fine Clothes to the Jew*. However, there is a far greater sense of a linear progression to the utterances of the voices in "Scottsboro Limited" than there is in *Fine Clothes to the Jew*. In this regard, for all its apparent differences, the play is more closely related to *Dear Lovely Death* than the collections of the 1920s. This sense of polyvocal, and often somewhat chaotic, progression would characterize much of Hughes's work until, at least, the 1950s, distinguishing it from his work in the 1920s.

"Scottsboro Limited" opens with a sort of prologue wherein the "Eight Black Boys" proclaim to the white "Man" their resolution to tell their story. The story they tell in flashback can be summarized as follows: eight black "boys" riding a freight train in search of work are stopped by a southern sheriff and charged with rape while an angry white "Mob" looks on, muttering threats; facing inevitable execution in the electric chair after a rigged trial, the "Boys" encounter the "Red Voices" of white Communists and are transformed into class conscious militants (or as the "8th Boy" says the "new Red Negro"); the "Boys" join with the "Red Voices" and, ultimately, the audience to escape their prison and fight for social justice singing the *Internationale*.

After the prologue section, the initial speech of the "Boys" is emphatically rural and vernacular ("I wish I had some sugar cane in ma mouth / I'se hongry"). The diction of the "Boys" becomes progressively more "standard" as their consciousness is raised. By the end of the play, their speech is indistinguishable from the "Red Voices" who are specifically identified as "white workers"—though the "Man" and the white "Mob" continue to speak in a southern regional vernacular.

Interestingly, the linguistic progression of the "Boys" is also associated with poetic production so that as they become class conscious they also speak more "poetically." In the prologue passage, the "Man" demands that the "Boys" "Stop talking poetry and talk sense." The form of the Boys' "poetic" speech is irregular. There are many end rhymes, but no regular rhyme scheme and often rhymes are not exact. The length of the lines varies considerably, though there are generally either two or three stressed syllables in each, often heavily alliterated line. Despite this formal irregularity, the "poetic" nature of the "Boys" speech is clearly announced by the generally "high" diction and the obvious rhymes:

> 8th Boy: (*As they line up on the stage*):
>> All right, we will—
>> That sense of injustice
>> That death can't kill
>
> Man: Injustice? What d'yuh mean? Talking about injustice, you coon?
>
> 2nd Boy: (*Pointing to his comrades*)
>> Look at us then:
>> Poor, black, and ignorant,
>> Can't read or write—
>> But we come here tonight.

(11)

Here the poetry of the "Boys" is interrupted by the prose of the "Man." In general, though the lines of the racist white characters (the "Man," the "Sheriff," the "Girls," the "Judge," and the "Mob") sometimes rhyme, their speeches are far more prosy than those of the "Boys." When the lines of the racist white characters do rhyme, frequently the rhymes are between lines spoken by different characters, so that the lines read together may be "poetic," but the speeches of the individual characters are not.

Thus there seems to be a clear relationship between "standard" (and even "high" "poetic") diction and knowledge in "Scottsboro Limited" that seems to be at odds with Hughes's work in the 1920s and 1940s. This relationship also seems to conflict with the CPUSA's Black Belt Thesis: the "Boys" are not northern black workers (for whom such a transformation would be perfectly consonant with the CPUSA position), but southern agricultural workers (who were members of the black "nation" with distinct "national" characteristics). In short, Hughes makes no essential distinction between African Americans in the North and those in South. (Though Hughes's notion in the play that there is a fundamental link between African Americans and the subaltern populations of European and North American colonies and semi-colonies in Africa, Asia, and Latin America [e.g., Haiti, Cuba, China] dovetails with the Comintern position.)

Hughes also seems to be making an implicit argument about the function of poetry in the proletarian literature movement. When it comes time for the "Boys" to speak the unvarnished truth about race and class oppression, they do so in speech emphatically marked as "poetic." In this regard, Hughes is arguing against both a sense within some quarters of the proletarian literature movement that poetry lagged behind fiction and reportage as a vehicle to express the realities of the class struggle as well as a similar sense among leading African-American critics that the 1930s was not an era hospitable to poetry.[21] Yet unlike Sterling Brown, who in many respects made a similar argument in *Southern Road*, Hughes seems to be rejecting vernacular black speech and "folk" music as the basis of a liberationist poetry in "Scottsboro Limited."

However, even in "Scottsboro Limited," a vernacular humor and energy is presented that speaks beyond the denotative meaning of the lines, and that undercuts the apparent subsuming of "folk" into "class." For example, in the overtly "folk" passages before the revolutionary transformation of the "Boys," there is a playfulness of tone:

3rd Boy: Uh-O! This train done stopped. Where is this?
7th Boy: Well, wherever it is, I'm gonna take a—
(*Turning his back*)

(13)

This implied rhyme of "this" and "piss" is not very interesting sonically in and of itself. But it is so brash that it calls attention to itself as a joke, interrupting a meditation on race and class by the "Boys." The rhyme in a sort of synecdoche also allows the black folk to "piss" on Scottsboro—and "moon" the audience.[22] The joking rhyme occupies a mediating position between this meditation and the appearance of the sheriff who will arrest the "Boys" for rape. Thus, between two of the most serious moments of the play, a play admittedly filled with serious moments, is an eruption of the folk voice that is outside the overt politics of the play. This eruption creates one of the few breaks in that politics and in the deadly serious tone of the play, expressing a playful ambivalence about the play's audience that is made complicit in the joke (as well as literally the "butt" of it) after the manner of a humorous folk story or even an African-American comic variety show (or white vaudeville for that matter).

There is a similar, though less obvious eruption in the middle of perhaps the most dramatic moment of the play. The "Boys," led by the words of the "8th Boy," complete their ideological transformation. Then in conjunction with the "Red Voices," they destroy their prison, including the instrument of their impending execution, the electric chair:

> 8th Boy:
> > No chair!
> > Too long my hands have been idle
> > Too long have my brains been dumb.
> > Now out of the darkness
> > The new Red Negro will come:
> > That's me!
> > No death in the chair!
> Boys: (*Rising*) No death in the chair!
> Red voices: (*Rising in the audience*) NO DEATH IN THE CHAIR!
> Boys: NO DEATH IN THE CHAIR!

> > > > > > (19)

The colloquial and gleeful "That's me!" is almost sweet in its enthusiasm, striking an odd note between the four relatively stiff and formal lines proceeding it and the solemn political chant following it. One could almost imagine in that moment that the "8th Boy" was actually Jesse B. Semple of Hughes's humorous "Simple" stories or Alberta K. Johnson of the "Madam" poems, both of which began to appear in print during the early 1940s.[23]

The point here is not that Hughes was secretly undermining the overt message of his play or that he was not "really" a Communist supporter. But even here, where Hughes seems to posit a progression from black rural folk culture as black workers join the struggles of the international working class, the individual folk voice persists, however obliquely. Anticipating his work in the late 1930s, 1940s, and early 1950s, Hughes's references to African-American expressive culture establish a continuum from Africa to contemporary African-American urban popular culture. This model of "authentic" African-American culture, comprehending folk culture *and* popular culture, is seen not simply in Hughes's use of African-American vaudeville, but also in the way that jazz underlies the play. For example, the stage directions to the trial scene read "The trial is conducted in jazz tempo: the white voices staccato, high and shrill; the black voices deep as the rumble of drums." Obviously a line is drawn here from Africa to the rural South filled with displaced agricultural workers to the urban centers North and South.[24]

In this respect, the phrase "new Red Negro," referring, obviously, to the New

Negro Renaissance, signals that Hughes sees "Scottsboro Limited" as a revision of his work in the 1920s, not a completely new enterprise. Hughes was not the first to use the phrase. William L. Patterson used it in a letter in the June 1928 *New Masses*, where he attacked the New Negro Renaissance in much the same way that he would at greater length in "Awake Negro Poets" in October of the same year. It seems likely that Hughes, who was already a contributor to *New Masses*, read Patterson's letter and article. But Hughes did not simply appropriate Patterson's notion that the bulk of the African-American writing of the 1920s was the work of aesthetes and dilettantes. Instead, the phrase the "new Red Negro" is an emblem of Hughes's mediation between the criticisms of the New Negro Renaissance by black and white Communists, such as Patterson and Mike Gold, demanding that the struggles of black laborers in the South—and North—be represented from the viewpoint of the folk and the body of work produced by African-American writers in the 1920s (of which Hughes's own work was such a prominent part). Hughes revised both the terms of the New Negro Renaissance and the Communist Left without negating either.

This attitude toward the southern folk expressed in the concept of the New Negro was quite close to that of the "new Red Negro" in "Scottsboro Limited." The difference was that the new Red Negro emerged directly out of the folk (with some prompting by the revolutionary vanguard) without a northern education, a stint on the Western Front, or any of the other transformative exiles from the folk milieu that typified the narratives of the New Negro. At any rate, Hughes clearly linked the play with his earlier writing and earlier African-American folk expression (and mass commercial culture) in ways that the style and subject of the play would seem to deny. In fact, the sly and oblique use of the folk voice in the poetry, as well as the development of a form that would allow the simultaneous (or near simultaneous) expression of a community of voices in a manner that is accessible to a large audience, is perhaps the most significant aspect of "Scottsboro Limited" in terms of the later development of Hughes's work.

Newsreel of a Dream Deferred: Modernism
and Mass Culture

Another aspect of Hughes's radical poetry of the 1930s that has been often overlooked is its formal link with earlier modernism. Generally speaking, critics since the 1940s have treated Hughes's poetry as if it were in an entirely separate sphere from the work of white modernist poets.[25] A number of the leading African-American critics of the New Negro Renaissance, such as James Weldon Johnson, considered Hughes, along with Jean Toomer, Anne Spencer, and Fenton Johnson, to be among the most "experimental" of the black poets of the 1910s and 1920s.[26] However, few even of these critics connected Hughes's Leftist poetry to the formal radicalism associated with modernism in the early twentieth century.

As noted earlier in this chapter, much of Hughes's early work featured a formal radicalism rooted in an American language that was akin to the work of William Carlos Williams in the same period. This polyvocality continued in many of his "revolutionary poems," which become increasingly engaged with the rhetoric of mass commercial culture to an extent that Hughes might be considered a premature postmodernist. For example, in the 1936 "Broadcast in Ethiopia," first published in the *American Spectator* during the journal's period of sympathy with the cultural Left, the opening lines appear to signal a formally conservative "serious" poem with a radical message. ("The little fox is still. / The dogs of war have made their kill.") After all, the diction here seems suitably "high," if somewhat clichéd, and the lines rhyme and, though of uneven length, are straightforwardly iambic. But then a section follows with an upper-class, slangy, and slightly English diction and wildly varying line length and meter where the overall impression is in sound that of a sort of grim nursery rhyme or child's doggerel ("But he has not poison gas—so he cannot last. / Poor little joker with no poison gas!). Suddenly, an all-capitalized fragment of a line from a popular song ("MISTER CHRISTOPHER COLUMBUS") is interpolated followed by an Associated Press news bulletin about the flight of Ethiopian Emperor Haile Selassie from the 1935 Italian invasion. Then the rest of the song's line appears ("HE USED RHYTHM FOR HIS COMPASS") just before two lines ("Hunter, hunter, running, too— / Look what's after you") whose initial trochees make them sound like a street rhyme and / or a metric variation on the initial anapests of a floating line ("Sinner Man, sinner man, where you going to run to?") from a number of spirituals. It additionally alludes to what is perhaps the most famous trochaic lyric in English (after "Twinkle, Twinkle, Little Star"), Blake's "The Tyger," connoting a just and inevitable retribution by the fearful tiger of the international working class and its allies among the colonized peoples of the world—a point emphasized by the following news bulletin, this time a United Press release about Communist electoral victories in France.

Then comes a passage in a generic vernacular American with what might be seen, especially given the fact that the author is a well-known black poet, as a faint African-American inflection, beginning:

> France ain't Italy!
>
> No, but Italy's cheated
> When any Minister anywhere's
> Defeated by Communists

> (*Good Morning Revolution*, 36)

Here the diction of poem, if not specifically African-American, is certainly "lower" and more passionate than that of the ironic and somewhat weary passage preceding the first news item. The structure of the latter passage resembles that of the former in its irregular use of end rhyme, near rhymes, internal rhyme, consonance, and assonance. But the second passage is more prosaic, or at least more like "natural" speech and less structurally "poetic" in that there are fewer end rhymes than in the first passage and much less use of alliteration.

After the rousing passage in which the vernacular voice (and, implicitly, the black vernacular voice) erupts, a bell is sounded and the radio broadcast is under control again. A fragment of "Mister Christopher Columbus" plays and the poem returns to a muted tone and more conservative form and diction corresponding to the abandonment of Ethiopia by the League of Nations (essentially European and North American "civilization") in the face of the Italian invasion:

> The British Legation stands solid on its hill
> The natives run wild in the streets.
> The little fox is still.
>
> Addis Ababa
> In headlines all year long.
> Ethiopia—tragi-song.

(36–37)

As is the case in *Scottsboro Limited*, "Broadcast on Ethiopia" ends in tragedy and loss rather than a note of revolutionary optimism.

One of the most interesting things about this poem is the use of the literary equivalent of the modernist montage: wild shifts of voice, typography, diction, rhythm, rhyme, line length, stanzaic form and its interpolation of song, prose items, expressions of mass culture, and sound effects often occurring simultaneously. Of course, the use of these typically modernist devices was certainly not restricted to Hughes, but was common among many left-wing poets, including Kenneth Fearing, Muriel Rukeyser, Joy Davidman, and, as will be examined in the next chapter, other black writers such as Frank Marshall Davis.

Hughes differed from a number of these Left poets, particularly Fearing and Davidman, in that Hughes's work in the 1930s basically argued that popular culture was a field of contestation with the ruling class, whereas Fearing and Davidman (and novelist Nathaniel West), like many American intellectuals of the Communist Left, saw mass culture as a hegemonic web of social control anticipating the later critiques of the Frankfurt School. Though they did not generally attempt to represent an alternate "people's" culture (as did Sterling Brown), Fearing and Davidman drew on mass culture in ways to show mass culture as an instrument of containment of revolutionary impulses (or genuine human feeling). In this respect, Hughes is essentially optimistic, even in his most despairing radical poetry, (such as "Broadcast on Ethiopia"), where Fearing and Davidman are pessimistic—as are a surprising number of Left poets in the 1930s. Hughes embraced the aesthetic possibilities suggested by Popular Front ideology very early when many other Left poets and artists retained a sort of Third Period aesthetic, preferring either pessimism, as did Fearing and Davidman, or else locating poetic value in "popular" forms of the "folk" supposedly outside of mass culture, as did writers Sterling Brown and Don West and the participants of the Left folk song movement of the Popular Front.[27]

While the modernist literature of the 1920s has often been opposed to the proletarian literature movement of the 1930s, to a large extent the older Left writers and readers associated with journals such as *New Masses* saw themselves as proceeding out of modernism, particularly in matters of form. Thus Hughes, in part, made use of a sort of pastiche or montage technique to reach an audience of the Left intelligentsia brought up on literary modernism. As in the case of "Broadcast on Ethiopia," it could argued that the coupling of modernist form and generic modernist sentiment ("Civilization's gone to hell") with the specific content of the poem was in itself a sort of assessment of "high" modernism, perhaps referring to Pound's engagement with Italian fascism.[28] Of course, reflecting Hughes's abiding interest in drama, many of the effects that seem modernist on the page can also be seen as instructions for oral performance in which the different voices would not seem so disruptive as on the printed page. Even so, the poems Hughes wrote and read for primarily African-American audiences in the early and middle 1930s, particularly southern black audiences, were more formally conservative than the "revolutionary" poetry. As seen above, the poetry Hughes wrote for southern African-American audiences in the early 1930s shared thematic concerns, and even broad formal strategies, with his "revolutionary" poetry. But where simultaneous voices existed, they were more explicitly labeled in such a way as to reduce the experience of fragmentation or dislocation than was the case with his explicitly "Left" work.

Is There a Speaker in this Text?: The African-American Popular Voice

Nevertheless, as was the case in *Scottsboro Limited*, a recognizably African-American voice was not entirely subsumed in the vision of an essentially raceless America that characterized Hughes's work appearing in the journals of the literary Left during the early and middle 1930s. Hughes's Left poems during this period often feature a racially ambiguous generically "hard-boiled" working-class speaker whose diction derives as much from pulp fiction and the movies as from any actually spoken English. But frequently an African-American voice erupts from within the address of the "hard-boiled" speaker, as it does in a section of "Advertisement for the Waldorf-Astoria":

NEGROES

Oh, Lawd, I done forgot Harlem!
　Say, you colored folks, hungry a long time in
　　135th Street they got swell music at the Waldorf-Astoria. It sure
　　is a mighty nice place to shake hips in, too. There's dancing
　　after supper in a big warm room. It's cold as hell on Lenox
　　Avenue. All you've had all day is a cup of coffee. Your
　　pawnshop overcoat's a ragged banner on your hungry frame.
　　You know, downtown folks are just crazy about Paul Robeson!
　　Maybe they'll like you, too, black mob from Harlem. Drop in
　　the Waldorf this afternoon for tea. Stay to dinner. Give Park
　　Avenue a lot of darkie color—free for nothing! Ask the Junior
　　Leaguers to sing a spiritual for you. They probably know 'em
　　better than you do—and their lips won't be chapped with cold
　　after they step out of their closed cars in the undercover driveways.
　　　Hallelujah! under-cover driveways!
　　　Ma Soul's a witness for the Waldorf-Astoria!

(Collected, 145)[29]

　As in "Scottsboro Limited" there is a satire on African-American vernacular language and cultural forms rooted in the rural South, notably that of the rural black church. The narrator adopts a pseudo-folk voice shouting about the glory of the Waldorf-Astoria, which he follows with the bracketed recitations of the harsh economic realities of African Americans and the subaltern peoples of European and American colonies. However, the satire is obviously in the first place a comment on the cultural consumption of wealthy white people who love spirituals and Paul Robeson and only secondly on the rural folk culture.[30] Thus the overall effect of the poem is similar to that of Sterling Brown's "Cabaret," where a commercialization of the folk for white consumption, both simultaneously marketing and obscuring the actual life of the folk, is followed by what might be thought of as riffs or fragments of the actual experience of the rural black poor. The difference is that Hughes is more ambiguous here about the rural folk culture that underlies his satirical verses than Brown, who is unabashedly a partisan of that culture. Hughes also makes a connection between the experiences of Africans on rubber plantations, black railroad workers in the South, and unemployed Harlem residents that Brown does not. Unlike the narratorial voice in "Cabaret," the speaker of "Advertisement for the Waldorf-Astoria" locates himself among the black folk, albeit in Harlem rather than the rural South. It is at this moment ("And here we stand, shivering in the cold, in Harlem") that Hughes's speaker steps out of a generic working-class vernacular American role and into a specifically African-American identity, using the pronoun "we" for the first (and virtually the only) time instead of "you." It is notable that in these bracketed passages in which the speaker identifies himself (or possibly herself, though the speaker's male-identified "hard-boiled" diction invites the reader to cast him as male) racially and situates himself in a specific urban African-American community, the work is most formally "poetic" and least "prosaic." The bracketed passages employ much alliteration, assonance, near-rhyme, and internal rhyme, and (with the notable exception of the word "nigger") a relatively "standard" diction. These devices are virtually absent in the unbracketed prose passage of this section of the poem. Thus, as in "Scottsboro Limited," there is an interrelation between plain truth, self-realization, and poetry cast in an unequivocally "poetic" form, as well as a sense that the African-American vernacular derived from southern black culture is something to be transcended even as a specifically African-American voice remains distinct.[31]

Of course, Hughes continued to write poems in an identifiably African-American vernacular voice and publish them in Left journals during the 1930s, particularly in the second half of the decade. There is a correlation between the beginning of the Popular Front period in 1936 and the return in Hughes poetry of the sympathetic black vernacular speaking subject who does not simply represent an early, relatively unconscious stage that will be transcended by a newly conscious black folk.[32] In some ways, this new engagement with the vernacular may seem to run counter to the direction of the Communist Left. Certainly, the Black Belt Thesis and the concomitant valorization of rural vernacular culture and language, while officially still CPUSA policy, was downplayed during the Popular Front, particularly in day-to-day political agitation in the *Daily Worker* and other CPUSA organs. However, in practice the literary and other cultural institutions associated with the Communist Left retained a strong interest in the issue of racism and in African-American popular culture. The difference was that these institutions were much

Hey!
Scenario For A Little Black Movie,
You say?
A RED MOVIE TO MR. HEARST
Black and white workers united as one
In a city where
There'll never be
Air raids over Harlem
FOR THE WORKERS ARE FREE

(40)

Yet the final note of the poem, unlike "Scottsboro Limited" or "Advertisement for the Waldorf-Astoria," is the assertion of an African-American identity in an African-American vernacular voice:

What workers are free?
THE BLACK AND WHITE WORKERS—
You and me!
Looky here, everybody!
Look at me!

I'M HARLEM!

(40)

The diction of the speaker is not transformed into either a "standard" "high" diction or a "standard" vernacular diction, but remains specifically marked as colloquial African-American by the phrase "looky here" (at least in the linguistic context of Harlem and New York City).

This language is bonded together once again by such devices as irregular end-rhyme and near-rhyme, assonance, slant rhymes, anaphora, and alliteration often obscured in lines of wildly differing length so that the poem seems to be a self-dramatized speech that one could encounter on a street corner or in a bar—though perhaps the poem does not succeed quite that well. It is worth noting that the implied not-quite-exact-rhyme of "past" and "ass" ("Into the dust of the Jim Crow past / And laughs and hollers / kiss my !x!&!'") causes attention to be focused on the language of the poem in a way that is outside of the overt political message of the poem in much the same manner as the already noted omitted rhyme of "this" and "piss" in "Scottsboro Limited." (These omitted rhymes, either verbally or visually, also recall many ribald blues recordings of the 1920s and 1930s, where the omitted rhyme was also frequently employed.) And as the opening exchange indicates, the apparently unitary speech contains multitudes which occasionally diverge from a unified voice, sometimes in the form of a policeman's racist counterpoint (*"You keep quiet / you niggers keep quiet"*), sometimes in an interrogating but ultimately sympathetic voice of what appears to be an individual member of the Harlem community, neither of whom in turn is clearly distinguished from either the community generally or the author. The narrating voice strangely alternates between an individual voice and a communal voice, between a folk voice, as signified in the subtitle by "black," and a voice produced by mass culture, as signified by "screenplay" and "movie," ending in revolutionary synthesis.

This period of Hughes's career as a "social poet" could be said to climax with the self-described "poetry play" "Don't You Want to Be Free," which was performed in Harlem in 1938 by the Suitcase Theater under the auspices of the International Workers Organization, a left-wing workers organization associated with the CPUSA. This play was notable among Hughes's activity as a revolutionary poet in that it was first performed in a black community and aimed at a black audience with considerable success.[34]

The play itself, like many of Hughes's more successful long poems of the 1930s, is filled with disparate voices—sometimes speaking, sometimes singing. It is loosely organized chronologically from the period of slavery to the play's present in Harlem against a background (and at times a foreground) of African-American music from spirituals to jazz, also roughly corresponding more or less to a particular historical period. The play is a vernacular portrait of the development of African Americans in the United States, focusing particularly on the community of Harlem, which ends, like "Scottsboro Limited" and "Air Raid Over Harlem," with a call for unity between black and white workers in the fight for social justice. However, unlike "Scottsboro Limited" and "Advertisement for the Waldorf-Astoria," and like "Air Raid Over Harlem," this call for unity and a new revolutionary consciousness among African Americans did not involve the negation of African-American vernacular culture, whether "folk" (as in the case of the work song and the spiritual) or "popular" (as in the case of jazz or the blues), although it is worth noting that the speech of the play's characters becomes more "standard" by the play's end.[35] Also, in addition to the portions of the play that were written originally for it, Hughes includes poems (and fragments of poems) that he had written over his entire career. Among these older works are poems from *Fine Clothes to the Jew*, such as "Brass Spittoons," which had so inflamed large sections of the African-American press and the African-American reading public in the 1920s, linking the New Negro to the New Red Negro and successfully presenting this overview to a primarily "mainstream" African-American audience.

Thus, while "Don't You Want to Be Free" has, like his longer revolutionary poems, a certain "uplift" aspect, it contains elements that are quite different from those of the poems Hughes usually presented to African-American audiences on his reading tours in the 1930s.[36] The play is far more radical politically, more "low-down" lyrically, and more formally diffuse than the poems he generally read. At the same time, the play is also anchored by African-American popular music (sacred and secular) and vernacular speech far more overtly than any of the earlier revolutionary poetry, including those poems published in the CPUSA's African-American-oriented journal *The Negro Liberator*, much less such journals as *New Masses* and the various regional publications of the John Reed Clubs.

In part, this change was due to the fact that the attitudes of the cultural institutions associated with the CPUSA, and the attitudes of the party itself, had changed during the Popular Front. Within the circles of the Communist Left, African-American popular culture, particularly that associated with the urban North and West, became much more acceptable within the context of serious literary production and intellectual consideration beyond the level of entertainment at fund-raising dances or parties where black popular music had always been acceptable to the CPUSA by and large. Certainly, as we have seen earlier, Hughes's work published in Left journals had been moving more in this direction. And, of course, the Popular Front success of such politicized musicals with loose plot structures as *Pins and Needles*, a collection of pro-labor skits and songs performed by members of the International Ladies Garment Workers Union, shaped the prospective audience for Hughes's play, as well as to a certain extent providing models for Hughes's work.[37] However, probably at least as important, especially to Hughes, was the development of an African-American audience that was able to accept a formally and politically radical play rooted in African-American popular culture—and willing to spend money (35 cents) to see a "serious" play consisting significantly of "serious" poems by a "serious" poet.[38] Perhaps for Hughes the greatest legacy of the "Red Decade," at least as far as his work was concerned, was the creation of this audience that allowed him to write a poetry that often would be formally daring, politically engaged, and aimed to a large extent at the "average" African American, in addition to larger national and international audiences, without having to balkanize his efforts. Thus while works of the 1940s and very early 1950s, such as *Shakespeare in Harlem* and *Montage of a Dream Deferred*, may seem to break with Hughes's work of the 1930s, they are logical extensions of his work in the 1930s and would, in fact, not have been possible without the work done in the former decade. And while lingering Third Period and modernist values among Left critics, particularly white critics, would cause them to review Hughes's poetry in the 1930s and 1940s ambivalently, it was Hughes's engagement with the aesthetics of the Popular Front in the 1930s and its influence on the African-American reading (and listening) public that allowed him to become the best-known and most popular African-American poet among "mainstream" African-American audiences, despite his mixed critical reception.

I Am Black and I Have Seen Black Hands

The Narratorial Consciousness and Constructions of the Folk in 1930s African-American Poetry

Remembering Nat Turner: The Dunbarian Heritage, the Reclamation of the Folk, and Diversity and Unity of 1930s African-American Poetry

Any argument for the coherence of poetry produced by African Americans during the 1930s has to contend with the formal and thematic variety of that poetry. In his *Negro Poetry and Drama* (1937), Sterling Brown claimed that "contemporary Negro poets are too diverse to be grouped into schools." Nonetheless, Brown went on to divide poets between those influenced by the modernist "new poetry revival" (to which Brown applied the pejorative "so-called"), those "bookish" poets writing after the manner of Victorian and Pre-Raphaelite poets, and those who "have taken folk-types and folk-life for their province." Brown clearly did not conceive of these as mutually exclusive categories. While he may have implicitly disparaged the "new poetry" by the tag "so-called," he also criticized contemporary African-American poets who "have left uncultivated many fields opened by modern poetry." He went on to say that "almost as frequently they have been unaware of the finer uses of tradition." At the same time, Brown posited a neoromantic concept of poetic expression in which "one of the cardinal rules of modern poetry is that the poet should express his own view of life in his own way." This romantic subjectivity as an authorial stance remained at odds with most theoretical statements of American modernism (whether in the criticism, editorials, and manifestos of imagism in the 1910s, objectivism in the 1920s, or social realism in the 1930s) that emphasized an antiromantic objectivity, whether of language, society, or perceived things, that transcended individual personality. In short, Brown set up as a model for African-American literature a poetry that closely resembled his own: a poetry that, while cognizant of the modernist heritage, combined a formally conservative neoromantic narratorial frame and a politically radical sensibility with folk expression and a folk subject rooted in the rural South.[1]

Whether or not one agrees with Brown's view of the relative weaknesses or strengths of African-American poets in the 1930s, his categories (and his initial reluctance to categorize) is in itself an example of the diversity of African-American poets in the 1930s, as well as how the work of even the most distant of these diverse poets can be linked to each other and to the ideological concerns of the decade. An interesting text in this regard is Lucy Mae Turner's *'Bout Cullud Folkses* (1938). For the most part, Turner's collection is an imitation of Dunbar's *Lyrics of Lowly Life*, mixing "high" neoromantic lyrics, such as "Mountains at Night" ("The mountains lift their hoary heads on high, / As up the slope we climb, my love and I"), with humorous or pathetic "dialect" poems, such as the volume's title poem, which opens:

I is allus very happy,
Dis ole world s jes' full o' fun,
An' at eve I'se feelin' better
Dan w'en the day has jes' begun.

Does you want to know de method
To keep joy aroun' de place?
All I say is, "Watch de antics
Ob de good ole cullud race."

(7)

Even Turner's relatively "proletarian" dialect poem, "Pay Day," which posits the life of a black foundry worker in Pittsburgh as a sort of new slavery, has much in common with Dunbar's treatment of northern urban life, particularly in his novel *Sport of the Gods*.

Like Dunbar with "We Wear the Mask" in *Lyrics of Lowly Life*, Turner signals to the reader that these dialect poems need to be reread with care when she ends the collection with a short poem, "Nat Turner, An Epitaph":

Nat Turner was a slave who stood
For a supreme great brotherhood
Where men did not each other buy;
But, missing that, he chose to die!

(64)

Obviously, to end the collection with such a poem forces the reader to reconsider even the collection's relatively happy invocations of slavery and post-Reconstruction sharecropping (or "debt peonage," as it was described in the Communist press), such as "'Bout Cullud Folkses." But this, as mentioned earlier, was nothing new in African-American letters, and was in keeping with the general Dunbarian influence on *'Bout*

Cullud Folkses. Perhaps more closely related to Turner's poem to Nat Turner than "We Wear the Mask" is Dunbar's elegy "Frederick Douglass" in *Lyrics of Lowly Life*, memorializing Douglass as a race leader in six-line stanzas that employ an extremely regular iambic pentameter and "high" diction.

However, Turner's memorializing of Nat Turner dovetailed with the relatively frequent use of African-American slave rebellions and leaders of these rebellions in 1930s and early 1940s African-American literature, including such works as Arna Bontemps's novel *Black Thunder* (1936), Robert Hayden's poem "Gabriel" (included in *Heart-Shape in the Dust* [1940]), Langston Hughes's poem "Scottsboro" (included in *Scottsboro Limited* [1932]), Randolph Edmonds's 1934 play *Nat Turner*, and Sterling Brown's poems "Remembering Nat Turner" (published in *The Crisis* in 1939) and "Memo: For the Race Orators."[2] As noted in chapter 1, this use of what the CPUSA called the "revolutionary tradition" of African Americans was very much a product of the attempt by the CPUSA in the late 1920s and early 1930s to commemorate, or (from a more cynical perspective) to create such a tradition. The "revolutionary" tradition was counterposed to more "reformist" and / or "accommodationist" traditions associated by the Communist Left with such individuals as Booker T. Washington and Howard University President Kelly Miller and such organizations as the Urban League and the NAACP. While both "reformists" and "radicals" honored Frederick Douglass, it was the Communist Left that actively promoted Nat Turner as a revolutionary hero on a national level in the 1930s.

Lucy Mae Turner, who was not well known in her own time, who had no apparent connection to the literary Left, and whose work falls into Sterling Brown's category of African-American poets apparently untouched by modernism or modern approaches to the folk and folk expression, closes her work with a poetic move that employs a Dunbarian dualism, but in a distinctly 1930s register. While Brown may be correct in suggesting that a wide diversity of work was produced in the 1930s, underneath this diversity, as Turner's work indicates, was a considerable sharing of theme, image, trope, diction, vertical and horizontal construction, and other formal elements influenced by the ideological concerns of the era. As noted earlier, these concerns fall generally within two interrelated though often opposed categories that I associate with Langston Hughes and Sterling Brown, respectively. The category I link with Hughes is defined by an urban internationalist and popular culture aesthetic, while the one I connect with Brown is essentially rural, local, and folkloric. Taken too rigidly, such categories, besides being obviously reductive, are problematic because the representations of the folkloric, whether by Lucy Mae Turner or even Brown himself, are significantly influenced by mass-culture versions of the folk. The influence of such versions was inescapable, however opposed to or subversive to those mass-culture products the works of Turner and Brown might be. Conversely, Hughes and such popular-culture-influenced poets as Waring Cuney and Frank Marshall Davis clearly conceive of their projects as at least partially folkloric in the sense that they are creating "realistic" portraits of the urban (and rural) folk and the expressive culture that is often opposed to mass culture, at least to the extent that an uneasiness about the purposes and effects of mass culture is registered. However, so forewarned, I use the categories, and Hughes and Brown as exemplars of those categories, as tools for investigating the conflicts, stresses, and commonalties of Left African-American poets (and to no small extent Leftist American writers) in the 1930s.

You Have Seen Their Voices: The Folk Documentary

The documentary impulse of the 1930s has been much discussed. As Richard Pells notes with respect to fiction during that decade:

> If some writers found it necessary to abandon fiction for journalism, there were others who tried to adapt the methods of the documentary to the traditional concerns of art. This was especially true of the "proletarian" novel, which, whether or not it was written from a truly revolutionary perspective, exhibited many of the techniques of reportage: a preoccupation with the factual details of modern life, an emphasis on the function and relation of groups and classes, an interest in social types and external events. Where it differed from conventional journalism was in the effort to invest contemporary facts and naturalistic description with poetic (as well as political) significance and thereby to raise brute facts and naturalistic description to the level of art. (202)

There was also a prominent documentary strain among Left poets generally during the 1930s. The clearest example of this is Muriel Rukeyser's long poem "The Book of the Dead" in her second collection *U.S. 1* (1938). As Walter Kalaidjian points out, "The Book of the Dead" is "an experimental fusion of poetry with nonliterary languages drawn from journalism, Congressional hearings, biography, personal interviews and other documentary forms."[3] The poem attempts to represent the Union Carbide Gauley Bridge scandal that arose when corporate greed led to a massive number of silicosis cases among miners digging a tunnel for a Union Carbide subsidiary. While Rukeyser's poem is perhaps the most formally radical in its employment of journalism and other "objective" or "nonliterary" discourses, the documentary impulse can seen in the poetry of many leading Left writers, such as Mike Gold's "Examples of Worker's Correspondence" and the previously noted "Broadcast on Ethiopia" by Langston Hughes.[4]

Of course, the CPUSA and its supporters did not generally see "objective" as contradistinct to "partisan." In their view, any discourse fundamentally represented the interests of a particular class. They understood their official ideology of Marxism-Leninism to be both a "science" of society and also partisan to the working class as well as to oppressed "peoples" generally. During the Third Period especially, the CPUSA tended to see various social discourses as monovocal in their class interests. Mass culture, for example, was often (though sometimes inconsistently) considered to be an expression of bourgeois ideology aimed at disarming the working class. In the Popular Front era, many social discourses, particularly those of mass culture, were allowed to be at least partially polyvocal and to be sites of popular struggle, as seen in the struggle to integrate professional baseball.[5] Nonetheless, despite changes of attitude throughout the decade, a general sense of the partisan nature of discourse remained a constant. Thus the notion of representing and recreating the "authentic" voices of the working class (and during the Popular Front, the "people" more generally) to counterbalance the bourgeois voices of "high" art and the mass media became a priority for Left artists. The task as it was generally envisioned was not simply to reveal the "facts" about the United States or even the working class, but to give voice to the worker, and the "nationally oppressed" African American, thus allowing those exploited by class and nationality to speak. For writers, this involved both the "accurate" ventriloquizing of the oppressed subject, as in V. J. Jerome's poem "A Negro Mother to her Child" (leaving aside for the moment the success of Jerome's rendering of the African-American vernacular subject), as well as the promotion of "authentic" voices of working-class or nationally oppressed subjects, as in the inclusion of songs by Aunt Molly Jackson and "Negro Songs of Protest" collected by Lawrence Gellert in the collection *Proletarian Literature of the United States*.[6] In either case, the project was in no small part linguistic; the representation and recreation of these working-class or folk voices in registers differing from what was perceived as standard literary diction was the objective as much as any "facts" that these voices might reveal. In short, the formal structures of "nonstandard" speech uttered by these recreated voices, whether in the stories of Meridel Le Sueur, the poetry of Don West, or the novels of Jack Conroy—or the urban fiction of Mike Gold or Henry Roth for that matter—declared in their very existence a resistance to class, regional, and/or national oppression.

Thus the problems of inauthenticity posed for authors by "bourgeois" "dialect" and "regional" literature, and popular music, film, and drama, were not strictly an African-American concern. Many of the non-African-American writers of the 1930s, especially those on the Left who often focused on particular subcultures, had similar problems in representing the "folk" or "working-class" speaking subject. Mike Gold had to contend with various mass-culture representations of the Jew, as well as such "high" culture representations as F. Scott Fitzgerald's Meyer Wolfsheim in *The Great Gatsby*.[7] Similarly, Don West labored under the weight of mass-culture constructions of the "hillbilly" and the "Okie" in addition to "high" culture constructions, such as the image of "Bonnie and Josie" dancing around a stump in Wallace Stevens's "Life is Motion." One of the most significant impacts of African-American literature (and African-American literary criticism) on American literature generally is that very early on it, as a body, engaged these questions of mass culture and "high" culture type and stereotype and of "realistic" or "authentic" representation in a manner that provided models for later non-African-American (and African-American) writers and that prepared audiences for "serious" literature in various forms of American vernacular language.

Among African-American poets such resistance to racial oppression by the representation of linguistic difference obviously antedated the Great Depression. As noted earlier, the project of Langston Hughes's *Fine Clothes to the Jew* is largely concerned with formal qualities of African-American speech as distinct from a "high," or standardly colloquial, American literary language. Other important works by black writers during the 1920s that invoke the formal qualities of African-American vernacular language, or as James Weldon Johnson said, utilized "a form which is freer and larger than dialect, but which will hold the racial flavor; a form expressing the imagery, the idioms, the peculiar turns of thought and distinctive humor and pathos, too, of the Negro," include Johnson's *God's Trombones* and Jean Toomer's *Cane*.[8] Even Countee Cullen, a writer known for his use of a "high" literary style, begins one of his bitterest poems, "Uncle Jim" (from the 1927 collection *Copper Sun*), with the line "'White folks is white,' says Uncle Jim." Cullen here sets the voice of the African-American folk subject in opposition to the "standard" voice of the speaker, whose "elevated" diction in responding to his Uncle ("'A platitude,' I sneer") emphasizes the concrete distinction between "high" literary speech and that of the folk subject. It is the formal distinctiveness of Uncle Jim's brief statement that gives power to the bitter weariness of the poem's meditation upon the vexed and irreducible persistence of racial, sexual, and class identity in modern American society.

As James Weldon Johnson points out in his prescription for the correct literary approach to the resources of African-American vernacular language, the problem of representing the African-American folk or popular voice was greatly complicated by a heritage of minstrelsy and "dialect" literature that was seen as essentially racist in the hands of white artists and readers and accommodationist in those of African-American writers and readers.[9] As we have seen in Turner's *'Bout Cullud Folkses* and Hughes's *The Negro Mother and Other Dramatic Recitations*, the model of Paul Laurence Dunbar was an overpowering presence well into the 1930s. Dunbar's influence remained strong far into the Depression era, not merely because of his status as the first truly "professional" African-American poet and of his popularity during his lifetime among black and white readers but also because of his representation within his work of an opposition between his "high" poetry, which is posed as his "true" work, and his "dialect" poetry, which is both a "mask" of his "genuine" poetry and his "authentic" self, as well as a prison in which the poet is incarcerated by his own success. This opposition remained a potent paradigm for the New Negro era with its concern for representing "authentically" the racial self without being imprisoned by the implicitly or explicitly racist expectations of white readers, actual or potential, or of variously accommodationist black readers.

Fundamentally, African-American writers who drew on a construction of the folk voice during the New Negro Renaissance attempted to solve the problem posed by the Dunbarian split in one of two manners. The most common solution, as exemplified by Johnson's *God's Trombones*, Toomer's *Cane*, and Cullen's "Uncle Jim," was to suggest the structure and "flavor" of African-American vernacular speech without actually directly attempting to reproduce that speech at any length. In this approach, the reader was forced to receive the material in a manner that would not allow him or her to interpret it through the conventions of minstrelsy and dialect literature.

The other solution, as exemplified by Hughes's *Fine Clothes to the Jew* and the early blues- and work-song-based poetry of Sterling Brown and Waring Cuney, was to attempt to reproduce vernacular speech, but also to place that speech within "authentic" African-American expressive forms, such as the blues, the work song, and the tall tale. Thus vernacular speech was reclaimed as literary diction through the certifiable authenticity of these forms. In a sense, the blues structure, work-song-structure, and so on of these poems served as a sort of reverse image of the "authenticating" letters appended to slave narratives by white "authorities" in the eighteenth and nineteenth centuries with the folk structures underpinning the poems serving as "authenticating" documents that distinguish the genuine expression of the Negro self from the faux Negro of dialect poetry and minstrelsy.[10]

Can I Get a Witness?: The Narratorial
Consciousness as Outsider

A crucial distinction among those African-American writers who attempted to represent and recreate the folk voice during the 1930s is that between the writers whose works were essentially elegiac in nature and those whose works were not. Many, perhaps most, writers of the New Negro Renaissance who attempted to recreate, or at least invoke, the folk voice did so with the sense that the voice issued from a dying, if oppositional, subculture that was disappearing under the pressures of modern life, particularly mass culture. In the case of James Weldon Johnson's *God's Trombones*, this passing is seen as the inevitable result of genuine progress.[11] In Jean Toomer's *Cane*, the African-American folk culture of the South is also pictured as doomed, but in this instance the results, the deracinated and impotent human products of modern society, are tragic. This elegiac approach to the folk voice in somewhat modified form remained a powerful influence through the 1930s and beyond. As noted in chapter 2, the work of Sterling Brown, particularly *Southern Road*, had a strongly elegiac cast resembling that of *Cane*, but without the overt primitivist aspect. The powerfully corrupting influence of modern society, identified as mass culture by Brown, on the folk culture is rendered in both Toomer's work and that of Brown as a generational split, suggesting the doomed, if heroic, nature of the rural folk. Interestingly, as the dominant construction of the African-American folk, or "people," is transformed during the course of the 1930s from rural to urban, such an elegiac approach remains powerful. Even a poet as commonly, if wrongly, seen as opposed to vernacular African-American language as Melvin Tolson, a product of the literary and political movements of the 1920s and 1930s who published his first collection in the 1940s, saw his neomodernist epic *The Harlem Gallery* (1965) as an attempt to "fix" (to use James Weldon Johnson's term) a vision of African-American community that is seen, like Johnson's "old-time preacher" in *God's Trombones*, with a certain sadness and affection stemming from its inevitable passing in a better, more egalitarian future.[12]

In addition to the elegiac approach to the folk voice, the other major approach during the New Negro Renaissance was that which attempted to fix the distinctive "nowness" of the folk or popular voice in its concrete particularity. The most notable example of this approach is Hughes's *Fine Clothes to the Jew*, which drew on the resources of the urban and "classic" blues and modern gospel music (as opposed to the "traditional" spirituals) to authenticate its representation of vernacular language. In Hughes's text, and in the vernacular poems of Waring Cuney and Helene Johnson in the 1920s, there is little sense of a lament for a passing culture. Where such a sense exists, as in Johnson's "Bottled," the lost or faded culture that is mourned is located in Africa and not the Deep South.

There was a certain amount of crossover between the elegiac approach and the "immediate" approach to the folk voice and the folk subject. As indicated in chapter

3, Hughes's verse play "Scottsboro Limited" is characterized by a sense that the African-American vernacular culture of the rural South would wither away in the new socialist order. Despite the fact that this withering is seen as "progressive," the liveliness of Hughes's representation of the folk voice suggests that his feelings about this future development were not unmixed.

One of the persistent problems facing African-American authors who attempt to represent and recreate the folk voice is where to locate the narratorial consciousness with respect to the folk voice. At one end of the spectrum of possible stances is that of the narratorial consciousness as a witness who is clearly distinct from the represented folk voice. An example of this stance is Ida Gerding Athens's 1940 collection *Brethren*, in which the narratorial consciousness is implicitly or explicitly (depending on the poem in question) that of a teacher in a school with a predominantly African-American student body. The poems of the collection consist largely of vernacular addresses to the teacher by the students and their parents, or observations of the students by the teacher. The documentary impulse of the collection, and an obsession with "authenticity," is emphasized by the introductory note by B. Y. Williams and the foreword by the author, both claiming the veracity of the poem's "portraits" on the basis of Athens's experience as a Cincinnati schoolteacher.[13] There is no overt move to either identify the narratorial consciousness with the folk or to represent a narratorial rapprochement with the folk except on the hierarchical basis of the narrator as social authority.

I say overt because the book begins and ends with vernacular statements in adult voices with no apparent addressees. In this the book closely resembles much Left African-American literature in the 1930s, beginning in Athens's title poem with a vernacular litany describing an interracial (though rhetorically masculine) utopia that is also an implicit critique of racism as the tool of class domination:

> White chile an' cullud chile plays togethah,
> If'n biggety folks leave dey be.
> White chile an' cullud chile learns togethah,
> If'n biggety folks leave dey be.
> White chile an' cullud chile friends fo' ebbah,
> If'n biggety folks leave dey be.
> White man an' cullud man suah to unnerstan'.
> White man and cullud man atween dem shinin' sea.
> White man and cullud man habitin' this geat lan'.
> White man an' cullud man togethah dey'll stan',
> If'n biggety folks leave they be.

> (13)

This opening stands at odds with the great majority of poems that follow in which the stance of teacher-poet-narrator as witness-authority is clearly delineated. Athens's approach to the folk is after the manner of Hughes rather than Brown, in that her urban "portraits" represent the people of the northern ghetto as genuinely "Negro" despite, or perhaps because of, a Dickensian cast to these portraits. (Physical sickness and the deformation of the children resulting from poverty are favorite themes of Athens.) But Athens differs from Hughes in her pronounced separation of narratorial consciousness and folk voice. Of course, Hughes often foregrounded the problem of where to locate the position of the narratorial consciousness with respect to the folk as seen in the beginning lines of "Air Raid Over Harlem" ("Who you gonna put in it? / *Me* / Who the hell are you? / *Harlem* / Alright, then") and later in the relationship between Jesse B. Semple and the narrator of the early "Simple" stories of the 1940s in which the formal and somewhat stiff narrator is clearly identified with Hughes. But even as he problematized this relationship, Hughes insisted on the inextricable connection between the narrator-author and the folk as African Americans.

This connection is almost entirely missing in Athens's work. Athens's claim for the "authenticity" of her work derives almost entirely from her position as eye- and ear-witness rather than from a common racial identification:

> I seen a show.
> Yes'm, *sawn* a show.
> An' in the show the captain said,
> "They's French ships out in the road stead."
>
> (30)

Here, in the poem "Conversation Piece," the implied teacher-narrator ventriloquizes, and implicitly corrects, the folk subject who in turn vainly attempts to reproduce the teacher-narrator's authoritative and explicit initial correction of the vernacular. This double ventriloquism and double correction coexist without any satire of the narrator as occur, for example, in similar exchanges between the narrator and Jesse Semple in Hughes's "Simple" stories.[14] Thus the teacher-witness's "neutrality" has a reciprocal relationship with the diction of the recreated folk voice, producing a further guarantee of the "authenticity" of the portraits: the folk voice is rescued from minstrelsy by the "objective" witness while the veracity of the observations of the outside witness is attested to by the recognizably "folk" diction in much the same way that visual details, say the overalls of African-American farm laborers in the 1930s, authenticate a vision of the essential African-American folk in many Farm Security Administration photographs during the 1930s.[15]

Those few moments of racial identification in *Brethren* on the part of the narratorial consciousness happen when the question of class differences among African Americans is raised. One of these moments takes place in "Lift Up Your Face," where a common racial identity among African Americans is advanced and then undermined by a series of class distinctions:

> "I ain't playin' with Gracie Haydie.
> She say, 'Last one in's a nigga baby.'
> She calls names, I is cullud, I is.
>
> "No, you ain' nither. Why'd you ruther
> Be call "cullud" like a Easter egg?
> Honey, you can look proud in the face
> 'Cause you belong to the Negro Race.
>
> (26)

As in "Conversation Piece," a double correction of the folk voice occurs. One might even say there is a triple correction since the poem begins with the correction of a (presumably) white child by a black child who is in turn corrected by another, almost certainly older African American, possibly an adult, who speaks in the first stanza. Beyond the linguistic correction by the older speaker lies the unspoken emendation by the narrator-teacher who overhears this conversation. In this, the second speaker is not unlike the speaker of "Conversation Piece" who when corrected says "sawn" instead of "saw." The second speaker cites only exemplars of a "high" Negro art in a speech that mixes folkish diction and figures of speech ("An' do you leave Miss Savage alone / See what she can do with a stone) with a neo-Garveyite rhetoric. This may seem unremarkable to us, living in the post–Black power, post-Malcolm X era in which such a nationalist mixture of the "high" and the "folk" became commonplace. But, as noted in chapter 1, Garveyite literary production tended to be formally "high" in the extreme, suggesting that while the second speaker may be ideologically "correct," he or she is not yet quite linguistically "correct," despite her own revision of the child's initial assertion of racial pride. Standing beyond the two speakers is the auditor-narrator-teacher who here is implicitly revealed as part of this African-American continuum that is a strange amalgam of race pride, uplift, and class difference.

As in Turner's work, and the work of all of the African-American poets of the 1930s for that matter, the figure standing behind these poems is Paul Laurence Dunbar. Dunbar is explicitly and implicitly invoked in *Brethren* as a model of the writer who attempted to navigate the contradictions of "high" and "dialect" literature while self-reflexively representing the problems of such a navigation. Athens is Dunbarian in that she upholds a "high," or "middle-class" if you will, literary standard while writing frequently in "dialect," which she often corrects. In keeping with the documentary spirit of the 1930s, Athens's vernacular portraits of the African-American poor of Cincinnati are far less overtly humorous than most of Dunbar's recreations of an African-American speaking subject. But there is a certain satire of the folk voice in nearly all the vernacular poems of the collection, even in such a sympathetic assertion of race pride as "Lift Up Your Face." Perhaps the most noteworthy, so to speak, is a series of twelve "notes" to the teacher-narrator that are written by parents, or by children for their illiterate parents, and in which the diction is to various degrees "nonstandard." What is most interesting about these notes is the way in which they foreground the problems of the written literary representation of the folk voice, particularly those problems amplified by the inheritance of previous "high" and "popular" literary representations of African-American vernacular language. The literariness of these notes, and by extension the book's recreation of the folk voice, is highlighted by the use of apostrophe marks (e.g., "an'," "clo'es," "'cause," "'tendance"), which clearly refer to literary conventions of representing the African-American folk voice rather than approximating any actual note that might be produced by a parent of a public school student. (In other words, if parents were unable to reproduce a "standard" English note, they would almost certainly leave the apostrophe mark out of "'cause," whatever spelling they might use.) These apostrophe marks call attention to the fact that there is a supervising consciousness between the reader and the represented folk, as well as reminding the reader of the conventions

sciousness" leading to a "new type of man" (the "new socialist man") and, even more, Popular Front notions of a new inclusiveness in which all would develop toward an ideal of a truly unified American people—though the typical Popular Front cultural production rarely had such a "high" and corrective notion of the ideal of citizenship. Thus a certain tension exists within the text between its fundamentally optimistic and strangely "high–low" Emersonian–Popular Front critique of society and its basically Dunbarian structure in which is embedded the far more pessimistic post-Reconstruction Dunbarian representation of the problems of African-American self-representation by the African-American artist.

This tension between this Emersonian–Popular Front optimism and Dunbarian pessimism is further complicated by the fact that the poems, whether "standard" or "dialect," witnessed by the correcting consciousness of a middle-class teacher-narrator and making up the overwhelming majority of the collection, are sand-wiched between vernacular poems in which there is no hint of the teacher-narrator-witness. As noted earlier, the opening title poem is a vernacular integrationist litany that implicitly links racism to the ruling class of the United States. Following "Afro-Madonna" is another series of vernacular poems, including several wry love poems reminiscent of the more light-hearted love lyrics of Langston Hughes and four po-ems inspired by African-American folk religion, ending with the millenarian "When de Trumpet Blows":

> When de Lawd say, "Is you sorry
> You been bad mos' ebery day?"
> I'se gwine bow me down—bow me down—
> "I done de bes' I could," I'll say,
> "Wid troubles dat I didn't borry."
>
> "An' den I'll say—I'll say—I'll say,
> "Good Lawd, does You-all membah?
> You-all's hongry on de mountain—
> Wid old Satan on de mountain—
> Smoov-mouf Satan on de mountain?"
>
> "Does you-all 'membah, Lawd," I'll say,
> "'Bout de foxes wid dey holes?
> An' de buh'ds of de air wid nes's?
> But you had no place fo' Yo' haid.
> You—You—Lawd no place fo' yo' haid."
>
> "You is done de bes' You could, Lawd.
> You de one kin onnerstan', Lawd,
> You de one los' all He fren's, Lawd,
> You de one kin see inside, Lawd,
> Inside, inside Yo' chillun's hah'ts."

(70)

The progression of the poem's logic is remarkable in several ways. The poem begins in a fairly typical Dunbarian manner with a sentimental folk vision of Judgment Day. However, when "de Lawd" asks the speaker to repent, rather than do so in the manner that most mainline Christian churches would dictate, the speaker proceeds to justify his or her actions, declaring he or she "done de bes' I could" in a society not of his or her ordering. Then even more remarkably, the speaker goes on to claim a commonalty with God on the basis of the experience of hunger, homelessness, and victimization by the power of the state (in the reference to Jesus' crucifixion in "You de one los' all He fren's, Lawd") that seems more than a bit condescending ("You is done de bes' You could, Lawd"). Finally, the speaker proclaims his or her worthiness and a certainty of the heavenly kingdom.

In the end, then, the reader is left with an assertion of pride by the folk subject that lacks any hint of correction or supervision by the narratorial consciousness and with the certainty of a better world in the future. While this sort of prophetic self-assertion has a long history in African-American religious culture, as Robin Kelley points out, such religious-based millenarian and egalitarian visions of a new society also typified the Left African-American subculture around the CPUSA, particularly in the South.[17] It too found an echo in the millenarian or apocalyptic rhetoric of the work of Left African-American writers, as in the endings of Margaret Walker's "For My People" and Langston Hughes's "Don't You Want to Be Free."

This is not to say that *Brethren* is the work of a militant Communist. The precise politics of the virtually unknown Athens are difficult to determine now. In any event, the enshrinement of an ideal middle class and a Dunbarian model of literary excellence that characterize most of the volume makes it unlikely, though not impossible during the Popular Front era, that the writer was an active Communist or closely connected to the CPUSA. However, as in the case of Turner's *'Bout Cullud Folkses*, it is notable that in such a work where the stance of the narratorial consciousness is so clearly distinguished from the folk subject, and is so dependent on Dunbar's representation of this split in everything from theme to diction, Athens feels compelled to give the folk the first and last words in a manner that is at odds with this narratorial stance. This folk frame, like the basic documentary claims made for the book in its prefatory materials, is a hallmark of Left-influenced African-American writing. In the final analysis, the reader is confronted with a reversal of the Dunbarian model (where "standard" poems, such as the rondeau "We Wear the Mask," force a rereading of the "dialect" poems), so that the envelope of "unsupervised" vernacular poems demands a rereading of the supervised "standard" and "dialect" poems, raising in a highly conscious manner the problems of the "authentic" literary representation of the folk, and troubling the narratorial authority of even the most supervised poems of the collection as evidenced in the self-reflexive punctuation of the series of "notes."

I Went Down Home: The Narratorial
Consciousness as Insider

Perhaps the most common narratorial stance toward the African-American folk subject during the 1930s is that of the insider. As we shall see in the next section of this chapter, African-American poets often have foregrounded the problems of the intellectual-artist speaking by, of, and for the folk. This was especially true of the collections of poetry published in the 1930s. However, in terms of how African-American poetry was available to readers, the stance of the unself-conscious insider was extremely important, particularly in Left-influenced media. This largely resulted from the facts that relatively few book-length collections of poetry by African Americans were published in the 1930s and that no important anthologies of African-American poetry, or African-American literature generally, appeared in the United States between the revised edition of Johnson's *The Book of American Negro Poetry* in 1931 and Brown, Davis, and Lee's *Negro Caravan* in 1941.[18] Many significant authors, including Gwendolyn Bennett, Helene Johnson, Claude McKay, Waring Cuney, Richard Wright, Owen Dodson, and Melvin Tolson, published no books of poetry during those years despite having written a considerable amount of poetry. Sterling Brown was unable to publish another collection after *Southern Road* in 1932. Langston Hughes did publish three collections, not including his collection for children, *The Dream-Keeper* (1932), but these were essentially self-published chapbooks—or in the case of *A New Song*, a chapbook published by a small Left press—that he sold on his speaking tours. This led some observers, such as Alain Locke in his annual literary survey in *Opportunity*, to bemoan the lack of poetic production after the prolific era of the 1920s New Negro Renaissance.[19]

However, there were many poems published by African-American writers during the 1930s. Journals, and anthologies that were not organized as "African American," such as *Proletarian Literature in the United States*, were by far the most important vehicles for the dissemination of African-American poetry. As a result of the prominence of journals and general anthologies as the vehicles for African-American poets, the manner in which readers had access to these poems was generally that of single poem, at most two or three. Thus the context for the poems that a collection or a specifically African-American anthology would provide was largely absent during the 1930s. This missing context was often to no small extent a narrative of the relationship of an alienated intellectual narratorial consciousness to the folk, recasting the old trope of the North-South axis (North to "freedom" in some larger "American" context; South to an essential African-American "folk" identity) and the problems that moves in either direction entail for African-American intellectuals. In some cases, particularly in the work of Sterling Brown after *Southern Road*, this simultaneous insider-outsider consciousness is apparent even in a single poem. However, in many other cases, such as Hughes's "Florida Road Workers," which first appeared in 1930 in the New York *Herald Tribune*, the initial periodical publication of these poems recreated the allegedly unmediated folk voice. But, as we have seen with "Florida Road Workers" in chapter 3, in the larger context of such poetry collections as *Dear Lovely Death* and *Southern Road*, these apparently straightforward "folk" poems became part of a self-reflexive narrative of the formal, ideological, and even moral problems of the intellectual-artist recreating or ventriloquizing the folk. In short, without the frame of the collections, the relationship between the folk subject and the narratorial consciousness was often fairly uncomplicated since the narratorial consciousness was invisible in many of the individual poems published in periodicals.

One of the most interesting aspects of the 1930s with respect to this stance of the narratorial insider is the attempt by many African-American poets to embody the folk speaker through various hybrids of poetry and other sorts of performative culture, particularly those forms associated with folk or popular culture, in order to address a folk or popular audience. Whether or not a folk or popular audience for the poetry actually existed, constructs of such an audience, as distinguished from "modernist" or "genteel" constructs of the audience for poetry, were central features of many poems that recreated the folk voice in the 1930s. Thus in Sterling Brown's "Ma Rainey" (which first appeared in the 1930 *Folk-Say* with two other of Brown's vernacular poems, "Southern Road" and "Dark of the Moon"), a community of meaning is proposed between the folk speaker of the poem and the potential folk audience for the poem, a community that would be analogous to the relation between Ma Rainey and her audience. (Of course, as suggested in chapter 2, the actual relationship between poet and audience proposed in the later collection *Southern Road*, in which "Ma Rainey" appeared, was far more complicated.) Brown's invocation of the popular singer and the truncated citation of the popular blues, like the use of blues lyrics by Hughes, Richard Wright, Waring Cuney, and others, are more than an attempt to create an authentically "Negro" poetry, but are also a poetry that could speak authentically to an imagined popular African-American audience.

The nature of the imagined audience varied considerably from author to author. As indicated earlier, Brown's conception of an "authentic" audience was rooted in a notion of a folk culture that was inherently antagonistic to mass commercial culture, including that consumed almost exclusively by African Americans. Brown's conception was largely shared by such writers as Waring Cuney and Helene Johnson. Johnson published seldom during the 1930s, but she apparently wrote a considerable number of poems in the 1930s (though it is often hard to date the unpublished work exactly), which are quite fascinating as examples of the formal transition between the New Negro and the New Red Negro. In many respects, the work that survives (contained in the archive of her cousin Dorothy West at Radcliffe College's Schlesinger Library) resembles her work in the 1920s, consisting largely of love sonnets, pastorals, and African-American minstrelsy-inflected semicomic vernacular pieces with a strong (though somewhat ironic) element of race pride. What is different in the 1930s is the appearance of vernacular poems much in the spirit of Sterling Brown, focusing on the southern African-American folk as authentic in opposition to the inauthentic industrial North, where before the opposition, as in "Bottled" had been between America and Africa (and sometimes between "high" and "low").

For example, Johnson's "Goin' North" presents a vignette of a migrant to the North. The speaker of the poem is the migrant himself who narrates the poem in the first person present. The speaker describes how he drops something while boarding the train. At first he is afraid that it is his wallet and ticket that has fallen. Instead it turns out to be the Bible his father has given him, much to his relief. ("Lord! Dat was sure a narrow escape, alright.") The migrant declares that he will buy another Bible as soon as he gets north. But it is clear that will never happen as the ties of family, community and southern culture are left behind.

Of course, as with the work of Brown, taken out of context, the story of the narrative poem could easily form a scene from such popular films of the era as *Hallelujah!*, *Green Pastures*, and *Emperor Jones*, which no doubt had a tremendous influence in the construction of the folk by black and white artists, and the reception of those constructions by black and white audiences—constructions that were nonetheless recognized as problematic by African-American artists. However, in an earlier poem, tellingly titled "A Southern Road," the relatively idyllic portrait of the southern folk is disrupted by Johnson with the representation of lynch violence, a representation obviously lacking in the popular film of the late 1920s and the 1930s:

> A blue-fruited black gum
> Like a tall predella
> Bears a dangling figure—
>
> (17)

Once again, the continuing influence of Dunbar is revealed here in that Johnson's most overtly "serious" utterances, even when representing the African-American subject, are formally "high," while her vernacular pieces, though far more "topical" than the "dialect" poems of Dunbar, are humorous in a way that her "high" ones are not. (As noted in chapter 2, this poem appeared in the short-lived journal *Fire* in 1926, antedating both Hughes's "Bound No'th Blues" and Brown's "Southern Road." Thus, both Hughes's poem and Brown's poem can be seen to be carrying on an argument with the "high–low" Dunbarian split of Johnson's work as well as contesting each other's reading of the essential "folk.")

On the other hand, Hughes, like Frank Marshall Davis, constructed an audience, whether on Beale Street, Railroad Avenue, or Lenox Avenue, that was largely urban and bound together by the products and institutions of popular culture. Obviously, these conceptions were not absolutely rigid: Brown acknowledged in such essays as "The Folk Blues as Poetry" and in such poems as "Ma Rainey" that it was impossible completely to separate authentic folk expression from popular commercial culture in modern society; Hughes, Davis, and others who drew on the resources of mass culture nonetheless foregrounded the contradictions of such a usage in their work.

Beyond the various adaptations of forms of "nonliterary" folk or popular expression to the printed page, the 1930s were notable for attempts to create hybrids of literature and popular culture that would be accessible to a mass audience and that would attempt to embody the folk voice in ways that were not possible on the printed page. While there obviously had been poetry readings and reading tours before the 1930s, the decade saw the rise of populist reading tours throughout all the regions of the United States to a degree never seen before in African-American letters. As discussed earlier in chapter 3, the 1930s were the decade in which Hughes launched his reading tours that took him across the country, especially the South. In the case of Hughes, many of his readings, particularly in the South, were not primarily to a working-class or farming audience, but to African-American college students and the local African-American intelligentsia. However, other readings, particularly those sponsored by the International Workers Order, were part of the Left cultural network of fraternal organizations, labor unions, Workers Schools, reading groups, and so on, discussed in chapter 1, exposing Hughes and other African-American poets to audiences inside and outside the African-American community that would not have generally appeared at such events before the 1930s.

In addition to the reading tours, there was an explosion of vernacular poetry-plays, dramatic monologues, and mass recitations created by African-American poets, including Hughes, Davis, and Owen Dodson. Some of these poetry dramas, such as Hughes's "Scottsboro Limited" and "Don't You Want to Be Free" and Dodson's *Divine Comedy* (1938), were actually performed to substantial audiences.[20] Others, such as Davis's "I Am the American Negro" (1937), probably were never performed, but involved a construct of oral performance and audience that was far more "popular" than that of typical "high" literary poetic production.

Even more striking were the large number of African-American folk music- and popular music-poetry hybrids of the 1930s that were actually performed on records, on radio broadcasts, in clubs, or on stage. There were precedents for this phenomenon in the interest in folk music by the "popular modernists" of the early twentieth century, notably Carl Sandburg and Vachel Lindsay. Similarly, during the 1920s Hughes attempted on at least one occasion to have a blues musician perform at one of his readings and began to work on "popular" and "high" poetry-drama works that would utilize the blues and other folk and popular musical forms.[21] But for the most part such hybrids by African-American writers in the 1920s were tentative, existing only in the implicit form of lyrics based on vernacular song and in projects that remained at best partially completed.

In the 1930s such projects were actually realized, often using the new technology and systems of distribution of mass culture. As with vernacular poetry on the printed page, these works tended toward either a "folk" model that, after the manner of Sterling Brown, privileged the "authentic" culture of the rural South or a "popular" model that was more urban, northern, and rooted in mass culture expressive forms— albeit forms associated with the African-American community. An example of the "folk" model can be found in a series of blues or blues-inflected poems written by Waring Cuney and set to music and recorded by Josh White in 1941.[22] In a sense, these poem-songs represent an attempt to create "folk" songs of struggle after the manner of those discovered, or allegedly discovered, by Lawrence Gellert. Interestingly, these poems on the printed page, as published in the Southern Negro Youth Congress's *Cavalcade* and other Left journals, formally resemble the work of James Weldon Johnson in their invocation of "folk" diction and structures without trying to exactly recreate the folk voice. "Hard Times Blues," for instance, rejects the stereotypical orthographic and syntactical markers of "dialect" literature for the most part:

> I went down home
> About a year ago,
> Things looked so bad
> My heart was sore.
> People had nothing
> It was a sinning shame,
> Everybody said
> Hard times was to blame.
>
> Great-God-A-Mighty
> Folks feeling bad,
> Lost all they ever had.

Cuney recreates the folk voice through a series of vignettes reporting on the folk condition—though even here the line "I went down home" suggests an "insider" returning from the outside rather than an "insider" who had never left. He also employs "folkisms" such as "Lawd," "ain't got," and "Great-God-A-Mighty" and certain folk cadences with the varied rhythm of the poem organized around a series of phrases rather than lines or stanzas. On the page, the narratorial consciousness is that of the insider-outsider who returns home and is able to document "objectively," but sympathetically the condition of the southern folk. The voice of the poem is folk inspired and yet seemingly distinguished from the folk—despite the title, the poem is not even formally a blues (though some of the poem–songs on *Southern Exposure*, especially "Bad Housing Blues" and "Southern Exposure," are formally closer to the typical twelve-bar blues).

Yet when Josh White performs the poem-song, the work takes on an entirely different cast. While the poem is not formally a blues, and the song itself sounds closer to a gospel number than the rural folk blues, White's acoustic blues guitar riffs frame Cuney's poem, and White's voice is that of the folk subject. White's performance on the record is interesting in that it seems more deliberately "folk" than his usual work. (He performs solo accompanied only by his guitar rather than by his more "urban" vocal group, "Josh White and his Carolinians," with whom he had recorded in 1940.) White's presentation is one that erases the distinction between the narratorial consciousness and the folk voice that exists on the printed page. It is "folkish" in a way that distinguishes it from more urban constructs of mass culture, though it does so through the mass-culture technology of the phonograph recording. And yet White's rendition is more "authentic" than such popular culture constructs of the folk as found in *Green Pastures* and *Hallelujah* through its more "accurate" use of folk forms (including nonverbal elements) and its documentation of the folk condition, thus avoiding the Dunbarian split of "high" and "low" and the problematic heritage of minstrelsy and "dialect" literature. In a sense, Cuney and White attempted to tap a new audience, black and white, shaped by the Left subculture of the 1930s, creating a popular form that appealed to its audience precisely because it appeared to reject mass culture and speak in the authentic voice of the folk subject.

The "popular" model was largely a product of the Popular Front era when many on the Left viewed mass culture as a field of contestation rather than simply a tool of bourgeois class interests. However, as we have seen, the impulse for the "popular" model antedates the Popular Front, and the Third Period for that matter, as attested by Hughes's half-realized attempts to write pieces for the popular musical theater during the middle and late 1920s, which, as Arnold Rampersad sums up, included "some broad satire and even low comedy, but also revealed elements of fantasy, pathos, and social protest, all of which Langston saw as significant in the often despised blues form."[23] This description of Hughes's failed attempts at musical theater in the 1920s would also serve as an apt summary of his 1938 self-described "poetry-play" "Don't You Want To Be Free," missing only the revolutionary ending of the later work.

One of the chief features distinguishing the "popular" model of the narratorial insider from those of the "folk" model is that instead of defining the "popular" in opposition to the "folk," the "popular" is linked to the "folk" on a cultural continuum from South to North. The "folk" in some sense authorizes the "popular" model, help-ing to sort out the "authentic" uses of mass culture from "inauthentic" appropria-tions.[24] For instance, in Richard Wright's blues "King Joe," as performed on two Okeh Records sides ("King Joe-Part I" and "King Joe-Part II") by Paul Robeson and the Count Basie Orchestra in 1941, a clear genealogy is established between the folk cul-ture of the rural South and the popular culture of the urban North.[25] "King Joe-Part I" begins with a clear invocation of the southern folk ("Black-eyed peas ask corn-bread, "What makes you so strong?")

In the second stanza of "King Joe-Part II," the literary landscape shifts to the ur-ban North of Cleveland, St. Louis, Chicago and Harlem. The closing stanza returns to the culture of the South, albeit within the context of the popular culture institu-tion of professional boxing ("Bullfrog told boll weevil: Joe's done quit the ring").

The movement of the poem-song is literally from the South of black-eyed peas and cornbread to the streets of Harlem and the cities of the urban North and back again. Similarly, a popular culture hero, the foremost African-American participant in mass-spectator sports in that era, is transformed into a John Henry–like folk hero. It is also telling that Wright picked a migrant from the South to the industrial North as this sort of hero.[26] On the formal level, in much the same way that Brown's "Southern Road" is a blues–work-song hybrid, Wright's "King Joe" is a hybrid of ur-ban blues, featuring the accompaniment of the most famous blues-based jazz or-chestra of the time, and rural southern folk rhymes, "badman" stories, and animal stories.[27] The choice of the Count Basie Orchestra for the record is telling in this re-gard, since the heavily blues-based urban jazz of the Kansas City scene from which the Basie band came is in itself an embodiment of the sort of the rural folk-urban popular continuum that Wright's lyrics invoke.[28] Thus Wright makes an argument for the essential continuity between North and South, "folk" and "popular" (a conti-nuity which, ironically, he problematizes in *Native Son* and, to a lesser extent, in *Lawd Today*). This notion of a continuum is related to the "folk" model in that it requires a construction of a southern folk in order to evaluate popular culture, but that nonetheless allows overt mass cultural forms, whether in the ring or on the jukebox, as far more viable arenas for "authentic" African-American expression than the older "folk" forms in and of themselves.

Snapshots of the Cotton South: The Narratorial Consciousness as Insider and Outsider

A third approach to documenting and recreating the folk is the narratorial con-sciousness as both insider and outsider. This narratorial stance is, at least initially, sufficiently "outside the circle," to use Frederick Douglass's formulation, to "objec-tively" see the structure and meaning of folk expression and the folk experience. Ultimately, there is a sort of conversionary identification with the folk. However, de-spite this identification, the narratorial consciousness remains paradoxically distinct. As many scholars have pointed out, the construction of the literate African American as an answer to the "mainstream" construction of the nonliterate (and consequently subhuman) African-American folk, and the ensuing paradoxes of exemplarity and representativeness, go back to the earliest days of African-American writing.[29] Yet, prior to the 1930s, African-American authors generally represented, with varying degrees of tension and contradiction, either an Emersonian progression from the folk culture associated with slavery, as did Douglass in his autobiographies, or a return to the folk, whether as a sort of intellectual missionary, as did Frances Harper in *Iola Leroy* (1893) and W. E. B. Du Bois in *The Souls of Black Folk* (1903), or as a reborn member of the folk, as did Claude McKay in *Banana Bottom* (1933). Few writers, if any, proposed a return to the folk in which the journeying subject did not serve either as an exemplar of the potential for self-development of the folk or as a representative man or woman whose separation from the folk represented a fall. Perhaps the closest in spirit to the paradoxical relationship of the narratorial consciousness to the folk that characterized much African-American writing in the 1930s is Jean Toomer's *Cane* (1923), in which the narratorial consciousness returns to the folk and is portrayed as both attracted and repulsed through a series of scenes of an alienated procreation on the part of the folk subject and an even more alienated impotence on the part of the intellectual subject detached from the land.

Such paradoxes of distinction and self-identification were not restricted to the works of African-American writers and intellectuals in the 1930s and 1940s. The ideological contradiction between the Leninist notion of the vanguard party by, of, and for the working class (forming and being formed by class values and class consciousness) and yet fundamentally unlike other working-class institutions was a permanent feature of the CPUSA during this period. Similarly, as discussed in chapter 1, the Communist view of the "national question" attempted to yoke nationalism to integrationism without erasing either category, resulting in uneasy and contradictory attempts to balance dual identities of "nationality" and class.

This insider-outsider stance characterized much of the work of Langston Hughes and Sterling Brown in the 1930s. In the case of Brown, the relationship between the intellectual-poet-narrator and the folk subject was one of near-equals: though the intellectual needed to rejoin the organic and authentic folk community in order to truly perform his (and I mean his) function, the folk needed the intellectual in order to develop a full national self-consciousness. In this, Brown had more than a little in common with Du Boisian (and Emersonian) notions of self-development, albeit in what Brown considered to be authentically African-American terms rather than Du Bois's raceless and international (if Eurocentric) brotherhood of Dumas, Shakespeare, Balzac, and Du Bois. Hughes, as mentioned earlier, also often posited a narratorial consciousness that was separate from and yet tied to the African-American folk, as in "Advertisement for the Waldorf-Astoria" and "Air Raid Over Harlem." But this consciousness was generally a tool of the folk spirit, a collective identity that literally directs the figure of the poet in "Air Raid Over Harlem," rather than being an equal or near-equal partner with that spirit.

Close to Hughes's insider-outsider narratorial stance, particularly Hughes's more bitter poems of the 1930s, such as "Advertisement for the Waldorf-Astoria," are many of the most powerful works of Chicago poet Frank Marshall Davis. Like Hughes in "Advertisement," though more cynically and more pessimistically, Davis modulates between an outraged, yet "objective" description and an identification with the African-American folk. For example, "What Do You Want America?" in the 1935 collection *Black Man's Verse* begins with a Whitmanic-Sandburgian question, followed by a catalogue with a tone of affectionate outrage also reminiscent of Sandburg:

> What do you want, America?
> Young bearded nation of the thick muscles
> that does not sleep
> against the breasts of past greatness—
> What do you want, America?
>
> Sprawling across a continent
> your feet washed in two oceans
> and your goal above high heaven
> Thousands of miles of steel veins
> through which flows your life blood
> hauled by bellowing freight engines
> Your brain at work in Wall Street, Washington
> telling the world to cut it out or keep it up
> through a thousand mouths
> at Geneva, London, Paris, Berlin, Rome, Tokyo
>
> (21)

The catalogue continues in the next stanza, suddenly modulating in mid-stanza to an identification with the African-American folk:

> Your six foot scientists smart enough to measure
> stars billions of miles around or split unseen atoms
> Swimming in a sea of gold
> strong men going from rags to riches to rags to riches
> Leading little nations by the hand
> Your army and navy a Medusa's head
> turning potential enemies to stone—
> Why search the Sahara
> for ME, one grain of black sand
>
> (21)

Davis's narrator then draws back from this identification into another, more outraged catalogue overlaid with a cynical stance strongly influenced by H. L. Mencken and by the later published works of the older African-American Chicago poet Fenton Johnson, only to reaffirm his connection with the black folk described at the end of the stanza:[30]

> Black scars disfigure
> the ruddy cheeks of new mornings in Dixie
> (lynched black men hanging from green trees)
> Blind justice kicked, beaten, taken for a ride
> and left for dead
> (have you ever heard of Scottsboro, Alabama?)

Your Constitution gone blah-blah, shattered into a
thousand pieces like a broken mirror
Lincoln a hoary myth
(How many black men vote in Georgia?)
Mobs, chaingangs down South
Tuberculosis up North
—so now I am civilized

(22)

The diction here is alternately self-consciously literary ("shattered into a thousand pieces like a broken mirror," "a Medusa's head"), self-consciously "hard-boiled" ("cut it out," "taken for a ride," "blah-blah"), and self-consciously clichéd after the manner of a newspaper headline with an explanatory subhead ("Black scars disfigure / the ruddy cheeks of new mornings in Dixie / [lynched men hanging from green trees]"). In fact, Davis's diction here, and in his longer poems, draws generally on the peculiar self-conscious mixture of "high" and "low," purple passion and "objectivity," cynicism and idealism, cliché and arresting coinage bordering on self-parody that characterizes mainstream print journalism—an unsurprising influence given Davis's long career as journalist. The shape of the lines themselves with their minimal punctuation and their alternation of headline- and subhead-like lines with a prosy enjambment ("shattered into a / thousand pieces") resembles the column construction of a typical news article, editorial, or newspaper feature as much as the work of Masters, Sandburg, Lindsay, or even Fenton Johnson. Even sonically Davis uses assonance, alliteration, and slant rhymes to bond his lines together, rather than end rhyme or any regular metrical scheme, in much the same way as the typical newspaper headline.

Davis employs the authority and "objectivity" of journalism to attest to the veracity of his portrait of the black folk with whom the narrator explicitly identifies. The poem closes as the speaker's voice shifts into equally authoritative Old Testament–Whitmanic anaphoric long lines (and perhaps invokes the figure of Br'er Rabbit):

Today I tell of black folk who made America yesterday, who
    make America now
Today I see America clawing me like a tiger caged with a
    hare
Today I hear discords and crazy words in the song America
    sings to black folk
So today I ask—
What do you want, America?

(23)

The result of this mixture is a strangely "high" and "low," ironic, cynical, objective jeremiad that implies a falling away without any vision of a redemptive path or a divine destiny.

Thus, along with Hughes and Kenneth Fearing, Davis is one of the earliest Left artists of the 1930s to engage mass commercial culture in a manner that is not entirely hostile.[31] In "What Do You Want America," for example, the achievements of African Americans in the "high" arts of poetry, painting, and "art" song are equated with achievements in vaudeville and popular music. Similarly, African-American athletes, such as the boxer Jack Johnson and the football player Fritz Pollard, are mentioned with the same respect as is accorded to illustrious political leaders W. E. B. Du Bois and Booker T. Washington. Mass culture, particularly journalism and pulp fiction, is more important to Davis as a model for poetic production than a typical pantheon of African-American heroes. Davis begins his 1937 "Snapshots of the Cotton South" with an implicit declaration of the superiority of journalistic representation of the African-American folk, the white folk, and their condition in the rural South to that which has been produced (or not been produced) by the tradition of "high" art. The speaker presents a set of editorial demands (as befits the years Davis spent as a newspaper and wire service editor):

> Listen, you drawing men
> I want a picture of a starving black
> I want a picture of a starving white
> Show them bitterly fighting down on the dark soil
> Let their faces be lit by hate
> Above there will stand
> The rich plantation owner, holder of the land
> A whip in his red fist
> Show his pockets bulging with dollars spilled
> From the ragged trousers of the fighting men
> And I shall call it
> "Portrait of the Cotton South"

(40)

The poem's speaker finishes with an even more pointed challenge to "high" art:

> See today's picture—
> It is not beautiful to look upon.
> Meanwhile paint pots drip over
> There is fresh canvas for the asking.
> Will you say,
> "But that is not my affair"
> Or will you mould this section
> So its portrait will fit
> In the sunlit hall
> Of Ideal America?

(45–46)

Davis makes the response of the addressed "drawing men" (clearly associated with "drawing room") superfluous since he has chosen to present his own representation of the condition of the "cotton South," giving his work a journalistic title, "Snapshots of the Cotton South," which supersedes the more genteel and more "high" title of "Portrait of the Cotton South" suggested by the speaker. Davis claims a greater artistic power for print journalism and the related art of photography than the "high" traditions because of the relative accessibility of the mass culture styles to the common person and the greater willingness of journalists, especially such left-wing journalists as John Spivak and Erskine Caldwell, to seriously engage the realities of race and class in the South.[32]

As Davis draws on the resources of mass culture, particularly journalism and pulp fiction, he also interrogates the problems of such a usage and of mass culture generally. One aspect of pulp literature and journalism, particularly journalism aimed at a working-class audience, is the highly stylized self-reflexive and self-parodic elements that were a crucial part of pulp literature, journalism, animated cartoons, and mass culture of the era generally, and that were recognized as such by the audience. Davis takes this aspect of journalism even further with his use of cliché; headline-like lines; the "hard-boiled" yet sentimental voice of the newspaper columnist; the ridiculous purple prose, assonance, slant rhymes, and alliteration of the sports pages; the onomatopoetic sound effects of the comics pages; and so on. In this, Davis, despite his characteristic cynicism, differs from contemporaries, such as Nathanael West in *Miss Lonelyhearts* and *Day of the Locust*, who view the consumers of mass culture as essentially passive recipients of naturalized mass-produced dreams. The problem, as Davis sees it, is not that the consumers of mass culture accept all they see, read, or hear as "nature," "truth," or even "news," but that part of the very power of the mass media is the ability to allow the consumer to see the machinery, giving the consumer a sense of agency while still influencing the consumer. Frequently in the work of Davis, as in Hughes's "Advertisement for the Waldorf-Astoria," the limits of mass culture are emphasized when the narratorial consciousness momentarily abandons the journalistic mode and identifies with the African-American folk (as it does in "What Do You Want America?"). Given the titles of Davis's collections of poems in the 1930s—*Black Man's Verse*, *I Am the American Negro*, and *Through Sepia Eyes*—such an identification is implicit even when it is not explicit in a particular poem.

In short, Davis enters the heated debate in Left circles about the nature of the influence of mass culture and the ability of the forms, and even the institutions, of mass culture to be used for liberationist or "progressive" politics. Relatively little theoretical work around the relationship of mass culture and more "serious" art was done by left-wing intellectuals in the United States during the 1930s until the rise of the group of intellectuals organized around the *Partisan Review* in its second "anti-Stalinist" incarnation in the late 1930s (and the attitude of the *Partisan Review* intellectuals to mass culture was decidedly negative—which is not surprising considering that the founders of this version of the magazine, Phillip Rahv and William Phillips, during their earlier affiliation with the CPUSA had been among the most extreme Third Period proponents of a revolutionary worker's culture).[33] Rather, the debate was conducted largely through the novels, short stories, poems, and plays of Left writers. What is interesting about this quite diverse group of writers is that few of them completely rejected mass culture, even during the Third Period, and few uncritically valorized it, even during the Popular Front. Rather more typically, Left writers of 1930s and 1940s drew on the resources of mass culture even as they questioned the function of mass culture within society and, indeed, the implications of their own use of mass culture. Thus, despite the claims to the contrary by Richard Pells and other scholars, a work such as Nathanael West's *Miss Lonelyhearts*, with its conscious formal debt to the comic strip while savagely critiquing mass culture, is a typical work of the literary Left during the 1930s.[34] Even a writer so antagonistic to mass culture as Sterling Brown nonetheless embraced the vaudeville and tent show singer Ma Rainey as a figure of the folk spirit. As mentioned above with respect to the problem of "authentically" representing racial, ethnic, and regional difference in the face of previously existing popular culture representations, African-American writers served as models for these complex "literary" interactions with popular culture because of the long history of such interactions by African-American writers dating back to, at least, Dunbar.

In order to make this simultaneous critique and reclamation of mass culture work, it is necessary for the narratorial consciousness to occupy a liminal position between insider and outsider. In the case of Davis, while there is explicit and implicit narratorial identification with the African-American folk, even to the extent of claiming to be *the* American Negro, the primary speaker rarely uses a specifically African-American vernacular; a stylized, generically "American" colloquial voice is assumed much more frequently. Of Davis's work collected in the 1930s, only "Jazz Band" is voiced in an identifiably African-American vernacular.[35] More typical would be the recreation of a blues-inflected African-American folk or popular secondary voice that is clearly distinguished from the alternately hard-boiled and "literary" voice of the primary speaker, as in "Notes on a Summer Night" from the 1937 *I Am the American Negro*:

> Twenty brownskin babies suckle the wet teats of gin bottles
> > at Mojo Mike's in Chicago
> Twenty gin guzzling gals gone to the dogs with a grin at
> > two bucks a throw
>
> (43)

When the folk or popular voice appears, it is not one of the rural South and "traditional" culture, but rather that of an urban African-American hipster whose voice is closely related to that of the commercial blues and the rhythm and blues "novelty song" and is sharply distinguished from the primary speaker:

> "Not now, anyhow" says the barber shop porter
> In a forty dollar suit ogling sheer frocked gals
> "Gimme a skinny chick
> When it's too hot to cover up nights
> They don't cut off no breeze
>
> (44)

The only possible moment of narratorial identification with the folk is an apostrophe by the primary speaker to "Mandy Lou" (whose name is typically "folk" and "Southern"). Even here it is a strangely culturally hybrid (and synaesthetic) moment, with the primary speaker and Mandy Lou encountering an un-natural pastoral scene in a small Illinois city where clouds playing a "mazurka" (suggesting European, particularly Eastern European, immigrant culture) on a "banjo moon" (suggesting rural Southern folk culture, black and white). Interestingly, it is at this moment when Davis is at his most "high literary" and least "hard-boiled pulp." This "high literary" assertion of common identity with the African-American folk is, as we have seen, typical of Davis in his longer poems (e.g., "Today I see America clawing me like a tiger caged with a hare"). So even at the moments of narratorial identification with the folk, a certain distance is formally maintained, a distance that is emphasized by those other moments where the folk voice is more clearly distinguished from the narratorial consciousness.

Conclusion: Countee Cullen and the End
of the New Negro Renaissance

Countee Cullen, the poet of the New Negro Renaissance most publicly acclaimed during the 1920s, virtually ceased to write lyric poetry after the early 1930s. As Gerald Early points out, there has been much speculation by critics as to why.[36] The general scholarly consensus is that this was due to a sort of emotional and artistic exhaustion.[37] A few have suggested that Cullen's relative poetic silence was part of a general end to optimism of the New Negro Period.[38] Yet in many respects Cullen was a public part of the Left literary subculture of the 1930s and the early 1940s. Like Langston Hughes and the black journalist, critic, and literary editor Eugene Gordon, Cullen signed on to the League of Professional Groups for Ford and Foster's *Culture and the Crisis*, a pamphlet supporting the CPUSA presidential ticket of William Z. Foster and James W. Ford in 1932. He was also involved with a number of Left-initiated Harlem cultural groups, such as Vanguard and the Harlem Cultural Committee. Cullen's later endorsement of a dinner for Benjamin Davis, one of the leading black members of the CPUSA (and later a successful candidate for New York City Council), was prominently featured in the CPUSA press. He was also an occasional contributor to *New Masses*.

Cullen's poem, "Scottsboro, Too, Is Worth Its Song" first appeared in the *Daily Worker* in 1933. This poem chastises American poets for their lack of support for the "Scottsboro Boys," the cause célèbre of the Communist movement before the Spanish Civil War, suggesting that racism is responsible for the relative silence compared to the outpouring during the Sacco and Vanzetti case in the 1920s:

> Here in epitome
> Is all disgrace
> And epic wrong,
> Like wine to brace
> The minstrel heart, and blare it into song.
>
> Surely, I said,
> Now will the poets sing.
> But they have raised no cry.
> I wonder why.

(*Medea*, 96–97)

Cullen was in part wrong, as he well knew, in the sense that there was a whole sub-genre of Scottsboro poems and verse plays. However, his point was correct to the extent that there was not the same public support of the Scottsboro defendants by white liberal writers and intellectuals that marked the Sacco and Vanzetti case. While in part this was no doubt due to the bitter battles between the NAACP and the CPUSA as to the conduct of the defense, Cullen's obvious implication is that it is because the Scottsboro defendants were black and Sacco and Vanzetti white. Cullen's choice of form is interesting because the poem is a sort of truncated version of an irregular ode with its variable meter, rhyme scheme, line length, and stanza length after the manner of Wordsworth's "Ode: Intimations of Immortality." Mirroring the denotative meaning of the poem, the form seems to promise some lengthy outpouring of feeling characteristic of the irregular ode and then pulls up short, withdrawing into a meaningful silence.

Yet this poem may say as much about Cullen as about "the poets." On a certain ideological level Cullen is very much "with" the writers whose work would dominate African-American poetry in the 1930s. In some ways, Cullen's public support of national CPUSA political candidates was a more radical public stand than most black poets of the 1930s ever made—including some who may have been CPUSA members.[39] However, Cullen continued to subscribe to the Dunbarian paradigm that opposed "high" poetry to "low" or "vernacular" poetry. As noted earlier in this chapter, Dunbar's opposition was not simple in that it appeared to valorize his "high" poetry at the expense of his "dialect" poetry while actually requiring the existence of both "high" and "low" in a symbiotic relationship in order for his poetry to fully work. Perhaps it would be more accurate to say that Cullen subscribed to Dunbar's fiction of the tragic African-American poet. Then, having adopted Dunbar's general paradigm, he formally rebels against enforced (by racist expectations) tragedy by rejecting commercially viable "low" poetry for the heroic stance of the "true" neoromantic poet who is his or her own romantic hero. Cullen himself was tricky in his adoption and adaptation of the Dunbarian paradigm in that he found it a congenial vehicle for his interior dramas of race, class, and sexuality. But, however complex Cullen's apparently reductive adaptation of Dunbar may have been, he was unwilling to alter completely the paradigm within which he wrote even as it became politically and aesthetically untenable in a climate in which the representation of the folk experience, the re-creation of the folk voice, and the location of the narratorial consciousness in some sort of relationship with the folk became a mark of "serious" poetry by African-American writers. In a formal sense, "Scottsboro, Too, Is Worth Its Song" is a postmortem for the end of the New Negro Renaissance, signaling an end, in Cullen's view, to one strain of the Dunbarian heritage.

The Left-influenced writers of the 1930s, particularly African-American writers, were intensely aware of the famous paradox that Marx expressed in *The 18th Brumaire of Louis Bonaparte*, where the inevitable use of past "names, battle cries and costumes in order to present the new scene of world history in time-honored disguise and borrowed language" (15) conflicts with the notion that social revolution in the present "cannot draw its poetry from the past, but only from the future" (18). Further, they recognized the irony that the latter sentiment was perhaps the most time-honored sentiment in American culture, resembling both Emersonian notions of self-devel-opment and more apocalyptic Protestant visions of a new order. The problem was how to create literature by, for, and of the people (or the related, but not identical, construct of the folk) during what those authors saw as late capitalism when tradi-tionally in American society, the practice of writing (and even reading) "serious" lit-erature separated the Left author from the people that he or she was trying to speak to, with and for.[40] The legacy of modernism was retained in an opposition to a fem-inized "genteel" literature, in a willingness to jettison or modify received "high" forms, and in a sense of vanguardism. Nonetheless, a paradigm was created that differed from "high" modernism in that "making it new" involved a formal and the-matic construction that theoretically issued from and was accessible to the "folk" or the "people," whether the model in question was a revolutionary model of folk strug-gle or a cultural struggle model of reappropriation from mass culture as authorized by the traditions of the folk.

As the decade of the 1930s wore on, African-American poets, like Left poets gen-erally, showed a greater willingness to draw on the resources of mass culture, creat-ing complex works that foregrounded the conflict between the possibilities and the limitations of mass culture, particularly in the face of previously existing mass cul-ture constructions of the African-American folk that necessarily informed the recep-tion of the work of the poets of the 1930s and early 1940s. In particular, these poets sought to find ways to render vernacular culture that were recognizably "authentic," popularly accessible, at least in theory, and that evaded the "high"–"low" split that they inherited from the still dominating presence of Paul Laurence Dunbar. This may explain, in part, the relative lack of productivity, or lack of publication, on the part of African-American poets active in the 1920s, such as Countee Cullen, Georgia Douglas Johnson, and Anne Spencer, who were unable or unwilling to approach the folk voice and the folk subject in these ways, even when, as in the case of Cullen, they were sym-pathetic to the Communist Left.[41]

5

Hughes's Shakespeare in Harlem and the Rise of a Popular Neomodernism

Langston Hughes is seldom mentioned as one of the authors who are part of the self-consciously "modernist" or "neomodernist" turn in African-American poetry during the 1940s and early 1950s. When Hughes's *Montage of a Dream Deferred* appeared in 1951, it was characterized as a rehash of earlier work or even old-fashioned.[1] This critique, which implicitly or explicitly compared Hughes's work unfavorably to that of other African-American writers considered incontestably "modern," such as Brooks, Tolson, and Hayden, was largely turned on its head during the cultural nationalist era of the 1960s and 1970s. In the "Black Arts" era, Hughes's proto-"Black Aesthetic" was praised and the "whiteness" and integrationist irrelevance of the "high" neomodernists were attacked.[2] However, contrary to the claims by such critics as Saunders Redding and Ralph Ellison that Hughes's art essentially remained the same throughout the 1930s and 1940s, Hughes attempted to create a "usable" African-American "neomodernist" poetry derived from popular African-American expressive culture, popular "literary" poetry, and "high" modernism.[3]

In part, Hughes's popular neomodernism of the early 1950s seemed to some observers a rehashing of his earlier work because it did in fact proceed from his development as a poet through the 1930s and 1940s. As noted in chapter 3, Hughes began the 1930s writing three types of poetry for three relatively discrete audiences—the "literate" African American, the literary Left, and the "high" literary—and ended the decade writing largely to an imagined, and to some extent realized, unified popular audience rooted in, but not restricted to, the African-American communities of the

North and West. This development saw a marked return by Hughes, like many other Left artists of the Popular Front, to the materials of popular culture, notably music, popular theatre, broadcast radio, and film. Also like other writers of that period, Hughes accompanied his use of popular culture with a questioning of the implications of such a use of materials and institutions that were part of a political and economic system that he saw as basically inimical to the interests of African Americans, and the mass of Americans generally. However, unlike the work by those writers associated with the more ironical and self-doubting model that I associate with Gwendolyn Brooks (as the most powerful example of a "high" neomodernist poet in the 1940s), Hughes's work is generally more sanguine about the ability of the poet to appropriate such popular culture discourses without being in turn appropriated, and to speak to and for the "people" as an insider—or at least to authentically represent and recreate the popular voice.

"If This Radio Was Good I'd Get KDQ": Popular Culture,
"High" Culture, and the Construction of a Popular
African-American Literary Audience

Hughes's *Shakespeare in Harlem* (1942), his first collection of poetry for adults with a "mainstream" publisher since the 1927 *Fine Clothes to the Jew*, seems in many respects a return to Hughes's poetics of the late 1920s with its heavy use of the blues lyric and a deemphasis of overt "protest." Many reviewers, particularly African-American and/or Left reviewers, including Eda Lou Walton and Frank Marshall Davis, did see the collection as a facile and conservative retreat from Hughes's more ostensibly militant poetry in the 1930s.[4] As noted earlier, such charges by Left reviewers had dogged Hughes since the 1920s. This criticism fails to take into account the full range of Hughes's "engaged" work of the late 1930s, particularly the play "Don't You Want to be Free," instead focusing narrowly on Hughes's earlier collections of poetry and his poems published in "major" journals.

When viewed in the context of his work in theater where Hughes made much use of vernacular musical forms, such as the blues and gospel, *Shakespeare in Harlem* is revealed not as a return to the 1920s but as a logical development of Hughes's work in the 1930s. Like "Don't You Want to Be Free," *Shakespeare in Harlem* is an attempt to create an "authentically" popular African-American poetry that is "modern," formally and emotionally accessible to a mass audience through the use of the resources of popular culture, and, despite Hughes's own claim in the prefatory note that the collection is "a book of light verse," engaged with the "social realist" tradition of 1930s Left poetry.

That Hughes's was attempting to translate the successful hybrid of poetry, popular theater, social protest, and vernacular music of "Don't You Want to Be Free" to the printed page is further emphasized by the stage directions that appear in the collection's author's note, "Blues, ballads, and reels to read aloud, crooned, shouted, recited, and sung. Some with gestures, some not—as you like. None with a far away voice." As Steven Tracy notes about *Shakespeare in Harlem*, "Having presented a series of dramatic monologues in a variety of forms using blues stanzas and rhythms in *Fine Clothes*, Hughes went one step further by explicitly inviting performance and audience participation in this volume; the invitation had been only implicit in the oral base of the earlier poems."[5] Such a construct of an oral poetry in which there is a call and response relationship among the poet, the popular voice, and the imagined audience was made quite explicit in much of Hughes's work in the 1930s from *The Negro Mother* and *Scottsboro Limited* to "Don't You Want to Be Free" and "Air Raid Over Harlem." However, *Shakespeare in Harlem* represents his first large-scale effort to establish such a relationship in a lyric form on the printed page. In short, *Shakespeare in Harlem* is in many respects one of the last pure expressions of the side of Popular Front poetics that imagined that such a popular, and popular culture–derived, poetry was possible.

This is not to say that Hughes viewed popular culture uncritically and simply opposed his optimistic take to the more ambivalent stance of Brooks and other Left poets, such as Kenneth Fearing and Joy Davidman. Hughes's best known belletristic critique of mass culture, "Note on Commercial Theatre," attacked what Hughes saw as "inauthentic" mass-culture appropriations of African-American popular culture. Yet even here Hughes, who, after all, wrote for the commercial theater, posited an authentic popular culture that could be utilized by a cultural insider. A similar critique is made in the "Mammy Songs" section of *Shakespeare in Harlem*. On occasion during the late 1930s and early 1940s, most notably in "Air Raid Over Harlem" and in the "Simple" stories (which first appeared in the *Chicago Defender* in 1943), Hughes created an authorial persona who was seen as distinct from the speaking folk subject. However, while this distinction was raised, ultimately the re-creation of the authentic popular African-American voice by the narratorial consciousness of the African-American poet who is willing to submit himself, or herself, to the folk is never really in doubt in the way that it is in Brooks's work.

The first series of poems in *Shakespeare in Harlem*, "Seven Moments of Love," establishes the basic framework for the collection in which "folk" or "popular" African-American forms of expressive culture are simultaneously paired with and set against "high" literary forms. The subtitle, "an un-sonnet series in blues," and the near-sonnet length of the individual poems ranging from thirteen lines to twenty lines— one is actually fourteen lines—force the reader to read the poems against the expectations for a traditional sonnet series much like the way that Wallace Stevens's long poetic series of near-sonnet length, such as "Le Monocle de Mon Oncle" and "Sunday Morning," almost inevitably have the first-time reader counting lines to see if the poems are "really" sonnets. At the same time, the subtitle also leads the reader to read the poems against the formal expectations for the blues, and the blues-based poetry that Hughes, along with Sterling Brown and Waring Cuney, pioneered in the 1920s and early 1930s. And while the subtitle privileges the vernacular or "popular" form over the "high" form, the interplay between the blues and the "traditional" sonnet sequence is far more reciprocal than the subtitle would indicate.

The most obvious conjunction between the blues, particularly the tradition of the commercially performed and recorded blues, and the sonnet drawn by Hughes (other than their mutual origin in song) is the common subject of an obsessive romantic love and its perceived betrayal. In choosing this subject, Hughes avoids the comparatively recent African-American subgenre of "protest" sonnets most famously associated with Claude McKay (and prominently continued in the 1940s by Margaret Walker). He also avoids the even more recent subgenre of the "protest" blues of which Waring Cuney's lyrics set to music on Josh White's 1941 recording *Southern Exposure* and Hughes's own "Red Clay Blues," co-written with Richard Wright and published in *New Masses* in 1939, are among the best-known examples.[6] In short, Hughes does not recast the folk voice of "Seven Moments of Love" in an overtly oppositional form that would supposedly stand outside and against mass commercial versions of the blues and the "genteel" "high" culture form of the love sonnet. Instead, Hughes chooses to adopt a construct of the folk voice that was much more consonant with mass-culture representations of the speaking folk subject and with "high"-culture representations of the middle-class (or middle-status-obsessed) subject with a unobtainable upper-class love object. While Hughes formally and thematically revises both the commercial blues and the "genteel" sonnet considerably, he essentially argues that both the blues and sonnet in their popular forms have been vehicles for indirect but telling social criticism. The blues content of the blues-sonnet hybrid transforms the bourgeois-lesser aristocratic social context of the sonnet sequence in English since Wyatt and Spenser into a specifically, and "authentically," African-American working-class one. At the same time the invocation of the sonnet tradition is used to claim genuinely "literary" status for the poems, and by extension the African-American popular lyric associated with the blues, and the African-American speaking subject. Thus the poems of the series are authorized both by their obvious, and self-proclaimed, differences from the sonnet sequence and by their less obvious—hence the need for the negative sign of the "un-sonnet sequence"—but nonetheless considerable affinity with the sonnet.[7]

However, despite the positive and negative expectations for the sequence with respect to the blues and the sonnet set up by Hughes's subtitle, it is obvious that the poems of the sequence are neither blues nor sonnets in any typical sense. As noted earlier, the number of lines in the poems formally restate the epithet "un-sonnet" with the near-sonnet length of the poems (and in one case sonnet length), invoking the sonnet while frustrating the most popularly known "rule" (and often the only "rule" observed in the modernist and postmodernist sonnet): a sonnet is always fourteen lines in length. Similarly, Hughes uses end rhyme in such a way as to suggest a certain regularity that vanishes on closer inspection. The couplet is the basic unit of end rhyme employed in the series with only the very occasional repetition of an earlier rhyme. However, interspersed among the couplets are tercets, as in the third poem in the series "Bed Time":

> Or if it wasn't so late I might take a walk
> And find somebody to kid and talk.
> But since I got to get up at day,
> I might as well put it on in the hay.
> I can sleep *so* good with you away!

> (5)

Not only is the use of end rhyme here both emphatic and apparently idiosyncratic, but the length of the lines themselves varys considerably and the lines are not easily scanned except those where Hughes indicates stressed syllables with italics. (In some poems, the idiosyncrasy of the rhyme scheme is further complicated by the occasional use of single unrhymed lines.) The reason that the lines are hard to scan authoritatively is in no small part due to the gloss that Hughes has already provided for the reader in both the author's note and in the subtitle for the section. The connection that Hughes draws between the blues (where the number of stresses in a typical line are regular, but placed in lines of often varying length according to the interpretation of the performer) and the poems in the series reminds the reader that a wide range of scansions for the poems are possible according to the emotional and artistic needs of the interpreter-reader who, as Steven Tracy notes, has been authorized by Hughes to create his or her own reading of the poem. This is a double authorization since in making the poems part of the process of popular expression, Hughes is given authority by a construct of the folk or the people in much the same way that he is by the personified community of Harlem in "Air Raid Over Harlem." At the same time, a bluesified "un-sonnet" with flexible scansion essentially validates the "popular" aspect of popular culture in that it demonstrates the ability of the "people" to evade both the restrictive confines of a "standard" cultural arbiter and the more alluring web of mass commercial culture in the sense that it is criticized in "Note on Commercial Theatre."

However, the poems of the "Seven Moments of Love" sequence are obviously not formally blues after the manner of *aab* stanza blues poems adapted from the typical twelve-bar blues that had been pioneered by Hughes in the 1920s. Instead, the claim to the blues announced by the series subtitle is made on the basis of the narrator's stance, the poems' ostensible subject (the disappointment in romantic love of an "average" African American as opposed to the more bourgeois or aristocratic speaker of the traditional love sonnet), their vernacular diction, and blues phrases and images (the sun going down, the missing trunk, the empty bed). On one hand, this invocation of the blues shows, contrary to some criticisms of Hughes as a simple mimic of the basic blues form rather than an innovator within the genre of blues poetry, a will by Hughes to stretch the boundaries of blues poetry nearly as much as he does the sonnet.[8] On the other, Hughes's calling attention to the blues in this series when there are far more "regular" blues lyrics elsewhere in *Shakespeare in Harlem*, not to mention the earlier body of "regular" blues poems by Hughes, seems to deliberately frustrate the formal expectations of the reader in much the same way the epithet "un-sonnet" does.

In addition to Hughes's formal evasions of the expectations for blues poetry that he played no small part in originally creating, Hughes grounds the sequence completely in an urban setting and in urban mass culture, as explicitly indicated in the author's note to the collection that locates the cultural context of the poems in "Harlem, Beale Street, West Dallas and Chicago's South Side." Here Hughes avoids any reference to a rural setting or rural origin of the blues, thus distinguishing his sequence not only from the more folkloric and rural constructs of the blues, particularly those of Brown, but also from most of the blues poems of Waring Cuney and Hughes's own early blues poetry. Where Hughes's earlier blues poems had largely recreated the voice of the new African-American emigrant to the urban North from the rural South, far more of the blues and blues-inflected poems of *Shakespeare in*

Harlem are in the voice of the urban native, North and South, whose rural origins, if any, are far in the past.

The "Seven Moments of Love" sequence itself is full of iconic markers of modern urban African-American life: furniture store installment plans, bus stations, brownstone stoops, radio broadcasts, rooming houses, the WPA, alarm clocks (also, and probably not accidentally on Hughes's part, a notable feature in the period's most famous work of literature by an African American dealing with urban life, Richard Wright's *Native Son*). The most telling reference to urban popular culture takes place in the poem "Bed Time" where the narrator imagines tuning into a jazz broadcast on the radio and listening to Count Basie. The Basie orchestra can be seen as a sort of totem for Hughes's poetry in the 1940s in that it played a heavily blues-based dance-oriented music that was indisputably modern, popular, and urban. That the Basie band was based in Kansas City, a city to which Hughes felt a strong connection from his childhood in Kansas, no doubt aided Hughes's artistic identification.[9] The use of the Basie band as emblem of African-American expressive culture also marked a continuity between Hughes's work in the 1930s and that of the 1940s. As noted earlier, the Basie band participated in various Left culture productions, including the "Spirituals to Swing" concerts in 1937 organized by John Hammond under the auspices of *New Masses* and other Left institutions. Hughes's identification with Kansas City jazz promoted on a national scale by the cultural Left also served as a bridge to his later work, since musicians associated with the Kansas City and Southwest "territory" bands, most famously Charlie Parker, Lester Young, and Charlie Christian, would be crucial to the rise of bebop, a music which was the declared inspiration for *Montage of a Dream Deferred* (1951).[10]

Thus Hughes's use of the formal and thematic resources of the blues in *Shakespeare in Harlem* is not simply a return to an earlier poetics, as a number of critics over the years have suggested, but in fact mirrors a development in jazz in which heavily blues-based dance music became immensely popular. The appeal of this music, which was popular, modern, urban, and yet retained a well-known continuity with the "folk" past of the blues, as an artistic model for Hughes is obvious. This musical model was simultaneously popular, avant-garde, traditional without being curatorial, serious, and humorous, encouraging the adaptation, alteration, and intermingling of "high" and "folk" culture. In short, it was the perfect vehicle for the sly, double-voiced, and yet, paradoxically, impassioned lyric that had long been a characteristic of Hughes's best work, including, as argued in chapter 3, much of his "revolutionary" poetry.

Perhaps, most important, the model of the blues that Hughes derived in large part from the Kansas City bands (along with his earlier conceptions of blues poetry) is one that allows a double-voiced commentary on sexual politics and the political concerns more commonly associated with Hughes's revolutionary poetry. In this Hughes anticipates the feminists of the 1970s, and echoes some within the CPUSA of the 1930s and 1940s, in connecting the domestic with "larger" social questions.[11] This sequence of love poems is saturated with references to the "larger" world of African-American life during the Great Depression—to unemployment, the hardness of work, poverty, poor housing, and racism. This is not to say that the poems are "really" about racism or class oppression, but that there is no separation between the domestic sphere and the social sphere within Hughes's blues model. Contrary to the typical conceit of the love sonnet sequence from Petrarch to Millay, there is no fiction on Hughes's part that these blues monologues by the narrator "Jack" express the author's actual feelings in any direct way. Neither is there an allegorical subtext of the hierarchy of aristocratic political power as sorted through the emotion of love that there is in Thomas Wyatt's loose translations of Petrarch or in Edmund Spenser's *Amoretti*. Instead, Hughes creates a unified political landscape in which even the most stereotypically domestic (and most normatively gendered) scene at the end of the series is marked by concerns of money, race, work, urban alienation, and displacement:

> So let's just forget what this fuss was about.
> Come on home and bake some corn bread,
> And crochet a quilt for our double bed,
> And wake me up gentle when the dawn appears
> Cause that old alarm clock sho hurts my ears.
> Here's five dollars, Cassie. Buy a ticket back.
> I'll meet you at the bus station.
>
> (10–11)

Here the speaker Jack writes a reconciliatory response to a similar letter from Cassie—at least as interpreted by Jack since the reader never actually sees Cassie's letter. The series ends with the folk or popular African-American subject provisionally reestablishing a community that retains roots in an older, rural African-American folk culture as signified by cornbread and homemade quilts. However, as the ending of the series makes clear, this community is definitely urban, marked by alarm clocks and bus stations. Jack's model of community is provisional in that a tension remains as the male subject attempts to dictate the terms of community to the female subject while implicitly recognizing the ability of the female subject to dissolve that community. In short, Hughes argues that the spirit of the blues, as he sees them, allows for the expression of female and male subjectivity within a genuine, if unstable, community of feeling that is at the same time "traditional" and "modern," incorporating both quilt making and radio broadcasts of urban big-band jazz. Like the title of the collection where "Shakespeare" is not privileged over "Harlem," the sonnet is invoked in the series by Hughes to declare the worth, and the formal flexibility of the blues model, which in turn captures, or recaptures, the lyric from the aristocratic (or pseudo-aristocratic) focus with which the lyric is traditionally associated. This vision of the lyric, like Jack's letter to Cassie, is closely related to Hughes's work in the late 1930s, and much of the more optimistic works of the literary Left in that period generally, in that it imagines that a literature (and audience) is possible that is both social and personal, authentically "folk" and authentically "popular," "literary" and "mass."

"I Guess I Ought to Know How I Want to Go:" Making the "Authentic" Literary and the "Literary" Authentic

Most of the sections of the *Shakespeare in Harlem* follow the pattern of pairing a "high" literary form with and against African-American folk and popular musical and verbal expression introduced in the opening "Seven Moments of Love." The "Declarations" section sets the aphorism with and against the blues and street rhymes. The "Ballads" section plays with "high" literary, popular or folk literary (e.g., the Scots ballads of Robert Burns and the *Constab Ballads* of McKay), and popular musical (specifically African-American popular musical) versions of the ballad, a literary form favored as a vernacular vehicle by New Negro Renaissance poets. "Death in Harlem" invokes the elegy, a staple of African-American literature from Dunbar's "Frederick Douglass" to the present, while also drawing much upon African-American popular song, particularly modern versions of the old "badman" story. For example, the poem "Sylvester's Dying Bed" in "Death in Harlem" is close in form and spirit to singer and guitarist Willie McTell's "Dying Crapshooter's Blues." McTell first recorded "Dying Crapshooter's Blues" in the 1940s for John A. Lomax for the Library of Congress. Despite the word "blues" in the title, the song was a blues-inflected popular music ballad in much the same manner as Cab Calloway's versions of "St. James Infirmary Blues" and "Minnie the Moocher." The lyrics of "Dyin' Crapshooter Blues" tell the deathbed story of a gambler and "rounder," Jess, who was shot down by the police on the streets of Atlanta. Sandwiched between a brief description of the shooting and a similarly short picture of the death of Jess, is basically the gambler's last testament filled with instructions for who will be mourners (prostitutes) and pallbearers (gamblers) and for the correct behavior in Jess's final minutes (dancing the Charleston). Hughes's poem a opens with a first-person image of a dying "rounder"

> I woke up this mornin'
> 'Bout half-past three.
> All de womens in town
> Was gathered round me.
>
> Sweet gals was a-moanin',
> "Sylvester's gonna die!"
> And a hundred pretty mamas
> Bowed their heads to cry.

(68)

Interestingly enough (particularly since McTell is somewhat famous for his evasive answers to a series of questions by John A. Lomax about race relations in the South), McTell's version is far more socially pointed and outraged (and poetically inventive) than Hughes's.[12] However, a similar movement can be seen in the two works as they move from a humorous hyperbole to an almost heroic pathos to a grim resignation. Whether or not Hughes ever heard McTell's song is unknown, and even unlikely; my point, however, is not that Hughes was influenced by McTell, but that he was operating here within the context of a type of African-American popular song of which McTell's song is one of the poetically most notable.

The invocation of "high" forms—the elegy, the sonnet, the ballad—much favored by previous African-American writers reminds the reader that Hughes is not just posing a simple opposition between "European" (and "Euro-American") high culture and "African American" folk and popular culture, but is also engaging earlier African-American strategies, including Hughes's own, to represent and recreate the

African-American subject in ways that an American audience (or American audiences) could recognize as both "authentic" *and* "literary." The problem that such strategies attempt to solve is not only that the qualities of universal "literariness" and of popular "authenticity" were (and are) seen by many readers as antagonistic, but also that the effectiveness of markers of "authenticity" vary from audience to audience and period to period. As noted earlier, the legacy of minstrelsy and other popular-culture re-creations of the African-American folk voice created (and create) various paradoxical expectations of "authentic" African-American culture. On one hand, certain conventions of the African-American popular voice—of orthography, syntax, tone, figuration, subject matter, and so on—existed (and exist) in popular American culture and clearly influence the ability of the reader-auditor to identify a particular representation–re-creation as "authentic." The conventions of such representations–re-creations vary according to period, stance of the author, and intended audience—though some conventions have been remarkably stable, such as the dropping of the "g" at the end of the gerund as a distinctive mark of African-American speech (as well as a convention of representing southern speech and working-class speech generally) when the "g" in a gerund is often dropped by many sorts of Americans in normal speech. On the other hand, the "authenticity" of the recreated folk voice, particularly by Left authors, African American and white, was (and is) attested to by the degree to which the re-creation differs from "mainstream" mass culture re-creations seen as degrading, old-fashioned, and patently "inauthentic." In other words, the authenticity of the "folk" poetry of Brown and Hughes is attested, as James Weldon Johnson argues, in no small part because its representation of vernacular speech visibly (and audibly) differs from the old conventions of "dialect" poetry.[13]

What makes the poetry of Hughes and Brown more authentic than the older dialect poetry, in the view of Johnson (and indeed, for the most part, the Communist Left to which Johnson was often antagonistic), was the alleged superiority of Brown and Hughes in the utilization of such "genuine" folk forms as the spirituals, the blues, and the tall tale. To this folkloric authentication was added, particularly in the 1930s, what might be seen as the documentary impulse that posed its "realism" against what were seen as the sentimental or primitivist fantasies of mass culture. As Walter Kalaidjian points out, a good example of this opposition of documented "reality" and mass-culture "fantasy" is found in cartoons from the May 1930 issue of *New Masses*, where a panel of "The White Bourgeois Version of the Negro" is posed against a panel "as the White Worker Knows Him." The first panel consists of various mass-culture images of the African-American folk—as gambler, dancer, musician, sexualized savage, criminal, religious "shouter," and so on—and the second of images of the African-American as worker—miner, agricultural laborer, porter, millworker, and so on—and victim of racist violence. This opposition is problematic in part because of its assumption of the ability of white workers to stand outside mass culture and because, as Kalaidjian argues, it excludes a huge range of African-American expressive culture, specifically jazz, popular dance, and religion, because of its connection to mass culture.[14]

The problem, however, is more complicated than Kalaidjian allows. This opposition is not limited to the "CP leadership" as Kalaidjian claims, but, as I have argued, is common among African-American artists and intellectuals inside and outside the literary Left. The obvious point needs to be recalled that the use of African-American expressive culture in American "high" culture and mass culture was far from benign, however lacking in nuance Siegel's cartoon might be; such usages were indeed linked, in Kalaidjian's terms, "to the racist stereotypes of the black minstrel tradition: the surreal world of Jim Crow, Zeb Coon, Amos n' Andy, plantation medleys, and "August Hams."[15] In short, one should not underestimate the difficulty of negotiating the representation of the African-American folk or popular subject that many in the Communist Left undertook in the late 1920s and early 1930s when viewing their efforts from the 1990s.

However, the artists and intellectuals of the 1930s and 1940s were forced to recognize that the reception and interpretation of even the most authentically "folkish" expressions are largely structured by mass culture as demonstrated by the "native" African dance that dissolves into an American ring shout at the beginning of the film adaptation of *The Emperor Jones*, suggesting to the audience a certain interpretation of the ancestry and meaning of African-American folk culture. Such forms as the urban blues, dance, and jazz are clearly even more a part of the web of mass culture. Thus, the paradox of "authentic" representation was that this tension between the positive and negative expectations set up by mass culture forced a constant renegotiation of what conventions were acceptable and how far from an unacceptable, but commonly held, convention one could stray.

In the case of Hughes and *Shakespeare in Harlem*, an example of this process of renegotiation is the fact that, as Steven Tracy notes, Hughes revised the poem "Down and Out," which first appeared in the October 1926 issue of *Opportunity* as "Down an' Out," so as to generally (though not always) make the orthography of the poem more "standard"—the exceptions having to do with the sonic arrangement of certain lines.[16] While it is impossible to know exactly why Hughes made these revisions, it seems obvious that by the late 1930s, he felt the original to be too close to conventions of "dialect" poetry and mass-culture re-creations of the folk that later seemed unacceptable. If that is the case, then it is likely that either Hughes felt constrained, at least at one time, to be influenced by those conventions of "dialect" or that the conventions were so ubiquitous that Hughes wrote within them unconsciously—at least until changes in conventions of "authenticity" made him sensitive to how much the older conventions influenced him. (Though a third possibility that there was a shift in the meaning of the older conventions, so that they came to be seen as solely patronizing or derrogatory, also needs to be noted.)

On the thematic level, the "Mammy Songs" section is another example of this paradoxical renegotiation. This titling of the section containing the most overtly "political" poems in the collection (including the book's most famous poems, "Sharecroppers," "Merry-Go-Round," and "Ku Klux") obviously attempts to recapture the "mammy" (and, by extention, the folk) from mass-culture representations of the "mammy," most notably the 1939 film version of *Gone With the Wind*. This point is further emphasized by the first "song" of the section, "Southern Mammy Sings":

The nations they is fightin'
And the nations they done fit.
Sometimes I think that white folks
Ain't worth a little bit.
  No, m'am!
Ain't worth a little bit.

     (75)

Here is what is supposed to be the authentic utterance of the "mammy," the words, perhaps, behind the glare that Butterfly McQueen gives Vivian Leigh in a scene in Scarlet O'Hara's bedroom in *Gone With the Wind*. However, clearly the power of this "authentic" utterance depends on the "inauthentic" folk persona created by mass culture.

Blues Men and Women: Gender, Community, and the Blues

In *Shakespeare in Harlem*, Hughes, to borrow Henry Louis Gates's notion of "Signifyin(g)," both interrogates and pays tribute to earlier literary attempts to represent and recreate the African-American folk subject within the unstable matrix of "high" culture, folk culture, and popular culture.[17] Thus, not only does Hughes pair "high" culture with (and against) "popular" culture but he also invokes, honors, and critiques other African-American literary strategies of "authenticity" that employ constructs of "folk" culture. The "Blues for Men" section, for example, is much in the spirit of Sterling Brown's "Tin Roof Blues" and such earlier poems of Hughes as "Po' Boy Blues" and "Homesick Blues" from *Fine Clothes to the Jew*, where the African-American emigrant to the urban North from the rural South regrets his rash move. Unlike the "blues" "un-sonnets" of "Seven Moments of Love," the poems in "Blues for Men" almost all adhere formally to the typical literary imitation of the twelve-bar blues with their six-line adaptations of the *aab* blues stanza. The poems of "Blues for Men" also differ from those of "Seven Moments of Love" in that the speakers of the former section frequently mention their origins in the South despite their present location in the North. Direct references to urban mass culture are far less obvious than in the other sections of *Shakespeare in Harlem*. As in Brown's *Southern Road*, the model for the authentic recreation of the folk voice is the itinerant male blues guitarist or pianist, not the jazz orchestra or the female "classic" blues singer backed by a jazz band.

  The one poem of "Blues for Men" not set in the North, "Mississippi Levee," utilizes the trope of the southern flood as a marker of authentic African-American culture in the South. In large part, the southern floods of the late 1920s were able to function as such a marker through the work of African-American blues artists, notably Bessie Smith's "Backwater Blues," which made the flood available to "literary" artists as a certified figure of the experience and culture of the southern folk. The flood trope found its most famous poetic expressions in Brown's "Ma Rainey" and "Cabaret." These poems from *Southern Road* represent African-American musicians representing the southern floods—with "Ma Rainey" advancing a vision of an authentic relationship between the folk artist and the folk audience and "Cabaret" depicting the "inauthentic" relationship between audience and artist resulting from an urban mass-culture appropriation of southern "folk" material. The flood trope as used by Brown declares an intertextual relationship between "high" literature and folk expression, notably the blues, in which the primacy of the southern folk experience and expression is clearly affirmed.

Thus Hughes's use of this trope connects the "Blues for Men" section not only to the experience, music, and religion (the "cold muddy waters" of Hughes's poem echoes descriptions of the Jordan River in the spirituals and black religious rhetoric) of a still existing African-American community in the rural South but, like the rest of section, also to that vision of African-American literature (of which Brown was the chief proponent), which argued (to take Raymond Williams's terms) for the development of an "emergent" oppositional culture through cultivation of a "residual" rural culture in the South.[18] However, having paid tribute both to those blues singers who used the flood trope and to Brown's appropriations of those singers and their representations of the flood, Hughes also signals his difference from Brown:

> Don't know why I build this levee
> And de levee don't do no good.
> Don't know why I build this levee
> When de levee don't do no good.
> I pack a million bags o'sand
> But de water still makes a flood.

> (46–47)

Taken by itself, the poem seems to adopt a stoicism that resembles that of the folk subject as a stoical and self-conscious "philosopher" found in much of *Southern Road*, notably "Memphis." However, when Hughes's poem is seen in the context of the other poems of the "Blues for Men" section, the effect is quite different. For one thing, "Mississippi Levee," as in much of the collection, is obsessed with work—the difficulty of it, the lack of it, looking for it, and so on—where labor does not figure as a particularly large part of *Southern Road* in a specific way. (Even in the title poem "Southern Road," the actual labor of the convicts serves as background, albeit a very significant background.) As with the "Seven Moments of Love" section, the marks of the Depression—the WPA, mass unemployment, urban hunger—appear throughout the section along with such more "traditional" blues themes as love, travel, and drinking.

Unlike Brown's poetry, and indeed, a number of Hughes's early blues lyrics, Hughes here does not pose the authentic South against the inauthentic North, folk culture against popular or mass culture. Instead, a continuum of experience and culture is advanced:

> Believe I'll do a little dancin'
> Just to drive my blues away—
> A little dancin'
> To drive my blues away,
> Cause when I'm dancin'
> De blues forgets to stay.

> (38)

It is interesting to compare this willful forgetting to that depicted in Brown's "Children's Children" in the "Tin Roof Blues" section of *Southern Road*. In both cases the process of forgetting by African-Americans in the North is connected to popular music. In the case of Brown's poem, the rejection of the folk heritage as embodied in the spiritual and the work song in favor of mass culture embodied by an unspecified popular music, probably jazz, is a mark of the northern African-American subject's alienation from the authentic folk experience and folk culture. In Hughes's poem, the act of forgetting through dancing to some form of urban popular music, whether urban blues or jazz, argues for a continuity of culture (and experience) between the South and the North, prefiguring Amiri Baraka's concept of the "changing same" or "the blues impulse transferred."[19]

At the same that a certain cultural continuity is argued, with the blues as an icon of authenticity, this continuity is such that it allows for a range of authentic expression, with the blues also as a emblem of cultural pluralism. Hughes's pluralism here is filled with tension between male and female, North and South, recently arrived immigrant from the South and long-time urban resident, "high" culture and "popular" culture, and so on. Nonetheless, Hughes does not define authentic African-American culture against ersatz African-American culture, except in the case of "outside" appropriations that remove the blues, spirituals, and other forms of African-American expression from the context of the African-American community either for the purpose of the box office or for that of ideologically reinforcing categories of racial hierarchy (or both). In short, not only is there a variety of "blues people," but their blues differ considerably in form, subject, theme, imagery, literary landscape, and narrative stance.

This variety is true not only of the encounters of the "blues impulse" with "high" culture, as in the "Seven Moments of Love," "Declarations," and "Death in Harlem" sections of *Shakespeare in Harlem*, but also of the apparently straightforward blues sections, "Blues for Men" and "Blues for Ladies." As the titles of the two "Blues" sections suggest, Hughes attempts to delineate distinctively "male" and "female" approaches to the blues. In order to make these distinctions clear, Hughes significantly breaks with his earlier efforts to recreate the speaking female African-American subject within the blues form (and within the body of work of the most famous female blues singers). In many respects, Hughes's "Blues for Ladies," as seen in the title itself, is based on a normative genteel, if somewhat ironic, model of femininity—despite the presence of prostitution, poverty, and a distinctly ungenteel diction.

Formally, the poems of both blues sections almost always adhere to the typical literary recreations of the "standard" twelve-bar blues mentioned above. Thematically, the "male" blues poems are often concerned with work. However, work does not figure in the "female" poems, except for the occupation of prostitute in "Midnight Chippie's Lament," despite the extraordinarily large numbers (compared to white women) of African-American women who were wage workers in the urban North in the late 1930s and early 1940s.[20] Instead, the "female" poems are most entirely centered by male-female relationships, even in a poem describing poverty ("Down and Out"), where a relationship is seen as a solution for financial hardship and in another where the emphasis is on emotional rather than financial need

("Midnight Chippie's Lament"). The "male" blues poems also often focus on love, but three of the nine poems in the "Blues for Men" section ("Evenin' Air Blues," "Out of Work," and "Mississippi Levee") are simply about work without reference to love and a fourth ("Hey-Hey Blues") is a self-reflexive commentary on the blues performance as folk process.

The "Blues for Ladies" poems are more purely urban than the "Blues for Men" poems. In the former section, there is no mention of the speaker's rural origins in the South, as there frequently is in the latter section. The "female" blues are also far less violent in their language than the "male" blues. Two out of the four male poems focusing on male-female relationships ("Brief Encounter" and "In a Troubled Key") involve the murder or threats of murder of the female partner by the male. The other two "male" blues about love ("Morning After" and "Only Love Blues") contain the almost gleeful insulting of the female by the male. By contrast, there is no such violence in the "female" blues; they remain mournful rather than angry in tone despite male insults and betrayal. These poems are quite different from the "women's" blues of *Fine Clothes to the Jew*, in which the expression of anger and revenge is a notable feature (as it is in the actual work of prominent female blues artists with which Hughes was familiar, such as Ma Rainey and Bessie Smith).[21] The poems of "Blues for Ladies" are much closer in spirit to the repertoire of popular female jazz singers of the 1930s and 1940s, notably Billie Holiday (whose nickname "Lady Day" may be alluded to in Hughes's title), in which (unlike the repetoire of many of the leading African-American male jazz singers) formal blues were relatively uncommon.

What Hughes does here is construct not only a model of "female" blues that is opposed to a "male" model but also a model of "female" blues poetry opposed to the prominent 1930s and early 1940s model of blues and blues-inflected poetry, such as Brown's "Southern Road," Cuney's "Defense Factory Blues," and Wright's "King Joe," in which active (and often violent) assertions of masculinity, race, and class are conflated. As noted earlier, in many respects Hughes here allows the earlier model of an active, often violent, and work-oriented "male" blues poetry to stand—with some significant revisions as to the symbolic geographical location of African-American folk tradition and vernacular culture. The section of mournful and relatively passive "female" blues seems to confirm the notion of action as the province of "male" blues. This passivity stands in contradistinction not only to Hughes's earlier blues poetry but also other vernacular poems of Hughes nearly contemporary with those of *Shakespeare in Harlem*, most notably the well-known series of "Madam" poems that began to appear in 1943.

The passivity of these "female" blues poems in *Shakespeare in Harlem* obviously reinforces the assumptions of a masculinist approach to representing and recreating the folk voice that characterized African-American vernacular poetry during the 1930s, including Hughes's own work. But they also propose a polyvocal model of the folk that may seem unremarkable now, but that was a considerable break from the masculinist practices of the 1930s. However much these poems accept notions of male action and female passivity, they also establish the voice of the female subject as an authentic folk or popular voice that is different from the voice of the male subject. And, unlike the representation and re-creation of the female folk subject from, at least, Du Bois's African "grandfather's grandmother" in the final chapter of *The Souls of Black Folk* to Bigger Thomas's mother in *Native Son*, the female folk subject in the "Blues for Ladies" section is not the embodiment of an anachronistic folk heritage that either is honored and transformed for current use, as in *The Souls of Black Folk*, or rejected and transcended, as in *Native Son*. Instead, the voice of the female subject in "Blues for Ladies" is as contemporary as that of the male subject (and even more urban), and is as much a part of the folk-popular continuum as signaled by the use of the blues form.

As in the "Seven Moments of Love" section, a model of the folk is set up that is not only polyvocal but also one where the different parts of the folk community, while obviously bound together, are in conflict with each other. Hughes consciously heightens the "masculinity" of the male subject and the "femininity" of the female subject so as to emphasize intracommunity difference. Gender differences stand in for other sorts of difference—economic class, skin color, sexuality, and so on—as well as standing for themselves, within the African-American community, in much the same way that a sense of sexual difference was displaced into racial difference in the work of Countee Cullen in the 1920s and early 1930s.

The final section of *Shakespeare in Harlem*, "Lenox Avenue" is a group of blues and blues-inflected poems dealing for the most part with heterosexual relationships, alternately from the perspective of the male subject and that of the female subject. In a few cases ("Lover's Return," "50–50," and "Early Evening Quarrel"), both the male and female voice are recreated in the same poem, though one voice is usually predominant. The section starts with "Shakespeare in Harlem," a pastiche of popular song and Shakespearean comic song, that begins:

> Hey ninny neigh!
> And a hey nonny noe!
> Where, oh, where
> Did my sweet mama go?
>
> (111)

The question is answered in the second stanza: the "sweet mama" has gone home to her "ma." Thus the section opens with the rupture of community—while at the same time affirming a network of gender ties with the sly differentiation and connection between "sweet mama" and the "ma" to whom the "sweet mama" returns in the second stanza of the poem.

But after a series of poems nearly always representing male-female relationships as struggle and often hostile negotiation, the section ends with a temporary erasure of that conflict in "Love":

> John Henry with his hammer
> Makes a little spark.
> That little spark is love
> Dying in the dark.
>
> (124)

Here the diction is the most overtly "literary" and least "folk" of any poem in the collection. At the same time it names the best-known figure of African-American folklore, a figure frequently invoked in the 1930s and 1940s by Left African-American poets, including Brown, Hughes, Robert Hayden, Melvin Tolson, and Margaret Walker. As in the beginning of the collection, the gaps between "folk" and "literary," male and female, modernity and tradition, are provisionally bridged in a sort of popular front where different communities of interest and sensibility agree to unite while maintaining a critical difference. This provisional unity maintains a continuity with visions of class unity that typified much of Hughes's work in the 1930s and anticipates the utopian vision of African-American race and class unity, where "high" culture and popular culture amalgamate, that surfaces in *Montage of a Dream Deferred* (1951) in "Projection" ("Paul Robeson / Will team up with Jackie Mabley").

Shakespeare in Harlem in many respects can be seen as a product of the Popular Front that maintains its ties, albeit critically, to the earlier "proletarian" and New Negro Renaissance moments while interrogating its own terms. It attempts to synthesize the "literary," the "folk," and the "popular" in a manner that does not simply accept any of those categories. It modifies the typical masculinist paradigm of the folk and the folk voice of 1930s vernacular poetry, even as it pays tribute to that earlier poetry, and helps to establish a new paradigm of the folk and authentic popular expression that is far less male—and far less homophobic. Ironically, the relatively passive female blues singers of *Shakespeare in Harlem* set the stage for the far from passive Alberta K. Johnson of the "Madam" poems. At the same time, the collection retains a concern for racial and class oppression that marked Hughes's poetry in the 1930s and would continue to do so however obliquely for the rest of his career. Hughes in *Shakespeare in Harlem* begins to develop a popular African-American modernism that takes into account the legacy of Third Period and Popular Front Left expressive culture, as well as the legacy of the African-American folk tradition and the demands of the fragmented world of the urban African-American experience that increasingly typified African-American life in the twentieth century.

"Hey Pop! Re-bop! Mop!": Toward *Montage of a Dream Deferred*
and a Popular Neomodernism

Hughes would not again attempt to create a poetic text that fully unified his various social and aesthetic concerns until *Montage of a Dream Deferred* (1951). His next collection, *Jim Crow's Last Stand* (1943), printed by the Negro Publication Society of America (an African-American press associated with the CPUSA) was aimed at an audience that was, at least conceptually, Left, popular, and largely African-American. As Arnold Rampersad notes, Hughes was not successful in unifying the collection as a whole, which ranged from journalistic pieces in a sort of "popular" doggerel to much more realized poems, such as "Note on Commercial Theatre" and "Daybreak in Alabama" (both of which were first published in 1940).[22] Probably the most ambitious poem in its combination of popular African-American expressive culture and a "mass" Left polemical style is "Good Morning, Stalingrad." Here sympathy for the Soviet Union and socialism generally and the struggle against fascism are connected with an antagonism toward Jim Crow.[23] This poem is an amalgam of the colloquial polemical style typical of columnists in the Left press (and columnists in the "mainstream" press, for that matter) and popular blues-inflected African-American song where the Left optimism replaces the pessimism of the original songs (e.g., "Good Morning, Heartache" and "Good Morning Blues") on which the poem draws:

> Goodmorning, Stalingrad!
> When crooks and klansman
> Lift their heads and things is bad,
> I can look across the sea
> And see where simple working folks like me
> Lift their heads, too, with gun in hand
> To drive the fascists from the land.
> You've stood between us well,
> Stalingrad!
> The folks who hate you'd
> Done give you up for dead—
> They were glad.
> *But you ain't dead!*

> (*Collected*, 298)

From an ideological standpoint this poem is interesting in that it challenges many assumptions about Left literature—especially Left literature published by a press run by CPUSA members and sympathizers—during World War II. The poem, and indeed the whole collection, is a militant attack on Jim Crow at a time when the CPUSA and its supporters were supposed (with some reason) to have down-played the "national question." It also promotes what is essentially the concept of the "Double V" (victory over fascism abroad, victory over Jim Crow at home) that was opposed as a slogan by the CPUSA on the basis that defeating fascism was the first priority. The speaker of the poem also voices support for the USSR using the language of class solidarity (rather than the rhetoric of democratic patriotism associated with the CPUSA during the war) and, implicitly, calls for a worker-led revolution ("When crooks and klansman / Lift their heads and things is bad, / I can look across the sea / And see where simple working folks like me / Lift their heads, too, with gun in hand / To drive the fascists from the land").[24] With respect to Hughes specifically, it is again possible to see that there is considerable continuity here from his work throughout the 1930s. And with respect to the literary Left generally, "Goodmorning, Stalingrad" serves as another reminder that the shift from the "proletarian" period in the early 1930s to the neo-Popular Front of the war years (and the intervening Popular Front and anti-interventionist years before the invasion of the USSR) is less abrupt, less discontinuous, and more uneven (in the field of literature at least) than has been argued by many scholars.[25]

Despite the elements of continuity in *Jim Crow's Last Stand* with Hughes's work in the 1930s, it was a departure from the course charted by *Shakespeare in Harlem* in that it did not engage "high" literature in the overt manner of the latter collection. Like *Shakespeare in Harlem*, it did attempt in a more consciously "politicized" manner to reach a mass Left African-American audience, or help create such an audience, through the use of popular African-American culture and vernacular rhetorical forms. In this way *Jim Crow's Last Stand* was of a piece with Hughes's other work during the period, notably his "Simple" columns in the *Chicago Defender* and his poetry. However, the sense of attempting to create a work that is authentically "modern," "popular," "political," and "literary" is missing. This, in different ways, is true of Hughes's collections of the late 1940s, *Fields of Wonder* (1947) and *One-Way Ticket* (1949). *Fields of Wonder* is a "literary" collection in which the "political," the "popular," and the "modern" are notably absent at least in any self-conscious fashion. *One-Way Ticket* is much more like *Shakespeare in Harlem* than either *Jim Crow's Last Stand* or *Fields of Wonder*. Nonetheless, the aggressive engagement with "literary" modernism that characterizes *Shakespeare in Harlem* is absent in *One-Way Ticket*, except as a negative presence.

Montage of a Dream Deferred is a different matter. It is a poetic series obsessively concerned with the modern, the literary, the political, and the popular. It promotes what might be thought of as a popular African-American neomodernist aesthetic that grows out of Hughes's earlier work and proposes an alternative to the neomodernism of those African-American writers, notably Gwendolyn Brooks (whose work Hughes admired) as well as Robert Hayden and Melvin Tolson (about whose work Hughes was much less enthusiastic), who were more influenced by the modernism promoted by the New Criticism and what might be thought the post-Trotskyist criticism found in *Partisan Review* and other journals influenced by the "anti-Stalinist Left" of the late 1930s and early 1940s. Certainly the facts that Hughes's text is rooted in African-American rhetoric (song lyrics, jokes, turns of speech, and so on) and is, as announced in the prefatory note, organized formally with the "conflicting changes, sudden nuances, sharp and impudent interjections, broken rhythms" of bebop in mind challenge the stereotypical model of the neomodernist text that draws back from the vernacular-influenced diction and "social realism" of the poetry of the 1930s and early 1940s.[26] Unlike other forms of American neomodernist art—abstract expressionist painting, for example—Hughes's work not only retains the stance of rebellion but also makes rebelliousness and potential rebellion quite explicit, most famously in "Harlem" ("What happens to a dream deferred"), which both psychologically contextualizes the Harlem riots of 1935 and 1943 and predicts future unrest.

At the same time it is necessary to point out that Hughes's choice of the word "montage" in the title of the poem signals his desire to connect his work with an earlier era of artistic modernism. As discussed in chapter 3, Hughes use of a polyvocal montagelike technique in *Montage of a Dream Deferred* has its origins in Hughes's earliest work and can be clearly seen in such poems of the 1930s as "Radio Broadcast on Ethiopia" and "Air Raid Over Harlem." But Hughes took this polyvocal technique further in *Montage* than he did in any of his earlier works, with the possible exceptions of his verse plays, notably the 1938 semimusical "Don't You Want to Be Free." Even in these plays the juxtaposition of the voices is less radical and the transition between scenes is usually less abrupt than the transitions of the *Montage* sequence. Of course, one can read a number of Hughes's earlier collections, notably *Fine Clothes to the Jew* and *Shakespeare in Harlem*, as essentially polyvocal montages of black America, but even in those collections there is a sense that the individual poems stand on their own far more than those of *Montage*, despite the relative fame of "Harlem." As Hughes indicates in his prefatory note to *Montage*, he saw this work as a single long poem or a poetic sequence rather than a collection.[27]

The use of the word "montage" in the title particularly links his book to the more politically radical side of international 1920s artistic modernism, particularly the German Expressionist photomontages of John Heartfield (the pseudonym of Helmut Herzfelde), and the early Soviet filmmakers, particularly Sergei Eisenstein and Dziga Vertov. However, the claim that the sequence is formally influenced by bebop—a claim thematized in many of the sequence's sections—asserts for *Montage* a modernism based on postwar urban African-American experience and expressive culture. While the protest elements of the sequence are often quite explicit, as in "Freedom Train" (which was removed from the "Montage of a Dream Deferred" section of the *Selected Poems* by Hughes and placed in the "Words Like Freedom" section), more often they are explicitly implicit. To put it another way, anger is prominently linked with fear and concealment so that the concealment of anger becomes the dominant theme of the sequence. Thus the first section of the sequence, "Dream Boogie," provides a guide to reading the rest of the text:

> *You think*
> *It's a happy beat*
>
> Listen to it closely:
> Ain't you heard
> something underneath
> like a—
>
> *What did I say?*
>
> Sure,
> I'm happy!
> Take it away!
>
> *Hey, pop!*
> *Re-bop!*
> *Mop!*
>
> *Y-e-a-h!*
>
> (3)

There is an obvious connection here to the longstanding African-American notions, seen both in literature and in the folk culture, of the need to conceal one's true identity from white people, particularly those who can exercise direct power over one. "Dream Boogie" is in many respects also a perfect product of the cold war era. (In fact, when one considers Hughes's later apologetic testimony before Joseph McCarthy's Senate Permanent Sub-Committee on Investigations in 1953, it is quite prophetic.)[28] In this section are sounded the themes of discontent transvalued into "nonsense" syllables and "wild" music in the face of a consensus compelled by force on those unwilling to accept that consensus otherwise. "Dream Boogie" both thematizes and embodies the enforcement of this consensus while making its shortcomings with respect to African Americans obvious. It maintains a link with Hughes's earlier "Communist" poetry, both in its representation of the Harlem community and its problems, which in many respects is quite "realistic," and in the implication of a coming explosion of the "dream deferred," which, while not perhaps quite as ideologically delineated as in his earlier work, is quite consonant with the calls for and predictions of social revolution in such works as "Air Raid Over Harlem," "Scottsboro Limited," and "Don't You Want to Be Free." In addition, one can also say that Hughes is making an argument for how such themes will be able to be expressed in the "high" cold war era in which it is not only dangerous to express radical political positions directly but also practically difficult, since the institutions, whether *New Masses* (which under the pressures of the period had retrenched from a weekly journal to a monthly and merged with the journal *Mainstream* in 1947) or the National Negro Congress (which folded in 1946), that had provided both a forum and form for such sentiments had collapsed or were becoming increasing isolated. As Hughes himself had already discovered and would soon be reminded even more sharply when he was subpoenaed by the McCarthy committee, even a past history of such direct expressions could be dangerous.

Hughes is often credited as the "father" of jazz-poetry, both in terms of the formal construction of his poetry and, along with Kenneth Patchen, of the reading of poetry to jazz accompaniment. Hughes's relative optimism about the possibility of representing and recreating an authentic African-American folk or popular voice has also been the subject of significant discussion. Less noted is Hughes's commitment to creating a popular modernism heavily engaged with mass culture and "high" literary culture, even as it interrogated the terms of that engagement. In this Hughes is an important if almost unconsidered progenitor of what came to be known as the New American Poetry, particularly the Beat and New York poets, and to a lesser extent, the Black Mountain poets. Hughes's influence on these poets is not merely as a forerunner to the now almost quintessential (at least in the popular conception) Beat practice of reading in front of a jazz band but also in the appropriation, however ironically or critically, of a model, or models, of authentically modern "American" diction, mass culture, and so on, that is an inheritance of the literary Left during the Popular Front. The invocation of the Shadow by Amiri Baraka (then LeRoi Jones) and his later use of jazz (and the Lone Ranger, for that matter), the "hydrogen jukeboxes" of Allen Ginsberg's "Howl," the bebop of Bob Kaufman's work, Frank O'Hara's use of James Dean and Lana Turner, not to mention the approach of all these poets to diction, within a broadly oppositional framework is in many respects closer to Hughes than those of the much more heralded American ancestors of the New American Poetry, notably Pound and Williams.[29] Hughes thus stands not only as an obvious and acknowledged forerunner of the Black Arts Movement of the 1960s but also as a significant, if unacknowledged, influence on the poetic reaction in the 1950s and 1960s against the New Critical sponsored neomodernism of the 1940s.

6

Hysterical Ties
Gwendolyn Brooks and the Rise
of a "High" Neomodernism

The project of connecting Langston Hughes's *Montage of a Dream Deferred* to the "red" spirit of the 1930s is relatively easy owing to the existence of Hughes's "revolutionary" poetry of the 1930s (with direct appeals to class consciousness, worker solidarity, proletarian revolution, and antifascist unity), published in unquestionably radical (often Communist) journals that can then be compared to his work in the late 1940s and early 1950s. Discussing Gwendolyn Brooks in this manner is obviously far more difficult, despite her association with Left-influenced organizations and individuals, since she does not have a similar body of overtly "radical" work. Nonetheless, on careful examination it is possible to see how Brooks's "high" neomodernist style in *Annie Allen* (1949), where there is a deliberate attempt by an African-American narratorial consciousness to create an "international" modernist documentation of the African-American subject, develops directly out of the formal and thematic concerns of the late 1930s and early 1940s transposed into the context of the "high" cold war. In many respects, Brooks is the cold-war poet of anger and self-repression par excellence.

One of the generally overlooked aspects of the early career of Brooks is the important role that the cultural network associated with the Communist Left played in Brooks's artistic development. Brooks's friendships with Leftists such as Theodore Ward, Margaret Walker, Margaret Taylor Goss (later Margaret Goss Burroughs), and former members of the South Side Writers Group, particularly Ed and Alden Bland, are often noted; sometimes her connections with such Popular Front organizations as the National Negro Congress and the League of American Writers are mentioned; and the impact on Brooks's career of Left-influenced literary institutions, such as the South Side Community Art Center, the journal *Negro Story*, and the *Negro Story* poetry awards (financed by a Left-led labor union, the United Electrical and Machine Workers Union, through the offices of the well-known African-American Communist Ishmael Flory), are frequently registered.[1] But rarely are the political affiliations of such individuals and organizations mentioned and when they are, it is implied that Brooks was a naïf who had little or no understanding of her involvement.[2] To these individuals and organizations directly linked to the Communist Left need to be added those writers and editors who promoted Brooks's career, such as Paul Engle and Edwin Seaver, whose literary sensibilities continued to be shaped in many ways by their experience in the literary Left of the 1930s, even though they had broken organizationally with the CPUSA in the 1940s. (For example, Seaver, a founder of *New Masses* and former literary editor of the *Daily Worker*, included work by Brooks in his important *Cross Section* anthologies in the middle and late 1940s.) While it is beyond the scope of this study to untangle the degree of Brooks's organizational connection with the literary Left of the late 1930s and early 1940s, it is worth keeping in mind the existence of such a connection while considering Brooks's first collection of poetry, *A Street in Bronzeville* (1945), in which all three narratorial stances outlined in chapter 4 (outsider, insider, and insider-outsider) are utilized to document the African-American community on the South Side even as they interrogate the limits of "authentic" documentation.

"Movie-time Approaches, Time to Boo": The Narratorial Insider-Outsider, Popular Culture, and Gender in *A Street in Bronzeville*

As pointed out in chapter 4, the narratorial stance of the insider-outsider who documented the "authentic" conditions of the African-American "folk" or "people" was a notable feature of much of African-American poetry in the late 1930s and early 1940s. Another common feature of that stance was a certain ironic detachment on the part of the narratorial consciousness, issuing largely from an engagement with popular culture that questioned the results of drawing on such cultural forms even as those forms were being used. Among the conditions *A Street in Bronzeville* documents, particularly in the first section, "A Street in Bronzeville," is the penetration of mass culture into all levels of life so that daily language is hardly distinguishable from commercial advertisement. In the second poem of the collection, "kitchenette building," the most basic aspects of existence are understandable only through the formulations of mass culture. The poem begins with a transposition of Eliot's "The Hollow Men" or "Gerontion" with their images of dreams and aridity, into the South Side: "We are things of dry hours and the involuntary plan."

While there are a number of concrete details in the poem documenting the "authentic" conditions of the South Side ghetto ("onion fumes," "fried potatoes," "garbage ripening in the hall," "the bathroom," "lukewarm water"), the language and images of advertising determine the reception of that reality. The very title of the poem, referring to the squalid and minuscule subdivision of larger apartments typical of the black South Side, points out the irony inherent in a realtor's euphemism that has become the commonly accepted usage for substandard slum housing. The "involuntary plan" of the Eliotic first line suggests furniture and appliance store "lay-away plans" as well as more obviously sinister plans of "deadlining" by banks, realtors, gangs, police, and politicians designed to contain the African-American ghetto, both types of plans being antithetical to the "dream." The phrases set in opposition to the "dream" are also those of commerce and advertising.

The speaker is strangely inside and outside the scene described because, even as the speaker imagines the possible reception and nurturing of the "dream," he or she can do so only in terms that are ironically close to that of advertising for household goods or kitchenware ("Had time to warm it," "keep it very clean"). In this way, though the tone of the poem is apparently lighter than that of its Eliotic ancestors, Brooks's poem is perhaps more despairing in that the narratorial consciousness of Eliot's poems can imagine itself outside of the decay it ironically describes so that when Eliot's speakers adopt the voice of commercial culture, it is clearly a momentary ventriloquism, whereas in Brooks's poem no such place outside mass culture exists where an oppositional "dream" can be clearly envisioned.

This web of mass culture is not restricted to the rhetoric of advertising and real estate, but even to street slang and African-American urban vernacular speech. Unlike Hughes's affirming stance toward street slang, Brooks's use of "hip" speech in *A Street in Bronzeville* is quite ambivalent. While such language can serve, as it almost always does in Hughes, as a medium of authentic African-American self-assertion, it can also be alienating. Here Brooks raises the problem of the Dunbarian split between "high" poetry and vernacular poetry where a mass culture construct of African-American vernacular language, which is to one degree or another abstracted from the African-American community, becomes an imprisoning medium of African-American expression. Thus the hipster described in "the soft man" is a figment of mass culture: "And calling women (Marys) chicks and broads,/Men hep, and cats, or corny to the jive."

The problem of the "soft man" is that his "hipster" persona, as marked by the "hip" language of the poem's first stanza, functions much like the advertising language of "kitchenette building." Rather than affirming a specific African-American "authenticity," the hipster persona has by the middle 1940s passed into the popular culture of the United States generally and was employed in various media as a means of parodically asserting a broadly "American" modernity.[3] (This sort of mocking mimicry is in fact also characteristic of the speaker of the poem.) The absorption of the "hipster" into the popular culture was also accompanied by a "whiting up" so that the figure of the African-American hipster as such rarely appears in "mainstream" film, cartoons, comics, and so on—though the African-American origins of the hipster were not forgotten by the consumers of popular culture. The hipster is faced with the contradictory task of reappropriating from the mass culture a stance that, extended to the whole bebop (or proto-bebop) subculture, was originally oppositional and in fact a means of limiting co-optation by mass culture.[4] Brooks's poem suggests that such a task is impossible from within the hipster's stance, which provokes "giggles" from others and self-disgust in himself.

Once again the whole question of the uses of vernacular and the Dunbarian heritage in the face of mass–culture appropriations of African-American vernacular is raised in a new register. Interestingly, the speaker resolves the split in the manner of Sterling Brown, despite the northern urban locale, by suggesting that there is a place outside of popular culture, at least to that point, where the African-American subject can be his or her authentic self, a church—though Brown would not have found that place in the church: "No one giggles where/You bathe your sweet vulgarity in prayer."

Unlike the resolution of a similar split in Ellison's *Invisible Man*, this gap is bridged in 1930s fashion within a communal space rather than a clean, well-lighted hole. Whether such a place can exist outside the charmed circle of "Sunday" remains more problematic. The situation of the "soft man" parallels that of the narratorial consciousness of the "A Street in Bronzeville" section in that the "soft man" is strangely inside and outside his own identity as the narratorial consciousness is an insider and outsider within the landscape it documents. Such "double consciousness" as to the contradictions of the representation of the African-American subject was, as we have seen, nothing new. Still, the increasingly bleak vision of the ability of the African-American narratorial consciousness to transcend the limits of its own subjectivity distinguished Brooks from many of the writers of the 1930s, and from the popular neomodernists of the 1940s, particularly Hughes (and from her own work during the Black Arts era of the late 1960s and early 1970s).[5]

A similarly ironic take on the "double consciousness" of assertion and alienation appears in "patent leather."

On one obvious level, the irony of the poem is that the "cat" with "patent-leather hair" has really made himself "it," and has transformed himself into a sort of product that the "cool chick down on Calumet" prefers to a "natural" model. On another level, the diction and form of the poem is analogous to this "process," so to speak; with its goofy irregular rhythm and rhyming couplets that generally come to a full stop after each line, it resembles a sort of hip jingle for "patent-leather hair." As in "the soft man," the hip language that guarantees authenticity in its re-creation of the popular African-American voice also reminds the reader that this "authentic" diction is bound up inextricably with the mass culture as are such African-American cultural practices as the "processing" of hair, which in turn are related closely to popular images of film, the mass circulation press, and the fashion industry.

On other occasions in A Street in Bronzeville, Brooks seems to allow more credence to what might thought of as the Popular Front notion of popular culture as an arena of struggle where African Americans are able to redefine popular cultural forms to serve their genuine interests rather than simply allowing mass culture to define them. The longest and perhaps best known poem of the collection, "The Sundays of Satin-Legs Smith," is essentially a revision of Sterling Brown's "Sporting Beasley," where Brown's ridiculous (and ridiculed) protagonist is transformed into something more ambiguous and more menacing. While much of Brooks's poem, with its over-the-top purple diction, is scathingly sarcastic toward the zoot-suited Satin-Legs Smith, it also persistently undercuts this sarcasm, undermining the judgment of the imagined reader and the narratorial consciousness itself. Unlike

"Sporting Beasley," where Beasley's sartorial splendor is an act of forgetting his "authentic" self, the reader in "The Sundays of Satin-Legs Smith" is constantly reminded of his or her own forgetfulness, or ignorance, in his or her judgment of Smith: "But you forget, or did you ever know."

The condescending, if possibly affectionate, critique of mass culture and its influence on the African-American subject that characterizes the speaker and, by extension, the reader of "Sporting Beasley" is changed into a more complicated relationship between the narratorial consciousness, the African-American subject, mass culture, and the "high" culture reader. In Brown's poem there is a sort of conspiratorial agreement between the speaker and the reader in which the speaker is a cultural insider who invites the reader, particularly the African-American reader, "within the circle," using the buffoonish Beasley to define the outside. While there is a considerable anxiety in *Southern Road* about the difficulty of the process by which the intellectual-poet-narratorial consciousness (and the reader of poetry) becomes an insider, there is not much doubt that there is a folk "inside" that can be opposed to a mass culture "outside" (and a "high" culture "outside"), and that the duty of the African-American intellectual is to return "inside."

In "The Sundays of Satin-Legs Smith," a similar agreement, albeit "high" cultured in tone, between the speaker and the imagined reader is persistently undermined. There is a tension between the speaker and the imagined reader in which the presumed censorious attitude of the reader toward Satin-Legs Smith is mocked, even as Smith himself is mocked. The anaphoric lines of "Sporting Beasley" beginning with "forget" are transformed here into the repeated "you forget." It is not that Smith "forgets" his oppression after the manner of Beasley; quite the contrary: "He sees and does not see the broken windows / Hiding their shame with newsprint."

By single-mindedly pursuing the most basic and immediate hungers, Smith is able to push down the details of the larger pattern of his life, but he is not able to actually forget these details in the same way that the extremely irregular rhyming of the poem suggests a pattern that is obviously present, but not quite apprehensible. It is the reader, not Smith, that needs to be reminded by the speaker about Smith's connection to these details. At the same time, the speaker's reminders serve as a warning to himself or herself, and to the narratorial consciousness, about the project of critiquing Smith. It is clear that such a critique exists. The fact that the speaker mocks the reader, and himself or herself, does not erase the fact that Smith is also mocked. And beyond the mockery is a sense of unease, and even horror, about the hungers of Smith (hungers largely shaped by mass culture) and the acts that Smith commits in order to satisfy those hungers. In this, the most important literary ancestor of "The Sundays of Satin-Legs Smith" is Richard Wright's *Native Son* in which a similar mockery and horror is registered with respect to the novel's protagonist Bigger Thomas. It is quite possible that the ringing alarm clock, the sound of a plane overhead, and the ambiguous moment in the movie theater in the poem are direct references to Wright's novel.[6] Like Thomas, Smith is clearly a victim of hungers induced or warped by mass culture, notably the movies.

Brooks's poem revises Wright's novel in that a particular horror is registered as to the gender implications of such hungers—implications that are present within

Native Son, but noted by Wright's narrator without much apparent distress. Brooks's poem ends in an ambiguous and somewhat sinister linkage of Smith, the reader, and the narratorial consciousness within the web of mass culture: "At Joe's Eats/You get your fish or chicken on meat platters."

The previously clear lines of demarcation between the speaker, the imagined reader, and Smith are blurred here, as the "you" at Joe's Eats comprehends all three, so that all become simultaneously insiders and outsiders. The body of the woman is transformed into a commodity to be consumed, and natural sexual hunger, like the hunger for food, becomes determined by the forms and the images of mass culture ("like new brown bread/Under the Woolworth mignonette"). Thus the narratorial consciousness, the reader, and the African-American popular subject, Smith, are united by their use of "high" or "low" culture-determined "hungers" to distract them from the details of their lives, hungers which are as alienating as they are comforting or oppositional. In the cases of the speaker, the narratorial consciousness, and the imagined reader, there is a further possibility of alienation suggested by the poem: if they are female, they can also place themselves in the position of the interchangeable, consumable female product. This double alienation is perhaps the most sinister aspect of the poem in which the male is reduced to a certain animal level and the female to an inanimate object.

At the same time, despite the very real mockery and critique of Smith, there is a certain grudging admiration, and even envy, of his refusal to be controlled by "good taste," and of his ability to contest the meaning of mass culture. One of the recurrent themes of the "A Street in Bronzeville" series of poems opening the collection is the imprisoning nature of a feminized "high" culture and "genteel" propriety, a theme particularly noticeable in "sadie and maud" and "a song in the front yard" ("I've stayed in the front yard all my life. / I want a peek at the back / Where it's rough and untended and hungry weed grows."). Until the "Hattie Scott" series, the female subject is the focus of laments, complaints, and gloomy portraits cataloguing loss, betrayal, and objectification, while rebellion is almost completely a male domain. The destructive nature of mass culture and the violent hungers induced in the ghetto by this culture is not negated in "The Sundays of Satin-Legs Smith." But Smith is not simply a passive consumer of mass culture. Instead he attempts to contest its ability to control him. If he is not able to escape the cage that he is in, he, and others like him, uses the occasion of the mass-culture event, especially the archetypal mass-culture form of the 1940s, the movie, to rattle the bars: "But movie-time approaches, time to boo/The hero's kiss, and boo the heroine."

Here, as in the early pages of *Native Son*, the film becomes an ambiguous moment of rebellion, displaced sexuality, objectification, and self-hatred.[7] However, despite the undeniably sinister aspects of the process that has already transformed the female body into a consumable product, the refusal of the zoot-suited Smith to accept passively his imprisonment within the ghetto and the restrictions of poverty and Jim Crow Chicago style is clearly admired and even envied, since such rebellion does not seem available to the narratorial consciousness of the poet-intellectual-woman. Nowhere is the Midwestern tradition of African-American letters to that point (reaching from Dunbar through Fenton Johnson, Wright, Frank Marshall Davis, and Brooks), in which popular culture is both used as a model of expression and sharply questioned as to the implications of its consumption by black people, clearer in the 1940s than here.

This doubleness is most pointedly revealed in "Negro Hero," in which the speaker is aware that he uses and is used by the institutions of mass culture ("But let us speak only of my success and the pictures in the Caucasian dailies/As well as the Negro weeklies. For I was a gem.")

Unlike Satin-Legs Smith, the "soft man," or the "cat with the patent-leather hair," the speaker here appears to be entirely aware of the doubleness of mass culture and of his own actions. The speaker appears to stand outside mass culture, as least as far as his subjective consciousness is concerned. Syntactically he is opposed not only to an unspecified "them" but also to "the caucasian dailies as well as the Negro weeklies"—in short, mass-culture institutions controlled by "them." In many respects, the argument here resembles the dominant analysis of mass culture by the Communist Left of the Third Period, in that mass culture is seen as the instrument of a ruling class that is not exactly defined by race (insofar as the "Negro weeklies" are not "white" and yet serve "them") and yet that is dependent on racial hierarchy. On a formal level, the speaker's voice seems far removed from the "popular" voice represented in "the soft man" or the "cat" in "patent-leather" in his straightforward, emphatic tone and diction that is not particularly "elevated," but is still relentlessly "standard." Similarly, the quirky slant rhymes, assonance, alliteration, stanza length, and the combination of Whitmanesque long lines with short end-stopped lines or phrases in conjunction with the regular rhymes at the end of each stanza and a cinquain in the second to last stanza frustrate any easy identification with "popular" forms produced either by an engagement with African-American-identified forms, such as the blues, or with more ambiguous forms, such as the ballad, which could be said to be both "high" and "popular."

Yet at the same time that the speaker of the poem is opposed to what might be considered the "folk" voice and the "popular" voice, the formal pastiche of the poem creates an ironic relationship to the "high" culture in which it appears to reside. The speaker uneasily tries to locate himself in relation to a construct of "democracy" that is both a landscape from which the speaker can be (and has been) excluded or in which the speaker can be (and perhaps will be) included and also the figure of a seductive and treacherous "high culture" white, and "white-gowned" woman ("Their white-gowned democracy was my fair lady./With her knife lying cold, straight, in the softness of her sweet-flowing sleeve.")

While the speaker (and by extension a construct of the poet) seems able to distinguish between "high" and "low" culture (and able trickster-fashion to use those coexisting spheres against themselves), the speaker persistently undermines this vision of self-conscious cultural competence in his (and her) inability to "remember entirely the knife." The problem, as stated by the title of the poem, which is the stuff of mass-culture newspaper headlines (in both the "white" and the African-American press) and "epic" "high culture," is that it is impossible to find a place outside of the ideological web of "high" and "low" culture from which "objective" observation (and action) is possible. Thus the final sense of the poem, and the collection to this point, is a formal and thematic insecurity expressed as irony and self-doubt alongside a contradictory imperative to represent collective identity, collective voice, and collective action. While in many respects the masculinist voice of the poem couched in terms of African-American "manhood" seems, as noted in chapter 2, typical of much of the literature and political rhetoric of the African-American Left in the 1930s and early 1940s, the sense of insecurity and instability in the poem calls into question that earlier model even as the model is invoked.

"Got Somethin' Interestin' on My Mind": The Narratorial
Insider, Popular Culture, and Gender in *A Street in Bronzeville*

Following "Negro Hero," the voice and narratorial stance of *A Street in Bronzeville* shifts radically in the "Hattie Scott" series. Closely resembling Langston Hughes's "Madam" poems, these poems recreate the voice of a Chicago domestic worker.[8] As D. H. Melhem points out, this series of poems formally engages the structures of African-American vernacular speech, vernacular music, and vernacular literature, as well as the "high" literary form of the ballad.[9] The use of the ballad by African-American writers as a congenial vehicle for vernacular literature, owing to its dual citizenship as a "high" form and as a "folk" or "popular" form, has been noted earlier in this study. Hughes's "Madam" poems also generally employ the *abcb* rhyme scheme of the ballad, though metrically Brooks's poems engage the traditional 4/3/4/3 iambic pattern of ballad meter far more closely than those of Hughes. (Brooks clearly intends to remind the reader of her knowledge of the "classical" ballad form, while Hughes seems unconcerned with such a demonstration.) The "Hattie Scott" poems also draw on the tone, diction, and imagery of the blues and other musical genres specifically identified with African-American culture. However, these folk or popular African-American forms are often invoked in an ironic or revisionist way, as in the case of the poem "at the end of the day" where the old phrase from many "folk" blues, "the sun's gonna shine in my back door someday" is transformed from a metaphor of release (both socially and sexually) into a metaphor of imprisonment and repression ("Yes, off, until time when the sun comes back. / Then it's wearily back for me").

There is no supervising narratorial consciousness here that mediates between the reader and the African-American folk or popular subject as there is in nearly all poems in *A Street in Bronzeville* to this point. This series is also the first time that a female subject is unabashedly and unconflictedly heroic. The sense of the tragically self-destructive (and anti-woman) nature of male rebellion that had characterized "the soft man," "The Sundays of Satin-Legs Smith," and even "Negro Hero" is missing. Interestingly, the Hattie Scott series is also the first time that the popular subject is clearly a worker in the Marxist sense. The other representations of the African-American subject in Brooks's collection to this point that are possible to fit into a Marxist spectrum of social class would appear to be *lumpen* or petty bourgeois—beauty shop owner, preacher, "fast woman," "soft man," landlord, prostitute, and so on. Not only is Hattie Scott a worker, but rebellion in the second poem of the section, "the date," is explicitly posed in terms of class as well as racial struggle: "Whatcha mean talkin' about cleanin' silver?/It's eight o'clock now, you fool."

The voice of the narrator is marked by an urban nervousness, emphasizing time as the measure of a job in staccato end-stopped lines. This voice ironically revises the familiar African-American trope of literacy, drawing on the working-class African-American tradition of lampooning "seditty" (pretentious) strivers with a dismissive aside about the city institution of the upwardly mobile, night school.[10] The spirit here is of the urban Chicago blues or rhythm and blues, with their frequent mention of money, work, and sex, rather than the folk blues ironically invoked in "at the end of the day." The voice of the poem is in many respects that of Third Period radical literature, full of class anger and revolt, recreating a working-class and "nationally oppressed" voice that is opposed to the bourgeois (and petty-bourgeois) "high" literary tradition. At the same time, the poem's emphasis on popular culture (expressed in the institution of "the date" itself) as resistance to oppression is, as we have seen, far more typical of the Popular Front era, and the neo-Popular Front politics of the post-Nazi invasion of the Soviet Union, post-Pearl Harbor era, than that of the Third Period. In Hattie Scott's use of mass culture for self-assertion (and class resistance), the self-destructive or self-distorting aspect apparent in the appropriations of mass culture by the male protagonists of previous poems is much muted, though not entirely absent. (There is a criticism of the self-distorting aspect of mass-culture consumption—for example, in the implication of "at the hairdressers" that the "processing" of Hattie Scott's hair, which refuses do naturally what she wishes it to do, is actually part of the processing of a human into a product much as in the case of the male protagonist of "patent leather.")

At the same time that the use and representation of African-American popular culture and vernacular language and the iconic naming of "typical" details of African-American life (e.g., "back porch," "lodge with banners flappin'," "grits") posit a folk community with roots in the rural South, the "Hattie Scott" poems set the individual speaking subject at odds with possible communities with which the subject might identify. The most obvious division is between male and female. The conflict between male and female and the deep unease, if not horror, at the use of the bodies of African-American women by African-American men for male rebellion and self-assertion felt by the supervising intelligence of the poet-narrator recurs throughout the collection. The "Hattie Scott" poems, however, differ from the earlier poems in that the supervising intelligence is silent, if not absent, and that Scott is not passive material to be worked or a victim—as is clear in the last poem in the series, "the battle," where Scott imagines killing the abusive husband of a passive neighbor.

While Scott exists entirely within a heterosexual universe in which homosexuality appears not to be a possibility, she reverses the relationship between men and women existing in the earlier poems, a type of relationship that she comments on in "the battle," so that the actions of men, like the actions of her employer, become occasions of her own self-assertion.

Nonetheless, though any easy notion of African-American community between men and women is put in doubt, the construction of a community of women, or even black women, is also questioned. While a network of women is invoked in the phrase "her landlady told my ma" in the first stanza of "the battle," four out of the five poems in the series feature explicit conflict between the speaker and other women. Even if the female (and presumably white) employer of "the date" is excluded, "at the hairdresser," "when I die" and "the battle" all feature conflict with and / or contempt for other African-American women. Thus Hattie Scott becomes a heroic figure in a sort of popular-culture romanticism where she is both authentically mass, authentically individual, authentically folk, and authentically female, standing both for and apart from the folk.

The female subject as a popular romantic hero is even more clearly revealed in the "blues-ballad" following the "Hattie Scott" series, "Queen of the Blues." The critic Stephen Henderson argues that the form Brooks employs here, the "blues-ballad," was originated by Sterling Brown."[11] Whether this claim is true—an argument could be made for Langston Hughes with such poems as "Ballad of Gin Mary," which antedated "Ma Rainey" and "Memphis Blues" in publication—Brooks's poem does seem to be in dialogue with Brown's most famous blues-ballad "Ma Rainey." Where the narratorial consciousness of Brown's poem adopts the voice of the folk insider who virtually erases Ma Rainey as an individual subject, Brooks's narrator is neither an obvious folk insider nor a "high" literary outsider. Instead Brooks's narrator, much like that of Hughes's "Advertisement for the Waldorf-Astoria," refuses to make a definitive move toward either position, choosing instead a "standard" colloquial diction that occasionally makes gestures both toward a specifically African-American colloquial diction (e.g., "hollered") and toward a "literary" diction (e.g., "She covered that grave / With roses and tears. / A handsome thing to see"). Where Brown's Ma Rainey is given only the vaguest sense of individual personhood by the narrator, Brooks's narrator is almost completely absorbed by the individuality of Mame.

In the opening stanzas, the primary narrator clearly represents Mame as a type of romantic hero-artist. Mame as a popular vaudeville and night-club blues singer participates in the network of popular commercial culture, particularly that associated with African Americans. As in Brown's "Ma Rainey," the commercial blues singer creates a symbolic communal space for African Americans, allowing a cathartic self-assertion in the face of racial oppression. Unlike Brown's Ma Rainey, Mame is shown to be isolated from all the normative bonds of community, particularly those of family. In a sort of Promethean gesture, Mame sacrifices herself for the communal expression in which she is unable to share.

What distinguishes Mame from the stereotypical romantic hero is that not only is the cost of playing the role of the artist-hero called into question but also any easy notion of a common cultural community. Once again, the investigations of popular culture by Left artists of the Popular Front era are recalled here. The relation among the singer, her audience, and the institutional space in which Mame's art is presented to the audience is extremely complex and extremely troubled, particularly when the singer's actual voice appears—or is recreated by the narratorial consciousness.

Mame adopts the voice of a domestic with sore knees while dancing in a wildly (and commercially) sexualized manner. She sings songs of male betrayal to a largely male audience within a institution that presents her as "Queen of the blues" while retailing her as a female sex toy for the audience that physically abuses her. Mame is conscious of this economic transaction as degrading, answering at least in part the question of the narrator, "What did she have to lose?," but skirting the unuttered question of "What else could she do?" Obviously, the notion of community between African-American men and women is interrogated. Somewhat less obviously, as in the "Hattie Scott" poems, community among African-American women is also problematized, particularly with respect to skin color. However, what is possibly most troubled, and troubling, is Mame's adoption of the voice of the domestic worker. D. H. Melhem argues that Mame's "position matches that of the woman who scrubs the kitchen floors and is manipulated by her boyfriend, the abused woman whose life she sings, and lives."[12] While it could be argued in some structural sense of the way race and gender operate in American culture that Mame "lives" the life of the black domestic, the lives of the blues singer and the domestic are quite different. Mame is no doubt exploited in a degrading manner. But if the position of blues singer was not superior to that of domestic worker, especially for someone with no considerations of family propriety like Mame (as she is represented by the speaker of the poem), then Mame could have cleaned houses and at least avoided the physical abuse that was part of her job description as a blues singer.[13] Thus Mame's ventriloquism of the domestic worker, essentially selling the worker to her audience, is uneasily close to Mame's selling of her physical and artistic self to the male audience.

Again, the question "For what did she have to lose?" gives rise to the unverbalized and unanswered question, "What else could she do?" This uneasiness is clearly of significance to Brooks's announced project of representing and recreating the South Side ghetto on the page. It is worth noting that Mame's ventriloquizing of the domestic worker (or Brooks's ventriloquizing of the colloquial narrator ventriloquizing Mame ventriloquizing the domestic worker) within the highly stylized structure of the blues rather than rhetorical forms of "everyday" speech immediately follows Brooks's representation of the domestic Hattie Scott, highlighting the relationship between Mame's project and that of Brooks. The "artfulness" of the singer's performance and the "literariness" of Brooks's representation of that performance on the printed page are emphasized by the line breaks. These breaks suggest the phrasing of a jazz or blues singer while at the same time calling attention to the poem as a literary production as the eye is arrested by the extremely short lines, particularly the two one-word lines consisting of "do." In short, the poem brings into question in a very complex manner the equally complex problem of how a literary artist speaks of, by, and for an imagined popular audience—again, unlike Brown's use of the figure of Ma Rainey in which there is a organic, and unconflicted, community among the literary artist, the represented folk artist, and the folk subject.

After all, Mame, the artist, misrepresents herself through the aegis of an institution that allegedly claims for her the status of a "queen" while retailing her as a commodity to an audience that responds to her mask of the domestic abused by employer and mate alike with further abuse. The unasked question, "What else could she do?" is never directly answered. Instead Brooks suggests that what the artist can do, again resembling many other Popular Front and neo-Popular Front artists, is continually raise the question, "For what did she have to lose?" with respect to the transactions between the structures and institutions of "high" art and "popular" art, between the individual and different constructions of community, and among the artist, the represented subject, and the audience. This is not to say, of course, that Brooks rejects the possibility of community—quite the contrary. Rather, she is concerned with reminding the reader that constructs of community are constructs that constantly need to be interrogated, not "natural" facts. Or perhaps it would be more accurate to say that Brooks is obsessed with asking what is "natural" and with determining what organic elements exist in the urban African-American community (e.g., is there a meaning of the blues that forms one of the bonds of "authentic" community? If so, is that meaning fixed and univocal or is it fluid and polyvocal according to the subject's location in the community/communities, taking into account such factors as class, gender, color, family ties, and so on?).

In this respect, "The Ballad of Pearl Mae Lee" perhaps best represents this provisional and shifting nature of community. A narrative poem, "The Ballad of Pearl Mae Lee" recounts the story of Sammy, an African-American man in the rural South seduced by dominant standards of beauty as embodied in a white woman who accused him of rape after having sex with him in the back of a Buick. This accusation results in Sammy's lynching. The speaker of the poem is an African-American woman who presumably loved Sammy, but who is apparently enraged by his willingness to be seduced. On one level, there is no real solidarity of any kind between the characters of the narrative on the basis of race, class, gender, or region except in the negative sense that Sammy was condemned on the basis of his transgression of racial lines, which that speaker suggests took place ideologically before it took place physically. There is a remarkable resemblance between the white male sheriff and the black female speaker in their insistence that Sammy got what he deserved. And yet beneath this negative enforcement of "natural" community through lynch mob violence, and the positive reinforcement of "unnatural" community through the promotion of relative "whiteness" as a marker of female beauty, there is real sorrow and real outrage about the murder of Sammy on the part of the speaker, indicating an attachment that the speaker is unable to deny despite her stated anger at Sammy ("Oh, dig me out of my don't-despair.")

The rural folk is pulled apart in the space of an archetypal "status" commodity of the 1940s, the Buick, and yet ties remain that the speaker is unable to forget despite her best efforts.

"And We Still Wear Our Uniforms": Modernism, Community, and the African-American Sonnet in *A Street in Bronzeville*

A Street in Bronzeville closes with a sequence of twelve off-rhyme sonnets, "Gay Chaps at the Bar," which invoke both the African-American speaking subject and the tradition of "high" literature as it is popularly understood and yet undermine those invocations. As in the "Hattie Scott" series, the narratorial consciousness is absent from what is represented as ostensibly the unmediated voice of an African-American officer, or series of African-American officers, at the front during World War II. However, the voice of the soldier is so clearly "literary" that the reader is constantly and consciously reminded that this mask is indeed a mask, as in the title sonnet that begins the series: "We knew how to order. Just the dash / Necessary. The length of gaiety in good taste."

The "literariness" of the speaker's syntax is clearly self-mocking. On the face of it, the speaker, a "middle-class," self-consciously sophisticated, college-educated African-American man, mocks his own "attainments" in the face of death. But, as mentioned earlier, the very literariness of the syntax, and the choice of the archetypal "high" literary form of the sonnet sequence, reminds the reader that this satiric voice is not the soldier himself, but a narratorial consciousness that, when seen within the larger context of the collection, the reader assumes to be female. That the sonnets are narratorial reconstructions (and distortions) is further emphasized by the epigraph, which is drawn from a letter to Brooks and which, while self-consciously literate, is far more chatty and less "literary" than the following sonnets.[14] The literariness of the poem's syntax is reinforced by the fact that a close reading inevitably draws the reader back to other poems in the collection. The lines "And we knew beautifully how to give to women / The summer spread, the tropics, of our love. / When to persist, or hold a hunger off" recall "The Sundays of Satin-Legs Smith" as the mannered self-control (and mannered abandon) of the speaker demands comparison with the uncontrolled hunger of the poverty-stricken Smith. While the narratorial consciousness is obviously not unsympathetic to the speaker of the sonnet, there is a certain critique of the middle-class individual whose self-aware sophistication lacks the spirit of rebellion of the working-class subject, a rebellion that is viewed by the narratorial consciousness with a horrified admiration. A similar critique is found in the relation of the ninth line "But nothing ever taught us to be islands" to the poems immediately preceding the sonnet sequence, in which the experience of black women constantly prepares them to be "islands."

Formally, the choice of the sonnet sequence to end the collection may seem at odds with the self-reflexive meditation on the relation between "high" culture and "mass" culture in the construction (and the destruction) of community that has characterized the collection, in that "mass" culture or "popular" culture seems virtually missing from these closing poems. However, on closer inspection, the choice of the sonnet is apt. For the "middle-class" American, black and white, with a reasonable amount of formal education, the sonnet as a literary form epitomized "high" culture. If an American of that era (or this one) were asked to name a type of poem (and could), he or she would almost certainly name the sonnet, unless they were among the relatively few avid readers of poetry (and even an avid reader of poetry would probably think first of the sonnet rather than, say, the sestina or the rondeau). In short, the sonnet as a form could be seen as a popular-culture emblem of "high" culture (and in turn a sort of commercial marketing strategy) in much the same way as the name "Shakespeare." That the sonnet was in the popular mind the archetypal "high" poetic form particularly associated with notions of a pre-modern or traditional "high" European culture made it a particularly inviting target for numerous American modernists, black and white, male and female, who variously attempted to capture, recapture, recast, deform, or destroy it.

The sonnet was a form especially favored by African-American writers in the twentieth century until at least the early 1950s.[15] Houston Baker Jr.'s concepts of "mastery" and "deformation of mastery" are both useful in considering this tradition, in which some African-American authors demonstrated their "mastery" of the archetypal "high" form in fairly straightforward fashion while others "deformed" the sonnet in various ways, often by writing overtly "political" or "social" poems rather than the love lyrics generally associated with the form.[16] Much more rarely do African-American poets "deform" the sonnet through the recasting of the sonnet in a representation of African-American vernacular speech and other forms of vernacular culture—though some have fragments with a double identity as vernacular speech (for example, "holler" in "gay chaps at the bar") embedded in them—with, as we have seen, Hughes's "Seven Moments of Love" section of *Shakespeare in Harlem* one of the few examples.[17] Sometimes the sonnets written by African-American writers do not follow exactly the rhyme scheme of either the Petrarchan or Shakespearian sonnets seen as most "traditional" by American readers and writers, as in the case of a number of poems in the "Vestiges" section of *Southern Road*. However, nearly all make use of exact rhyme and are conservative in their use of typography, line break, punctuation, and so on—unless, again, one counts Hughes's "un-sonnet sequence." This relative African-American formal conservatism contrasts with the formal radicalism of the sonnets of many white modernists, notably e.e. cummings and Wallace Stevens. If one can speak of the African-American sonnet tradition, it is one that can be generally seen as both self-consciously "deformative" in content and conservative in its execution of formal "mastery"—at least on the printed page since, as noted in chapter 1 with respect to McKay, a spoken version might be another thing.

Thus, while it is worthwhile to link, as D. H. Melhem does, Brooks's use of the sonnet here to the sonnets of various New Negro Renaissance writers (though why Melhem leaves out earlier writers, notably Dunbar, in her brief genealogy of the African-American sonnet is puzzling), Brooks's sonnets are formally quite different from those earlier sonnets. This difference is most obvious in Brooks's avoidance of exact end-rhyme, employing instead near rhyme, slant rhymes, assonance, alliteration, and, on occasion, no suggestion of rhyme.[18] This avoidance of end-rhyme calls attention to the rhyming conventions of various types of sonnets while avoiding them even as the conventions are invoked, particularly when the rhyme scheme of the not-quite rhymes fits, or nearly fits, the pattern of a "typical" sonnet, as in the seventh poem in the series, "the white troops had their orders but the Negroes looked like men," which would be a regular Petrarchan sonnet if the not-quite-rhymes were exact. These sonnets self-consciously remind the reader of a "regular" sonnet, the popular middle-class icon of "high" literature, and the use of the various sonnet forms by African-American writers, and yet evade that regularity. This studied invocation and evasion parallel both the mocking "literariness" of the syntax of the "middle-class" African-American soldiers speaking—in fact writing—and also the horrified inability of these soldiers to quite put all their sophisticated understanding of the rules of sports, love, college and "good" grammar back together again in the face of the war.

As Ann Folwell Stanford points out, the war here is not simply the war in Europe and the Pacific but also the war "at home" against racism, with the sonnets embodying the slogan of the "Double V" (victory abroad and victory against Jim Crow at home) first popularized by the African-American newspaper *The Pittsburgh Courier*.[19] Perhaps the sonnets also, as Stanford claims, "are, finally, prophetic warnings: They look back at the devastation of war, and forward toward a time of revolution and rebellion that was to come in the Sixties" (though this seems to remake Brooks from the standpoint of her later participation in the Black Arts Movement of the late 1960s and early 1970s).[20] There is a sense of past and present apocalypse in the sonnets, particularly in the final sonnet:

> How shall we smile, congratulate: and how
> Settle in chairs? Listen, listen. The step
> Of iron feet again. And again wild.

(75)

But the sonnets also explore the difficulties and contradictions of such revolutionary moments where apocalyptic events have dislocated past knowledge of community and identity determined by the interface of race, region, class, and gender. This identity crisis is seen as good in many respects since the old system of social identity was oppressive in the extreme, especially for the African-American subject. And yet such a crisis is profoundly unsettling, notably for the "middle-class" black subject who feels he or she has something to lose as well as gain. Thus these subjects in the sonnets are preoccupied with often imprisoning social guideposts—etiquette, religion, patriotism, racial and economic caste, romantic love—that they feel they are losing even as they desperately try to retain them so that their lives can continue to make sense. In this, the ending of Brooks's collection is closely related in spirit to Hughes's *Montage of a Dream Deferred*, in which a spirit of edgy rebellion and fear pervades. The problem for the individual is coming to terms with what it would mean to win the wars at home and abroad, with what such a world would look like, and with how community, and the identity of the individual within the community, could be imagined.

The relation of this to Brooks's own project is obvious. *A Street in Bronzeville* is obsessively concerned with the problems of the literary representation of the individual African-American subject in an "authentic" manner that is also "literary" and of the relation of the "folk," "popular," and "high" discourses to social hierarchy and social power. Much of the collection before the final sonnet sequence calls upon the resources of these various discourses while investigating what the cost of such usages might be. The stance of the narratorial consciousness in these meditations on the problems of "authenticity" and artistic "achievement" is quite ambivalent. A sort of Faustian pact is seen as necessary to create the poems, with the narratorial consciousness aware at all times of the cost—not the least of which is the inability to speak with absolute sincerity and conviction. The sonnet sequence prominently links the question of the process of artistic construction to the recurring themes of manners, tradition, and belief in the construction (and reconstruction) of identity with the inevitable attention to form that the adoption and unusual adaptation of the sonnet as a poetic vehicle inevitably entails for even a casual reader. Finally, the narratorial consciousness is able to imagine the breakdown of tradition, manners, and language itself. But it is unable to imagine the new order; the "iron feet" bring dread, not elation—which is not to say that this inability to see a clear future means that this chaos is bad, simply that it is terrifying. In this respect, Brooks's sonnets here have to be among the most successful poems dealing with the terror of modernity in American letters.

Margaret Walker's claim that she was a "thirties" writer, while Brooks was essentially a "forties" writer, has a certain validity insofar as Brooks was considerably removed from the 1930s folkloric–high culture model associated with Sterling Brown and shaped in the ideological debates of the late New Negro Renaissance and the Third Period.[21] Yet as we have seen, her work is closely related in form and in spirit to the self-reflexive work of many writers during the Popular Front, including such African-American writers as Hughes and Frank Marshall Davis, who were concerned with issues of class, racial, and/or gender oppression while meditating on the problems of attempting to write for a imagined popular audience in a way that was authentic, literary, and truly popular. There is an obvious, and much remarked, relationship of *A Street in Bronzeville* to the "modernists," which became even more pronounced in *Annie Allen* (1949) as the cold war intensified. But this relationship did not distinguish Brooks from many writers of the literary Left who had similarly complicated relationships to "high" modernism.[22] While Brooks in *A Street in Bronzeville*, like the writers of the Popular Front, is concerned with issues of social justice and injustice, she creates a model where constructs of counter-hegemonic community, racial and class solidarity, and a simultaneously "popular" and "literary" discourse are provisional, imperfect, and unstable. This does not mean that this community is not "real," only that it needs to be constantly questioned with the result that the narratorial consciousness of the poems and the African-American speaking subjects which the poems attempt to represent and give voice to are never easy in communal identification. Neither is there the certainty—as there is generally is in Hughes's work—that the narratorial consciousness of the poet-intellectual-outsider is able to authentically recreate the folk or popular voice if he or she is sufficiently honest and receptive.

Brooks examined critically within an African-American context many of the thematic and formal concerns of Left writers in the 1930s: the connection of political vanguardism and artistic vanguardism; the problems of "realistic" formal representation and re-creation of the working-class–popular subject by a non-working-class artist; the relationship of "high" modernism and folk or popular modernism; the nature of mass culture; the relationship of class, gender, race, and nationality and the construction of community; the compatibility between a jeremiadic revolutionary or apocalyptic rhetorical mode and a liberal, progressive rhetorical mode. In this *A Street in Bronzeville* is not very far in spirit from *Native Son*, despite its diametrically opposed gender perspective, in that Wright also questions the practices and concerns of the literary Left of the 1930s without rejecting the Left ideologically or organizationally (at that point).[23] Brooks is both the inheritor of 1920s discussions among African-American artists and intellectuals of how to represent and recreate the African-American popular subject and 1930s discussions, initiated in no small part by the "proletarian literature" debates of the Third Period, of how the working-class subject or, later, the popular subject is represented.[24]

7

The Popular Front, World War II, and the Rise of Neomodernism in African-American Poetry of the 1940s

*D*espite the obvious differences between the "popular" neomodernism exemplified by the work of Hughes in the 1940s and the "high" neomodernism of which Brooks was the leading exponent, both neomodernist tendencies had in common an urban and largely northern landscape in which the ghetto, rather than the plantation or tenant farm, increasingly became the locus of authentic African-American culture. African-American communities in the North, notably Harlem and the South Side of Chicago, were seen not as either a "refuge" or as a place of alienation where the ur-culture of the rural immigrant is distorted or destroyed, but instead as "home" (as Amiri Baraka was to later title a collection of essays describing his intellectual journey to cultural nationalism mirroring his physical journey from the Lower East Side to Harlem). If life in the ghettos of the North and West was depicted as alienating, it was an alienation that was seen increasingly as typical of African-American life in the United States.[1]

There were, of course, certain empirical pressures for such a redefinition of "home," the most important being that by the 1940s African Americans in the cities outnumbered those in the country for the first time in U.S. history. By the end of the decade, 62 percent of the African-American population was urbanized.[2] In the 1940s, changes in agricultural technology greatly reduced sharecropping. At the same time, the new demand for labor by the war industries and the relatively egalitarian policies of the CIO unions, particularly those led by the Communist Left, vastly increased the number and status of African-American industrial workers.[3]

Yet these changes do not entirely explain the transformation of the dominant model of the folk from a rural southern one in the 1930s, particularly during the Third Period, to an urban northern and western one in the 1940s. After all, the process of urbanization and migration to the North had been a much noted phenomenon since the beginning of World War I, continuing even during the depths of the Depression.[4] And, despite urbanization, more than two-thirds of the African-American population lived in the South as late as 1950—albeit increasingly in cities and towns.[5] One might argue that the African-American poets of the 1940s, who were, in the main, urbanites and college-educated and who were almost all (with the exception of Margaret Walker) raised outside the states of the Old Confederacy, wrote about the communities with they were familiar and with which they felt a rapport that they could not with rural communities in the Deep South. But the poets of the 1930s (other than Richard Wright) had more or less the same backgrounds. Certainly, the urban northern and western background of many African-American writers and intellectuals after the cultural nationalist period of the late 1960s and early 1970s (and a much more urbanized and much less southern African-American population) did not stop a considerable revival of models of the southern folk culture as the ur-culture of African-Americans—and indeed the revival of the CPUSA's Black Belt Thesis in various forms by a number of African-American nationalist organizations.[6] Thus the new approach to reconstructing the "folk" or the "people" emphasizing a northern and urban model resulted from an altered ideological landscape during the Popular Front that was not unrelated to the material changes in the lives of African Americans, but which did not inevitably flow from those changes.

The Popular Front, the Rural Folk, and Neomodernism: The Case of Margaret Walker

In many respects, Margaret Walker is an anomalous figure among African-American poets in the 1940s. She is set apart from most of her contemporaries in her early upbringing in the Deep South—though this upbringing was urban for the most part, primarily in Birmingham and New Orleans, and her secondary education at Northwestern University and the University of Iowa Writers Program was northern. She is set apart also by her conscious identification in her essays and in her early poetry with the "socially conscious" writers of the 1930s, whom she contrasts with the more "formally" oriented African-American authors of the 1940s.[7] Walker describes her literary and political development during the late 1930s and early 1940s as being significantly influenced by the literary milieu of the Popular Front in Chicago—the Federal Writers Project, the organization of the CIO industrial unions, the League of American Writers, and so on. But in many respects Walker's poetry in the late 1930s and in the 1940s is closer in spirit to the poetry of the early and middle 1930s, which valorized the southern rural folk as the "authentic" African-American culture. In this she differs considerably from her contemporaries, such as Robert Hayden and Melvin Tolson, with whom she claims a kinship as writers who published in the 1940s but who "belong to the 1930s."[8] Rather, Walker's recreation of the folk and folk voice is more akin to the vernacular poetry of Sterling Brown and Waring Cuney in the 1930s and early 1940s. At the same time, Walker's narratorial stance resembles that of Langston Hughes in that the narratorial consciousness of the poems is, at least at first glance, a cultural insider who seems to see no serious division between the narratorial consciousness and the represented and recreated folk.

As Walker herself notes, she essentially writes three types of poems in *For My People*: long-lined and anaphoric biblical-Whitmanic-Sandburgian "prophetic" poems; narrative "folk" poems rooted largely in African-American "badman" songs; and documentary sonnets.[9] Each type is more or less grouped together in the collection, forming three rough sections: prophetic poems, folk poems, sonnets. In all three types or sections, the collective folk or the individual folk subject is represented and the identification of the narratorial consciousness with the folk is affirmed. However, the location of the narratorial consciousness with respect to the represented folk varies. Typically, the speaker-narratorial consciousness of the long-lined prophetic poem emphatically asserts a commonalty with the southern folk, emphasizing a spiritual oneness with the folk while linguistically maintaining a certain distance from 1930s conventions of recreated folk speech. The drama for the speaker-narratorial consciousness is not the prodigal alienation of the intellectual-poet from the folk, and the subsequent return of intellectual-poet to the folk, that marks the work of McKay, and even Brown to some extent. Rather, these poems are marked by the exodus of the folk, as embodied in the poet-intellectual-speaker, from the land and by a prophetic vision of a folk return to the land, as in the poem "Sorrow Home":

> My roots are deep in southern life; deeper than John Brown
>   or Nat Turner or Robert Lee. I was sired and weaned
>   in a tropic world. The palm tree and banana leaf,
>   mango and coconut, breadfruit and rubber trees know
>   me.
>
> Warm skies and gulf blue streams are in my blood. I belong
>   with the smell of fresh pine, with the trail of coon, and
>   the spring growth of wild onion.
>
>   (*This Is My Century*, 12)

As in Brown's poetry, here the home of African Americans is located in the Western Hemisphere, not in Africa—though Africa is often conflated with the South of the United States though a kinship of landscape, weather, blood, and music in Walker's prophetic poems. Walker's South, however, is more extensive than that of Brown, comprising the entire African diaspora in the Americas rather than simply the former slave states of the United States. Nonetheless, like Brown in *Southern Road*, Walker establishes a clear hierarchy of country and city, of South and North, of "folk" music (especially the spirituals) and "popular" music.

In the prophetic poems, there is a Whitmanic merging of the speaker-poet's body (which is also the body of the folk), music, and the southern rural landscape, a conflation or "fusion" that takes place most explicitly in "Southern Song:"

> I want my body bathed again by southern suns, my soul
>   reclaimed again from southern land. I want to rest

again in southern fields, in grass and hay and clover
bloom; to lay my hand again upon the clay baked by a
southern sun, to touch the rain-soaked earth and smell
the smell of the soil.

(11)

Here, as elsewhere in the prophetic poems, music, particularly the spirituals, is a constant referent. Unlike nearly all her other African-American contemporaries who similarly connected the "folk" voice to music, Walker almost never attempts in *For My People* to draw directly on the formal resources of African-American vernacular music, except in her use of the folk ballad for her vernacular "folk" poems. Instead, particularly in the prophetic poems, music is invoked without any direct attempt to represent music on the printed page. The "popular" music of the urban centers, notably jazz, is not mentioned. Even the blues are mentioned only in passing, often obliquely—as in the speaker's admonition to herself in "Sorrow Song" "to strike no minor key."

Once again, notwithstanding Walker's well-known connections to Wright and Hughes (who, despite quite different narratorial stances, frequently recreated popular culture products in their works), Walker is closer to Brown in her valorization of rural "folk" music as the "authentic" vehicle of the militant folk voice at the expense of urban "popular" music. In a move that recalls the Communist slogan "Promote Negro Culture in Its Original Form with Proletarian Content," Walker invokes existing "folk" music as the authentic expression of the "folk" spirit and then calls for a new and more highly conscious music to be developed from the old. Like the Communist position itself, Walker's model of African-American literary and artistic expression also draws on New Negro notions of folk culture, especially music, as the ore that needs to be refined into a new high culture. The creation of this new music out of the old, a concept most clearly expressed in "The Spirituals," serves, as it did for many of Walker's African-American predecessors from, at least, Du Bois, as an analogue to the process of developing a new, militant African-American self-consciousness:

Cotton pickers sing your song. Grumblers weed and
hoe the corn. Let the dirge of miners and
rebellious stirring road songs keep on ringing.

(13)

Here "Cotton pickers sing your song" recalls Sterling Brown's "O Ma Rainey, / Sing yo' song" in "Ma Rainey." Again, like Brown she argues for a literary model in which the "literary" artist assumes the stance of the "folk" artist who speaks from, to, and for the folk, though Walker's work here lacks Brown's sense of how contradictory and difficult, but necessary, such a model is for the literary artist.

The poem ends literally on a militant, martial, and somewhat open-ended note ("And our sorrow / songs now rise to bolder measures"). This note typifies Walker's prophetic poems where the endings are revolutionary and sometimes apocalyptic calls after the manner associated with many Left works of the "proletarian" era, such as Clifford Odets's *Waiting for Lefty*, Hughes's "Scottsboro Limited," and Meridel Le Sueur's "I Was Marching." And, as discussed in chapter 3, with respect to a similar apocalyptic optimism in the endings of many of Hughes's "revolutionary" works in the 1930s, Walker also tapped into a long tradition of African-American Christian millenarianism of which the spiritual was one of the most notable cultural vehicles.

The "prophetic" poems appear to be relatively straightforward in proposing a model where the author-narratorial consciousness is able to "authentically" speak for and to the "folk" as an insider without any serious difficulty. However, the group of "folk" poems that follows the "prophetic" poems complicates this model considerably, especially when also seen against the concluding group of poems that consists largely of documentary sonnets. The most obvious complication is the change between the "standard" diction of the "prophetic" poems and African-American colloquial diction of the "folk" poems. This change in diction undermines the authority of the narratorial consciousness with its claim to be one with the folk in both the "prophetic" poems and the "folk" poems; since the diction of the "folk" poems is clearly distinct from the "literary" diction of the "prophetic" poems, the reader is formally reminded that a gap might exist between the represented and the representer. Again, the high-low split of Dunbar is invoked indirectly.

The "folk" poems are most often in ballad form. They are essentially a series of "badman" stories (or, in the case of "Molly Means" and "Kissie Lee," "bad woman" stories) derived from similar stories, or in some instances (such as "John Henry" and "Bad-Man Stagolee") from actually existing "badman" stories, originating among African-Americans in the South. The one exception is "Long John Nelson and Sweetie Pie," which is a narrative ballad of love gone wrong after the manner of the traditional folk ballad "Frankie and Johnnie"—albeit without the murder of the original song. As in the "prophetic" poems, there seems to be no distance between the narratorial consciousness of these "folk" poems and their speakers, who narrate the stories using a diction clearly marked as African-American and southern, as in "Bad-Man Stagolee":

> That Stagolee was an all-right lad
> Till he killed a cop and turned out bad,
> Though some do say to this very day
> He killed more'n one 'fore he killed that 'fay.
> But anyhow the tale ain't new
> How Stagolee just up and slew
> A big policeman on 'leventh street

(28)

The clearest indication of a distinction between the narratorial consciousness of the poem and its speaker is the brief note appended to the poem explaining that "Stagolee" is "pronounced Stack'-a-lee." The note is a move toward establishing the poem's authenticity as folk re-creation and toward presenting the credentials of the author-narratorial consciousness as a cultural insider. An argument is made both implicitly and explicitly at various times in *For My People* that the author-narratorial consciousness is at home in a variety of discursive worlds as a sort of Gramscian organic intellectual who can simultaneously observe the folk, participate in the folk culture, evaluate the strengths and weaknesses of that culture and its members, and interpret the culture to outsiders without any conflict of identity. However, the note, like the distinction in diction between the "prophetic" poems and the "folk" poems cannot help but problematize the easy identification of the narratorial consciousness with the folk. In short, there is a self-consciousness about the role of the intellectual and a vanguardism common among the literary Left, and indeed the nonliterary Left, in the 1930s and early 1940s. As discussed in chapter 2, the peculiar self-consciousness and vanguardism of the Leninist Left produced a dualism in which the revolutionary party (e.g., the CPUSA) was both of the working class and yet ahead leading the working class. This dualism was fraught with tensions arising from fears of an "ultra-left" detachment from the working class at one extreme and a "right deviationist" or "spontaneous tailing" behind the natural "economist" demands of a working class lacking a revolutionary leadership at the other. Similarly, in the work of many artists of the literary Left, and the critical writings of many intellectuals associated with the Communist Left, the problematic relation of the Left intellectual-writer to the working class (and, during the Popular Front, to the people) is raised again and again. This is particularly true in the work of African-American writers, such as Brown and Wright in their different ways, where an identification with the folk is asserted along with a vanguard role for the African-American intellectual; then the two assertions are questioned both sharply and uneasily.[10] In the case of Walker, the formal distinction between the "prophetic" poems and the "folk" poems calls into question the identification between the narratorial consciousness of the poems and the represented and/or recreated folk, though this commonalty is never questioned by the denotative sense of Walker's poems.

This implicit structural questioning of the poet-speaker's easy identification with the folk subject is further heightened by the six sonnets that close *For My People*. The first four sonnets—"Childhood," "Whores," "Iowa Farmer," and "Memory"— are documentary poems of both "eye"- and "I"-witness in which a relatively "objective" poet-witness-speaker recounts his or her observations of a scene from the far or near past of the poet-speaker. This use of the sonnet form for such documentary purposes was unusual even in the 1930s, since the "factualness" of the speaker-witness's claims is undermined by the "literariness" of the sonnet. (There was some precedent for such a use of the sonnet in Claude McKay's more descriptive sonnets of the of the late 1910s and the 1920s [as opposed to his famous didactic sonnets of protest], such as the "The Harlem Dancer" [1917].)

In the testimonies of the first four of Walker's sonnets, the poet-speaker places herself in the foreground in a manner that locates her among that which she sees and describes while maintaining a considerable distance of identity from what she observes:

> When I was a child I knew red miners
> dressed raggedly and wearing their carbide lamps.
> I saw them come down red hills to their camps
> dyed with red dust from old Ishkooda mines.

(46)

Here, in "Childhood," as in all the sonnets, the diction is relatively plain and declarative, occasionally striking a colloquial note (as in the word "croppers" in the poem's second stanza). The plainness and "objectivity" of the diction is further heightened by the left margin of the lines where only the first-person pronoun and the beginning of sentences are upper-cased, suggesting a column of prose—perhaps a newspaper column. Unlike the lines of the "prophetic" poems and most of the "folk" poems, the lines of "Childhood" and the other sonnets are frequently end-stopped, again heightening the sense of declarative straightforwardness and accessibility to a mass audience already suggested by the diction. At the same time, the "high" literary nature of these poems is marked through the choice of the sonnet form. The use of the sonnet also signals Walker's engagement with literary modernism where the overt engagement with and evasion from the formal expectations of the sonnet was a common move of literary modernists both black and white—as we have seen with respect to Hughes's "Seven Moments of Love" sequence in *Shakespeare in Harlem* and in the final sonnets of Brooks's *A Street in Bronzeville*. In the case of Walker, the most obvious evasions or deformations of the formal expectations for the sonnet take place in the frequent absence of exact rhyme (or even consonance, assonance, or near-rhyme) except in the final couplet (and not always then) and her often idiosyncratic rhyme schemes that seem sometimes completely orthodox (as in "Childhood"), sometimes nearly orthodox (as in "Our Need"), and sometimes random (as in "Iowa Farmer"). This approach to rhyme compels the reader to carefully examine the formal construction of the poems in a way that belies the apparent straightforwardness and transparency of the poems' diction.

A conscious attempt is made to downplay the importance of racial distinction in the sonnets. In much the same way that the position of the poet-speaker with respect to the folk subject is blurred, and the formal design of the sonnets uneasily hybrid the preoccupation with racial identification (and racial self-identification) of the preceding poems in the collection is frustrated in the sonnets. It is impossible to tell who is what so far as categories of race are concerned. The miners from the hills are red; whether they are black, white, or a group of black and white is hidden by the by-product of their shared labor. There is no certain way of telling into which racial category the prostitutes of "Whores" fall.[11] The poor city-dwellers of "Memory" are similarly unmarked racially. The "croppers" of "Childhood" and the farmer and his son in "Iowa Farmer" remain racially indeterminate except through the reader's assumptions about southern sharecroppers (of whom a considerable number were white) and Iowa farmers. Differences of North and South, urban and rural, male and female, industrial worker, farmer, whore and farm laborer are more clearly noted and yet ultimately collapsed by their proximity in the series of sonnets or, as in the case of "Childhood," within the individual sonnet. What the reader is finally left with resembles the Popular Front sense of the "people" who are set in struggle against an enemy rather like the personified sins of medieval allegory—though in this case the sins are Hunger, Racism, Poverty, and Alienation rather than Pride, Sloth, Lust, and so on. Interestingly, the "people" to this point in the sonnet section does not include the poet-speaker who as an eye-witness goes among the miners, whores, sharecroppers, farmers, and slum-dwellers and yet remains an "I" apart who simply witnesses and never acts.

This distance between the speaker-poet and those whom she witnesses disappears in the final two sonnets that close the book, "Our Need" and "The Struggle Staggers Us." These final poems are not documentary or reportage, but a sort of lyric didacticism with echoes of Whitman's "Song of Myself":

> There is a journey from the me to you.
> There is a journey from the you to me.
> A union of the two strange worlds must be.

(51)

Here a common condition between the observer and the observed is proposed. The division between the two remains, transformed from "I" and "they" (or "he") to "you" and "me":

> Out of this blackness we must struggle forth;
> from want of bread, of pride, of dignity.
> Struggle between the morning and the night.
> This marks our years; this settles, too, our plight.

(51)

A need for the recognition of a common condition and a common program of action is proposed in the pronoun "we." The sonnet is in essence a plea for unity and action, but addressed to whom? What "union of two strange worlds" must take place? Is it an appeal for racial solidarity? For black-white unity? For a farmer-labor party? For a multiclass democratic front against fascism and / or the "economic royalists" (to take Franklin Roosevelt's phrase)? For the joining of "folk," "high," and "popular" art? And to what end? Socialism? Neo-Jeffersonian democracy? The welfare state? Perhaps what is strangest about the poem is this call to arms that refuses to name who is calling, who is being called, and for what cause the call is being made.

That the collection ends on such a militant and indeterminate note is perhaps not so strange. In many respects, the early poetry of Walker, along with that of Owen Dodson, represents one of the last attempts in the late 1930s and early 1940s to fuse the folkloric model for recreating the folk voice associated with Sterling Brown (who after all begins *Southern Road* with a vernacular poem and ends with a section largely of sonnets) with the "popular" model associated with Hughes in the late 1930s, while incorporating newer neomodernist influences. Though there is a certain progress in the book from the folk to the people and from the dichotomy of observer and observed to a common identity that (potentially) erases that dichotomy, ultimately the parts of the book never quite cohere. A "strange journey" is indeed proposed thematically and formally, from biblical prophecy to "badman" story to documentary sonnet to didactic exhortation in sonnet form, but never quite enacted. What is left is a diffuse text that sounds a note of rebellion that resists specific definition and addresses an audience that is similarly unclear. If the text as a whole seems less coherent than other later texts, such as *A Street in Bronzeville* and *A Montage of a Dream Deferred*, it is perhaps because Walker does not foreground consciously the uneasiness and uncertainty of such a formal and thematic hybridity in the way that Brooks and Hughes do. Ironically, then, Walker's text seems less coherent because it lacks the unifying theme of fragmentation that characterizes the other two texts.

The Schedule of Delivery Is Tentative: Robert Hayden's *Heart-Shape in the Dust*

Robert Hayden's participation in the literary Left of the 1930s and early 1940s is clear, if sketchily described by scholars to this point. Whether or not Hayden was a CPUSA member is uncertain. Nonetheless, Hayden's work on the Federal Writers' Project (FWP), including his publication in the anthology of FWP writers *American Stuff*; his activity in the Detroit chapter of the John Reed Clubs; his energetic support of CIO organizing drives (including the reading of his poetry at United Auto Workers Union meetings); and his job as the music and drama critic for the Left-influenced African-American newspaper the *Michigan Chronicle* (whose editor Louis Martin arranged for the publication of Hayden's first collection *Heart-Shape in the Dust* [1940]), place Hayden within the Left network of cultural activists and institutions.[12]

Also clear, though even more sketchily described (if described at all), is Hayden's homosexuality or bisexuality.[13] As we have seen with Countee Cullen (and will see with Owen Dodson), despite the masculinist and often homophobic constructions of the working class and the folk by the Left, an identification with the Communist Left and its cultural organizations did not preclude writing relatively open gay poetry. Hayden was also religiously inclined (as were many African-American participants in the Communist Left, particularly after the adoption of the Popular Front strategy by the CPUSA), first as a Christian and later as a Baha'i. It appears that it was in fact Hayden's religious sensibility rather than his early radicalism that conflicted most seriously with his sexuality.

If Walker's *For My People* is a broad survey of African-American Left poetry in the 1930s, embracing the "folk," the "popular," the "high," and the "modern," then the early work of Hayden that is collected in *Heart-Shape in the Dust* ranges even further over the terrain of modern African-American poetry, directly invoking the work of the New Negro Renaissance as well as the chief Left poetic forms, themes, and tropes of the 1930s. As Fred Fetrow notes, the long "mass chant" that ends the book, "These Are My People," is in itself practically a compendium of Left African-American writing of the 1930s.[14] Hayden later repudiated most of these poems after a conversion to the Baha'i religion in the mid-1940s, ostensibly on the basis of an ideological shift from his earlier radicalism and of his sense of the poems' formal inadequacies—and, I suspect, to distance himself from the fairly open homoeroticism of some of the early poems.

Most of Hayden's critics have accepted Hayden's judgment of *Heart-Shape in the Dust* as not worthy of serious consideration owing to the book's juvenile and imitative nature.[15] It is certainly true that the poems of *Heart-Shape in the Dust*, particularly taken as a whole, lack the coherent self-assurance that marks the highly polished neomodernist style that would characterize Hayden's work from the mid-1940s to the 1960s. But these early poems are fascinating in that the separate (and often apparently contradictory) parts that would make up Hayden's mature style are clearly displayed in an unsynthesized form, revealing their indebtedness to thirty years or more of African-American poetry. At the same time, these poems are rarely simple imitation, but often are in critical dialogue with various African-American literary predecessors. This is not to say that the reader cannot discern the influence of non-African-American writers, such as Millay, Wylie, Crane, Sandburg, and Whitman. But it is hard to think of a black poet of the 1930s and 1940s who so openly and thoroughly engages earlier African-American writing.

The literary ancestor whose work Hayden most clearly invokes is Countee Cullen. It is not surprising that a radical religious gay or bisexual African-American poet with large literary ambitions and considerable negative feelings about his sexuality would see an important forerunner to himself in Cullen, a religious gay poet who was acclaimed as the premier poetic voice of the New Negro Renaissance and who was an endorser of numerous radical causes. Hayden shares with Cullen a racialized and often primitivist homoeroticism that conflicts with a deeply held religious sense of the sinfulness of homosexuality, a penchant for Christian imagery and tropes (including the figuration of lynch victims as Christ), a neo-Pre-Raphaelite morbidity and exoticism, and an often elevated literary diction. Moreover, a number of individual poems in *Heart-Shape in the Dust* consciously engage individual poems of Cullen.[16] For example, Hayden's "Southern Moonlight" closely resembles Cullen's "Tableau":

> Oh moon, moon, hide your light—
> That he is black
> And I
>   am white.

(16)

Like Cullen's poem, Hayden's poem displaces homosexuality into a construct of miscegenation that allows for the expression of transgressive sexual relations in a manner relatively acceptable within the African-American community (and the somewhat overlapping Left literary community). At the same time, in a move typical of Hayden's poetic conversation with Cullen, Hayden introduces an element of practical politics, sexual and otherwise, into Cullen's utopianism. Where Cullen's black and white male lovers proudly walk "locked arm in arm" in an urban (and presumably northern) landscape in the bright sun, Hayden's lovers creep out at night in an explicitly southern landscape, fearing even the moon and a scrutiny that could result in their destruction, both physically and socially.

Similarly, "Poem for a Negro Dancer" speaks directly to Cullen's "Heritage," with a passing reference at the end to Cullen's "Shroud of Color":

> Your beauty should be
> A high festival,
> A carnival of blackness
> To hold in thrall
> Strong-limbed warriors
> Whose hands would bear

Sun-colored blossoms
For your hair.

You should live naked,
Naked and proud,
Where black skin is neither
God's curse, nor a shroud.

(41)

Again, like Cullen, Hayden uses an imagined African exoticism to figure homoerotic desire. Hayden's speaker refuses to clearly reveal the gender of the dancer who holds the "strong-limbed warriors" in thrall, but suggests a male identity in the lines "Your blood should sing / With pride our fathers knew." It is this male homoerotic element that distinguishes the relation of this poem to Cullen's poem from its relation to other poems, such as Helene Johnson's "Bottled," Waring Cuney's "No Images," and Claude McKay's "The Harlem Dancer," which use the primitivist figure of the black dancer to figure an ur-black identity.[17] But as in "Southern Moonlight," Hayden does not simply recapitulate Cullen's poem, but instead invokes Cullen in order to criticize what Hayden sees as an unnecessary shame over racial identity and sexual preference as it has been displaced into categories of race.

Perhaps the most telling exchange directed from Hayden to Cullen is Hayden's "Essay on Beauty," which critiques, somewhat unfairly, Cullen's neo-Keatsian invocations of beauty abstracted from social relations (as in Cullen's "To John Keats, Poet. At Spring Time"):

> **There is not more blood-burning loveliness to me**
> **Than slaves at Valley Forge fighting for liberty,**
> **Than Toussaint's freedom-dream, the Douglass memory.**

> And know that all your beauty's pentecostal tongues
> Fall mute before the urgent fact of T.B.-riddled slums
> And bloody cottonbolls and justice-klansman eyed.

(29)

At first glance the poem could almost be a 1920s nationalist response to Cullen, emphasizing black pride in a "literary" diction that might have appeared in a poem in the Garveyite *Negro World*. Or it could have been an early poem by Hughes along the lines of "Proem" from *The Weary Blues*. But on closer inspection, voices of the 1930s break into the conversation with Cullen. The phrase "T.B.-riddled" (rather than a more "literary" description, such as "consumptive") silences the "high" diction of the poem in a colloquial, almost hard-boiled moment that replicates the failure of aesthetic (and personal) beauty before the actual fact of the ghetto in the North and poverty and racist violence in the South, resembling the failure of "high" art in Frank Marshall Davis's "Snapshots of the Cotton South." Similarly, the allusion to Toussaint and the Haitian revolution recall previously noted Third Period attempts to create a "revolutionary Negro tradition" (a theme that is developed at more length in the poem "Gabriel," which pays tribute to the leader of an abortive Virginia slave rebellion in 1800). Reference to slaves fighting for American freedom at Valley Forge echo Popular

Front efforts to portray African-Americans as active participants in the creation of the United States and American democracy.[18] And, as in the work of Hughes, there is a continuity between the folk in the South and in the North with specific details ("T.B.-ridden," "cottonbolls," "klansman") having a quality of engaged reportage that characterized many of Hughes's shorter works in the 1930s. In short, the dialogue with Cullen moves jarringly from the 1920s into and across the 1930s.

If Cullen is the literary forerunner from the New Negro Renaissance era with whom Hayden engages most strongly, then, not surprisingly, it is Sterling Brown and Langston Hughes who play that role for the 1930s. It is with Brown in particular that Hayden carries on a critical literary conversation much as he does with Cullen. As noted above with respect to "Essay on Beauty," one of the themes of *Heart-Shape in the Dust* sounded again and again is the continuity of African-American culture between the rural South and the urban North. A concurrent theme is the northern black consciousness of that continuity. Hayden writes directly against Brown's notion of the "great migration" as a disruption and degradation of "authentic" African-American culture in *Southern Road* and *No Hiding Place*. For example, Hayden's "'We Have Not Forgotten" appears to be a direct response to Brown's "Children's Children," with the title and opening phrase of Hayden's poem answering the anaphoric "They have forgotten" of Brown's poem:

> We have not forgotten the prayers you prayed,
> Black fathers, O black mothers, kneeling in
> The cabin-gloom, debased, yet in your hearts
> Bearing high springtime pageantries of faith.
> We have not forgotten your morning hope,
> More burning than the sun of cottonfields
> Upon dark, shackled limbs, nor songs your anguish
> Suckled.

(10)

Where Brown posits the culture of the northern ghetto as a fall from the ur-folk experience of the South, Hayden uses a similar valorization of the African-American culture of the rural South as a means of affirming the culture and spirit of the working-class black culture of the North through its link to the southern culture, a link that is proudly and consciously acknowledged. It is worth noting that Hayden's construction of the southern folk to which the northern urban speaker so fervently affirms his or her connection is, unlike nearly all the constructions of the folk in 1930s (including Brown's), not gendered as either male or female, but is firmly male and female without the symbolic division of labor between the commercial and the domestic that often marked even those African-American constructions of the 1930s that did try to encompass both.

A similar cultural connection, one that is in a sense less conscious and more felt, is argued in "Sunflowers: Beaubien Street":

> **O sun-whirled, tropic tambourines**
> **That play sad juba songs in dooryard loam,**
> **Recalling chain-gang heat and shimmering pines;**

> O sunward cry of dark ones mute within
> The crumbling shacks; bright image of their will
> To reach through prayer, through long belief the sun
> Fixed in the heavens like Eziekiel's Wheel.

(12)

Where the northern ghetto-dwellers of Brown, particularly in the "Tin Roof Blues" section of *Southern Road*, are obsessed with forgetting their earlier lives, the lives of the working-class residents of black Detroit in Hayden's poems are organized around remembering: even the gardens are memorials to a past life and past home. (Beaubien Street was an important thoroughfare in the old Paradise Valley ghetto in which Hayden grew up.) Like the liveliness and propulsive energy of the new urban blues that filled the African-American neighborhoods of the North, particularly in Detroit, a major terminus of black migration from the Mississippi Delta, where blues clubs thrived on Hastings Street during the 1930s and 1940s, the "brightness" of the sunflowers embodies a transformed and transforming cultural memory that allows the African-American folk or popular subject to negotiate an oppressive past and impoverished present.[19] Hayden also alludes to the most famous literary sunflower in Blake's *Songs of Experience*, ironically reversing Blake so that Hayden's urban-dwellers, unlike Blake's, find in the sunflower a "down home" emblem of their ability to transcend (temporarily) their urban prison. Here also is seen something like Hayden's mature style where a rococo diction and combination of slightly abstract, but suggestive metaphors ("phonographs of poverty" and "blues-chorale of torsioning despair") mix with closely observed and often homely local detail containing an emotionality that threatens to overwhelm the poem's tight control.

If Hayden engages Cullen and Brown in a manner that is both critical and tributary, then Hayden's relationship to his older friend Langston Hughes would seem to be relatively uncritical or, to use Henry Louis Gates Jr.'s notion of "signifyin(g)," "unmotivated."[20] After all, Hughes was certainly the leading African-American writer on the Left to posit, like Hayden, a continuum between North and South, city and country, while remaining rooted in the urban landscape of the North. Indeed, *Heart-Shape in the Dust* contains a number of blues-inflected vernacular monologues that are fairly straightforward imitations of Hughes:

> Man at Cadillac
> Said: Gwan back home.
> Went an played me a number
> But it wouldn't come.
>
> Asked for a shovel
> On the W.P.A.,
> Man said: Uncle Sam
> Ain't handin out today.

(42)

Here in "Shine, Mister," Hayden's pastiche of the blues, a shoe shine cry, Depression landmarks in urban Detroit as signified by the names of automobile manufacturers

(Briggs, Cadillac, Ford), the W.P.A., and the street culture of the numbers and craps games could have been one of the less interesting poems in Hughes's *Shakespeare in Harlem*. At the same time, however derivative in its particular features, the poem, like the other vernacular monologues of the collection, "Bacchanale" and "Jim Crow," anticipates Hayden's extensive use of the monologue in his mature poetry, as in "The Ballad of Nat Turner" (which was among the group of poems for which Hayden won the Hopwood Award for Poetry in 1942) and in the vernacular semimonologue of "Aunt Jemima of the Ocean Waves" from *Words in the Mourning Time* (1970).

However, though the relationship here to Hughes's work seems uncritically imitative when examined through the lens of these vernacular poems, the relationship becomes more complex when the collection is seen as a whole. The poems that most clearly and consciously share Hughes's construction of the continuum between the urban North and the rural South, such as "Sunflowers: Beaubien Street" and "'We Have Not Forgotten,'" are written in a "literary" style that is quite different from that of Hughes. As in the work of Walker and Brooks, the narratorial consciousness-poet as both inside and outside "literature," as well as the folk it attempts to recreate, is foregrounded in the formal construction of the poem. In a sense, Hayden at this point in his career is located somewhere between Walker and Brooks. At times Hayden's "literary" poems are self-consciously pre-modern, as in "Sonnet to E," a Shakespearean sonnet, and in "Elegy (For Elinor Wylie)"—which, as noted with respect to Walker, can be seen as part of a modernist move toward pastiche or formal heteroglossia when framed by the clearly "high" modernist poems and "popular" or "folk" poems of the collection. At other times the "literary" poems of *Heart-Shape in the Dust* are quite intentionally "modern," as in "The Departure" with its obvious influences of literary surrealism and cubism along the lines of Pierre Reverdy:

> Headlines flare in our embrace,
> black flags enshadow
> the valedictory of your parting gaze.
> Violence, an interval suspended
> waits to fall.
>
> (50)

A semi-opaque doubleness, or tripleness, inheres in these lines: Is it an antiwar poem? Is it about the racial violence that was endemic to Detroit in the 1930s and 1940s? Is it a poem about a transgressive, perhaps gay romance? This poem is perhaps too slight and too neat to sustain much interest in and of itself. Nonetheless, its "high" modernity along with the collection's other poems which are consciously "high" modern or "high" pre-modern, in a sense critiques Hughes's work with its implicit insistence that Hughes's location of the narratorial consciousness-poet as an insider (or a potential insider) is simplistic and in fact is a capitulation to an oppressive race identity imposed on African Americans.

In the end, the literary figure that most haunts Hayden's work is Dunbar. In many ways, despite its clear formal and thematic links to the body of Left African-American writing in the 1930s, *Heart-Shape in the Dust* is a return to the Dunbarian split of "high" and "low," or "literary" and "popular," that marked much of the New

Negro Renaissance poetry.[21] There is no clear demarcation here between Hayden's "real" work and his "popular" work as there is in Dunbar's work. But, as when attempting to assess Dunbar's *oeuvre*, it is crucial to see the "high" poetry and "popular" poetry as a whole rather than simply accepting (or rejecting) the Dunbarian paradigm at face value. The "high" poetry forces the reader to reevaluate the "popular" and vice versa. Whether Hayden's work here is as realized as Dunbar's (it is not), Hayden did not try solve the problem of the Dunbarian spit in the "high" premodern modern manner of Cullen in the 1920s and early 1930s by essentially eschewing any attempt to recreate the folk voice, or in that of Brown in the 1930s by rooting representations of the folk by a semi-alienated, returning narratorial consciousness in authentic folk forms of the rural South and in verified reportage, or that of Hughes in the 1930s and 1940s by a similar use of folk documents and reportage combined with a use of urban popular culture to recreate a more broadly popular African-American voice. Instead, Hayden chose to use forms that are "high" in both "modern" and "premodern" ways, as well other forms that are broadly "low," popular, and vernacular, with the result that the narratorial consciousness-poet of the collection is revealed as deeply divided and deeply troubled as to his or her own relation to the African-American subject. This divide, and a recurring interest in communal memory, communal history, and communal voices of Africans and their descendants in the American diaspora that issues from the concerns and aesthetic imperatives of the 1930s, marks Hayden's poetry for the rest of his career. This division between "high" and "low," "literary" and "popular" in *Heart-Shape in the Dust* obtains for the most part between individual poems rather than within poems—though, as seen in "Sunflowers: Beaubien Street," there are instances of the split in single poems. In Hayden's later, mature work, this divide occurs within individual poems where a highly polished neomodernist style emphasizes the alienation of the African-American narratorial consciousness-poet from the African-American communities, experiences, heroes, and so on (often including a representation of the poet as a young man) that the narratorial consciousness obsessively recreates, recalls, and elegizes.

Soapbox of the Red Apocalypse: Proletarianism,
the Popular Front, and "High" Modernism
in Melvin Tolson's Early Works

Melvin Tolson's early career demonstrates complexities of the literary Left in the 1930s and 1940s that often evade scholars of that period. Though Tolson did not begin to publish in periodicals until the 1930s (and did not publish a book until 1944), he was of the generation of writers of the New Negro Renaissance. (Born in 1900, he was older than Countee Cullen and Langston Hughes.) Tolson taught English, coached the debate team, and directed the school drama group at the historically black Wiley College in Texas during the years covered by this study. He was long a sympathizer of the Communist Left, retaining an identification with Marxism to the end of his life.[22] Yet, as noted in chapter 1, he also had a close intellectual friendship with V. F. Calverton, an early anti-Stalinist who broke with CPUSA over the issue of Trotsky's demonization by Stalin and the Comintern in 1929. Calverton played a major role in Tolson's literary development; Calverton's *Modern Monthly* (later *Modern Quarterly*) was virtually the only journal to publish Tolson's poetry during the 1930s.[23] Tolson also helped organize the Socialist-led Southern Tenant Farmers Union during the 1930s. From 1937 to 1944 he wrote a popular column, "Caviar and Cabbage," for the African-American newspaper *The Washington Tribune*.[24] With the possible exception of Sterling Brown, Tolson had formally studied the works of earlier African-American authors more rigorously than any of his literary contemporaries; Tolson's master's thesis at Columbia University, "The Harlem Group of Negro Writers," was one of the earliest serious academic surveys of the writers of the New Negro Renaissance. In short, Tolson's literary and political activities during the 1930s challenge our received notions about what was possible for a public intellectual teaching at an all-black college in the South and what sort of relationships were possible among participants in the literary Left.

The great controversy about Tolson has long been the degree to which his work, particularly the diction of his later works, *Libretto for the Republic of Liberia* (1953) and *Harlem Gallery* (1965), is authentically African-American.[25] Such a questioning of Tolson seems strange considering that Tolson's career, including his many years as a teacher at historically black colleges in Texas and Oklahoma, his four terms as mayor of the all-black town of Langston, Oklahoma, and his stint as a columnist for the African-American press would seem to locate him solidly within the African-American community. And, in fact, not only was Tolson's life "black" but also his work was shaped by the aesthetic concerns that marked the majority of African-American poets of the time.

Like most of the African-American poets of the 1930s and 1940s, including Brooks and Hayden, Tolson's work of that era is both aesthetically and politically vanguardist and elegiac.[26] As noted earlier, this combination issued from an intersection of the discourses of nationalism, "high" modernism, and communism, in which uncovering (or recovering) and commemorating a usable tradition, whether of the Songhai empire, the Holy Roman Empire, or Spartacus's revolt against the empire is a major feature. This combination of vanguardism and elegy, which often characterized "Left" white writers such as Mike Gold and "Right" white writers such as Ezra Pound, as well as African-American writers, created an obvious contradiction of nostalgic and progressivist rhetoric. This contradiction can be traced back in the Marxist tradition to Marx and Engels and their appropriation of the Hegelian notion of a spiral development of history, in which certain social features of one epoch are repeated in other epochs on a higher level. Often in the work of both "Left" and "Right" writers, this contradiction of progessivism and nostalgia is negotiated through a notion of revolution or apocalyptic change that will produce a society that is both "new" and "traditional." What marks Tolson's work is the single-minded energy that he devotes to both sides of the elegiac-vanguardist contradiction and his sensitivity, or pandering in the view of his harshest critics, to various redefinitions of the vanguard. It is this single-mindedness that explains in large part the dramatic shifts in Tolson's work from his unpublished (until 1979) *A Gallery of Harlem Portraits* (completed in 1935) to *Rendezvous with America* (1944) to *Libretto for the Republic of Liberia* (1953).

The manuscript of *A Gallery of Harlem Portraits* was begun around 1932 and completed in 1935, just as the Comintern's Popular Front policy was being inaugurated.[27] Thus the collection can be seen as a product of the post-*Southern Road*, post-"Scottsboro Limited" Third Period of Left African-American letters. This Third Period influence on Tolson's work appears most clearly in the end of the last poem in the collection "The Underdog" (published in the Autumn 1939 issue of *Modern Quarterly* as "Kikes, Bohunks, Crackers, Dagos, Niggers"):

> Kikes and bohunks and wops,
> Dagos and niggers and crackers . . .
> Starved and lousy,
> Blind and stinking—
> We fought each other,
> Killed each other,
> Because the great white masters
> Played us against each other.
>
> Then a kike said: *Workers of the world, unite!*
> And a dago said: *Let us live!*
> And a cracker said: *Ours for us!*
> And a nigger said: *Walk together, children!*
>
> (*A Gallery of Harlem Portraits*, 230)

In essence what Tolson is articulating here is the concept of the workers' "united front" against capitalism, a political formulation of the Comintern that preceded the notion of a multiclass "popular front" against fascism as the dominant guiding principle of the international Communist movement. The African-American folk tradition is placed in the revolutionary tradition of Marx, Sacco and Vanzetti, and the often violent labor struggles of the early 1930s (e.g., the general strikes in San Francisco and Minneapolis and giant textile industry general strike, all in 1934).

This location of the African-American folk experience within a context of class and the development of class consciousness (as opposed to racial or ethnic consciousness) follows a long and ironic racial self-assertion by an African-American speaker using a diction that is an amalgam of journalism, hard-boiled fiction, "high" literature, advertising, and what might be thought of as "white" vernacular racism:

> I am sambo, the shine,
> In the St. Regis Iridium,
> The Cotton Club,
> The Terrace Room of the New Yorker.
>
> I am the nigger, the black son of a bitch,
> From the Florida Keys to Caribou, Maine;
> From the Golden Gate
> To the Statue of Liberty.
>
> I know the deafness of white ears,
> The hate of white faces,
> The venom of white tongues,
> The torture of white hands.

This poem clearly attempts to end the collection on a note of revolutionary optimism with a resolution of the formal contradictions and political contradictions (including the contradiction between racial and / or ethnic identity and class interest) seen in the varying discourses that make up the earlier part of the poem. Yet it seems at odds formally and thematically with the elegiac portraits that make up the vast majority of the collection.

The poem "Harlem" (an abbreviated version of which was published with the title "Vergil Ragsdale" in the Winter 1939 issue of *Modern Quarterly*) sets the tone of prophetic elegy that marks Tolson's work throughout his career. By prophetic elegy I mean that Tolson's work from *A Gallery of Harlem Portraits* to *Harlem Gallery* is marked by a sense of satirical nostalgia for an African-American culture that Tolson envisions as vanishing, but that has not in fact vanished. As noted earlier, such a nostalgia was based on the presumed inevitability of the disappearance of aspects of African-American culture—a presumption that also characterized the work of a number of African-American poets of the New Negro Renaissance era, most notably James Weldon Johnson and Jean Toomer. But where Toomer and Johnson represent and recreate a rural folk culture that they see in the process of disappearing, Tolson takes a similar stance toward all African-American communities North and South, rural and urban. "Harlem" serves as a sort of introduction to Tolson's project of fixing an African-American community, a cultural moment (or a series of linked cultural moments, types, and actual individuals) bound to disappear in a progressive future that the narratorial consciousness-poet anxiously awaits. Thus appropriately enough for the elegiac nature of Tolson's project, the poem opens with two deaths:

> Diamond Canady
> Was stabbed in bed by Little Eva Winn.
> Deacon Phineas Bloom
> Confessed his adultery on his deathbed.
>
> (3)

The satiric edge of the narratorial consciousness-poet's elegiac voice is established with widely varying prosy free-verse lines bonded sonically through alliteration, assonance, and repetition and employing an ironic, often hard-boiled diction.

This satiric voice then modulates into a sort of apostrophe invoking and commemorating the African-American folk spirit:

> Dusky Bards,
> Heirs of eons of Comedy and Tragedy
> Pass along the streets and alleys of Harlem
> Singing ballads of the Dark World
>
> (3)

The tone here is partially satiric, but not entirely. What appears to be a simple statement is also an invocation to the folk spirit to sing, or to sing through the poet, recalling and revising within a secularized, urban landscape James Weldon Johnson's well-known poetic tribute to the creators of the spirituals, "O Black and Unknown Bards" (1908). The inflated diction of "Dusky Bards, / Heirs of eons of Comedy and

Tragedy," following the hard-boiled and "realistic" opening stanza, rings humorously, mocking its own pretensions (and the pretensions of "high" art), while at the same time genuinely elevating the "folk" or "popular" expressions that follow to a level comparable to that of the highest of "high" culture.

The folk expressions that follow are a long series of blues and blues-inflected lyrics that are supposed to be the actual folk voice emerging from the text. These lyrics fall into roughly three categories: the popular blues, the social satire blues, and the protest blues. The popular blues are those lyrics rendered in both male and female voices that treat the traditional subject of popular blues recordings, love and sexual politics:

> When a man has lost his taste fer you,
>   Jest leave dat man alone.
> Says I . . . a dawg won't eat a bone
>   If he don't want de bone.

(3)

The social satire blues are those lyrics that lampoon some aspect of African-American society:

> Preacher called to bless my home
> An' keep it free from strife.
> Preacher called to bless my home
> An' keep it free from strife.
> Now I's got a peaceful home
> An' de preacher's got my wife.

(3)

Here, under the guise of a popular blues of love and gender relations, the folk-speaker is making a pointed commentary about morality, power, and social stratification within the African-American community. Of course, the philandering minister is a familiar figure both of black folklore and of black literature. However, rarely does this figure appear so overtly in the popular blues.

Finally, there is the protest blues and blues-inflected lyric:

> Rather be a hobo, Lawd
> Wid a stinkin' breath
> Dan live in de Big House
> Workin' folks to death.

(3)

This category seems largely derived from the genre of African-American songs proposed by the folklorists and musicologists of the Left, notably Lawrence Gellert in his collection *Negro Songs of Protest*. These blues affirm an African-American folk tradition of overt popular struggle against race and class oppression. Again, as with Tolson's blues of social satire, such a tradition may have existed, as evidenced by the recent release of a number of Gellert's field recordings, but the protest elements of popular blues records in the 1920s and 1930s were almost always far more oblique with respect to race and class, if not gender.

In short, Tolson has deliberately recast the blues to form an expressive vehicle that is simultaneously or by turns humorous, satiric, personal, broadly social, and politically radical. These categories are not posed by the narratorial consciousness as mutually exclusive. As in Brown's vernacular poems in *Southern Road*, the constitutive principles of Tolson's blues poetry closely resemble the previously mentioned slogan of the Communist Left, "Promote Negro Culture in Its Original Form with Proletarian Content." However, Tolson's blues differ from Brown's blues poetry in Tolson's attempt to incorporate the bawdy side of popular commercial blues, which Brown eschews, into his construction of the folk voice. In this incorporation of an overtly popular culture aspect into his blues poetry, Tolson is closer to Hughes, though the direct-protest aspect of Tolson's blues fragments is far more pronounced than in the work of Hughes who, despite his many militantly radical poems, wrote few protest blues as such—the best known of which, "Red Clay Blues" (written with Richard Wright), appeared four years after Tolson completed *A Gallery of Harlem Portraits*.

The fragments of the blues and other vernacular musical forms serve as a sort of alternate narrator, or as a folk chorus in *A Gallery of Harlem Portraits*. As Robert Farnsworth suggests in his biography of Tolson, blues fragments are used to link together formally a sprawling group of individual portraits that make up the bulk of the collection.[28] Farnsworth points out that the blues serve also as a reality check for Tolson's "most optimistic and imaginative speculations on his future," which imagine a raceless and classless utopia.[29] The blues are similarly employed as a counterpoint to the "high" culture or epic ambitions of Tolson's work, and by extension, vanguardist art.

This use of the blues as an alternate speaker that questions the authority of the narratorial consciousness-poet to represent, recreate, and critique the folk voice and the folk-popular African-American community is further emphasized by the figure of the consumptive "high" Vergil Ragsdale and his unread epic *An African Tragedy*. The work of Ragsdale, "dishwasher poet," is "proletarian" in sympathy and alternately hard-boiled and "literary" in diction. In short, the work of Ragsdale is much like that of Tolson:

"Harlem, O Harlem,
I shall not see the quiet Dawn
When the yellow and brown and black proletarians
Swarm out of stinking dives and fire-trap tenements,
Pour through canyon-streets,
Climb Striver's Row and Sugar Hill,
Erase the liveried flunkies,
And belly-laugh in the rich apartments of the Big Niggers.

"I shall not see the unwashed mob
Hoofing the Lindy Hop in Madame Alpha Devine's drawing room,
Guzzling champagne in Banker Calverton's library,
Bouncing their unperfumed butts upon Miss Briffault's silken beds,
Gorging the roast chicken and eclairs in Editor Speare's kitchen.

(4)

Ragsdale's poetry is like Tolson's work, only taken to the point of self-parody and pathos: the apostrophes, the neoromantic stance of the poet, the Sandburgian catalogue, the Menckenesque sarcasm, the mixture of "high" and "low" suggested by Vergil Ragsdale's name are pushed until the poem is more than faintly ridiculous. The satire on Ragsdale's neoromantic literary stance is further emphasized (in a move resembling the ending of Wallace Thurman's novel *Infants of the Spring*) when Ragsdale's Harlem landlady, Big Sadie, orders her husband to destroy the manuscript of *An African Tragedy*, after the poet has suffered a suitably tragic and "poetic" death from tuberculosis; the poet's "epic," is rejected by a rooming-house landlady, one of Ragsdale's "unwashed mob," as "trash." While Big Sadie, like the African-American community in general, is depicted by Tolson as lacking discernment with respect to "high" art, particularly modernist art (a theme that would be sounded to an even greater extent in *Harlem Gallery*), the "high" artist and the intellectual who adopt a "vanguardist" politics and art compounded of Marxism and modernism are also rendered as at least slightly ridiculous and more than slightly pompous.

"Harlem" ends with a return to the voice of the original speaker-poet-narratorial consciousness:

> Radicals, prizefighters, actors and deacons,
> Beggars, politicians, professors and redcaps,
> Bulldikers, Babbitts, racketeers and jig-chasers,
> Harlots, crapshooters, workers and pink-chasers,
> Artists, dicties, Pullman porters and messiahs . . .
> The Curator has hung the likenesses of all
> In *A Gallery of Harlem Portraits*.

(4)

This catalogue is a typical example of Tolson's jarring juxtaposition of different dictions—the archaically "poetic" ("harlots"), the hard-boiled ("bulldikers"), colloquially African-American ("dicties"), the literately journalistic ("Babbitts")—that borders on self-parody and that partially undermines the "social realist" aspect of the representations hanging in the "gallery"—if one takes a certain unified and flattened out accessibility of voice to be a mark of "social realism."

As we have seen, Tolson's earliest work is marked by an extremely contradictory doubleness, a doubleness that throughout Tolson's career provides a continuity to what many have seen as a formally disparate body of work marked by rapid aesthetic "conversions." The presence of apparently opposed qualities—of satire and sympathy, of "high" and "low," of an artist who stands simultaneously among and beyond "the Dark Masses," of a Menckenesque sarcasm that is aimed at the represented subjects and at the poet himself, of a folk voice that has an authority that stands outside the narratorial consciousness and yet that itself is a subject of ridicule, of a Christian–Third Period vision of a revolutionary apocalypse (and the rising of new society in which racial and class divisions shall wither away) and an intense, if premature, nostalgia for the culture that will disappear into that new society—is the most prominent feature of Tolson's work throughout his career. Tolson recognizes that this sense of a self-conscious doubleness has a long tradition in African-American intellectual history; it is not accidental that the most famous articulator of the concept of African-American "double-consciousness," W. E. B. Du Bois, is repeatedly referred to directly and indirectly in Tolson's *Harlem Gallery*. However, Tolson differs from Du Bois in that the doubleness of Tolson's work is ultimately unreconciled—and even the foreseen reconciliation of the new society is troubling.

This doubleness is also apparent in Tolson's first published book, *Rendezvous with America* (1944). In a number of respects, *Rendezvous* is an atypical work for Tolson. It is the only book of Tolson's to make extensive use of rhyme and "traditional" "high" poetic forms, particularly the sonnet. Tolson's signature mocking and self-mocking satiric tone is much muted except in a few of the shorter poems of the collection, such as "An Ex-Judge at the Bar." The democratic optimism of the collection is relatively untempered by the elegiac quality that marks *A Gallery of Harlem Portraits*, *Harlem Gallery*, and, to a lesser extent, *Libretto for the Republic of Liberia* (1953). As in the other book-length works by Tolson, there is a vanguardist ideological cast to *Rendezvous*, but the ideological vanguard is decidedly that of the Popular Front with its inclusive rhetoric in which the "people" are invited to join together more or less as they are rather than as they should be.[30] While African-Americans are pointedly included by Tolson among the "people," there are far fewer attempts to recreate the folk or popular African-American voice than in *A Gallery of Harlem Portraits* (or in *Harlem Gallery*, for that matter). Interestingly, despite the frequent invocation of the "people" and popular culture, popular culture, including African-American commercial forms such as the blues, as a formal resource for poetry is virtually absent from the book.

Nonetheless, on a formal level, foregrounded and unresolved oppositions of the "popular" (in the sense of the "popular" poetry of, say, Sandburg rather than that of mass commercial culture) and the "high" and of the "modern" and the "traditional" remain. Metrics, patterns of rhyme (or lack of rhyme), line length, arrangement of lines on the page, and so on vary widely even with a single poem. With respect to metrics, for example, as Mariann Russell points out, Tolson employs monometer, dimeter, and trimeter, as well as more "traditional" tetrameter and pentameter. Even in the lines that are essentially in iambic pentameter, Tolson plays considerably with the stresses and number of feet.[31]

Visually, the radical juxtaposition of "traditional" and "modern" elements is even more striking, particularly in the often shocking transition between sections:

> I see America in Thomas Paine,
> As he pinnacles the freedoms that tyrants ban;
> In young Abe Lincoln, tanned by prairie suns,
> As he splits his rails and thinks the Rights of Man.
>
>   V
>
>   A blind man said,
>   "Look at the kikes."
>   And I saw
> Rosenwald sowing the seeds of culture in the Black Belt,
> Michelson measuring the odysseys of invisible worlds,

Brandeis opening the eyes of the blind to the Constitution,
Boas translating the oneness in the Rosetta stone of mankind

(6)

Here among the relatively unsurprising democratic figures of neo-Popular Front politics (particularly Paine and Lincoln), and the equally unsurprising catalogues of democratic sentiments derived from Whitman and Sandburg (also Popular Front icons), is a sudden transition from a fairly standard *xbyb* quatrain to three unrhymed lines centered on the page to a proselike block of four lines. Another somewhat disturbing element here among an otherwise predictable and even slack diction is, as Joy Flasch points out, Tolson's proclivity for changing the normative grammatical function of a word, particularly using a noun ("pinnacles") as a verb.[32] The massive accumulation of these noun-verbs over the course of the collection disrupts the generically "popular" voice of many of the poems, introducing a distinctly "literary" and "modern" note. At the same time, the use of nouns as verbs has been associated with African-American vernacular speech, particularly by Tolson's contemporary, Zora Neale Hurston.[33] Thus, as often is the case in Tolson's work, a link to popular African-American expressive culture is found even in those places where diction and allusive detail seem far removed from any specifically African-American identity.

The "popular" voice of Tolson's poems is also disrupted by the frequent allusions, often piled on one another in catalogues, and epigram-like lines. (Of course, in this regard, the great forerunner of Popular Front poetry, Whitman, and the somewhat less drawn upon icon, Blake were no strangers to the enigmatic epigram or aphorism.) It is perhaps in the allusively learned catalogues that the double-edged satire that characterizes Tolson's work is most clearly present in *Rendezvous*:

Messiahs from the Sodoms and Gomorrahs of the Old World,
Searchers for Cathay and Cipango and El Dorado,
Mystics from Oubangui Chari and Uppsala,
Serfs from Perugia and Tonle Sap,
Jailbirds from Newgate and Danzig,
Patriots from Yokosuka and Stralsund,
Scholars from Oxford and Leyden,
Beggars from Bagdad and Montmartre,
Traders from the Tyrrhenian Sea and Mona Passage,
Sailors from the Skagerrak and Bosphorus Strait,
Iconoclasts from Buteshire and Zermatt.

(3)

This catalogue from the title poem of the collection no doubt expresses a multicultural vision of America that dovetailed with a neo-Popular Front ideology and certainly with the editorial vision of *Common Ground* magazine in which the poem was first published in 1943. It also establishes the authority of the narratorial consciousness-speaker who leaves the reader with no doubt that he or she knows where Oubangui and Uppsala are without looking at an atlas. Nonetheless, while the catalogue unquestionably is intended seriously, it also contains a certain satire of the speaker who would make such claims to geographical authority and, perhaps, of a reader who might receive the catalogue and pretend not to need an atlas. The very sound of the listed names has a sort of doubleness in which the outlandishness of the names (for American readers) clashes with a sense of cultural inclusiveness, provoking a nervousness on the part of the reader, and perhaps on the part of the poet, as to whether a name such as "Skagerrak" or "Tonle Sap" is funny. In any event, it is hard to believe that a poet as invested in comic naming as Tolson (e.g., "Vergil Ragsdale" and "Hideho Heights") was not playing humorously with the associations of names containing such sounds as "sap," "skag," and "bang" for American audiences.

The use of epigram-like lines usually uttered in near oracularity also adds to the disruptive doubleness of the text. Sometimes these lines erupt in the middle of otherwise "popularly" voiced passages. Often whole passages, and even whole poems, employ this oracular and epigrammatic voice:

> The hoary druid Time
> Leans upon his mace,
> Discerns the odyssey of the tiny dace,
> Sees the *raison d'être* worming from the slime,
> Discovers the vigils of a soul-rived clod
> In a rendezvous with God.

(107)

This voice is clearly at odds with the formal expectations of a "typical" Popular Front artistic work, despite the fact that Popular Front ideology informs nearly all the poems of the collection. In short, even the most "popular" of Tolson's poems is a long way from "The House I Live In" or "Ballad for Americans."

By the mid-1940s, Tolson was clearly moving toward his "high" neomodernist style, which he would fully adopt in *Libretto for the Republic of Liberia* (the first draft of which he completed in 1947).[34] He also moved away, temporarily, from attempts to represent and recreate the African-American folk voice and folk experience and toward a more allusive, oracular, epigrammatic style that would become denser as his career progressed. (It is worth noting that Tolson himself did not see this as moving away from the folk, but instead as making an intellectual and aesthetic journey that the African-American artist in the twentieth century who truly wished to represent the folk in its totality and complexity would have to make.) Nonetheless, the sort of formal and thematic doubleness of self-doubt and self-assertion, which had characterized his earlier work, would continue to be a defining feature of Tolson's work for the rest of his career. This combination of populism and vanguardism, which in no small part issued from the Left cultural politics of the 1930s and early 1940s, maintained a formal and thematic unity between works that might otherwise seem quite disparate.

Conclusion: Owen Dodson and the End of the Populist Front

Such assessments as exist about Owen Dodson's poetry of the 1940s arrive at no consensus as to Dodson's place in African-American poetry. In fact, these assessments are often diametrically opposed. For example, Margaret Walker places Dodson (along with Robert Hayden, Melvin Tolson, and herself) as part of a group of "1930s" poets who published in the 1940s. By "1930s," Walker refers to "social protest" and, somewhat covertly, to a sympathy with the Popular Front rather than a simple chronological definition of "1930s."[35] Conversely, Blyden Jackson opposes the "strong individual inclination" of Dodson's first collection of poems, *Powerful Long Ladder* (1946), to Walker's "racialism" in *For My People*.[36] James V. Hatch's biography of Dodson frequently touches on Dodson's participation in the Popular Front cultural Left (and the neo-Popular Front of the World War II period) while almost completely eliding the Left character of these activities and their impact on his work.[37]

On close reading, one is inclined to agree with Walker in her assertion of the affinity of Dodson's *Powerful Long Ladder* to the work of Hayden, Tolson, and herself in the 1940s. As in the 1940s collections of the other three poets, Dodson's collection ends with a plea for interracial "peoples'" unity for progressive ends ("Brothers, let us enter that portal for good / When peace surrounds us like a credible universe. / Bury that agony, bury this hate, take our black hands in yours" [103]). The synecdoche of the "black hands" also recalls the ending of Hayden's first collection and Wright's famous poem of the 1930s, "I Have Seen Black Hands," proposing a further genealogy of Left African-American poetry than that suggested by Walker.

Dodson shares with Hayden, Walker, and Tolson not only Walker's "note of social protest" but also the stylistic diversity (or even diffuseness) that marks the texts of these other authors, as well as Brooks's *A Street in Bronzeville* (which Walker pointedly distinguishes from the work of "1930s" 1940s poets).[38] In this diversity, Dodson is clearly a poet of the early and middle 1940s, whatever his proclivity for "social protest." Like these other texts, *Powerful Long Ladder* is by turns, or simultaneously, self-consciously "modern," "high," "folk," and "popular." The poem "Black Mother Praying," for example, is a virtual anthology of earlier tropes of the African-American folk (including the figure of the black mother and the figure of the black Christ) in the service of the popular slogan of the "Double V":[39]

> You know bout this war that's bitin the skies and gougin out the earth.
> Last month, Lord, I bid my last boy away to fight.
> I got all my boys fightin now for they country.
> Didn't think bout it cept it were for freedom;
> Didn't think cause they was black they wasn't American;
> Didn't think a thing cept that they was my only sons,
> And there was mothers all over the world
> Sacrificin they sons like You let Yours be nailed
> To the wood for men to behold the right.

> (8)

The poem itself is a stylistic pastiche that does not quite cohere. End-stopped conversational lines mix with Whitmanic catalogues of racist oppression and black self-sacrifice and with flowing biblical apocalyptic millenarianism, united largely by the speaker's "folk" diction, which often seems forced. However, the poem is a striking departure from most invocations of the figures of the Negro Mother and the black Christ, in that there is a historical specificity to the poem, citing and describing particular instances of wartime racist violence that earlier usages of these tropes (even by radical authors) generally lacked.

Yet despite this undeniable commonality with other writers of the early 1940s and continuity with the writers of the 1930s, the position of Dodson's work can be seen as analogous to that of an older poet who never successfully negotiated the transition between the 1920s and the 1930s: Countee Cullen. On one level, Dodson's affinity to Cullen, like that of Hayden's, is easily seen. In addition to Dodson's actual friendship with Cullen (Dodson was a pallbearer at Cullen's funeral in 1946), whom Dodson elegizes in "Countee Cullen," Cullen's work was a model for the expression of homoeroticism for Dodson—though Dodson was less morally troubled about his homosexuality than either Cullen or Hayden.[40] Like Hayden's *Heart-Shape in the Dust*, *Powerful Long Ladder* contains a considerable number of homoerotic poems that draw formally on Cullen's work. For example, as James V. Hatch notes, Dodson's "Circle One," a poem dedicated to Dodson's close gay friend Gordon Heath, is clearly indebted to Cullen:[41]

Why we sailed and how we prosper
Will be sung and lived again;
All the lands repeat themselves,
Shore for shore and men for men.

(75)

While Dodson's homoerotic poems are generally his most Cullenesque, there is also often a sense of playful humor about them, as seen here in humorous and deliberately corny invocation of colloquial speech ("shore for shore") and in the double entendre of the last line "men for men," lacking in the work of Cullen. This deflating playfulness in "Circle One," which breaks the mechanically "classical" sound of the trochaic tetrameter quatrains, is to some degree a satire on what is seen as the overwrought seriousness of Cullen's homoerotic poetry and a considerable amount of Dodson's own elegiac love poetry.[42]

However, Dodson's resemblance to Cullen is not so much in these clear ties of sympathy, form, and narratorial stance, but in the position that Dodson's poetry occupies in African-American poetry of the 1930s and 1940s. As Cullen's 1935 *The Medea and Some Poems* signals a personal ending and a metaliterary comment on the passing of a general literary era, so too does Dodson's collection mark a long hiatus in Dodson's poetic career and an end to a period of African-American letters. Though Dodson was in the midst of a long and productive career in the theater, shortly after the publication of *Powerful Long Ladder* he essentially ceased writing poetry for more than a decade (and would not publish any real collection of poetry until the 1970s).[43] Written during the neo-Popular Front era of World War II and its immediate aftermath, and published as the cold war began in earnest, *Powerful Long Ladder* is also the last major example of the formal diversity that marked many texts by African-American writers in the 1940s.

The formal and thematic diffuseness of *Powerful Long Ladder*, in which the different parts never quite come together, shows many of the political and aesthetic stresses—really the politico-aesthetic stresses—that marked black poetry during World War II, both before and after direct American participation in the war. As noted above, this was a quality that Dodson shared with many of the other important African-American poets of the time. However, in the years following the publication of Dodson's collection, a number of African-American poets, including Brooks, Tolson, and Hayden, moved toward a unified "high" neomodernist style. Others, most notably Hughes, created a unified "popular" neomodernist style. (And in the case of Hughes, his "popular" neomodernism existed mostly as a prominent, but rather singular, alternative to "high" neomodernism, which would be directly influential for the most part in the later "postmodern" works of the New American Poetry and the Black Arts Movement rather than in the late 1940s and early 1950s.) Some poets, such as Walker, would like Dodson essentially fall silent or devote themselves to other literary genres, at least until the rise of the African-American cultural movements associated with the civil rights and cultural nationalist periods of the 1960s and early 1970s.

The issue of modernity may be the defining issue for the black poets who came of literary age in the late 1930s and early 1940s, as was the issue of authenticity in the re-creation of the folk or popular voice for the previous generation. In much the same way that formerly productive poets, such as Cullen, who were unwilling or unable to attempt to recreate the folk or popular African-American voice, largely stopped writing (or publishing at least) after the early 1930s, perhaps the relative decline of such productive poets of the 1930s as Sterling Brown, Waring Cuney, and Frank Marshall Davis, and of such 1940s poets as Walker and Dodson as poets (as opposed to novelists or playwrights) until the 1960s, was due to a failure (for whatever reasons) to renegotiate their relationship with modernism. As with the passage of the 1920s into the 1930s, the one African-American poet active in the 1930s to remain productive throughout the 1940s into the 1950s was Langston Hughes. Hughes was successful in no small part because he was able to create a popular neomodernist style that grew organically out of the aesthetics and ideological concerns that marked his poetry in the 1930s.

The younger poets (at least with respect to career, if not chronological age) who produced and published a sustained amount of work through the decade and beyond moved for the most part toward a "high" neomodernism that drew considerably on the general neomodernist revival in the United States supported by the unlikely anti-Communist alliance of the New Critics and a significant section of the intellectuals associated with the anti-Stalinist Left. However, all these poets came from a milieu significantly informed by the politics and cultural expressions of the Communist Left, and their work retained many continuities with the Left literary subculture, even when (as in the case of Hayden and Brooks) the poets themselves left these ties behind, sometimes denying that they ever existed or that the poets truly understood during the 1930s and 1940s what the ties meant.[44] Among what the poets retained was a polyvocality that included the direct recreation of the African-American folk voice; a concern with the location of the narratorial consciousness-poet with respect to the

African-American folk or people, an obsession with the relation of mass, folk, and "high" culture; a historical social sense that focused on the recovery and preservation of a specific African-American experience; and the desire to mediate the contradiction between populism and vanguardism that generally characterized the political and cultural activities of the Communist Left, particularly after 1935.

Conclusion

"Sullen Bakeries of Total Recall"

I acknowledge the demands of Surrealist realization. I challenge
Apollinaire to stagger drunk from his grave and write a poem about
the Rosenbergs' last days in a housing project . . .

—BOB KAUFMAN, "SULLEN BAKERIES OF TOTAL RECALL"

Commentators often have characterized the immediate post-World War II era of African-American letters and culture generally as cautiously optimistic, save for some lingering anxiety over potential nuclear armageddon and McCarthyism.[1] In these accounts, the neomodernist strains of postwar African-American literature are largely an "integrationist" expression of this optimism and a rejection of the "protest" literature of the 1930s and early 1940s. It is certainly true that the wartime breaches in Jim Crow, particularly in terms of employment, housing, and public accommodations, were not completely nullified in the "reconversion" period that followed the war.

However, the actual experiences and attitudes of African-Americans were far more mixed than such labels of qualified optimism would suggest. As George Lipsitz points out, "reconversion" often had a disastrous impact on urban women workers and black workers employed in the mass-production industries.[2] In the South, Jim Crow remained largely intact and the attitude of southern segregationists became more belligerent in the face of the new challenges to the system brought on by the war. While there was a decline in "traditional" racist violence, notably lynching, the postwar era featured an intense (and often brutal) repression of militant anti–Jim Crow organizations (particularly in the labor movement) that had been active in the South during the late 1930s and early 1940s.[3]

This repression, was not, of course, limited to the South. One ironic feature of the early cold war era was that the same ideology that was authorized by the international competition of the American-led "Free World" with the Soviet-led "People's

208

Democracies" gave advocates of African-American civil rights an increased leverage while severely limiting the organizational forms and methods of that advocacy. Thus the period was characterized by the frequent red-baiting and isolation of militant civil rights advocates and organizations, many of which *had* been associated with the Communist Left, even as certain advances against the Jim Crow system were registered, such as Truman's 1948 order abolishing segregation in the Armed Forces. Similarly, much of the labor movement, particularly the CIO, publicly supported the end of Jim Crow even as those Left-led unions that were most militantly antisegregationist and pro–civil rights were expelled from the CIO in 1949 and subsequently isolated, dismembered, and largely destroyed by "raiding" AFL and CIO unions. Covert or overt racist appeals to white workers by anti-Communist "raiders" not infrequently marked the campaigns against the expelled unions, especially in the South.[4]

For African-American artists and intellectuals (and community and labor activists), one of the largest sources of anxiety during the cold war had to be the near-complete repression of the domestic Communist Left with which many had been connected in the 1930s and early 1940s.[5] The late 1940s and early 1950s witnessed high-profile federal interrogation and / or persecution of many of the African Americans who were (or had been) most prominently linked to the CPUSA, such as leading black Communists Benjamin Davis and Henry Winston, W. E. B. Du Bois, Paul Robeson, and Langston Hughes. There were also many lower-profile or covert disruptions of the lives of various black artists and intellectuals deemed "disloyal."[6] One particularly effective method of less public intimidation was the harassment and / or questioning of African-American writers and intellectuals, including Sterling Brown and Frank Marshall Davis, by FBI agents.[7] At the same time, Left-led black organizations, such as the Southern Negro Youth Congress, the National Negro Labor Council, and the Civil Rights Congress, were denounced as "Communist fronts," isolated, and destroyed.

By the early 1950s virtually no major African-American poets were willing to be associated publicly with the Communist Left. Some poets, like Robert Hayden and Langston Hughes, publicly renounced their earlier connection to the literary Left of the 1930s and the 1940s. Others, like Sterling Brown, Frank Marshall Davis, and Melvin Tolson, seem to have retained many of their earlier political sympathies, but became distant from the remaining cultural institutions of the Left. (Davis literally distanced himself from those institutions by moving from Chicago to Hawaii at the end of 1948—though that did not prevent more harassment of Davis by the FBI.) Still others, such as Gwendolyn Brooks and Margaret Walker, did not so much renounce their earlier associations as downplay them. There were a few young poets, notably Lance Jeffers and Audre Lorde (as well as Lorraine Hansberry, whose first important publications were a couple of poems in *Masses and Mainstream*), who were affiliated with the Communist movement in the 1950s, but their connection, as far as I can tell, was of a far lower profile than the African-American poets of the previous twenty years.[8]

This is not to say, of course, that the distance these poets put between themselves and their former ties to the Left was due to mere political expediency. It is only to point out that the political repression of the domestic Communist Left during the cold war, along with factional strife and the ensuing disillusionment among many CPUSA members and supporters (particularly after the Soviet invasion of Hungary and the revelations of Krushchev's secret 1956 speech about the crimes of Stalinism), forced a sharper end to the era of 1930s and 1940s African-American literary radicalism than would have been the case otherwise. For example, it may be true, as Arnold Rampersad argues (and as Hughes himself would claim before the McCarthy committee), that Hughes drew away from the Communist Left during the 1940s. However, Hughes continued to occasionally lend his name to CPUSA-initiated campaigns and organizations and to publish works in such CPUSA-identified or Communist-influenced journals as *New Masses*, *Harlem Quarterly*, *Mainstream*, and *Masses and Mainstream* until (at least) 1950.[9] It was not until his "friendly" appearance before the McCarthy Committee in 1953 that he completely broke with his radical past. (And even then, Hughes continued to criticize McCarthyism somewhat more obliquely, particularly in a number of the "Simple" stories he wrote after his appearance before the committee.) In this regard, it is worth noting that though the CPUSA never again became anything like the cultural force it had been during the 1930s and 1940s, once the domestic cold war had somewhat receded, journals initiated by the Communist Left, notably *Mainstream* and *Freedomways*, and various other "Old Left" institutions and individuals, had a modest, but significant impact on African-American letters in the 1960s.[10] That a considerable number of African-American artists and intellectuals who had been identified with the Left during the 1930s and 1940s were willing to be associated with *Freedomways* and other Old Left–influenced institutions and functions suggests that perhaps their ideologies had remained fairly constant, whether or not they still saw the CPUSA as an important vehicle for social change.

At the same time, the work of those African-American poets who came of age during the 1930s and early 1940s remained marked by the formal and thematic concerns of the 1930s and 1940s, which were in turn largely shaped by the ideological concerns of that era, even as the poets moved away from the Left organizationally. It is hard to think of an African-American poet before the 1930s, with the partial exceptions of Langston Hughes and Jean Toomer, who attempted to represent an actual African-American community in any extended or specific manner. After the 1930s and 1940s, such representations are common, whether Hughes's Harlem, Hayden's Paradise Valley, Brooks's Bronzeville, or Tolson's Harlem. Similarly, there are few examples by black poets prior to the 1930s of any detailed engagement with history, or even contemporary events, other than generalized tributary poems to historical figures, as in Dunbar's "Frederick Douglass." (Even Du Bois's well-known "A Litany of Atlanta" responds to the violence of the 1906 Atlanta riot with much outrage but little historical specificity.) After the onset of the cold war, a concern for the recovering and dramatizing of a "people's history" or "revolutionary Negro tradition," which was so much a part of 1930s and early 1940s African-American literature, remained a significant element of the work of even a poet like Robert Hayden, who wrote such historical poems as "The Ballad of Nat Turner," "Frederick Douglass," and "Middle Passage" in the 1940s as he was moving away from the Communist Left. (Hayden continued to write such poems for the rest of his career.)

Another mark of the 1930s and 1940s that continued to be displayed in the following period of African-American poetic production was a concrete internationalism, particularly with respect to the nations and cultures of the African diaspora, and also with the anticolonial struggles, and anti-neocolonial struggles of Asia, Africa, and Latin America. This internationalism remained distinct, for the most part, from the generalized, and often primitivist, constructs of Africa that marked black literary internationalism before and during the New Negro Renaissance. While a certain idealization of Africa was often present in poetry written after the beginning of the cold war (as was the case in Margaret Danner's poetic meditations on African art), it was an idealization that was authorized by observations of actual artifacts or by drawing on various cultural texts, thereby attempting to ground the idealizations in a "real" cultural frame. This anti-colonialism would be an important bridge between the poetry of the 1930s and early 1940s and the cultural nationalist poetry of the 1960s.[11]

However, the most important continuity is the manner in which the old problem of how to represent and recreate the folk or popular voice was solved. Of course, the problem was not worked out in the same way by all the poets in question. Yet it is impossible to overemphasize the importance of the relatively obvious fact that after the 1930s the direct recreation of the African-American folk or popular voice, as opposed to the indirect representation of that voice that dominated New Negro Renaissance poetry and criticism, became an accepted practice by African-American poets, even by those poets, such as Brooks, Hayden, and Tolson, accused of having an overly "difficult" and essentially "white" style in their work produced from the late 1940s until the middle 1960s.

What made many of these recreations "difficult" was the degree to which they were embedded in poems that attempted to render the popular African-American voice within the context of a postwar, cold war, urban ghetto America, simultaneously drawing on the discourses of modernism, popular culture, and a residual folk heritage (which throughout the nineteenth and twentieth centuries had been problematically bound up with American popular commercial culture). This difficulty in no small part derives from many poets' perceptions of the difficult and contradictory nature of the cold war era. It is hard to see how *Montage of a Dream Deferred* or *Annie Allen* can be construed as optimistic affirmations of the time. In fact, a strong case can be made for considerable ideological continuity between much earlier "protest" poetry and neomodernist poetry, both "high" and "popular," in a radically uncertain time when a general resistance by African Americans to being "reconverted" to their prewar racial roles existed alongside a sense of the riskiness inherent in the direct expression of such resistance.[12] An analogy might be made (and indeed was made by some of the poets themselves—as did Hughes in *Montage of a Dream Deferred*) between the work of many postwar poets and the musicians of the bebop revolution who created a music that was definitely (and defiantly) modern while rooted in interlocking popular commercial culture and folk expression. Like much of the neomodernist poetry, whether "high" or "popular," this music was erudite, populist, self-reflexive, humorous, angry, ironic, exuberant, meditative, parodic, historically minded, radically new, and deeply traditional. As we have seen, this sort of eclectic aesthetic that sharply and openly interrogated its own grounds was a hallmark of

212 The New Red Negro

much African-American Left writing during the 1930s and 1940s, particularly after the beginning of the Popular Front. The bebop mode would have a profound effect on such postmodern African-American writers as Amiri Baraka throughout his career, and on the development of much of what became known as the New American Poetry generally. This sense of the authorial consciousness as both an insider and an outsider to the recreated folk, which marked African-American poetry (and much of the fiction) of the cold war era was, as we have also seen, one of the strongest characteristics of African-American poetry of the early 1930s and 1940s.

The influence of the 1930s and 1940s extends beyond those poets who came of literary age or produced significant work during that era. It goes beyond those poets, such as Margaret Danner, Bob Kaufman, Dudley Randall, and Ray Durem, who were products of the 1930s and 1940s Left milieu to one degree or another, but did not begin to publish to any extent until after World War II. It extends to many African-American poets, such as Amiri Baraka and the Umbra Poets (including Calvin Hernton, Ishmael Reed, David Henderson, and Askia Muhammed Touré), who appeared in the late 1950s and early 1960s. The ideology of the Communist Left in its various permutations linked nationalism and integrationism, emphasized a cultural model rather than a biological model of African-American identity, and insisted on the crucial role of that culture in shaping American culture. This cleared a space for African-American poets to be both "black" and "artists," and at least partially escape the Dunbarian split of "high" and "low."(One aspect of the cultural McCarthy era that began in the postwar period was the increasingly frequent move by conservative and liberal anti-Communist critics and scholars of African-American literature to return to the old hierarchical paradigms of "low" and "high" and the related "Negro" and "universal"—with perhaps the ultimate horror reserved for the Popular Front–associated "middlebrow," which blurred these distinctions. Nonetheless, the notion of African-American poetry as both national expression and art survived this assault.)[13] The somewhat contradictory Leninist vanguardism of the CPUSA (and of the organized Trotskyists), which projected a political organization that was both of and ahead of the working class, also provided a model that combined aesthetic and political vanguardism with an identification with the folk or the people. This model was clearly influential on a range of African-American writers, including neomodernists such as Hayden, Brooks, and Tolson, as well as postmodernists such as Baraka, Kaufman, and Cleveland concretist Russell Atkins, even after the decline and isolation of the CPUSA and its cultural institutions in the postwar era.

As has been argued throughout this study, this exchange between African-American poets and the organized Left and its literary institutions was not a unilateral set of instructions from the Left to the poets. Neither was it simply a case of African-American artists making use of the cultural institutions of the Left to replace the patrons and institutions of the New Negro Renaissance that disappeared in the economic crisis of the 1930s. Certainly, there were plenty of instructions from various levels of the leadership of the Communist Left—though the centrality of the "Negro question" in the U.S. Communist movement after 1928 gave African-American CPUSA members and sympathizers a considerable tool to inspire, alter, or resist the instructions of party leadership, if they so wished. And there is no question that the practical support of the literary Left was avidly sought (and found) by African-American poets. But these African-American poets also played a crucial role within the literary Left that is often overlooked.

The work of the Left African-American poets of the 1930s and 1940s, drawing on a long history of literary responses to popular-culture representations of the African-American folk and re-creations of the folk voice, served as important models for the representation and re-creation of ethnic and/or working-class subjects by non-African-American authors. When one considers the examinations of the troubled relationship between constructs of "high" traditional poetry, "high" modernist poetry, popular commercial culture, and folk or working-class cultural practices at least partially outside of popular commercial culture—examinations that were such a large part of Left or Left-influenced poetry during the 1930s and 1940s—it is hard to think of poets who undertook this more rigorously, more energetically, and more profoundly in their different ways than Langston Hughes, Sterling Brown, Gwendolyn Brooks, and Frank Marshall Davis. Hughes in particular, with his development of a popular neomodernist style that evaded New Critical standards (not art, as some have claimed), emerges as a particularly important progenitor of much postmodern poetry by black and white poets of the 1950s and 1960s. This influence is especially pronounced in the more linguistically based, more vernacularly oriented poetry of the 1950s and 1960s, including many of those poets connected with the New York School and the Beats, such as Allen Ginsberg, Jack Kerouac, Gregory Corso, Bob Kaufman, Frank O'Hara, Kenneth Koch, James Schuyler, Amiri Baraka, Ted Berrigan, Ron Padgett, and Anne Waldman. While William Carlos Williams may be rightly credited as a patron saint of these writers, along with a pantheon of French surrealists and Russian futurists, the lyric insouciance and polyvocality that mix American popular culture and modernist dislocation and juxtaposition with a sly lightness of touch that variously distinguishes much of the work of these authors are far closer to the work of Hughes than that of Williams, who himself was much marked by the literary Left of the 1930s and 1940s. Even the clearly surrealist-influenced work of many of these "postmodern" authors is often couched in an American diction and imagery that seems nearer to Hughes and the poetics of the American Popular Front than the early Eluard or Desnos.

Of course, when these New American poets were asked to list their literary ancestors, few, if any, of the white poets at least ever named Langston Hughes. In a sense, the contribution of Hughes and other African-American poets of the 1930s and 1940s is so large and ubiquitous (and the notion of black literary [though not musical] ancestors for white writers still so anathema) that the influence of Hughes, Brown, Cuney, Walker, Brooks, and Hayden remained invisible, an invisibility that was appropriately and doubly ironic, given the famous foregrounding of the African-American invisibility trope in American literary discourse by Ralph Ellison in 1952. That Hughes was one of the progenitors of the poetry reading with jazz performance that became an icon of the Beat subculture was occasionally, if infrequently, noted by commentators during the 1950s. What was missed, however, was the degree to which this mixed-media popular culture–literary hybrid was a hallmark of the 1930s and 1940s literary Left, most notably of African-American writers such as Hughes,

Cuney, and Wright. And beyond this actual hybrid of popular media and literary production was the aesthetic and ideological hybrid of literary artists who drew on the resources of popular culture that also characterized much Left literature of the 1930s and 1940s, especially after the Popular Front. Again, African-American artists such as Hughes, Davis, Brooks, Tolson, and Wright were at the forefront of this undertaking. In short, much of what we today think of as the postmodern New American Poetry was heavily influenced by Left aesthetics of the Popular Front (which in turn had many continuities with Third Period aesthetics) that were drawn on, knowingly or unknowingly, in reaction to the dominant New Critical literary models. And, as argued above, African-American poets played a crucial role in the development and practice of these aesthetics.

Once again we are brought back to ideology and Left concepts of the "national question." Can one speak of the African-American poets of the 1930s and 1940s, as part of a tradition of African-American writers stretching back to Phillis Wheatley and the earliest captivity and conversion slave narratives? Can one productively situate these writers within the discursive field of a broad Left literary discourse? Can we do both? The answer to each of the above questions, which we are learning ask again with respect to the whole body of African-American writing and its role in the constitution of an "American" literature, as would have been obvious to most of the participants of the literary Left of the 1930s and 1940s, is yes. No doubt, as with those earlier writers and intellectuals, our framing and interpretation of these answers will be the subject of intense debate and scholarly conversation. As mentioned in the introduction to this study, it is not with false modesty that I see this work as an attempt to further open this conversation not to close it off with a gesture of critical definitiveness. While I am convinced that my claims here are often debatable and are subject to correction, clarification, and deeper analysis, I remain equally convinced that the subject of the study is crucial to our understanding of African-American literature and culture, American literature and culture generally.

Notes

Introduction

1. A few of these studies are Arnold Rampersad's *The Life of Langston Hughes*, George Kent's *A Life of Gwendolyn Brooks*, James Hatch's *Sorrow Is the Only Faithful One: The Life of Owen Dodson*, and Joanne Gabbin's *Sterling A. Brown: Building the Black Aesthetic Tradition*.

2. Baker, *The Harlem Renaissance and Modernism* (106).

3. For example, Langston Hughes writes in *The Big Sea* (1940):

That spring for me (and, I guess, for all of us) was the end of the Harlem Renaissance. We were no longer in vogue, anyway, we Negroes. Sophisticated New Yorkers turned to Noel Coward. Colored actors began to go hungry, publishers politely rejected new manuscripts, and patrons found other uses for their money. The cycle that had charlestoned into being on the heels of *Shuffle Along* now ended in *Green Pastures* with De Lawd. (334)

4. Huggins (190).

5. Murphy (138–147); Foley, *Radical Representations* (54–63); Ellison, *Going to the Territory* (199).

6. For an extremely useful article discussing the development of the study of popular culture in the 1980s, see Denning, "The End of Mass Culture."

7. Denning (8). Denning here is speaking of the 1980s, but I think that it was also essentially true of the 1930s and 1940s.

8. While a minor part of African-American literary production from the 1920s through the 1940s, one could add to the category of "high" literature what might be thought of as "al-

ternate high literature" of various non-European cultures. One example of this would be Lewis Alexander's haikus—a form to which Richard Wright would devote much effort late in his career. Of course, T. S. Eliot's interest in Indian literature and culture and Ezra Pound's interest in Chinese literature and culture suggest that this could be considered a more generically "modernist" move than a specifically African-American one.

9. Harlem's claim as a literary and cultural center lies in no small part in its distinction as one of the most important loci of gay life in America. As George Chauncey points out, gay social and cultural networks played a crucial role in energizing the Harlem literary scene (264–266).

10. This is not to deny, as George Hutchinson points out, that Harlem, and New York generally, as a site of cultural production allowed the New Negro Renaissance to flourish in ways that would not have been possible in Washington, Boston, Chicago, or Philadelphia— though Hutchinson sometimes ignores examples of interracial intellectual and artistic cross-fertilization outside of New York (such as the important gatherings of black and white artists and intellectuals at V. F. Calverton's home in Baltimore) in order to emphasize the uniqueness of such interactions in New York (Hutchinson, *The Harlem Renaissance in Black and White*, 5–6).

Chapter 1

1. Despite an obsessive anti-Communism that sees the CPUSA as simply an appendage of Soviet foreign policy, practically the only in-depth scholarly studies of the early years of the CPUSA remain Theodore Draper's *Roots of American Communism* and *American Communism and Soviet Russia*. For accounts of the early years of the CPUSA from Communist points of view, see William Z. Foster's *History of the Communist Party of the United States* and William Weinstone's "Formative Period of CPUSA." For an interesting discussion of the problems of ethnicity, "Americanization," and "Bolshevization" in the CPUSA during the 1920s, see Buhle, *Marxism in the USA: Remapping the History of the American Left* (125–135).

2. For an account of the radical origins of the postwar use of the concept of the "New Negro," see Ernest Allen Jr. For another take on the "New Negro," which argues that the figure of the New Negro goes back to, at least, the late nineteenth century, see Gates, "The Trope of a New Negro."

3. The Comintern theory of the Third Period divided the post–World War I era into three periods: a First Period of crisis for the capitalist system immediately following the October Revolution; a Second Period of partial recovery and prosperity beginning in 1923; and a Third Period of capitalist production outstripping demand, leading to an economic collapse. In this scenario, the predicted collapse would produce a revolutionary situation in which the various "reformist" groups (in the American context most notably the SP, the American Federation of Labor, and, within the African-American community, the NAACP) would inhibit the development of the necessary consciousness on the part of the working class.

In this regard, as in other areas, the directives of the Comintern found a responsive audience among American Communists. The rhetoric of "social fascism" was certainly wildly sectarian. But this antagonism had local roots in the bitter struggles that American Communists waged with the SP leadership in the trade union movement before the Sixth Congress and in the past resentments of many of the older CPUSA activists toward the SP leadership dating back to the expulsion of IWW militants from the SP, the split in the SP over the American participation in World War I, and the effective disenfranchisement of the Foreign Language Federations at the 1919 SP Convention. See Perry Anderson (150–151) for a brief discussion of how the carrying out of Comintern Third Period and Popular Front directives varied according to the specific histories of local social democratic parties and their relationship to

Communist Party national leaders and rank-and-file members in particular countries before and after the October Revolution.

4. See Draper, *American Communism and Soviet Russia* (429–436) and Klehr, *The Heyday of American Communism* (3–27) for the "orthodox" assessment of the CPUSA's situation at the beginning of the Depression and Ottanelli (9–16) for a "revisionist" view.

In addition to the SP, these other Left groups included A. J. Muste's Conference for Progressive Labor Action, which—after a brief incarnation as the American Workers Party— would later join with various Trotskyists to form the Workers Party in 1935, the Proletarian Party, the Trotskyist Communist League of America, and Jay Lovestone's Independent Labor League, as well as the older Socialist Labor Party and the Industrial Workers of the World. Of course, these groups, other than the SP, were mostly minuscule. However, the fact remains that even with the CPUSA's international connections, it would have been hard to predict in 1928 the dominance that the Communists would achieve on the Left in a few years. It is also a reminder, if one is needed, that the growth of the CPUSA in membership and influence was not due to the lack of political alternatives on the Left.

5. There were groups associated with the early CPUSA, notably the African Blood Brotherhood, which took a more nationalist stance with respect to the "Negro question." For a sense of the often murky history of the African Blood Brotherhood, see Moore; Naison, *Communists in Harlem* (5–10); and Solomon (80–83).

6. Foner and Allen (37).

7. Gold, "Where the Battle is Fought" (37). Gold's 1926 article resembles later critiques of the New Negro Renaissance by African-American Communists and Communist sympathizers (e.g., William Patterson's "Awake, Negro Poets" and Richard Wright's "Blue Print for Negro Writing," as well as Sterling Brown's stance toward the "Harlem Renaissance"), particularly in the opposition between effete "dilettantes" and a hyper-masculine "mass of peasants and factory workers."

8. Schuyler (662).

9. *New Masses*, February 1928 (32).

10. For accounts of the CPUSA's work among African Americans in the 1920s, and of the CPUSA as a center of African-American radicalism during that period, see Draper, *American Communism and Soviet Russia* (315–356); Foner and Allen; Joyce Moore Turner's "Richard B. Moore and His Works" in Moore (27–60); Naison, *Communists in Harlem* (3–30); Solomon (151–175); and Cruse (115–146).

11. Nelson, *Repression and Recovery* (101); Kalaidjian (52).

These anthologies stand not only as a genealogy of the literary Left generally but also of an African-American presence in this Left since nearly all include contributions by African Americans: *May Days* (Claude McKay); *Poems for Workers* (McKay and Langston Hughes); *Justice Arraigned* (Countee Cullen); *An Anthology of Revolutionary Poetry* (Cullen, Paul Laurence Dunbar, Hughes, Fenton Johnson, Georgia Douglas Johnson, James Weldon Johnson, and McKay); *Unrest* (Hughes); *Proletarian Literature* (Hughes and Richard Wright); *This Generation* (Sterling Brown); and *Seven Poets* (Hughes).

12. For valuable essays discussing the relation of the Communist Left (and 1930s literary radicalism) to the New Negro Renaissance, see Maxwell, "The Proletarian as New Negro," and James A. Miller. Maxwell's dissertation "Dialectical Engagements" is also an important contribution to rethinking the links between African-American literary production in the 1920s and that of the 1930s.

13. See the May 17, 1932, *Daily Worker* for a list of "ministers and representatives of the motion picture industry, writers, lawyers and artists" who signed a petition against the Japanese invasion. Other African Americans besides Walrond on the list, which is virtually a Who's Who

of intellectuals and artists associated with the CPUSA, include Langston Hughes and Eugene Gordon.

Toomer on occasion would also lend his name to Left organizations and causes in the 1930s, such as the Committee for the Release of Jacques Roumain in 1935. For a collection of correspondence between the Committee for the Release of Jacques Roumain and Toomer, see Jean Toomer Papers, Box 1, Folder 33.

14. See Nelson and Hendricks (9) for a reproduction of an ad in the *Daily Worker* for the "Red Poets Nite" that lists Hughes ("famous Negro Poet") among the readers.

15. Wilcox (47, 88–90).

16. For a summary of the politics of the Rebel Poets, see Wixson (159–184).

17. For examples of such studies, see Lewis, Huggins, *Harlem Renaissance*, and Wintz.

18. Kelley, *Hammer and Hoe* (119–192); Naison, *Communists in Harlem* (169–284). Of course, as noted elsewhere, Michael Honey claims that the Left and interracial union organizing never really got off the ground in Memphis, another city with a long history of segregation and brutal repression of Left and trade union activities, until the Popular Front.

19. In addition to the many articles in the CPUSA press about these issues, particularly after 1930, this conviction that the "national question" was central to the revolutionary process in the United States can be seen easily in the curriculum at CPUSA educational institutions all across the country in the early 1930s. For example, the "Workers' Calendar" in the November 15, 1930, *Daily Worker* lists "Workers Forums" in Cleveland, Philadelphia, Baltimore, and New Haven, discussing the "Negro question," including such topics as "The American Negro and the Struggle for Self-Determination" and "The Negro Worker in the Class Struggle," during a single week.

20. The CPUSA had persistent problems during the late 1920s and early 1930s with "Language Group" members who tried to exclude African Americans from "Language Group" events. The best known example became publicized as a result of the "Yokinen trial." The defendent in this public trial was a Finnish-American Communist who was held responsible for the ejection of African Americans from a dance at the Finnish Workers Club in Harlem. Other examples of "white chauvinism" in the "Language Groups" that received considerable attention from the CPUSA English-language press involved Lithuanians in Chicago and Russians in Gary and in Philadelphia. See Naison, *Communists in Harlem* (47–59) for discussion of the Yokinen trial; see "White Chauvinism in Chicago" in the July 17, 1930, *Daily Worker*, and "Smash the Ugly Head of White Chauvinism" in the May 18, 1932, *Daily Worker* for other examples of "white chauvinism" among CPUSA-connected "Language Groups."

21. Naison, *Communists in Harlem* (17).

22. For various essentially negative assessments of the Black Belt Thesis, see Klehr, *The Heyday of American Communism* (324–348); Draper, *American Communism and Soviet Russia* (320–350); Naison, *Communists in Harlem* (5–20); Solomon (80–155). However, Paul Lyons's study of former rank-and-file CPUSA members in Philadelphia suggests that the Black Belt Thesis and the "Negro nation" were actually quite important to African-American Communists, at least in Philadelphia, well into the 1950s (78–79). For more positive assessments of the Black Belt Thesis, see also Gerald Horne's "The Red and the Black: The Communist Party and African Americans in Historical Perspective" and *Black Liberation/Red Scare* (66–72); and Foley (170–212).

23. For a discussion, albeit quite preliminary, of the influence of Herder on African-American writers and intellectuals, see Bell (16–31). See also Solbrig.

24. Locke, *The New Negro* (5–16); James Weldon Johnson, *The Book of American Negro Poetry* (9–48).

25. For an account of Hughes's relation to American Left critics, see Rampersad,

"Langston Hughes and his Critics on the Left." An instructive example of the relative esteem in which Hughes and Brown were held by the Communist Left is Clay's (Eugene Holmes's) "The Negro in Recent American Literature," in which highly qualified praise of Hughes is followed by a lionization of Brown. Interestingly, the response to Hughes's poetry by Soviet reviewers appears to be far more enthusiastic than those American Left reviewers as evidenced by Lydia Filatova's 1933 article "Langston Hughes: An American Writer" in *International Literature*, where she proclaims Hughes to be "one of the important writers of America today" (99).

26. For brief discussions of how black intellectuals found the CPUSA notions of "self-determination" inspiring, see Kelley, *Race Rebels* (114–121); Naison, *Communists in Harlem* (5–20).

27. See the first volume of Rampersad, *The Life of Langston Hughes* (140–146), for a summary of the reviews of *Fine Clothes to the Jew*. For a large selection of the reviews of *Native Son*, see John Reilly (39–99).

28. An early articulation of this perceived tradition of revolutionary struggle is the Op-Ed article "Revolutionary Negro Tradition" by Gilbert Lewis, an African-American TUUL organizer, in the January 9, 1930, *Daily Worker*. It is also during this period that the CPUSA begins to claim African-American abolitionists as revolutionary heroes, as exemplified by Otto Hall's front-page article honoring Frederick Douglass in the February 12, 1930, *Daily Worker*. See also Aptheker's *American Negro Slave Revolts*.

This emphasis is quite different from that of even the most militant black writers of the 1920s who rarely, if ever, raised the slave revolts or mentioned the names of Nat Turner or Gabriel in their work.

29. Robin Kelley, *Hammer and Hoe* (92–100).

30. Ad in January 9, 1930, *Daily Worker*.

31. Gates, *Loose Canons* (26–28). See also the review of *Anthology of American Negro Literature* by Bernard Smith in the February 1930 *New Masses*.

For an account of the break between Calverton and the CPUSA, see Aaron, *Writers On the Left* (339–343).

32. McKay began his career as a "dialect poet." In his *Constab Ballads* (1912) and *Songs of Jamaica* (1912), McKay was perhaps the first "serious" Jamaican poet to attempt to represent and recreate the speaking Jamaican "folk" subject. However, he would not attempt such a recreation of the "folk" or "popular" voice in his later published poetry associated with the United States. (Though when one hears McKay actually read the sonnets "If We Must Die" and "St. Isaac's Church, Petrograd" in a distinctly Jamaican voice, one wonders if one of McKay's projects was to place the "folk" voice within the metropolitan "high" form rather than to efface that voice. After all, McKay was certainly capable of adopting an "Oxbridge" accent. For a recording of McKay reading his poems in the 1940s, see the 1961 Folkways recording *An Anthology of Negro Poets*). For a discussion of McKay's "dialect" poetry, see Cooper (36–54).

33. For example, Bishop I. E. Guinn's 1921 poetry broadside, "Our Home in Africa" begins, "Watch ye therefore ye know not the day."

34. For an example of such a use of "dialect," see Ernest Jones's humorous prose "Letters from Freckles from Bricktop" (filled with "eye" dialect and misspellings), which appeared in the *Bronzeman*, a popular magazine aimed at an upwardly mobile "striver" audience.

35. Again, this opposition of the "authentic" folk culture and ersatz popular culture "borrowings" from the folk culture by black intellectuals goes back, at least, to Du Bois's chapter "Of the Sorrow Songs" in *The Souls of Black Folk*.

Very few writers of either the New Negro Renaissance or the literary Left of the early 1930s attempted to use the model of African-American minstrelsy and minstrelsy-influenced musical theater, such as the comic song and dance of Bert Williams and George Walker (and the musical comedies of Bob Cole and Paul Laurence Dunbar), as a strategy of negotiating the heritage of white blackface minstrelsy. One of the few exceptions was Helene Johnson, whose 1927 "Poem" ("Little brown boy, / Slim, dark, big-eyed, Crooning love songs to your banjo / Down at the Lafayette / Gee, boy, I love the way you hold your head") confuses the speaker's stance (ironic, condescending, or naively genuine—or some combination of the three) toward a minstrelsy-inflected representation of the African-American folk subject after the manner of the minstrel performers themselves.

36. For a discussion of "race records" and their production, distribution, and reception in the 1930s, see Oliver, "Sales Tax On It."

37. See the exchange between Lomax and Gellert in the December 11, 1934, *New Masses* for an early example of this debate. It now appears that Gellert's work was legitimate as his field notes and field recordings, which he concealed to protect his sources, have been discovered by Bruce Conforth of the Indiana University Archives of Traditional Music. For examples of Gellert's field work and Conforth's liner notes, see the Rounder Records recordings *Negro Songs of Protest* and *Cap'n You're So Mean.*

38. For an example of Gellert's direct influence on the recreation of the African-American folk voice by left-wing authors, see the scene of Herbert Klein's play *John Henry* in the May-June 1934 issue of *Left Front.* In this scene, John Henry teaches his fellow convicts on a chain gang to sing songs that Klein credits to Gellert in a footnote.

39. Hughes, *The Big Sea* (228).

40. For a more in-depth look at how the Depression affected the institutions that supported the Harlem Renaissance, see Johnson and Johnson (97–124).

41. This was not a strictly African-American phenomenon. White artists connected with the Left, such as Woody Guthrie and Aunt Molly Jackson, also reworked "white" folk songs, hymns, and country tunes into vehicles of social protest. For a fuller treatment of this process, see Serge Denisoff's "Religious Roots of the Song of Persuasion" in his *Sing a Song of Social Significance.*

42. For an extremely valuable discussion of White and his role in the cultural Left of the 1930s and 1940s, see Denning, *The Cultural Front* (348–361).

43. For a discussion of the relation of the popular African-American musical theater to black writers during the Harlem Renaissance, see Graziano. As Graziano notes, however much *Shuffle Along* and other musicals inspired young African-American writers, notably Langston Hughes, almost none of these artists were involved as writers with musical theater actually produced during the 1920s.

44. As Michael Denning points out in *The Cultural Front*, this "high culture"–"folk culture" hybrid becomes even more complicated since it seems likely that Gutherie was invoking the commercially successful "hillbilly" version of "John Hardy," a folk "outlaw" song, recorded by the Carter Family, one of the seminal progenitors of modern country music (270).

45. See Gold, et al.

46. For the most definitive account of the John Reed Clubs to date, see Eric Homberger's *American Writers and Radical Politics, 1900–1939: Equivocal Commitments* (119–140).

47. See Note #4 of the Sterling Stuckey Introduction to *The Collected Poems of Sterling Brown* (14); Gabbin (61).

48. Some perceptive scholars of the Left, notably Michael Denning, make the claim that the JRC was not a CPUSA "mass organization" in the way that was, say, the League of Struggle for Negro Rights. Rather, in this view, the JRC was a fairly autonomous (and contentious) organization in which only a quarter of the members belonged also to the CPUSA. This is a plausible claim, but one that underestimates, as Denning generally does, the role of the CPUSA and CPUSA activists. For Denning's view, see *The Cultural Front* (205–212).

49. For a differing argument that *New Masses* was less interested in African-American culture and more interested in "class issues" as it adopted a more "party-line" stance in the late 1920s, see George Hutchinson, *The Harlem Renaissance in Black and White* (268–275).

50. See Conroy's Introduction to *Writers in Revolt: An Anvil Anthology* (ix–xxi). According to Wixson, some 3,000 copies of *The Anvil's* circulation of 4,500 in 1935 were distributed by the CDA (318).

51. Rampersad, *The Life of Langston Hughes, Volume I* (356–358); Crusader News Service releases, week of April 28, 1938 (4).

For a brief history of the IWO, particularly of what might be thought of as its cultural politics, see Keeran, "National Groups and the Popular Front."

52. For a description of CPUSA educational institutions in New York, see Gettleman; for accounts of the Abraham Lincoln School, see Frank Marshall Davis, *Livin' the Blues* (283–290), Patterson, *The Man Who Cried Genocide* (149–155), and Wixson (453–455). See also the Gwendolyn Bennett Papers for materials on the Carver School as well as Bennett's activities at the CPUSA-led School for Democracy in New York.

53. For details of the network of the CPUSA subculture in a particular community (Philadelphia), see Lyons (61–69). For more specific accounts of the network of CPUSA "cultural" institutions, see Lieberman (14–24) and Rubinstein.

54. Walker, *Richard Wright* (68–85) and Frank Marshall Davis, *Livin' the Blues* (244–249).

55. For a useful review of many of these journals as well as the "proletarian," "Left modernist," and "proletarian regionalist" journals mentioned elsewhere in this chapter, see Denning, *The Cultural Front* (211–222).

56. For the best, and practically the only, in-depth study of the important radical literary activity in the Midwest during the 1920s, 1930s, and 1940s, see Wixson.

57. In the early and middle 1930s, founding editor Harriet Monroe issued periodic editorials against "proletarian literature" until her death in 1936. Nonetheless, in the early 1930s it was still possible to see an exchange in *Poetry* like that between the CPUSA member Morris U. A. Schappes and Communist sympathizer Louis Zukofsky in the May 1933 issue (117–118). Zukofsky, responding to Schappes's claim that the objectivist poet failed to "ally oneself with the revolutionary proletariat," supported his defense of objectivism with a quote from Lenin's *Left-wing Communism*. Schappes replied to Zukofsky also using Lenin for support.

Two other issues of *Poetry* that were fundamentally Left in character were the "Social Poets Issue" of May 1936, guest-edited by Horace Gregory and the "Federal Poets Issue" of July 1938, featuring poetry, articles, and reviews by members of the FWP, edited by Willard Maas and including poems by Margaret Walker and Sterling Brown. The journal also published many individual left-wing poets during this period in addition to Brooks, Hughes, and Walker, including George Oppen, Norman MacLeod, Eda Lou Walton, Muriel Rukeyser, H. H. Lewis, Horace Gregory, Edwin Rolfe, and James Rorty. Nonetheless, it should be noted that *Poetry* did not publish any African-American writers between the appearance of Hughes's series of poems "The Quick and the Dead" in October 1931 and Walker's "For My People" in November 1937.

58. This raises the question of whether there was a relationship between an institution's organizational attachment to the CPUSA and its relative openness to African-American writing. Radical journals and institutions were all influenced by the degree to which the CPUSA elevated the "Negro question." Any journal or institution with an interest in or sympathy with "proletarian" or "revolutionary" literature was forced to at least consider its relation to the "national question" and African-American literary expression. This was true even of those Left journals and institutions opposed to the CPUSA.

Nonetheless, there often seems to be a correlation between the closeness of a Left jour-

nal or institution to the CPUSA and the interest with which it considered African-American literature and culture. Generally speaking the correlation was the closer the formal relationship
with the CPUSA, the more active the interest in African-American writing. For example,
Windsor Quarterly, which considered itself part of the revolutionary literary movement and yet
was not formally linked to the CPUSA, never published any work by African-American authors
and never reviewed or seriously discussed any works by African Americans. Conversely, *New
Masses* featured articles, poems, stories, one-act plays, theoretical pieces, reviews, and / or artwork by African-American authors as well as articles, poems, one-act plays stories, translations,
theoretical pieces, reviews, and / or artwork about African Americans by white Americans in
the vast majority of issues, particularly in the 1930s. And, whether tokenism or not, there was
almost always at least one African American listed on the masthead during the entire history
of *New Masses*. (There were exceptions to this rule. *The Anvil* actively searched out African-
American writers. On the other hand, *Dialectics*, a quasi-official CPUSA journal of literary criticism published by the "Critics Group" of the Communist Party of New York in the late 1930s,
never considered African-American literature.)

An interesting point of comparison is *Partisan Review*, which as a journal of the JRC and
the Communist Left from 1934 to 1936 published—and reviewed—works by African-American
authors, though never to the same degree as *New Masses*. These works included poems by
Sterling Brown (which were actively solicited by Alan Calmer, one of the leading literary activists of the Communist Left), a poem and reviews by Richard Wright (who during the period
of the *Partisan Review–Anvil* merger in 1936 was listed on the masthead as an associate editor),
and translations by Langston Hughes. During this period *Partisan Review* reviewed Arna
Bontemp's *Black Thunder* and Hughes's *The Ways of White Folks*. After a hiatus of eighteen
months, *Partisan Review* reappeared in December 1937 as a journal of what came to be known
as the "anti-Stalinist Left." From that point, as far as I can tell, nothing written by an African-
American author appeared in the journal until James Baldwin's "Everybody's Protest Novel,"
a patricidal assault on Richard Wright and the Communist Left via *Uncle Tom's Cabin*, in June
1949. During the same period, no African Americans were included on the masthead of *Partisan
Review* and only three reviews of books by African-American authors (a review of Wright's
Uncle Tom's Children in 1938, a brief review of *Native Son* in a survey of current fiction in 1941,
and a longer review of *Black Boy* in 1945) were published.

For an account of the relationship between *Partisan Review* and African-American intellectuals, see Teres, *Renewing the Left* (204–229).

59. For an account of *Common Ground* as a Popular Front journal, see Denning, *The
Cultural Front* (447–449).

60. Klehr, *The Heyday of American Communism* (347). For two extended treatments of the
FWP, see Mangione, *The Dream and the Deal*, and Penkower.

61. Mangione (255–257).

62. For an account of Brown's activities at the FWP, see Gabbin (67–85).

63. For some figures regarding African-American membership in the CPUSA nationally
and in Harlem during the 1930s, see Klehr, *The Heyday of American Communism* (348).

64. Kelley, *Hammer and Hoe* (107–108).

65. Ottanelli (42); Glazer (174).

66. Naison, *Communists in Harlem* (210–211).

67. See Stepto, "I Thought I Knew These People: Richard Wright and the Afro-American
Literary Tradition."

68. Wright, *Later Works* (313–365).

69. Healey (125–126).

70. Mitford (106).

71. Kelley, *Race Rebels* (111–112).

72. Naison, *Communists in Harlem* (209); Rampersad *The Life of Langston Hughes, Volume I* (358–359).

73. For discussion of the Crusader News Agency, see Horne, *Black Liberation / Red Scare* (45–46).

74. For a brief account of the *People's Voice* and the key roles of such CPUSA members as Wilkerson, Marvel Cooke, and Ollie Harrington on the staff of the newspaper (as well as the unofficial role of CPUSA leader Benjamin Davis), see Rachleff (25–27).

75. For the best scholarly treatment of the South Side Writers Group, see Bone, "Richard Wright and the Chicago Renaissance."

In addition to his participation in the Chicago activities of the National Negro Congress, Bontemps, who is often described as apolitical during the 1930s, was also a part of national NNC events, appearing along with Richard Wright and Langston Hughes on a "Negro Culture and History" panel of the first NNC convention in 1936 (National Negro Congress, "Fight for Negro Rights," unpaged).

76. While the importance of Chicago's South Side Writers Group is beginning to be recognized, the crucial role of the "306 Group" (which grew out of the [Augusta] Savage School of Arts and Crafts and met in the studio of Left artist Charles Alston at 306 W. 141st Street in Harlem) has yet to receive any sustained scholarly attention. Nonetheless, this circle included a wide spectrum of Harlem's intellectuals and artists (including Langston Hughes, Claude McKay, Ralph Ellison, Gwendolyn Bennett, Jacob Lawrence, Romare Bearden, and lyricist Andy Razaf) as well frequent visits from white artists and intellectuals ranging from William Saroyan to Bing Crosby. For a very brief account of the "306 Group," see Kenkeleba House (20–21).

77. For a discussion of the political evolution of *Challenge* into *New Challenge*, see Johnson and Johnson (112–120). For brief accounts of Stark's poetry workshop, the South Side Community Arts Center and *Negro Story*, see Johnson and Johnson (135–142); Kent, *A Life of Gwendolyn Brooks* (59–60); and Bone (463–466).

In the case of *Negro Story*, a number of the editors and "advisors" on the journal's masthead had ties to the Communist Left, particularly Gayden and Earl Conrad, a white journalist who joined the staff near the end of the magazine's existence. Jack Conroy also provided much assistance to the journal and was frequently mentioned in its pages. Other evidence of the ties of the *Negro Story* to the Left includes the 1945 *Negro Story* Poetry Prize awarded to Gwendolyn Brooks, which was funded by the Left-led United Electrical and Machine Workers Union through the efforts of the African American Communist Ishmael Flory. See March-April 1945 issue (2) for the details of the prize. For the best study of *Negro Story* to date, see Bill Mullen, "Popular Fronts: *Negro Story* Magazine and the Literary Resistance to World War II."

78. For a brief account of the *Michigan Chronicle* and how it came to publish Hayden, see Louis Martin. For an example of Martin's willingness to publicly associate himself with the Communist Left, despite his description of himself as a "New Deal Democrat," see his endorsement of *New Masses* in the September 21, 1943, issue of *New Masses* (2). For a collection of Hughes's columns in the *Chicago Defender*, see Hughes, *Langston Hughes and the Chicago Defender*. For a selection of Tolson's columns in the *Washington Tribune*, see Tolson, *Caviar and Cabbage*.

79. Rampersad, *The Life of Langston Hughes, Volume I* (363), and John Lewis (78).

80. Though, as Robin Kelley points out, on a less "elite" literary level, there was a considerable commonalty between Garveyite poetry and poetry written by rank-and-file African-American Communists published in CPUSA journals such as the *Liberator* (Kelley, *Race Rebels*, 103–111).

81. Wright's poem ends:

Lingering as a duty after my command is shouted:
DEFEND THE U.S.S.R.!
I haunt the doors of your mind until I am taken in:
SELF-DETERMINATION FOR MINORITY PEOPLES!
I am the one red star in the workers' black sky:
TURN IMPERIALIST WAR INTO CIVIL WAR!
I AM A RED SLOGAN,
The crest of the wave that sweeps to victory:
ALL POWER TO THE SOVIETS!

82. Denning, *The Cultural Front* (211–222).

83. The standard account of the decision to end the JRC and found the LAW is found in Aaron (297–308). See also Kutulas, *Long War*, and Homberger (139–140).

84. While some would argue, with some justification, that this article was a mark of Wright's unwillingness to follow the CPUSA "line," nonetheless it does demonstrate that such differences remained even among those writers and intellectuals who were, as Wright was, party members. It is also worth noting that if Margaret Walker's comments on "Blueprint" are true and the article was in large part the product of collective discussion among the members of the South Side Writers Group, then it further indicates the engagement of left-wing African-American writers and intellectuals with Communist conceptions of a nationhood and national culture of African Americans rooted in the South. See Walker, *Richard Wright, Daemonic Genius* (355–356).

85. The most authoritative book-long articulation and defense of the Black Belt Thesis from the Communist perspective, James S. Allen's *The Negro Question in the United States* (1936), appeared during the Popular Front period. Even Browder in his 1936 *What Is Communism* energetically defended the Black Belt Thesis (186–187).

86. Crusader News Agency, week of February 8, 1937 (10).

87. Sillen (23–24).

88. Outside of New York and Los Angeles, LAW chapters, appear to have been much more "grassroots." Also, as Judy Kutulas points out, LAW nationally became open to virtually any writer willing to join after 1937 ("Becoming 'More Liberal,'" 73).

89. One example of the attachment of Left writers to the "working class" is the well-known debate following Kenneth Burke's speech to the 1935 American Writers' Congress in which he suggested substituting the "people" for the "masses" or "workers" in Left propaganda. While the overwhelmingly negative response to the speech is often cited as an example of CPUSA sectarianism and heavy-handed authoritarianism, it seems unlikely that the party leadership directed such criticism. (Given the politics of the emerging Popular Front that motivated the formation of LAW, one suspects that party leaders would have been inclined to counsel a less sharply critical stance toward an important sympathetic, non-Communist intellectual.) Rather, such criticism is much more indicative of a continuing allegiance to notions of class, ethnicity, and "nationality" on the part of many Left writers regardless of CPUSA policy. For an account of Burke and the first American Writers' Congress, see Aaron, *Writers On the Left* (304–308).

90. Probably the most famous examples of this phenomenon of simultaneously downplaying and emphasizing African-American difference were the concerts of Paul Robeson, where Earl Robinson and John Latouche's "Ballad for Americans" ("I'm just an Irish-Negro-Jewish-Italian-French and English-Spanish-Russian-Chinese-Polish-Scotch-Hungarian-Litvak-Swedish-Finnish-Canadian-Greek and Turkish and Czech and Double-Czech-American")

would appear on the program side by side with spirituals and work songs. Of course, Robeson and others would no doubt have claimed that work songs and spirituals were "American," but nonetheless they were received as statements of ethnic or national assertion (of "his people" as Robeson said) by the audience and were intended as such.

91. Wright and Brown were elected to the National Committee of LAW at the first American Writers' Congress (Hart, *American Writers' Congress*, (188); Hughes later became a vice president of LAW (Rampersad, *The Life of Langston Hughes, Volume II*, 23); Frank Marshall Davis was the secretary of the Chicago chapter (Davis, *Livin' the Blues*, 245–249).

See Kutulas, *The Long War*, for the most in-depth examination of LAW to date, albeit one that always assumes the worst motives for the actions of Communists and the best for the "progressives" who were sometimes antagonists of the Communists in LAW. Kutulas also ignores the role of African Americans in LAW except for a passing mention of Wright. See also Folsom for an interesting first-hand, though anecdotal, account of LAW by one of its leading officers.

92. See Davis, *Livin' the Blues* (277), and Rampersad, *The Life of Langston Hughes, Volume II* (216).

93. Naison, *Communists in Harlem* (294).

94. See Isserman (141–143) and Keeran, "The Communist Influence on American Labor" in *New Studies in the Culture and Politics of U.S. Communism*.

Similarly, Gerald Horne suggests in "The Red and the Black: The Communist Party and African Americans in Historical Perspective" that assumptions of the CPUSA's decline in African-American membership and in influence on the African-American community during World War II needs to reexamined.

One valuable, though unreliable, new source of information about the CPUSA's work among African Americans during World War II is the recently released *The FBI's Racon* (1995), a collection of FBI files concerning, as the title suggests, racial conditions in the United States during the war, compiled and edited by Robert A. Hill. While FBI files are notoriously unreliable largely owing to selective releases and editing by the bureau, the frequent fantasies or vendettas of informants, and the desire of agents to please Hoover by "discovering" extensive Communist activities where none existed, nonetheless *Racon* suggests the degree to which the CPUSA in many locales pursued what was essentially a "Double V" strategy even as they officially attacked the slogan.

95. An example of this is Countee Cullen's "Mad Song"—described by Cullen as "a provincial Southern air as sung by Senator Rankin and coterie"—in the June 30, 1944 issue of *New Masses*:

> Before I'd let a nigger vote,
> Or match me place for place,
> With my own hand I'd cut my throat
> To spite that nigger's face.
> I'd raise my hand in Holy Heil,
> March with the Nazi knee to knee.
> Niggers may be Americans
> But Hitler's white like me!

Cullen's "Mad Song" was also used as part of the script of *New World A-Coming* that Owen Dodson wrote for the neo-Popular Front Negro Freedom Rally at Madison Square Garden in 1944. For a copy of the poem's text and the context of its performance at the rally, see Hatch (112-115).

96. One mark of the continuity of *Freedomways* with African-American literary culture of the 1930s and 1940s was its inclusion of two previously unpublished poems written by

Sterling Brown during the late 1930s in its Summer 1963 issue, marking Brown's first "new" publication of poetry in a journal in decades.

97. Wilcox (244).

98. *Sunday Worker* (April 14, 1940), Section 2: 4, 6. Davis's view of *Native Son* was mixed. While quite critical of the portrayal of the Communists in the novel and of Bigger Thomas as a representative of the northern ghetto, Davis nonetheless praised Wright's book as the most important novel of 1940.

99. The terms "regional" and "regionalist" are somewhat loaded in this context, since they were apparently used by some East Coast Left critics to attack the works of various Midwestern writers. For an account of this antagonism that sometimes veers toward nativism, see Wixson (377–378). For a statement of Left Midwestern regional exceptionalism, see Le Sueur's speech to the first American Writers' Congress, "Proletarian Literature and the Middle West" (135–138).

100. For a discussion of the Left folk music scene focusing on one of the key participants, Huddie Ledbetter, see Wolfe and Lornell (200–256). For another look at Left cultural movements of the mid-and late 1940s through the lens of the People's Songs movement, see Lieberman. See also Denisoff, *Great Day Coming*.

101. For an interesting account of Burnshaw's somewhat covert relationship to Stevens (and a fascinating re-reading of Stevens's writing in the 1930s), see Filreis.

102. For example, during Hughes's appearance before the Senate Permanent Sub-Committee on Investigations in 1953, Roy Cohn, chief counsel for the Sub-Committee, touched on Langston Hughes's radical 1930s poetry, particularly "One More 'S' in the U.S.A." and "Goodbye Christ," but did not discuss anything from the 1951 *Montage of a Dream Deferred*, even though *Montage* was hardly the portrait of steadily improving race relations in which Hughes claimed to believe under Cohn's questioning. For a summary of Hughes's encounter with McCarthy's committee, see Rampersad, *The Life of Langston Hughes, Volume II* (207–221).

103. For an in-depth history of the various aspects of the cold war destruction of the Left in the United States, see Caute. For studies dealing with the particular impact of the cold war on African Americans, see Horne, *Black and Red: W. E. B. Du Bois and the Afro-American Response to the Cold War 1944–1963*, and *Communist Front?: The Civil Rights Congress, 1946–1956*.

104. This figure would continue to appear in the Left press, particularly with respect to the Scottsboro case. The worldwide tour of Ada Wright, mother of Scottsboro defendants Roy and Andy Wright, was clearly posed in these terms by the *Daily Worker* and other Communist journals—in fact, Ada Wright was often referred to simply as the "Negro Mother."

Another example of this persistence of this figure in the Communist Left is the previously mentioned "A Negro Mother to her Child" by V. J. Jerome. As is often the case with invocations of the Negro Mother, Jerome's figure is a transmitter of culture and historical memory telling her son the story of his jailed "bolshevik" father. However, the mother is essentially passive with all action arrogated to the male: the jailed father is apparently going to have to wait until his son grows up before anyone will set him free. This poem first appeared in a 1932 issue of *The Rebel Poet* (a radical, but nonsectarian journal) and was much reprinted in the CPUSA press, including the *Daily Worker*, *New Masses*, and *The Liberator*.

However, the Negro Mother does not seem to have been used much by African-American poets as a positive figure during the 1930s, even in their own Scottsboro poems. Thus it can be argued that this is one example where African-American writers from an earlier period influenced Left writing and iconography during the 1930s, reversing the usual formulation of literary influence where such influence flows from white to black.

105. Sundquist (581–592).

106. While some of the identities of the distant, and not so distant, African past that the

speaker of "Proem" recalls are not so clearly gender-specified, their link to American social roles overwhelming associated with men (bootblack, construction worker, ragtime musician, lynch victim) mark them also as male. Tellingly missing are such identities associated with African-American women (e.g., cook, domestic, wet nurse, victim of unwanted sexual contact by white master or male employer).

107. Carby, *Geneaologies of Race, Nation, and Manhood.*

108. Du Bois (276).

109. Gilbert and Gubar (125–164); Huyssen (44–62).

110. Locke, *The New Negro,* (49).

111. For example, the ratio of men to women published in *The Crisis* and *Opportunity* during the 1920s was close to equal. Women poets fared less well in anthologies and critical assessments during the New Negro Renaissance—but far better than they did in retrospective anthologies, such as Nathan Huggins's anthology *Voices from the Harlem Renaissance,* and criticism, such as Jean Wagner's *Black Poets of the United States from Paul Laurence Dunbar to Langston Hughes,* where women writers are virtually absent.

By contrast, the antagonisms among white modernists were often couched in a rhetoric of masculinity as exemplified by Williams's famous threat to kick Eliot "in the balls" (Mariani, 571) Similarly, the conflict of Pound—and Williams and Hemingway—with Amy Lowell was articulated by the former writers, in terms that referred both to Lowell's gender and to her transgressions of a normative feminine identity. See Hemingway's poem "The Lady Poet with Footnotes" in the November 1924 issue of the journal *Der Querschnitt* for a macho attack on Lowell and other female modernists. The final line "One lady poet was big and fat and no fool" (6) and the footnote "She smoked cigars all right, but her stuff was no good" (6) referred to Lowell. Of course, the poem with its footnotes was also a crude parody of Eliot with the obvious implication that Eliot was a kind of "lady poet." For a discussion of this poem and the relationship of literary modernism to gender, see Gilbert and Gubar (125–162).

112. Hull (7–13).

113. Though once again it needs to be mentioned that the sense of African-American literary community during the period was such that while the more formally "conservative" tradition was emphasized, Cullen did include such vernacular-based poems as Brown's "Maumee Ruth," Hughes's "Homesick Blues," Helene Johnson's "Bottled," and Toomer's "Cotton Song."

114. For an example of the CPUSA's opposition to Garveyism, neo-Garveyism, and other forms of organized African-American nationalism, see Naison's discussion of the CPUSA's initial opposition to the Harlem Boycott Movement of the mid-1930s led by nationalist Sufi Abdul Hamid in *Communists in Harlem* (116–122).

115. Marx and Engels, *The German Ideology* (40); Lenin, *Selected Works, Volume I* (745–752).

116. See Hicks, *The Great Tradition;* Freeman, Introduction in Hicks et al. (9–28).

117. Gold, "Wilder: Prophet of the Genteel Christ;" For accounts of Gold's contradictory relationship to literary modernism, see Bloom (113–118); James Murphy (66–68); and Rubin (145–219).

Gold's assault on Proust, which is often cited as evidence of the CPUSA-influenced critics' animus toward modernism, was not universally supported by Left critics. Joseph Freeman, in his introduction to *Proletarian Literature in the United States,* speaks of "Proust's superb study of a dying aristocracy and a bourgeoisie in full bloom (Hicks et al., 13). In fact, it would be hard to read Freeman's comment as other than a pointed, if belated, response to Gold's dismissal of Proust. For a similar, though more brief, comment on Proust, see Hicks's *The Great Tradition* (122). Richard Wright also cites Proust—and James Joyce, T. S. Eliot, and Gertrude Stein—as a part of the "heritage of the Negro writer" in "Blueprint for Negro Writing" (60).

Pound himself was a frequent contributor to Left and Left-influenced journals in the late 1920s and early 1930s. For an example of such a contribution, see Pound's pro-Communist and pro-Soviet "Address to the John Reed Club of Philadelphia" in *Left Review*, the organ of the Philadelphia JRC.

118. See Kalaidjian's provocative discussion of this topic where he claims that the use of such masculinist images and figures "stand not so much as phallic icons of working class hegemony but as uncanny symptoms of its absence" in *American Culture Between the Wars* (138–159). For a considerable selection of IWW androcentric images, see Kornbluth.

119. Conroy, Introduction to *Writers in Revolt: An Anvil Anthology* (ix–xxi); Cowley, *Exile's Return*.

120. Huyssen (51). For an influential example of such a masculinized criticism of mass culture with particular significance for the consideration of African-American expressive culture, see Maxim Gorky's "Fat Men's Music," which appeared in *Pravda* in 1928.

It is worth noting, however, that here, as in other areas concerning mass culture, the consistency of the Communist opposition to the "popular arts" during the Third Period has been somewhat over estimated by such historians and critics as Walter Kalaidjian and Mark Naison. While one can find articles such as S. B.'s "The Movies As a Weapon Against the Working Class" in the May 20, 1930, *Daily Worker* attacking the movie industry and proposing a sort of "dual-union" strategy of alternative workers' films, at the same time the *Daily Worker* frequently included brief summaries, often favorable, of popular movies, theater, and vaudeville reviews.

121. Rabinowitz (35). This invisibility of gender as a category is even more striking in theoretical considerations of the "Negro question" during and after the Sixth Comintern Congress. For a considerable selection of these documents, see Foner and Allen (161–200) and Foner and Shapiro (1–146). Similarly, as Paula Rabinowitz notes, outside of the work of Grace Hutchens, few theoretical articles on the "Woman Question" in CPUSA journals consider "race" except to compare the category of "Woman" with that of "Negro" without much thought to the intersection of the two categories (Nekola and Rabinowitz, 190).

122. CPUSA events during the early 1930s frequently featured African-American choirs performing work songs, presumably as an alternative tradition to the longstanding tradition of formal concerts of spirituals by choirs from African-American colleges, such as Fisk and Tuskegee. For example, one of the most prominently advertised features of the 1930 John Reed Memorial Meeting in the *Daily Worker* was the Hall Johnson Singers performing work songs. Another CPUSA response to the spirituals can be seen in the ironic invocation of the form in the poem "They Burn Children in Alabama" by "Hap," published in the January 16, 1932, issue of *The Liberator*. The poem carried the subtitle "'Spiritual' for the Struggle for Negro Rights" with the quote marks around "Spiritual" revealing all one needed to know about the author's attitude toward the spirituals. "Stop Foolin' Wit' Pray," a more direct vernacular assault on the spirituals, and folk religion generally, appeared in the March 13, 1932, issue of *The Liberator*. This attitude changed considerably after the beginning of the Popular Front, most notably in the concerts of Paul Robeson, which prominently featured spirituals, though Richard Wright's attitude toward folk religion and its cultural expression in *Native Son* is not too different from that of "Hap."

For an example of the critical opposition of African-American popular culture and "authentic" African-American folk culture by an African-American intellectual during the 1930s, see Sterling Brown's "The Blues as Folk Poetry" in the 1930 edition of *Folk-Say, A Regional Miscellany* (324–339). Brown, however, is forced to admit in his article that this opposition is somewhat problematic in that some commercial artists, such as Ma Rainey and Bessie Smith, "seem to be of the folk" so that "it is becoming difficult to tell which songs are truly folk and which are clever approximations. . . . Even with the flood of new Blues one finds still traces of the same folk imagery and attitude found in the earliest noted examples. One finds lines from the older spirituals. There has been such an assimilation that one might say: If these are not by the folk, they ought to be" (324–325).

Ironically, this opposition of authentic rural folk culture and contaminated urban mass culture became a subject of popular culture itself during the 1930s, particularly in film. One of the better known examples of this is Marc Connelly's 1930 play (and 1936 film) *Green Pastures*, where heaven is an eternal fish fry and Babylon is a jazz cabaret. In Eugene O'Neill's play *The Emperor Jones*, the corruption of the Pullman porter Brutus Jones, is represented as a fall from the rural folk into an urban money mass culture. The essential folk culture in the 1933 film version of O'Neill's play (with the screenplay written by Dubose Heywood) is figured in the opening credits where African dancers dissolve into a ring shout at a rural southern church. The scene of Jones's initial temptation and fall is a series of urban jazz clubs and barrel houses. Interestingly, in the film both the folk culture and the corrupting mass culture are gendered female with the folk embodied in Jones's church-going girlfriend back home and the mass culture in a series of "fast" women. Thus the corrupting mass culture here, as in Sterling Brown's work, is feminized as a sort of seductress interested only in money and pleasure. Jones as an agent of mass culture himself is shown to be initially irresistible. But ultimately Jones is destroyed by his alienation from the folk culture, now represented as masculine through the power and authority of male "witch doctors, and, by extension, nature as Jones goes mad in the jungle with the drums of the "natives" beating in the background.

123. See Brown, "The Blues as Folk Poetry."

The CPUSA's position on jazz in the early 1930s is contradictory. Contrary to what some scholars, such as Mark Naison, have claimed, the CPUSA was not universally hostile to jazz before the Popular Front. Though it was not until the Popular Front that *New Masses* began to seriously and favorably review jazz records and CPUSA-influenced organizations began to organize concerts of jazz, gospel and other urban African-American vernacular music, many pre-Popular Front Left functions featured dances with prominent jazz artists, including Chick Webb, Cab Calloway, Duke Ellington, Fletcher Henderson, Benny Carter, and Bessie Smith. However, it is true that the Left cultural critics associated with the CPUSA often tended to be ambivalent, if not hostile, to jazz because of its association with mass culture and hence its role as a secular opiate of the masses. Among some African-American writers and intellectuals associated with the CPUSA this attitude did not end with the beginning of the Popular Front since jazz in Richard Wright's *Native Son* is seen as just another product, and instrument, of the false consciousness of mass culture in much the same manner as detective stories, Hollywood movies, and the popular press. For the best accounts of the politics of jazz during the 1930s and 1940s and the relation of jazz to the Communist Left, see Stowe (50–93), and Denning, *The Cultural Front* (328–338).

124. Kelley, *Race Rebels* (112).

125. It is also worth noting that in his "Forewarning," which serves as preface to the volume, Davis proclaims in a rather "high" manner his intention of introducing the intrepid reader to the reality of the African-American folk using, as we have seen in other places, a gendered construction of the masculine reality of the folk and, by extension the author, that is opposed to feminine and genteel "white" literary culture:

Fairy words . . . a Pollyanna mind
Do not roam these pages.
Inside
There are coarse victuals

A couch of rough boards
Companions who seldom smile

126. For example, Cuney's 1941 blues-inflected "Uncle Sam Says" (as sung by Josh White on the record *Southern Exposure*)begins:

Well, aeroplanes fly across
Land and sea,
Everybody flies them
But a Negro like me.

A somewhat different version appeared in the October 1941 issue of *Cavalcade*, the journal of the Southern Negro Youth Congress.

127. For a more extended examination of Chicago as a major locus of African-American writing in the 1930s, see Bone, "Richard Wright and the Chicago Renaissance."

Chapter 2

1. Ad in *New Masses*, December 25, 1945: (31).

2. The other winners were Dr. Mary McLeod Bethune (education), Benjamin Davis (public life), Dean Dixon (music), Dr. Charles Drew (science), W. E. B. Du Bois (history), Arnaud d'Usseau-James Gow (for the play *Deep Are the Roots*), Duke Ellington (music), Jacob Lawrence (art), Canada Lee (theater), Alain Locke (criticism), Joe Louis (sports), Carlton Moss (writing), Pearl Primus (dance), Paul Robeson (citizen), Malcolm Ross (chairman, Fair Employment Practices Commission), Hilda Simms (theater), Frank Sinatra ("For his courageous fight on behalf of all minorities"), and Ferdinand Smith (labor leader).

3. For example, as far as I can determine, only thirteen of the forty-eight poems in Brown's unpublished collection *No Hiding Place* appeared in the 1930s and 1940s, mostly in Left or Left-influenced journals. These publications include "Transfer," "Old Lem," "Conjured," "Colloquy," "Bitter Fruit of the Tree," and "Glory, Glory" in the "American Revolutionists" section of Walton and Anderson's anthology *This Generation*; "Bitter Fruit of the Tree" in *The Nation*; "Old Lem" in *New Challenge*; "Sharecroppers" in *New Masses* and later in Calmer's *Get Organized*; "Break of Day" and "Master and Man" in *The New Republic* while Malcolm Cowley was still close to the CPUSA; "The Young Ones" in the special "Federal Poets Number" of *Poetry*; "Southern Cop" and "Transfer" in the *Partisan Review* when it was still associated with the CPUSA; "All Are Gay" in the *American Stuff* anthology of FWP writing. The only publications of poems from *No Hidin' Place* in journals not associated with the Left in the 1930s and early 1940s are "Let Us Suppose" in *Opportunity*, "Glory, Glory" in *Esquire*, and "Remembering Nat Turner" in *The Crisis*.

4. Brown's papers show him to be an active part of the literary Left during the 1930s and 1940s, corresponding with such well-known Left cultural figures as Malcom Cowley, Eda Lou Walton, Richard Wright, Isidor Schnieder, Sol Funaroff, Stanley Burnshaw, Elie Siegmeister, Lawrence Gellert, James Farrell, and Alan Calmer. But Brown's period of greatest visible connection with the Communist Left was during the Popular Front era, when he was active in the League of American Writers. Brown was a member of LAW's National Committee. He participated in major LAW forums, such as "The Negro as a Force in American Literature" at New York's Midtown Music Hall in 1938, where he appeared along with Hughes and Jessie Fauset. Brown was also active in the Left-initiated National Negro Congress. Brown, for example, chaired the session on "Culture" at the second national convention of the NNC in 1937. Crusader News Agency releases, week of October 25, 1937 (9), and week of November 14, 1938

(4). Brown was also a supporter of many other Left-initiated organizations, such as the Harlem Cultural Committee, the Committee for the Release of Jacques Roumain, the Southern Negro Youth Congress, the American League for Peace and Democracy, and the Labor Poets of America, as well as a frequent lecturer at Left schools, camps, and forums, such as Camp Unity in New York and the Philadelphia People's Forum. Brown was denounced as a "communist" in both the U.S. Senate and the House of Representatives for the essay "The Negro in Washington," a militantly antisegregationist and antiracist analysis of the Washington, D.C. African-American community, which opened the Federal Writers' Project guide, *Washington: City and Capital* (1937). For Brown's comments on the controversy, see Rowell (808). For a recent reprinting of the essay, see Brown, *A Son's Return* (25–46).

Brown's move left is hard to date exactly. Brown came into contact with the group of radical writers associated with the *The Rebel Poet* as a graduate student at Harvard University in the early 1930s. (June 8, 1932, letter from Seymour Glink, a leader of the Cambridge Poetry Forum and member of the *The Rebel Poet* national executive committee, and the August 3, 1932, letter from *Rebel Poet* editor Jack Conroy in Box 7 of the Sterling Brown Papers.) However, Brown's close friend and colleague Eugene Clay Holmes, one of the leading black intellectuals of the Communist Left in the 1930s, was much more important in Brown's political development and in bringing Brown to the attention of Left literary circles. (For an idea of Holmes's political and literary interests in the early and middle 1930s as he communicated them to Brown, see the many letters in Box 7 of the Sterling Brown Papers.)

5. For other examples of the high estimation of Brown's work by the Communist Left, see Clay, "The Negro in Recent American Literature" (149–151); Clay, "Sterling Brown: American Peoples' Poet;" Ford (192); and Haywood, *Negro Liberation* (149).

6. Ford and Patterson (166–172).

7. See Brown's "The Negro in Literature, 1925–1955" for his clearest written statement on the Harlem Renaissance.

8. Gabbin (41); Redmond; Wagner (477).

9. For a description of the Popular Front and the new attitude toward the black intelligentsia in Harlem, see Naison, *Communists in Harlem* (169–226).

10. It is also likely that Brown was invoking Helene Johnson's "A Southern Road," an ironic pastoral variation on the "Black Christ" lynching poem that was a significant subgenre of African-American poetry and art in the 1920s and 1930s. Johnson's poem appeared in the journal *Fire* in 1926 and is discussed at more length in chapter 4 of this study.

11. While what distinguishes a "folk" blues from other more commercial or more urban forms of blues is ambiguous, the folk blues is generally considered to be marked by the use of a common stock of traditional themes, images, phrases, and rhetorical devices. One aspect of the folk blues (and other forms of the blues for that matter) that makes blues poetry both difficult and distinctive is that while the typical twelve-bar blues is generally regularly stressed (four stresses to a line), these stresses are unrelated to line length. Thus in Brown's blues poetry, and other vernacular poetry, lines usually contain the same number of stresses but often in irregular intervals. For a good discussion of this subject, see the "Defining the Blues" chapter in Steven Tracy's *Langston Hughes and the Blues* (59–140).

12. See Hughes's comments in the liner notes to the Spoken Arts record *Langston Hughes Reads and Talks About his Poetry*.

13. *Fine Clothes to the Jew* as a whole represents the experience of the migrant to the North as far more difficult and contradictory than a reading of "Bound No'th Blues" alone would suggest. This is especially true in the "Railroad Avenue" section of Hughes's collection, which is an important predecessor to the poems in the "Tin Roof Blues" section of *Southern Road* with the difference that Hughes is far more sympathetic to the northern migrants than Brown.

14. Gabbin (122); Gates, *Figures in Black* (231–232).

15. Wagner (489–490); Gabbin (121–123).

16. In this respect it is interesting to compare Brown's poem to Waring Cuney's "Chain Gang Chant," which also appeared in the 1930 issue of B. A. Botkin's *Folk-Say* where "Southern Road" was first published. Cuney's poem begins:

> How long, how long,
> Oh, tell me how long?
>
> I call ma mother,
> But she don't answer me.
> No, Lawd.
>
> (280)

Cuney's poem presents a very similar list of disruptions of the speaker's connection to family and community, but, unlike Brown's poem, lacks any mention of the new black community in which the convict is located except in the title. While the repeated phrase "No Lawd" in the Cuney poem may be the response of the work gang to the leader, there is no clear address by the poem's speaker to his fellow convicts framing the poem in the way that there is in the first stanza of Brown's poem. Thus the narrative consciousness of Cuney's poem is more akin to that of Hughes's "Bound N'oth Blues" than to that of "Southern Road" despite their proximity in *Folk-Say* and their ostensible similarity of subject, which invites the reader to consider them together.

17. Wagner (496–503); Locke (90).

Hughes's own poetry in the early 1930s would change with respect to the possibility of African-American community in the South, though his vision, as in "Scottsboro Limited," where the "Boys" unite with white workers, is far more interracial than that of Brown during the same period.

18. For a differing view of the relationship between "Big Boy" Davis and the folk culture in which it is Davis rather than the poet-persona who is alienated from the folk, see Benston (40–42). For Brown's description of Davis's largely academic audience at these sessions, see Gabbin (34–35).

19. While the dominant tone of the Third Period CPUSA was definitely antireligious, there was considerable internal debate over how flexible Communists should be with respect to religious expression, particularly in work among African Americans. An interesting example of this debate is the "Party Pre-Convention Discussion" exchange between William F. Kruse and H. E. Kaye of the Chicago District in the February 18, 1929, *Daily Worker* (3). In this respect, the problem of the CPUSA was the problem of Brown: how does one favorably recreate and represent the folk while criticizing the religious values that you see as essentially accommodationist, but that are a critical portion of the folk heritage?

20. An early forerunner of Brown's notion of the role of the black intellectual in resisting the "northernizing" of the South in which earlier forms of southern racism are grafted to a new mass industrial "mammonism" is Du Bois's *The Souls of Black Folk*, particularly in the chapter "On the Wings of Atalanta." Brown's vision is obviously far from the "talented tenth" of Du Bois, but his sense of the dangers of commercialism and mass culture is quite similar to Du Bois's.

21. Jean Wagner also notes the close affinity of Brown to McKay:

> This also put him [Brown] in splendid position to denounce all the false portraits of the people and of their art, and the poems that tackle these problems show

him to be extraordinarily close to Claude McKay. In either writer, perhaps because they remained so closely rooted in the soil, one discovers the same scrupulous respect for the racial heritage, and the same commitment to defend the purity of its memory against those whose behavior jeopardized it. (479)

However, it needs to be noted that the shared commitment of McKay and Brown to which Wagner alludes arises in part because of the separation of the intellectual from the folk at some point in the past. McKay's poetry and novels, as well as Brown's poetry, posit a narratorial persona who is not "rooted in the soil" but alienated from the folk and "the soil." As a result, the works of Brown and McKay become a process of return for the intellectual-artist, both figuratively and literally. While both writers indicate that such a return will be salutary for both the alienated intellectual and the folk, Brown's sense of the importance of the intellectual for the folk is far greater than that of McKay. Thus the narratorial consciousness of many of Brown's poems does not simply defend the "purity" of the "racial heritage," but feels free to pointedly criticize it, albeit from a sympathetic point of view. For example, as Wagner himself notes (490–496), the narratorial consciousness clearly attacks what is seen as an accommodationist tradition of African-American folk religion as in "Maumee Ruth" in *Southern Road* and "The Young Ones" in *No Hidin' Place*. Brown's sympathetic yet critical attitude toward the folk, particularly with respect to religion, is quite consonant with the construction of the African-American folk by the CPUSA during the era of the Third Period.

22. For a brief description of this stock type and the "blackface" or "Ethiopian" minstrel tradition generally, see Southern (88–96). For a much deeper discussion of minstrelsy and its role in the formation of American culture, particularly of a sense of class identity among white workers, see Lott, *Love and Theft*.

23. For an account of the critical reception of *Harlem Shadows*, including rave reviews by James Weldon Johnson and Walter White in the African-American press, see Cooper (164–166).

24. Wagner (479–480).

25. The onomatopoeic and synaesthetic lines "Da, da, / Da, da, da!" confusing music, dance, and language authorize the apparently conflicting instructions (White folks, laugh! / White folks, pray!) to the white patrons of a Harlem club as to whether they should be amused, afraid, humiliated, or all of the above.

26. Brown, "The Blues as Folk Poetry" (339).

27. It should be noted that Brown admired some of these other more urban "classic" singers in his critical writing. For an example, see Brown, "The Blues as Folk Poetry" (324).

28. Gabbin (117–172).

29. According to Lawrence Levine, counternarratives of the Cain and Abel story were a part of African-American culture in the antebellum South—though apparently these stories tended to attribute the lineage of white people to Cain rather than to rehabilitate Cain (85).

It may also refer to Toomer's *Cane*, which Brown admired immensely. If so, then the poem can be seen as both a tribute of sorts to Toomer in which the problem of the split between mind and body (and between city and country, nature and civilization, and so on) posed by Toomer's novel is corrected by a utopian vison in which the tiller of the mind and the tiller of the land are one.

30. An example of this tradition would be the stride pianist Willie "the Lion" Smith's claim that he could "play Chopin faster than any man alive;" Spellman (5).

31. Eliot, *Selected Essays* (3–11)

32. Locke, "Sterling Brown: The New Negro Folk Poet" (92).

33. While Brown in "The Blues as Folk Poetry" sets up a rigid theoretical opposition of the "authentic" folk and the commercial, he admits that the practical situation is more com-

plex: owing to the market's demand, noting that the music industry recorded the most "primitive" folk utterances, and eminently commercial performers, such as Bessie Smith and Ma
Rainey, frequently captured the "authentic" folk spirit in their recordings and performances.

34. Wagner (490).

35. For a discussion of the conjunction of nationalism and masculinity in the poetry of
the *Negro World* and the Communist Party (CPUSA) journal *The Negro Liberator*, see Kelley, *Race
Rebels* (103–121).

36. This transformation is seen most clearly in the endings of the two poems. A version
of the actual folk ballad included in Brown, Davis, and Lee's anthology *Negro Caravan* ends with
Frankie declaring:

> "Put me in that dungeon,
>   Put me in that cell,
> Put me where the northeast wind
>   Blow from the southeast corner of hell,
>   I shot my man, 'cause he done me wrong.
>
>   (462)

Brown's poem in *Southern Road* concludes:

> Frankie, she was spindly limbed with corn silk on her crazy head,
>   Johnny was a nigger, who never had much fun—
> They swung up Johnny on a tree, and filled his swinging hide with lead,
>   And Frankie yowled hilariously when the thing was done.
>
>   (35)

37. Huggins, *Harlem Renaissance* (190–243).

38. It can be argued that there is a relation between the vernacular dialogue poems of *No
Hidin' Place* and the common practice of blues singers such as Leadbelly & Lightnin' Hopkins,
who intersperse a spoken narrative with sung blues refrains or blues stanzas (or interrupt the
song with a spoken gloss on the events described in the song).

39. An example of Third Period apocalyptic rhetoric can be found in CPUSA Chairman
William Z. Foster's *Toward Soviet America* (1932):

> The capitalist chain, with the progress of the general capitalist crisis, is becoming
> full of weak links. The entire chain is weakening. As we have seen, among the es-
> pecial weak links are Germany, Spain, Poland, China, India, etc. So far has the capi-
> talist crisis developed in these countries that the toiling masses may make a revolu-
> tionary break through at any time, with disastrous results upon the whole chain. (64)

The definitive, or at least the most authoritative, articulation of the Popular Front perspective
of the CPUSA toward revolution is CPUSA General Secretary Earl Browder's *The People's Front*
(1938):

> For the broad masses also, socialism is not the issue today, but rather the issue is,
> whether to move on the reactionary road toward fascism, or to struggle to maintain
> democratic rights, living standards and peace. For the Farmer-Labor Party move-
> ment the issue is not between socialism and capitalism, but whether to move on the
> reactionary or progressive roads. We Communists, throwing in our lot with the
> Farmer-Labor Party movement, agree to fight for the road of progress under capi-
> talism, together with those who are not adherents of socialism as we are; while at

the same time we point out that the only final guarantee of progress is to abolish capitalism and move to socialism. (32)

40. Naison, *Communists in Harlem* (193–206).

41. While Brown here stakes out a position against a certain aspect of Jazz Age modernism, his rhetorical stance recalls that of much "high modernism." The obvious overtones of emasculation of the black male body in "Roberta Lee" is far more nightmarish than the commodification of the female body. Once again, the female gaze, in essence the vision of the "lady poet" of modernist vituperation, is linked to a lingering nineteenth-century aesthetic that is even more objectionable to the narratorial consciousness than the modernist gaze of her male counterpart.

42. For example, during this period John Hammond began to write a regular jazz column in *New Masses*, first under the pseudonym Henry Johnson and later under his own name.

43. Wright, "Joe Louis Uncovers Dynamite."

44. The speaker also differs from the white woman in the poem who knows that Turner existed, but is confused as to the details of Turner and the rebellion he led. As Brown points out in an interview, the woman conflates Turner with John Brown (Rowell, 803).

45. As noted earlier, it is often stated with some justice that the Communist Third Period ideology is hostile to organized religion and various forms of expression associated with African-American folk religion. But it is important to recognize that strong African-American millenarian traditions of folk religion dovetailed quite well with the apocalyptic rhetoric of the Third Period. Thus the expression of millenarian visions of revolution and the end of capitalism can be said to accommodate the folk culture more readily than Popular Front gradualism, even if the overt expression of religious sentiments was tolerated more readily by the CPUSA during the Popular Front.

46. Naison, *Communists in Harlem* (212–213).

Much of the African-American folklore collected during the Popular Front, such as the work that Arna Bontemps and Jack Conroy did in the Illinois Writers Project, was of urban folklore, where the earlier collectors had dealt overwhelmingly with rural folklore. For that matter, the folk music boom itself was an urban phenomenon where the musicians, whether Woody Guthrie in Los Angeles or Leadbelly in Dallas and Houston, had considerable experience in big cities, whatever their rural origins, before their arrival in New York City.

47. Once again, Brown's experience can be put into the larger context of the literary Left. Difficulties negotiating the new cultural emphases of the Popular Front period were not restricted to Brown or African-American writers generally, as the experiences of Jack Conroy and other white authors who were lionized during the "proletarian" period can attest. For an account of the impact of the changing cultural politics of the Left on Conroy, see Wixson (396–402).

Chapter 3

1. Both Thurman in *Infants of the Spring* (1932) and Tolson in *Harlem Gallery* (1965) create characters modeled on Hughes. The character Hideho Heights, the "vagabond bard of Lenox Avenue" in *Harlem Gallery*, is a closet modernist who publicly declaims populist poems of the Harlem lowlife and vernacular culture while secretly writing allusive and difficult poems of existential despair. The poet Tony Crews in *Infants of the Spring* is declared by the narrator to have "no depth whatsoever, or else he was too deep for plumbing by ordinary mortals" (Thurman, 231).

2. For an early example of this type of criticism of Hughes, see Fearing, "Limiting

Devices." For more recent examples, see Huggins, *Harlem Renaissance* (221–227); Robert Stepto's Introduction to Fisher and Stepto; and O'Meally.

3. For the best history of Hughes's sometimes troubled relationship with the Left during the 1930s, see Rampersad, *The Life of Langston Hughes, Volume I* (211–395).

4. Arnold Rampersad divides Hughes work during the period into "radical, commercial and racial-genteel"(*Life of Langston Hughes, Volume I*, 223).

5. For examples of these reviews see Clay, "The Negro in Recent American Literature," and Walton.

However, it is necessary to make a distinction between the critics associated with the CPUSA and what might be thought of as the general Left reading public. Anecdotal evidence— individual testimony of the impact of Hughes's readings, the willingness of Left cultural institutions to print and / or perform Hughes's work, the use of Hughes's work by Left organizations (see the broadside of Hughes's "August 19" published by the Communist Party of Alabama), and so on—suggest that Hughes's work was much more popular among Left readers, and Left organizations, than among Left critics.

6. For a brief account of these responses, and Hughes's reaction to them, see Rampersad, *The Life of Langston Hughes, Volume I* (140–146).

7. Rampersad, *The Life of Langston Hughes, Volume I* (223–234).

8. The promotional blurb on the cover of the book reads that the poems in the collection, "passionately lyrical presentations of widely known and well-beloved Negro characters delineated in a broadly popular manner not associated with Negro poetry since the death of Paul Laurence Dunbar, are suitable for recitation by amateurs in schools, churches and clubs." This blurb was presumably written, or at least approved, by Hughes, since the book was basically self-published.

9. Harper's best known work, the novel *Iola Leroy* (1893), contains a number of such characters of whom the most prominent is Aunt Linda, whose "folkishness" is marked by her obstinate refusal to learn to read.

10. The stage instructions for this section of the poem read: "Tearing off his clown's suit, throwing down the hat of a fool, and standing forth, straight and strong, in the clothes of a modern man, he proclaims himself" (11). These instructions and the poem itself are accompanied by a Prentiss Taylor graphic that shows the discarded clown costume while the revealed black man stands proudly in a wide-lapelled suit and vest.

11. For an account of the success of Hughes's first southern reading tour and the sales of *The Negro Mother*, see Rampersad, *The Life of Langston Hughes, Volume I* (223–234).

12. For examples of such IWW songs, including "Solidarity Forever" and "We Have Fed You All for a Thousand Years," see Kornbluth.

13. Jemie (131).

14. See Vendler; Wagner (433–437); and Jackson and Rubin (58) for examples of negative assessments of Hughes's revolutionary poetry; see Baraka, "The Revolutionary Tradition in Afro-American Literature" in *Selected Plays and Prose of Amiri Baraka / Leroi Jones* (248) for a far less common positive judgment.

15. One notable exception is Cary Nelson, whose *Repression and Recovery* (1989) briefly, but provocatively, raises the relationship between text, illustration, and typography in Hughes's "Advertisement for the Waldorf-Astoria" as it first appeared in the December 1931 issue of *New Masses* (209).

Another exception is Martha Cobb, who formally links Hughes's revolutionary poetry of the 1930s with his work in the 1920s, claiming that "what marks much of his poetry in the decades of the thirties and early forties is not the fact he is protesting injustice but the way in which he continues to adhere to racial styles—the spiritual, the gospel, the blues" (76).

16. For an example of such an assessment, see Wagner (437).

17. Pinsky (122–139).

18. Section XVII of *Spring and All* ends:

That sheet stuff
's a lot a cheese.

Man
gimme the key

lemme loose—
I make 'em crazy

with my harmonies—
Shoot it Jimmy

Nobody
Nobody else

but me—
They can't copy it

(*Collected Poems of William Carlos Williams*, Volume 1, 216)

It is possible that Hughes's poem is a commentary on that of Williams in that both represent the same type of American vernacular language largely for itself, but that Hughes ties it to a less exotic and less abstract activity.

19. "Scottsboro Limited" here refers to the play itself, while the italicized *Scottsboro Limited* denotes the 1932 Golden Stair Press collection that included the play. All page citations are from the collection.

20. The first American use of the "mass chant" or "mass recitation" was in Michael Gold's 1926 play "Strike." However, the left-wing German-language theater Proletbuehne is generally credited as introducing the form as a regular feature of radical drama in the 1931 play *Scottsboro*. (Hicks, et al., 262; and Ira Levine, 89). Levine defines the mass recitation as "a simple narrative, often a poem, that built to a direct exhortation of the audience, normally to organize strike or fight. It was chanted, contrapuntally or in unison, by actors who were either formally arranged or moved rhythmically" (89). Another example of a Scottsboro mass chant, which may have been influenced by Hughes's play, was Jack Haynes "Scottsboro Mass Chant," which appeared in the October-November-December 1932 issue of *The Rebel Poet*.

21. For examples of the elevation of reportage, see the Preface to the "Reportage" section of Hicks, et al. (261–264); and Joseph North, "Reportage." For an example of the sense of the relatively unfavorable climate of the era for poetry in the 1930s, see Locke, "The Eleventh Hour of Nordicism" (11–12).

22. On a very simple level it also allows the audience to engage in an active reading after the manner suggested by Wolfgang Iser in "The Reading Process: A Phenomenological Approach" in *The Implied Reader*, or, to put it more squarely within an African-American tradition, the withheld rhyme functions a sort of "call" to which the audience can enthusiastically respond. With respect to the element of "mooning," it is possibly significant that most of the audiences for the performances of the plays, generally by local CPUSA groups as part of their agitation around the Scottsboro case, were predominantly white.

23. In fact, the ending of the poem "Madam's Calling Cards," as published in the 1949 collection *One-Way Ticket*, uses the same phrase, albeit to proclaim Alberta K. Johnson's American-ness rather than her identification with the international proletariat:

There's nothing foreign
To my pedigree:
Alberta K. Johnson—
American that's me

      (*Collected*, 302)

Interestingly, as Arnold Rampersad and David Roessel remark in their notes to their edition of Hughes's collected poems, the original publications of "Madam's Calling Cards" in *Poetry* (1943) and *Negro Story* (1945) end on a note of racial and female pride through individual self-affirmation ("*Madam*, that's me") rather than through the national affirmation of the *One-Way Ticket* version. Obviously, the change is motivated by ideological considerations, but, as usual with Hughes, the precise meaning of the shift is elusive since it could either represent a sort of retreat before the increasing domestic cold war or an attack on McCarthyism along the lines of Paul Robeson's assertion of his American-ness and the House Committee on Un-American Activities' own un-Americaness during Robeson's testimony before HUAC in 1956.

    24. For a brief discussion of *Scottsboro Limited* as a jazz play, see VèVè Clark's interview with Amiri Baraka in Charlie Reilly.

    25. In fact, Nathan Huggins does claim in *Harlem Renaissance* that Hughes places himself outside mainstream (read "high modernist") serious American literature of the twentieth century (226–227). Arnold Rampersad similarly, though more approvingly, claims that "poetic modernism, as defined by elitism, hyper-intellectualism, and a privacy of language was not for Hughes" (*The Life of Langston Hughes, Volume I*, 102–103).

    26. For example, Johnson writes in his headnote on Hughes in the 1931 edition of *The Book of American Negro Poetry*:

> Hughes is a cosmopolite and a rebel, and both of these attributes are reflected in his poetry. As a cosmopolite, he takes his subject matter from any level of life that interests him. His forms are for the most part free, and his subject matter is often from the lower strata. (232)

For another assessment of the early Hughes as an "experimentalist" by an African-American contemporary, see Brown, *Negro Poetry and Drama* (71).

    27. For an example of this pessimistic strain in the work of Davidman, see "Twentieth Century Americanism" in the 1938 collection *Letters to a Comrade*.

    28. Hughes's line "Civilization's gone to hell" recalls Pound's "For an old bitch gone in the teeth / for a botched civilization" in *Hugh Selwyn Mauberly* (1920) (*Selected Poems*, 64).

    29. For a brief but suggestive discussion of the complex interplay between the visual and verbal elements of the poem as originally published in the December 1931 *New Masses*, see Nelson, *Repression and Recovery* (219).

    30. "Advertisement for the Waldorf-Astoria" was obviously written before Robeson's public identification with the CPUSA. For a more detailed instance where Hughes used Robeson, along with Du Bois, Countee Cullen, and Carl Van Vechten, as an icon of a patronizing Harlem Renaissance spirit that Hughes came to reject, see the short story "Slave on the Block" in *The Ways of White Folks*.

    31. Despite the obvious differences in stance toward African-American culture between Hughes and Richard Wright, this notion of transcending the folk heritage while retaining a distinctly African-American identity is essentially the same in *Native Son*, particularly as represented by the relation between Bigger Thomas and the folk inheritance as embodied in his mother and the black church.

    32. Though Hughes would still occasionally use what might be thought his Third Period

paradigm of the transcendence of "folk" qualities (seen as the products and markers of the old social order) by the folk, as in "Broadcast on Ethiopia" and, to a lesser extent, "Don't You Want to Be Free."

33. In addition to concerts, African-American popular culture, particularly swing music, was the subject of many articles, speeches, forums, lectures, and classes within the press and the cultural and educational institutions of the Communist Left during and after the Popular Front era. For a brief look at the Popular Front approach to black popular music and sports in New York City, see Naison, *Communists in Harlem* (211–214).

34. Rampersad, *The Life of Langston Hughes, Volume I* (356–360).

35. It is interesting with respect to gender that the "Young Man," who has a role similar to that of the "Eighth Boy" in "Scottsboro Limited," as the figure of the new transforming consciousness, or what might be thought of as the New Negro Socialist Man, by the end of the play speaks in the most "standard" diction, while the "Wife" speaks in what is clearly seen to be a specifically African-American diction.

36. For a brief sketch of the typical Hughes program for a southern black audience during his first reading tour of the South in 1931, see Rampersad, *The Life of Langston Hughes, Volume I* (223–224).

37. For a valuable discussion of *Pins and Needles* and the Popular Front, see Denning, *The Cultural Front* (295–309).

38. In fact, "Don't You Want to Be Free" apparently was far more successful in Harlem than later, when it played downtown in front of a predominantly white, and Left, audience, at least as far as the critical responses are concerned. For a description of the early staging and responses to the play, see Rampersad, *The Life of Langston Hughes, Volume I* (356–360).

Chapter 4

1. Brown, *Negro Poetry and Drama* (79–80).

2. For a discussion of the literary representations of Nat Turner and Gabriel in the 1930s and 1940s, see Stone (192–216, 229–238).

3. Kalaidjian, *American Culture Between the Wars* (160).

4. Gold's poem begins:

> Indianapolis, Ind.
> We held a red funeral for a child who died of hunger.
> We marched in thousands to her grave.
> Red roses came from the Communist Party
> A wreath of lillies from the Unemployed Councils.
> Our banners flashed in the sun
> But our hearts were dark with anger.
>
> (Hicks et al., 161)

Whether or not Gold doctored or invented this "correspondence," the very datelines of Indianapolis and Ashtabula, Ohio, are clearly chosen to document to the "authenticity" of these voices from the American heartland.

5. For a brief account of the role of the Communist Left in the struggle to end the segregation of professional baseball, see Tygiel (36–37).

6. This obsession with authorial credentials of authenticity among Left writers is seen perhaps most clearly in the contributor's notes in literary journals of the time, where almost invariably various "proletarian" jobs and experiences are listed.

7. For a discussion of Mike Gold, as well as fellow interwar American Jewish writers Samuel Ornitz and Daniel Fuchs, and the use of the figure of the gangster as a means of negotiating mass culture and "high" culture representations of the Jew, see Rubin.

8. James Weldon Johnson, *God's Trombones* (8).

9. Ibid. (7).

10. Of course, the tradition of "authenticating" letters of white authorities attesting to the veracity of works by African-American authors continued into the 1930s and beyond. Examples of this are Mike Gold's Introduction to Hughes's *A New Song*, Stephen Vincent Benét's Foreword to Margaret Walker's *For My People*, and B. Y. Williams's note to Ida Gerding Athens's *Brethren*. A revision of this tradition common in the 1930s was the attestation to the authenticity of the work by the author or an African-American authority, as in Hughes's brief prefatory note to *Shakespeare in Harlem*, Wright's "autobiographical sketch," "The Ethics of Living Jim Crow," which opened his 1938 collection of four novellas *Uncle Tom's Children*, and James Weldon Johnson's Introduction to *Southern Road*.

11. James Weldon Johnson, Preface to *God's Trombones* (1–11).

12. Tolson wrote in one of his notebooks, "The Gallery is an attempt to picture the Negro in America before he becomes the giant auk of the melting pot in the dawn of the twenty-second century" (cited in Mariann Russell, 9).

13. Williams writes; "This author has done for these inconspicuous young Americans what John Steinbeck did on huge scale for the Okies. No person reading her lines will ever again be oblivious to this particular stratum of our complex existence" (Athens, 4).

14. See the opening of "Jazz, Jive, and Jam" in Hughes's *The Best of Simple* (239–245), for a typical exchange of this sort between the narrator and Simple.

15. This is not to say that such a vision is exactly false, but merely to make the obvious point that overalls serve an iconic purpose that would be undermined by a picture of the same laborers dressed up to go out on a Friday or Saturday night. An interesting juxtaposition, for example, is the photos of southern black farmers and agricultural workers taken by Ben Shahn and Arthur Rothstein for the Farm Security Administration with independently taken photographs by Walker Evans in the South in 1934. In the photos of Shahn and Rothstein, we see the dominant vision of the southern African-American folk: farm laborers and their families on the land in worn work clothes and plain and sober "good" Sunday clothes. Among the pictures by Evans, we see a laborer dressed up in what might be called a "premature bebop" outfit including round sunglasses (Evans, 99). In general, Evans's pictures of African Americans in the South are surprisingly absent the "typical" image of the farm laborer in overalls—in contrast to his famous portraits of white sharecroppers. For interesting discussions of the politics of African-American dress in the 1930s and 1940s, see Kelley, *Race Rebels* (49–51, 161–182).

It is also worth noting that such claims of authenticity on the basis of eye- and ear-witness, often contained in the phrase "knowing the Negro," was a common defense of works representing and recreating the African-American folk by white artists, generally southern white artists, who were clearly influenced by minstrelsy. For examples of this sort of defense, see Roark Bradford's Introduction to his *John Henry* and the interview with King Vidor in Seward where Vidor discusses the making of the film *Hallelujah* (1929).

16. The book is filled with poems about children who cannot attend classes despite their parents' wishes, owing to sickness, lack of clothing, and so on—in short, crises caused by poverty. The clearest articulation of the relation of material conditions to psychic or cultural development is "The Children's Dole":

> Next, a group of pretty, older girls,
> Good future mothers—if fed better.
> Silently the children pass along the way,

Enduring, hoping for the comfort of school fires,
The welcome of the kindly, casual greeting—
Wistful, grateful recipients of abstracted smiles;
Hungry for this meager dole, so transient, fleeting
American citizens of the coming day.

(53)

17. Kelley, "Comrades, Praise Gawd for Lenin and Them!" (61–63).

18. Though it was important in promoting a sense of political and artistic community among black writers in the Americas, Africa, and Europe, Nancy Cunard's *Negro* (1934) was published in Britain and had a miniscule readership. Beatrice Murphy's *Negro Voices* (1938) seems to have been a semi-vanity publication, despite the appearance of lesser poems by a few established poets, such as Langston Hughes.

19. Locke, "We Turn to Prose" (40)

20. See Hatch (44–54) for a short account of the production of Dodson's play, an attack on Father Divine first performed at the Yale Drama School in 1938 and, later, something of a staple of theater groups at historically black colleges.

21. For a brief mention of the poetry reading in which Alain Locke substituted a more "respectable" musician for the desired blues singer, see Rampersad, *The Life of Langston Hughes, Volume I* (123). For a somewhat longer account of Hughes's attempt to write for a popular "revue" and his plans with collaborator Zora Neale Hurston for a jazz and blues "opera," see Rampersad, *The Life of Langston Hughes, Volume 1* (133–134).

22. Cuney's attempt to reach a "folk" audience was not limited to these recordings and the poems published in *Cavalcade*. He was also a member of Southern Negro Youth Congress-sponsored Caravan Puppet Theater, which toured the rural South in 1940 performing skits aimed at a sharecropping audience (Kelley, *Hammer and Hoe*, 208–209; Crusader News Agency file).

23. Rampersand, *The Life of Langston Hughes, Volume 1* (133–134).

24. Thus it is possible for Hughes to write in "Note on Commercial Theatre" (1940):

You've taken my blues and gone—
You sing 'em on Broadway
And you sing 'em in Hollywood Bowl,
And you mixed 'em up with symphonies
And you fixed 'em
So they don't sound like me.

(*Collected*, 215)

While it may seem ironic for an author who in fact wrote for the commercial theater to produce such a poem, the complaint of the African-American speaker is not rooted in an opposition between mass commerical culture and folk culture, but the separation of essentially commercial forms, such as the blues in 1940, from their folk roots.

25. A "literary" printed version of "King Joe" did not appear, as far as I can tell, before the December 1971 issue of *New Letters*—though the sheet music for the song was published in 1942. The order of the stanzas on the recorded version differ considerably from those of the printed version—there are also some minor differences between the wording of the stanzas in the recorded text and the printed text in *New Letters*.

It is important to remember that, unlike the case of a number of the poem-songs on Cuney-White's *Southern Exposure*, no printed version was available when the record was issued so that there would be no discrepancy between the diction and orthography of the record and the printed poem. For example, "strong" and "born" would be a much more regular end-rhyme as sung by Robeson on the original recorded version than they would be in the later *New Letters* version.

For a description of the recording session of "King Joe," see Fabre, *The Unfinished Quest of Richard Wright* (237). According to Fabre, the record, which was distributed to juke boxes in northern African-American neighborhoods, was fairly successful commercially—the advance order was 40,000 copies.

26. Louis was born in Alabama and moved to Detroit with his family. In Detroit, virtually all the male members of the Louis family (including Joe Louis for a brief period in 1934) worked for the Ford Motor Company River Rouge plant in Dearborn at one time or another. Wright emphasizes Louis's experience as part of the newly proletarianized folk at the Rouge plant in a stanza that was not included on the record (but which appeared in the *New Letters* version).

27. The link between Wright's work and urban blues and popular African-American music is strengthened by the fact that "King Joe" was contemporary with a number of commercial blues and popular songs about Joe Louis such as Jack Kelly's "Joe Louis Special" (1939).

28. For an oral history of the Kansas City musical scene in the 1920s and the 1930s, see Pearson.

29. For an influential discussion of this subject, see Gates, *Figures in Black* (3–58).

30. The influences of Sandburg, Masters, and Lindsay have been often noted by commentators on Davis's work, including Davis himself. The influence of Johnson on Davis, who knew Johnson in Chicago in the 1920s and 1930s, has been less remarked on but is considerable. After all, Johnson had attempted to utilize a populist free verse derived from Sandburg, Masters, and Lindsay to represent an African-American subjectivity a decade before Davis. "What Do You Want, America" seems particularly indebted to Johnson's much anthologized poem "Tired," which ends "I am tired of civilization." For a brief account of a writers group that both Davis and Johnson participated in during the late 1920s, see Frank Marshall Davis, *Livin' the Blues* (130–131).

31. In addition to his work as a journalist in the African-American press, Davis taught one of the first courses in the history of jazz at the CPUSA-initiated Abraham Lincoln School during the 1940s. For a description of Davis's activities at the Lincoln School, see Frank Marshall Davis, *Livin' the Blues* (283–290).

32. For an example of this journalism, see Caldwell's "Parties Unknown in Georgia" in the January 23, 1934, *New Masses*.

33. Though, as Michael Denning points out in *The Cultural Front*, leftists of various stripes did produce significant studies of the mass-culture industries, such as James Rorty's *Our Master's Voice: Advertising*, Lewis Jacobs's *The Rise of American Film* (1939), and Elizabeth Hawes's *Fashion is Spinach* (1938).

The "anti-Stalinist Left" and the "New York Intellectuals" have received a large amount of scholarly attention over the last decade. For the most in-depth account of their political trajectory, see Wald, *The New York Intellectuals*. For an amusing, if hardly disinterested, portrait of Rahv and Phillips during the 1930s, see their long-time antagonist Jack Conroy's "On Anvil."

For the best known example of the antimass culture bent of the *Partisan Review* circle in its early anti-Stalinist days, see Clement Greenberg's "Avant-Garde and Kitsch." It is worth noting that while Greenberg's article may have been, as Serge Guilbaut suggests, "an important step in the 'de-Marxization of the American intelligensia,'" in its binaries of "avant-garde" and "kitsch," "authentic culture" and "ersatz culture" it resembles nothing so much as the more extreme versions of Third Period cultural Leftism with the important difference, of course, that the CPUSA, and Communism generally, is associated with "kitsch" or mass culture rather than the bourgeoisie. This association of the CPUSA with mass culture, particularly during the

Popular Front and after, remains a central tenet of the "New York Intellectuals" long after the 1930s, causing even as serious and sympathetic an observer of popular culture as Robert Warshow much anxiety, particularly in his early writings as evidenced by his 1947 essay "The Legacy of the 30's." In fact, this anti-Communist–mass culture anxiety continues to survive somewhat covertly among the remnants of the first generation of "New York Intellectuals," as seen in William Phillips recent attack on the "New Black Intellectuals" where he somewhat hysterically rejects comparisons of the "New York Intellectuals" to the "New Black Intellectuals" largely on the basis of the engagement of many prominent African-American intellectuals with mass culture (Phillips, "The New Black Intellectuals").

34. Pells (222–223). See Barnard for an account of the evolution of *Miss Lonelyhearts* from West's original concept of a comic strip novel. Of course, given West's representation of the consumers of mass culture as essentially passive, or nihilistically violent, what this formal use of mass culture for "serious" literature means is extremely complicated. Yet I would argue that representing the contradiction of the perceived necessity of drawing on mass culture in order to reach beyond what Clement Greenberg calls, not altogether pejoratively, the "mandarinism" of high culture, and to be authentically modern while attempting to examine the function and results of mass culture (not the least in the choice of the author to draw on that culture), are typical moves of Left writers or the era.

35. The opening stanza of "Jazz Band" reads:

Play that thing, you jazz mad fools!
Boil a skyscraper with a jungle
Dish it to 'em sweet and hot—
Ahhhhhhhhh
Rip it open then sew it up, jazz band!

(*Black Man's Verse*, 35)

The diction of the rest of the poem continues in this manner for the most part, though even here the speaker lapses into a journalistic-literary hard-boiled diction more typical of Davis's work, as in the line "Make 'em shout a crazy jargon of hot hosannas to a fiddlefaced jazz god."

36. Cullen, *My Soul's High Song* (56).

37. Huggins (214); Wagner (290); Early, Introduction to Cullen, *My Soul's High Song* (56–57).

38. DeJongh (78).

39. Barbara Foley claims that Cullen "joined the Party for about a year in 1932," though she does not document her claim (203).

40. Thus we find in Richard Wright's *Black Boy* a description of how even the least formally educated and most impoverished in origin of all the major African-American writers of the 1930s and 1940s experienced a sense of what he calls "emotional isolation" from other black CPUSA members at a party meeting caused by his identity as an intellectual and a writer (Wright, *Later Works*, 313–314). For a scholarly analysis of this passage that argues that it that it is a record of Wright's isolation from African-American vernacular culture generally, see Stepto, "I Thought I Knew These People."

41. An interesting exception to this phenomenon is Mae Cowdery, whose collection *We Lift Our Voices* was published in 1936 with an introduction by the dean of "genteel" poetry anthologists of the 1910s and 1920s, William Stanley Braithewaite. Cowdery's collection consists for the most part of "high," often overtly lesbian love lyrics and pastorals with occasional race conscious "primitivist" poems, generally written in the 1920s. An example, of her "primitivist" mode is "Longings," winner of the Krigwa Prize in 1927, which ends:

To croon
Sweet weird melodies
Round the cabin door
With banjoes clinking softly—
And from out of the shadow
Hear the beat of tom-toms
Resonant through the years.

(10)

Yet, like Lucy Mae Turner's collection, *We Lift Our Voices*, which seems such a throwback to an earlier period of poetic production, suddenly shifts gear at the end of the collection with a decidedly unexotic short tribute to the folk spirit ("Heritage"), a short lyric of youthful revolt ("Contrast"), two militantly antiwar poems ("To Veterans of Future Wars" and "Unknown Soldier"), ending finally on a note of near apocalyptic rebellion ("We Lift Our Voices"):

We must clear this humid air
Of vows and promises never kept
Of fear and false confidence
That we may fill our lungs
Of our youth with the cold wind
The clean wind of courage

O audience
So unaware of our music
We are a symphony reaching the final movement
FORTISSIMO!!!

(67–68)

What we are left with at the end of this poem is a call to collective rebellion that is in spirit, and even in diction, close to what is now seen as the stereotypical call to action in the Left literature and drama of the 1930s. It is as if somehow the ending for *Waiting for Lefty*, which after all ends in similarly purple speech by the character Agate, was appended to a collection of poetry by Countee Cullen. And while the diction of the poem is not precisely typical of the poetry examined elsewhere in this chapter, the poem contains phrases ("strength of the earth," "our broad shoulders") that are closely akin to Left visual and literary figurations of the folk and of the working class.

Chapter 5

1. As Rampersad notes, Babette Deutsch's review in the May 6, 1951, *New York Times* was particularly scathing in its denunciation of *Montage* as "cultivated naiveté" (Rampersad, *The Life of Langston Hughes, Volume II*, 196–197; Deutsch, 32).

2. For examples of such attacks on neomodernist African-American poetry, see Sarah Webster Fabio's "Who Speaks Negro?" (on Tolson's *Harlem Gallery*) and Don L. Lee's "On *Kaleidoscope* and Robert Hayden." Brooks was largely excepted because of her public conversion to the Black Arts Movement, though even in her case, her early work was occasionally attacked.

Hughes was viewed ambivalently by the Black Arts Movement. Nonetheless, he was viewed far more favorably than Tolson and Hayden. For example, virtually every essay on poetry in Addison Gayle Jr.'s *The Black Aesthetic*, a crucial collection of Black Arts literary and cultural criticism, has a positive view of Hughes's work.

3. Redding, "Old Forms, Old Rhythms, Old Words." For Ellison's assessment of Hughes's lack of growth as an artist, see Rampersad, *The Life of Langston Hughes, Volume II* (286).

4. Rampersad, *The Life of Langston Hughes, Volume II* (40–42); Walton.

5. Tracy (4).

6. For discussions of the "protest" sonnet and the use of the sonnet by Harlem Renaissance writers generally, see Emanuel, "Renaissance Sonneteers."

7. See Kennedy (195–280) for an account of the politics of the early English sonnet.

8. For an example of the view of Hughes as mimic, see Stepto, "Sterling A. Brown: Outsider in the Harlem Renaissance?" (78), and "Teaching Afro-American Literature: Survey or Tradition" (14).

9. Hughes claimed in print on a number of occasions that he first heard the blues as a boy in Kansas City (*Langston Hughes and the Chicago*, 212–214)—though elsewhere he claimed that Lawrence, Kansas, was where he first encountered the blues (Hughes, *The Big Sea*, 215). See Tracy (105–107) for a brief discussion of Hughes and the Kansas City blues style.

In any event, Hughes had as a child an important emotional attachment to Kansas City, where his mother lived for a time (while Hughes stayed with his grandmother in Lawrence) as well as his uncle Desalines Langston. For an account of this period of Hughes's life, see Rampersad, *The Life of Langston Hughes, Volume I* (11–20).

10. See Pearson for an oral history of the Kansas City jazz scene and its importance to the origin of bebop.

11. For discussions of debates about the "woman question" within the CPUSA, see Foley (213–248), Rabinowitz *Labor and Desire*, and Nekola and Rabinowitz.

12. For an account of the exchange between McTell and Lomax, see Tony Russell (72–73).

13. James Weldon Johnson, Preface to the 1931 edition of *The Book of American Negro Poetry* (6).

14. Kalaidjian, *American Cultures Between the Wars* (63–65).

15. Kalaidjian, *American Cultures Between the Wars* (65). I would add that such usages were more closely related to the black-face minstrel tradition than the African-American minstrel tradition.

16. Tracy (238–245).

17. Gates, *Signifying Monkey* (xxvi).

18. Raymond Williams, *Marxism and Literature* (121–127).

19. Baraka, *Selected Plays and Prose* (157).

20. In 1930, the proportion of gainfully employed African-American women living in the Northeast and the Midwest was close to 50 percent. For more on the employment patterns of African-American women during the 1920s and 1930s, see Jacqueline Jones (152–232).

21. Examples of such blues include Rainey's "Cell Bound Blues" (1925) and Smith's "Aggravatin' Papa (1923).

22. Rampersad, *The Life of Langston Hughes, Volume II* (59–60).

23. Hughes was not unique in making this connection in his poetry. For example, Henry Binga Dismond's "To the Men of the Soviet Army," from his 1943 collection *We Who Would Die*, draws on the familiar figure of the Negro Mother to make essentially the same argument as Hughes ("A Red, my son, / Is one / Who died that you might live"). In another poem of the same collection, "The Mixed Brigade," a black speaker and his Jewish friend, both veterans of the antifascist International Brigades of the Spanish Civil War ("We crossed the sea; we fought in Spain / In that Brigade that died in vain / All bigotry and hate to end"), call upon the reader to join a "New Brigade" against the Nazis.

24. For a history of the CPUSA during the 1940s, see Isserman.

25. In fact, one can trace a "Good Morning" genealogy from "Good Morning, Revolution" to "Good Morning, Stalingrad" to the "Good morning, daddy!" which opens *Montage of*

a Dream Deferred that demonstrates in minature a number of the changes and continuities between Hughes's work in the early 1930s and that in the early 1950s.

26. See Walker, "New Poets," for an early articulation of such a model.

27. In keeping with Hughes's original sense of *Montage* as a long poem, I refer to "sections" rather than "poems," even though many of these sections were published as individual poems.

28. For a description of Hughes's encounter with Roy Cohn and the McCarthy Committee, see Rampersad, *The Life of Langston Hughes, Volume II* (209–216).

29. In this regard, it is noteworthy that a number of the older poets in Donald Allen's seminal anthology *The New American Poetry* (1960), including Allen Ginsburg, Frank O'Hara, and Stuart Perkoff (as well as Bob Kaufman, who was not in Allen's anthology), had connections to the CPUSA. See Damon for a brief mention of the relation of Kaufman to the CPUSA and Gooch (28–29, 425–427) for mention of O'Hara's "Old Left" sympathies.

Chapter 6

1. Folsom (7); Melhem (9); Kent *A Life of Gwendolyn Brooks* (45–75); Bone, "Richard Wright and the Chicago Renaissance" (463–466).

2. George Kent, for example, sketches out some of Brooks's connections to the Left through the Blands, Goss, Ward, and, indirectly, Richard Wright, but then proceeds to undercut the influence of the Left on Brooks (53–57). For that matter, Brooks herself has promoted this notion of her political naiveté. For an example of Brooks's description of herself as politically naive before her association with the Black Arts Movement in 1967, see *Report from Part I* (175).

3. For example, in a "Little Audrey" cartoon of that period (a cartoon series that contained some of the most racist characterizations of the "mammy" figure in modern American culture), a hip Mother Goose argues for the relevance of "Mother Goose Land" to "modern times" by declaring: "You're in for a surprise; we sing; we jive; we're quite alive; what you'll see will open your eyes."

4. For recent discussions of the political implications of various aspects of the bebop / zoot suit subculture, see Lott, "Double V, Double-Time," and Kelley, *Race Rebels* (161–181).

5. Even Wright in *Native Son*, which critically engages many of the same concerns of 1930s politics and literature as does *A Street in Bronzeville*, projects no doubt about the ability of the narratorial consciousness to represent the popular consciousness. In fact, Wright goes out of his way to demonstrate the "authenticity" of Bigger Thomas as a popular type in the lecture "How Bigger Was Born." (The lecture was later published as an essay in magazine form, as a pamphlet by Harper, and finally as an introduction to editions of *Native Son*, beginning in 1942.)

6. According to George Kent, Brooks added the "The Sundays of Satin-Legs Smith" to the original manuscript of *A Street in Bronzeville* as the result of a suggestion that Wright made as a reader of the manuscript for Harper & Brothers. Wright had responded enthusiastically to Brooks's poems, but felt that the collection would be strengthened if she included "one real long good one, one that strikes a personal note and carries a good burden of personal feeling" (Kent, *A Life*, 62–63). In addition to Wright's direct influence on Brooks's manuscript, Brooks was apparently much impressed by *Native Son*, which she read in a single sitting (Kent, *A Life*, 65).

7. Wright, *Later Works* (472–477) A similar moment takes place in Brooks's novel *Maude Martha* (1953) in Chapter 18 ("we're the only colored people here"), when going to a movie in a "white" theater in downtown Chicago becomes the occasion for an amalgam of liberation, shame, fear, rebellion, and deference on the part of the protagonist Maude Martha and her husband Paul.

8. An interesting question is whether Hughes's poems in part inspired Brooks's poems or vice versa. According to George Kent, Hughes apparently heard and commented favorably on the Hattie Scott poems when Brooks read them at Inez Cunningham Stark's poetry workshop at the South Side Community Center, which ran from the summer of 1941 to the spring of 1942 (Kent, *A Life*, 59–60). Hughes wrote the first two "Madam" poems at the end of 1942 and the poems began to appear in journals in 1943.

9. Melhem (36–37).

10. While the trope of literacy in African-American literature has received much scholarly attention, what might be thought of as the trope of the "educated fool" who is not literate in African-American vernacular culture has gathered considerably less comment despite the frequency with which the latter trope appears in African-American literature.

11. Henderson (51); Melhem (37).

12. Melhem (39).

13. This is not to say that the sexual abuse of African-American domestic workers by their employers was not a serious, well-documented problem much represented in African-American literature, only that sexual abuse is not formally and publicly a part of the job of the domestic in the manner that Brooks portrays public abuse by men as part of Mame's work as a blues singer. Certainly the issue of sexual abuse by male employers does not figure in Brooks's "Hattie Scott" poems.

14. The epigraph reads, "and guys I knew in the States, young officers, return from the front crying and trembling. Gay chaps at the bar in Los Angeles, Chicago, New York. . . . "

15. For discussions of the sonnet in African-American literature, see Blount, "Caged Birds: Race and Gender in the Sonnet;" and Emanuel, "Renaissance Sonneteers."

16. Of course, "political" sonnets have a long history in the English language—as Milton's sonnet on the massacre of the Waldensians in Italy attests. Nonetheless, in the twentieth century, the sonnet was unquestionably associated with the love lyric in the popular mind. This is not to say that such love lyrics are not political. Many American women writers in the first half of the twentieth century, notably Millay, and indeed Brooks, were undoubtedly drawn to the sonnet precisely because its history as a love lyric make it a congenial vehicle for the exploration of sexual politics. Cullen's use of the sonnet for homoerotic love lyrics could be considered in a similar vein.

17. There were a few other earlier examples of this sort of "deformation" of "traditional" lyric forms. One example is Ruby Baker's "The Market Woman (A Rondeau)," in which a street vendor's market cries ("Nice celery, celery! No decay! / Come buy! It's fresh and so will stay.") are rendered as a rondeau. This poem appeared in the 1931 anthology *Dundo*, published by the January Club, a black literary group active in Cleveland from 1929 to (at least) the middle 1930s. Given Hughes's close connections to Cleveland and its literary circles, it is quite possible that he had read the poem.

18. Melhem (41).

19. Stanford (197).

20. Stanford (203).

21. Walker, "New Poets" (348–352); *Walker, Richard Wright, Daemonic Genius* (77).

22. See Filreis for his discussion of the attachment of a number of poets and critics of the Communist Left to Wallace Stevens despite Stevens's professed admiration for Mussolini.

23. Wright's ambivalent portrait of white Communists generally in *Native Son*, and the absence of any African-American Communists, has been much discussed by scholars and is beyond the purview of this study. However, the name Wright chose for the white Communist dilettante and victim Mary Dalton is also significant. As Michel Fabre notes, Mary Dalton was also the name of an actual mid-level CPUSA leader (*The Unfinished Quest of Richard Wright*, 170). The historical Dalton had been one of the famous (within CPUSA circles) Atlanta Six,

Communists who were charged with "insurrection" and faced the death sentence in Georgia for their work supporting the Gastonia textile strikers in 1930. The use of Dalton's name was not, as Fabre suggests, a "subtle allusion" that only a select few would appreciate, but would be recognized by many who had been in and around the CPUSA in the early 1930s. Whatever Wright's reason for such a choice, it is noteworthy that Mike Gold wrote a very favorable review of *Native Son* in the *Daily Worker* despite the fact that he certainly recognized Dalton's name. Even the review of leading African-American Communist (and Atlanta native) Benjamin Davis, while critical of Wright's treatment of the CPUSA and the black community generally, also contained considerable praise of Wright's work. I would suggest that this response to Wright's novel was not merely because the CPUSA wanted to bask in the glory of its association with Wright, but also that such questioning, if perhaps not as organizationally pointed as Wright's, marked Left literary efforts, particularly by African-American writers, during this period.

24. The most famous example of this discussion among African-American intellectuals of Harlem is Du Bois's 1926 *Crisis* column "A Questionnaire" soliciting the opinions of readers of the *Crisis* with regard to the representation of African Americans by black and white authors and the ensuing responses. Probably the most noted example of the debate among Left artists in the 1930s as to the nature of proletarian literature is the "Authors Field Day" symposium in the July 3, 1934, issue of *New Masses*, in which various writers, mostly not "regular" *New Masses* writers, responded to the "regular" critics of the journal.

Chapter 7

1. For a study of the evolution of the literary landscape of Harlem from refuge to everyghetto, see De Jongh.

2. Johnson and Campbell (125).

3. Jacqueline Jones (260–261); Meier and Rudwick (212–213).

4. Johnson and Campbell (95).

5. Johnson and Campbell (125–127).

6. Diverse examples of this new valorization of the "authentic" southern folk include much of the work of Toni Morrison, the critical positing of Zora Neale Hurston, and Sterling Brown as the ancestral eminences of "vernacular" African-American literature (e.g., Gates, *The Signifying Monkey*, 177–180); and Albert Murray's essay "Black Pride in Mobile, Alabama" (Murray, *The Omni-Americans*, 189–202).

7. Walker, "New Poets" (348); Walker, *Richard Wright, Daemonic Genius* (77–78).

8. Walker, *Richard Wright, Daemonic Genius* (68–79).

9. Walker, *This Is My Century* (xvi).

10. For the clearest example of this uneasy transaction between the African-American intellectual and the African-American folk in Wright's work, see the second part of *Black Boy* (Wright, *Later Works*, 249–365). As noted in chapter 1, Wright's representation of his troubled relationship with the CPUSA in Chicago turns more on this transaction than on ideological problems or even practical problems with national CPUSA leadership.

11. According to Walker, the genesis of the poem was a result of her observations of the black and white prostitutes of Division Street in Chicago while she worked for the Federal Writers Project (Giovanni and Walker, 90–91).

12. For a brief description of Hayden's involvement with the literary Left during the 1930s, see Hatch (12–14). For a useful discussion of the need to contextualize Hayden's early work within the larger field of Left literary production, see Wald, *Writing from the Left* (192–198).

13. As with Countee Cullen until very recently, accounts of Hayden's early life allude generally to his difficult childhood marked by his essential abandonment by his birth parents, domineering foster parents whose behavior today would be considered abusive, severe near-sightedness, and concomitant doubts about his masculinity and his self-worth without probing this identity crisis rooted largely in a conflicted sense of appropriate gender roles and sexuality. Instead, Hayden's early life is more or less glossed over, except with respect to his formal education, passing on to Hayden's marriage to Erma Morris who, in rather stereotypical fashion, "saves" Hayden from the generally unspecified negativity and confusion of his past (in other words, his homosexuality or bisexuality).

14. Fetrow (55–56). In addition to the intertextual relationships that Fetrow notes (with Wright's "I Have Seen Black Hands," Brown's *Southern Road* (particularly "Strong Men"), Walker's "For My People," and Hughes's "Let America Be America Again"), one could add Hughes's own mass chant "Scottsboro Limited" and Davis's "Snapshots of the Cotton South" and the list would not be nearly exhausted.

15. For examples of this critical response, see Fetrow (8–13) and Hatch (95–105).

16. See Pontheolla Williams (173) for a brief description of Hayden's negative feelings about his bisexuality as revealed by him to Williams in an interview near the end of his life.

17. While I think this distinction between the relationship of Cullen and Hayden and that of Hayden and other Harlem Renaissance figures holds, one can certainly make an argument, as does Gregory Woods, that McKay's homosexuality plays a crucial role in his poetry. For example, in "The Harlem Dancer," there is a clear element of female homoeroticism present that in turn may be a displacement of a male homoeroticism in much the same way that Katrina Irving argues Willa Cather displaces her own lesbianism in ethnicity and male homosexuality.

18. For examples of such Popular Front efforts, see the essays in Herbert Aptheker's *Essays in the History of the American Negro* (1945), especially "The Negro in the American Revolution," which were released as political pamphlets between 1938 and 1941.

19. For a brief description of the pre–World War II Detroit blues scene, see Oliver, *The Story of the Blues* (80–82).

20. Gates, *The Signifying Monkey* (xxvi).

21. For a poetic analysis of Dunbar's importance to Hayden's literary development by Hayden himself, see the belated elegy "Paul Laurence Dunbar" in *American Journal* (*Collected Poems*, 156–157).

22. The continuity of Tolson's Marxist–Popular Front sympathies from the 1930s until his death in 1966 is suggested by Tolson's notes on a chance meeting with Ralph Ellison at an event held by the American Academy of Arts and Letters just before Tolson's death:

> "The ideological battle is the most bitter and devastating battle there is. Ex-Communist turns on Communist. Ellison knows that I know; but he knows that I cannot be bought. I haven't changed; he has." (Cited in Farnsworth, *Melvin B. Tolson*, 299)

23. For a brief description of Tolson's friendship with Calverton and its importance in Tolson's literary evolution, see Farnsworth, *Melvin B. Tolson* (57–61).

24. For a selection of Tolson's columns in the *Washington Tribune*, see Tolson, *Caviar and Cabbage*.

25. See Fabio for the most famous (or infamous) assault on Tolson in this regard. This debate continues to inform the discussion of Tolson's work as seen in Michael Bérubé's *Marginal Forces / Cultural Centers*, which takes the debate as a starting point for a discussion of Tolson's *Harlem Gallery* and the cultural politics of literary institutions and the canonization process.

26. This vanguardism can be seen in Tolson's critical and autobiographical writings as

well. Tolson's career as a journalist and intellectual was marked by periodic pronouncements of the need of African-American writers, and American writers generally, to be "modern," whether that "modernity" was Sandburg, Frost, Masters, and Robinson, as was the case early in Tolson's career, or Pound and Eliot, as was the case later. For examples of such comments by Tolson, see Farnsworth, *Melvin Tolson* (42) and (143–145); Bérubé, *Marginal Forces / Cultural Centers* (63–64). For by far the best discussion of Tolson's later work and his concept of the role of the avant garde, see Bérubé, *Marginal Forces / Cultural Centers* (63–206).

27. For an account of the writing and the (non)publication history of *A Gallery of Harlem Portraits*, as well as brief looks at some individual poems, see Farnsworth, *Melvin B. Tolson* (40–61).

28. Farnsworth, *Melvin B. Tolson* (43–44).

Tolson himself wrote in an elegiac tribute to Bessie Smith in a 1937 "Caviar and Cabbage" column:

> Selma, Alabama ought to give her most famous daughter [Bessie Smith] a monument. She was a true artist with a heart as big as charity itself. The blues came from the common folk, like the airs of Old Ireland, and like them they have a universal heart. They have humor and pathos and artistry. It took some highfalutin Negroes a long time to see that. (Tolson, *Caviar and Cabbage*, 239)

29. Farnsworth, "Afterword in Tolson," *A Gallery of Harlem Portraits* (266).

30. While this Popular Front rhetoric dominates the text, it is worth noting that the rapid changes in the world situation and the policies of the Comintern (which was formally dissolved in June 1943), and consequently the policies of the Communist Left in the United States, from 1939 to 1944 create some interesting tensions in Tolson's book. For example, the politics of "Dark Symphony," written in 1940 during the "Yanks Aren't Coming" reaction to the Popular Front by the Communist Left (after the signing of the German-Soviet Non-Aggression Pact and before the Nazi invasion of the Soviet Union in 1940), has much in common with earlier Third Period "proletarian" stances—particularly in its general call for working-class unity and its specific delineation of a revolutionary African-American tradition in the first stanza of Part IV. At the same time, the title poem of the collection was written in the neo-Popular Front period that followed the invasion of the Soviet Union and the bombing of Pearl Harbor and employs a far less "Leftist" rhetoric than "Dark Symphony." Of course, as has been seen in many of the works considered in this study, such tensions marked many works of the 1930s and 1940s. Nonetheless, the sense of ideological disjuncture (within an overall Left context) is great in *Rendezvous With America*.

31. Mariann Russell (50).

32. Flasch (54).

33. Hurston, *The Sanctified Church* (51).

34. Farnsworth, *Melvin B. Tolson* (138).

35. Walker, *Richard Wright* (78).

36. Jackson and Rubin (69–70).

37. A very partial list of these activities include the publication in journals associated with the Communist Left, such as *New Masses*, *New Challenge*, and *Cavalcade*, his production of Hughes's "Don't You Want to Be Free" and other "socially conscious" plays at the Spelman College Atlanta Summer Theater in 1939; his script for the Negro Freedom Rally at Madison Square Garden in 1944; and his role as a contributing editor of *Harlem Quarterly*. For an account that clearly places Dodson within the cultural orbit of the literary Left, see the elegiac memoir "Remembering Owen Dodson" by Aaron Kramer, himself a long-time mainstay of Communist cultural circles.

38. Walker, "New Poets" (348); Walker, *Richard Wright* (78).

39. Appropriately enough, this poem appeared in its entirety as a part of the script Dodson wrote and directed for the Negro Freedom Rally, promoting a united war effort and the fight against racism (Hatch, 114). As noted in chapter 1, such adaptations of these tropes also characterized literary production by black and white Left writers in the 1930s, even finding their way into "nonliterary" political discourse as in the promotion of the tour of Ada Wright in support of the Scottsboro defendants.

40. Hatch (178–183).

41. Hatch (135).

42. This deflating satire on an overwrought "high" homosexual emotionality is seen further in the next poem of the collection "Circle Two":

Everywhere I go the same,
The same ole land to dig an sow,
Love winkin dressed in scarlet red,
Dancin in an out the do.

(76)

43. Hatch (141–143).

In fact, Dodson did not publish any new poem in a periodical after 1950 until the 1970s, as far as I can determine. Even during the 1960s, the only new poetry that Dodson published is the frequently anthologized "Yardbird's Skull" (which apparently first appeared in Arna Bontemps's 1963 anthology *American Negro Poetry*) and a group of poems in Rosey Pool's 1962 anthology, *Beyond the Blues*.

44. This effacement of public Left ties in the 1940s was a common practice of Left organizations and institutions themselves, generally in the cause of "unity" toward some larger object. An example of this phenomenon with respect to the literary Left is the journal *Negro Story*, which, as Bill Mullen has shown, claimed to be nonpolitical, while it was clearly tied editorially and organizationally to the Left (7).

Conclusion

1. For a few examples of this assessment, see Jackson and Rubin (85); Johnson and Johnson (125); and Bone, *The Negro Novel in America* (160–163).

2. Lipsitz (345–341).

3. For a view of this cold war repression in Birmingham, a relative stronghold of the Left and the CIO in the South during the 1930s and 1940s, see Kelley, *Hammer and Hoe* (226–227). See also Honey, *Southern Labor and Black Civil Rights* (245–277).

4. Kelley, *Hammer and Hoe* (227); Korstad and Lichtenstein (801–806); Honey, *Southern Labor and Black Civil Rights* (263–270).

5. This extreme anxiety about the cold war and the contradictions of the postwar era can be seen in Margaret Walker's 1950 *Phylon* article "New Poets." The essay, in large part an example of an "optimistic" assessment of 1940s African-American poetry and its relation to U.S. society, nonetheless begins its conclusion:

What is the future of the Negro writing poetry in America? It would seem from these remarks that the outlook is bright and hopeful. It is a fact that some of the most significant poetry written in American during the last two decades has been written by Negroes. Now, what is the promise? Is there hope that it will be fulfilled? Is the Negro as a poet doomed to annihilation because he is part of a doomed

Western world, or is that Western culture really doomed? Is our society already a
fascist society? If it is, what hope has our literature? (354)

6. For an example of how broadly the federal government construed "disloyalty" in this
era, see Dudziak, who examines largely successful attempts by the U.S. government to dam-
age the career of Josephine Baker.

7. Frank Marshall Davis, *Livin' the Blues* (325–327); Gabbin (51).

8. As Alan Wald pointed out to me, the situation was a bit different among African-
American novelists and theater workers, many more of whom were actively involved with the
Left than was true of black poets. Lorraine Hansberry in particular is an example of someone
whose greatest success took place during the McCarthy era, even though she did not hide her
links to the Communist Left. Wald's answer to why there seems to be a greater impact on the
poets is that there may have been what he calls the "exhaustion of a generation," insofar as the
Left African-American poets of the preceding period tended to have joined the political Left
earlier than the younger black theater activists who were part of a newer Left activity in popular culture. This seems plausible, though I would also point out that for various reasons the
repression of the Communist Left and its sympathizers was more idiosyncratic (and much less
thorough) in the theater than in many other areas of "high" and popular culture, and so possibly theater workers felt they could take more chances.

9. For an account of Hughes's earliest move away from his "revolutionary" work of the
1930s, see Rampersad, *The Life of Langston Hughes, Volume II* (4–5).

10. *Mainstream*, more or less the official cultural journal of the CPUSA in the early 1960s,
published the first significant collection of the proto–Black Arts Umbra Poets (outside of the
Umbra Poets' own journal) in its July 1963 issue. *Freedomways* was quite open in its affiliation
with the Old Left circles of Harlem and the South Side—even the name intentionally recalled
Paul Robeson's newspaper, *Freedom*. One can also find less obvious Old Left–New Black connections in such important proto–Black arts journals as the *Liberator* in New York, *Dasein* in
Washington, D.C., and, I suspect, *Free Lance* in Cleveland. Another significant example of this
Old Left–New Black enterprise is the 1969 anthology *For Malcolm*, a collection of tributary po-
ems and eulogies to Malcolm X edited by Dudley Randall and a long-time veteran of the 1930s
and 1940s African-American Chicago Left (and an old friend of Gwendolyn Brooks), Margaret
Gosse Burroughs. This anthology was crucial in the founding of Broadside Press as an important publisher of African-American poetry. (For that matter, one could consider Broadside
Press itself as an example, though we will have to await Melba Joyce Boyd's biography of
Randall to get a clearer sense of Randall's connections to the Old Left.) One of the most dramatic moments of a product of the Old Left acting in the black power era is Ossie Davis's eulogy for Malcolm X. (Davis's eulogy, a conversion narrative in which black manhood is reclaimed from "Negro" emasculation with its power largely deriving from Davis's willingness
to put himself in the narrative as a sort of deracinated sissy, is not unlike an earlier essay of
Davis's "Purlie Told Me" [1964] in *Freedomways*, where Davis himself undergoes a similar conversion while writing the play *Purlie Victorious* [1961]). One can also read Gwendolyn Brooks's
story of her "conversion" to the Black Arts Movement at the 1967 Black Writers Conference at
Fisk University as a similar, if differently gendered, example. (Although, as we have seen,
Brooks's relationship to the Old Left is more difficult to tease out than Davis's and her "conversion" in some senses occasioned a rejection of Popular Front poetics.)

One could find numerous other connections. The significant 1969 anthology *The New
Black Poetry*, edited by Clarence Major, was published by International Publishers, a Communist Party imprint. Various poets and cultural entrepreneurs who still had ties to the
Communist Left, such as Walter Lowenfels and Art Berger, were also important figures in
bringing many of the New Black Poets to a national audience.

In short, the direct influence of the Old Left and its remaining political and cultural in-stitutions on the New Black literature in the 1960s, and indeed on what came to be known as the New American Poetry, is a worthwhile, but largely untold story. No scholar has yet traced the continuities between the old literary Left and the new literary radicals of the 1950s and 1960s in the way revisionist scholars, such as Maurice Isserman, have done between the Old Left of the 1930s and 1940s and the New Left of the 1960s. For an article that contains glimmers of how productive such an approach might be, see Michel Orens's brief history of the Umbra Poets in which members or sympathizers of the "Old Left," particularly the CPUSA, clearly play an important role in the development of the group and the political context in which the group is formed.

11. For example, the Cuban revolution had a certain catalyzing effect on the nascent Black Arts Movement in New York City during the early 1960s. See Orens (179); Baraka, *The Auto-biography of Leroi Jones* (168–169).

12. Brooks articulates such a politics of oblique protest in the "Womanhood" section of *Annie Allen* (1949). Poem XIV begins:

People protest in sprawling lightless ways
Against their deceivers, they are never meek—
Conceive their furies, and abort them early;
Are hurt, and shout, weep without form, are surly;
Or laugh, but save their censures and their damns.

(*Blacks*, 138)

13. An example of the survival of this notion of national expression that is on the pe-riphery and at the center of American culture is Karl Shapiro's Introduction to Tolson's *Harlem Gallery*, in which he makes his famous, or infamous, statement, *"Tolson writes in Negro"* (em-phasis Shapiro's).

Works Consulted

Archival Sources

Gwendolyn Bennett Papers, Schomburg Center for the Research of Black Culture
Sterling Brown Papers, Moorland-Springarn Research Center, Howard University
Crusader News Agency Papers, Schomburg Center for the Research of Black Culture
Owen Dodson Papers, Moorland-Springarn Research Center, Howard University
Fantasy Magazine Papers, Beineke Library, Yale University
Langston Hughes Papers, Beineke Library, Yale University
Victor Jeremy Jerome Papers, Sterling Memorial Library, Yale University
James Weldon Johnson Collection, Beineke Library, Yale University
Joseph North Papers, Mugar Memorial Library, Boston University
Jean Toomer Papers, Beineke Library, Yale University
Dorothy West Papers, Schlesinger Library, Radcliffe College
Richard Wright Papers, Beineke Library, Yale University

Books, Articles, Broadsides, Pamphlets, and Dissertations

Aaron, Daniel. *Writers on the Left*. New York: Harcourt, Brace, 1961.
Aaron, Daniel, and Robert Bendiner, eds. *The Strenuous Decade: A Social and Intellectual Record of the 1930's*. New York: Anchor, 1970.
Allen, Donald M., ed. *The New American Poetry*. New York: Grove Press, 1960.
Allen, Ernest, Jr. "The New Negro: Explorations in Identity and Social Consciousness, 1910–1922." In *1915, the Cultural Moment*, edited by Adele Heller and Lois Rudnick, (48–68). New Brunswick: Rutgers University Press, 1991.

Allen, James S. *The Negro Question in the United States*. New York: International, 1936.

Allen, James S., and James W. Ford. *The Negroes in a Soviet America*. New York: Workers Library Publishers, 1935.

Anderson, George, and Eda L. Walton, eds. *This Generation*. New York: Scott, Foresman, 1939.

Anderson, Jervis. *This Was Harlem: A Cultural Portrait, 1900–1950*. New York: Farrar, Straus, 1982.

Anderson, Perry. "Communist Party History." In *People's History and Socialist Theory*, edited by Raphael Samuel, (145–156). London: Routledge and Kegan Paul, 1981.

Aptheker, Herbert. *American Negro Slave Revolts*. New York: Columbia University Press, 1943.

———. *Essays in the History of the American Negro*. New York: International, 1945.

Athens, Ida Gerding. *Brethren*. Cincinnati: Talaria, 1940.

Baker, Houston A., Jr. *Afro-Poetics*. Madison: University of Wisconsin Press, 1988.

———. *The Harlem Renaissance and Modernism*. Chicago: University of Chicago Press, 1987.

Bakhtin, Mikhail. *Problems of Dostoevsky's Poetics*. Edited and translated by Caryl Emerson. Minneapolis: University of Minnesota Press, 1984.

Baraka, Amiri. *The Autobiography of LeRoi Jones*. New York: Freundlich Books, 1984.

———. *Selected Plays and Prose of Amiri Baraka / Leroi Jones*. New York: Morrow, 1979.

Barksdale, Richard. *Langston Hughes*. Chicago: American Library Association, 1977.

Barnard, Rita. *The Great Depression and the Culture of Abundance: Kenneth Fearing, Nathanael West, and Mass Culture in the 1930s*. New York: Cambridge University Press, 1995.

Baskerville, Stephen W., and Ralph Willett, eds. *Nothing Else to Fear: New Perspectives on America in the Thirties*. Manchester: Manchester University Press, 1985.

Bell, Bernard W. *The Folk Roots of Contemporary Afro-American Poetry*. Detroit: Broadside, 1974.

Benston, Kimberly W. "Sterling Brown's After-Song: 'When De Saints Go Ma'ching Home' and the Performances of Afro-American Voice." *Callaloo* 5,1–2 (February-May 1982): 33–42.

Berger, Art. "Negroes with Pens." *Mainstream* 16,7 (July 1963): 3–6.

Berry, A. W., Williana Burroughs, Benjamin Carreathers, et al. *The Road to Liberation for the Negro People*. New York: Workers Library Publishers, 1937.

Berry, Faith. *Langston Hughes: Before and Beyond Harlem*. Westport: Lawrence Hill, 1983.

Bérubé, Michael. *Marginal Forces / Cultural Centers: Tolson, Pynchon and the Politics of the Canon*. Ithaca: Cornell University Press, 1992.

Bessie, Alvah, ed. *The Heart of Spain*. New York: Veterans of the Abraham Lincoln Brigade, 1952.

Dismond, Henry Binga. *We Who Would Die*. New York: W. Malliet, 1943.

Bloom, Harold, ed. *Langston Hughes*. New York: Chelsea House, 1988.

Blount, Marcellus. "Caged Birds: Race and Gender in the Sonnet." In *Engendering Men: The Question of Male Feminist Criticism*, edited by Joseph A. Boone and Michael Cadden, (225–238). New York: Routledge, 1990.

———. "The Preacherly Text: African American Poetry and Vernacular Performance." *PMLA* 107,3 (May 1992): 582–593.

Boelhower, William, ed. *The Future of American Modernism: Ethnic Writing Between the Wars*. Amsterdam: VU University Press, 1990.

Bogardus, Ralph F., and Fred Hobson. *Literature at the Barricades: The American Writer in the 1930's*. University, Ala.: University of Alabama Press, 1982.

Bone, Robert. *The Negro Novel in America*. New Haven: Yale University Press, 1965.

———. "Richard Wright and the Chicago Renaissance." *Callaloo* 9,3 (Summer 1986): 446–468.

Bontemps, Arna. *Black Thunder*. New York: Macmillan, 1936.

———. *Personals*. London: Paul Breman, 1963.

Bontemps, Arna, ed. *Golden Slippers: An Anthology of Negro Poetry for Young People*. New York: Harpers, 1941.

————, *The Harlem Renaissance Remembered: Essays.* New York: Dodd, 1972.

Botkin, Benjamin A., ed. *Folk-Say, A Regional Miscellany: 1930.* Norman: University of Oklahoma Press, 1930.

————. *Folk-Say, A Regional Miscellany, 1931.* Norman: University of Oklahoma Press, 1931.

————. *Folk-Say IV, A Regional Miscellany.* Norman: University of Oklahoma Press, 1932.

Bradford, Roark. *John Henry.* New York: Harper, 1931.

Breman, Paul. "Poetry into the Sixties." In *The Black American Writer*, edited by C. W. E. Bigsby, (99–109). Deland, Fla.: Everett / Edwards, 1969.

Breman, Paul, ed. *You Better Believe It: Black Verse in English from Africa, the West Indies and the United States.* Baltimore: Penguin Books, 1973.

Brewer, John Mason, ed. *Heralding Dawn: An Anthology of Verse.* Dallas: June Thomason, 1936.

Brooks, Gwendolyn. *Annie Allen.* New York: Harper, 1949.

————. *Blacks.* Chicago: The David Company, 1987.

————. *Maud Martha.* New York: Harper, 1953.

————. *Report from Part I.* Detroit: Broadside Press, 1972.

————. *A Street in Bronzeville.* New York: Harper, 1945.

Browder, Earl. *The People's Front.* New York: International, 1938.

————. *What Is Communism?* New York: Vanguard, 1936.

Brown, Michael E., Randy Martin, Frank Rosengarten, and George Snedeker, eds. *New Studies in the Politics and Culture of U.S. Communism.* New York: Monthly Review, 1993.

————. Brown, Sterling A. *A Son's Return: Selected Essays of Sterling A. Brown.* Boston: Northeastern University Press, 1996.

————. "The Blues." *Phylon* 13 (Fall 1952): 286–292.

————. "The Blues as Folk Poetry." In *Folk-Say, A Regional Miscellany: 1930*, edited by Benjamin A. Botkin, (324–339). Norman: Univeristy of Oklahoma Press, 1931.

————. *The Collected Poems of Sterling A. Brown.* New York: Harper, 1980.

————. "Negro Folk Expression." *Phylon* 11 (Fall 1950): 318–327.

————. "Negro Folk Expression: Spirituals, Seculars, Ballads and Works Songs." *Phylon* 14 (Winter 1953): 45–61.

————. "The Negro in Literature, 1925–1955." In *The New Negro Thirty Years Afterward*, edited by Rayford Logan et al. (57–72). Washington, D.C.: Howard University Press, 1956.

————. *Negro Poetry and Drama.* 1937. New York: Arno, 1969.

————. *Southern Road.* New York: Harcourt, Brace, 1932.

Brown, Sterling A., Arthur P. Davis, and Ulysses Lee, eds. *The Negro Caravan.* New York: Dryden Press, 1941.

Bryan, T. J. "The Published Poems of Helene Johnson." *Langston Hughes Review* 6,2 (Fall 1987): 11–21.

Bryson, Clarence F., and James H. Robinson, eds. *Dundo: An Anthology by Cleveland Negro Youth.* Cleveland: January Club, 1931.

Buhle, Paul. *C.L.R. James: The Artist as Revolutionary.* New York: Verso, 1988.

————. *Marxism in the USA: Remapping the History of the American Left.* London: Verso, 1987.

Butcher, Margaret. *The Negro in American Culture.* New York: Knopf, 1956.

Cain, William. "From Liberalism to Communism: The Political Thought of W. E. B. Du Bois." In *Cultures of United States Imperialism*, edited by Amy Kaplan and Donald Pease, (456–473). Durham: Duke University Pres, 1993.

Caldwell, Erskine. "Parties Unknown in Georgia." In *New Masses: An Anthology of the Rebel Thirties*, edited by Joseph North, (New York: International, 1969. (153–157).

Calmer, Alan, ed. *Get Organized.* New York: International, 1939.

Calverton, Victor F. *Anthology of American Negro Literature.* New York: Modern Library, 1929.

Campbell, Susan. "'Black Bolsheviks' and Recognition of African-America's Right to Self-Determination by the Communist Party USA." *Science and Society* 58,4 (Winter 1994): 440–470.

Cannon, David W., Jr. *Black Labor Chant and Other Poems.* National Council on Religion in Higher Education, 1939.

Capeci, Dominic J., Jr., and Martha Wilkerson. *Layered Violence: The Detroit Rioters of 1943.* Jackson: University Press of Mississippi, 1991.

Cappetti, Carla. *Modernism, Ethnography, and the Novel.* New York: Columbia University Press, 1993.

Carby, Hazel. *Genealogies of Race, Nation, and Manhood.* W. E. B. Du Bois Lectures. Harvard University, 1993.

Carter, Dan T. *Scottsboro: An American Tragedy of the South.* Baton Rouge: Louisiana State Univeristy Press, 1969.

Caute, David. *The Great Fear: The Anti-Communist Fear Under Truman and Eisenhower.* New York: Simon and Schuster, 1978.

Chauncey, George. *Gay New York: Gender, Urban Culture and the Making of the Gay Male World, 1890–1940.* New York: Basic, 1994.

Childs, John Brown. "Concepts of Culture in Afro-American Political Thought, 1890–1920." *Social Text* 4 (Fall 1981): 28–43.

Christgau, Robert. "Rah, Rah, Sis-Boom-Bah: The Secret Relationship between College Rock and the Communist Party." In *Microphone Fiends: Youth Music and Youth Culture,* edited by Andrew Rose and Tricia Rose, (221–226). New York: Routledge, 1994.

Clark, Suzanne. *Sentimental Modernism: Women Writers and the Revolution of the Word.* Bloomington: Indiana University Press, 1991.

Clay, Eugene. "The Negro in Recent American Literature." In *American Writers' Congress,* edited by Henry Hart, (145–153). New York: International, 1935.

———. "Sterling Brown: American Peoples' Poet." *International Literature* 2 (June 1934): 117–122.

Cobb, Martha. *Harlem, Haiti and Havana: A Comparative Study of Langston Hughes, Jacques Roumain and Nicolás Guillén.* Washington, D.C.: Three Continents Press, 1979.

Cohen, Lizabeth. *Making A New Deal: Industrial Workers in Chicago, 1919–1939.* Cambridge: Cambridge University Press, 1990.

Coiner, Constance. *Better Red: The Writing and Resistance of Tillie Olsen and Meridel Le Sueur.* New York: Oxford Univeristy Press, 1995.

Communist Party, U.S.A. *The Communist Position on the Negro Question.* New York: New Century, 1947.

———. "Slogans for Scottsboro." *Daily Worker* (January 20, 1932): 1.

Connelly, Marc. *The Green Pastures.* New York: Farrar and Rinehart, 1930.

Conroy, Jack. "On Anvil." In *The Little Magazine in America: A Modern Documentary History,* edited by Elliott Anderson and Mary Kinzie, (111–129). Yonkers: Pushcart, 1978.

Conroy, Jack, and Curt Johnson, eds. *Writers in Revolt: The Anvil Anthology 1933–1940.* New York: Lawrence Hill, 1973.

Conroy, Jack, and Ralph Cheney, eds. *Unrest: The Rebel Poets Anthology for 1929.* London: Arthur H. Stockwell, 1929.

———. *Unrest: The Rebel Poets Anthology for 1930.* London: Braithewaite and Miller, 1930.

———. *Unrest: The Rebel Poets Anthology for 1931.* New York: H. Harrison, 1931.

Cook, Mercer, and Stephen Henderson. *The Militant Black Writer in Africa and the United States.* Madison: University of Wisconsin Press, 1969.

Cooney, Terry A. *Balancing Acts: American Thought and Culture in the 1930s.* New York: Twayne, 1995.

———. "Cosmopolitan Values and the Identification of Reaction: *Partisan Review* in the 1930's." *Journal of American History* 68,3 (December 1981): 580–597.

———. *The Rise of the New York Intellectuals: Partisan Review and Its Circle, 1934–1945.* Madison: University of Wisconsin Press, 1986.

Cooper, Wayne F. *Claude McKay: Rebel Sojourner in the Harlem Renaissance.* Baton Rouge: Louisiana State University Press, 1987.

Cowdery, Mae V. *We Lift Our Voices and Other Poems.* Philadelphia: Alpress Publishers, 1936.

Cowley, Malcolm. *The Dream of the Golden Mountains: Remembering the 1930s.* New York: Viking, 1980.

———. *Exile's Return.* 1934. New York: Viking, 1951.

Cromwell, Otelia, Lorenzo D. Turner, and Eva B. Dykes, eds. *Readings from Negro Authors for Schools and Colleges.* New York, 1931.

Cruse, Harold. *The Crisis of the Negro Intellectual.* 1967. New York: Quill, 1984.

Cullen, Countee. *Ballad of a Brown Girl.* New York: Harper, 1927.

———. *The Black Christ and Other Poems.* New York: Harper, 1929.

———. *Color.* New York: Harper, 1925.

———. *Copper Sun.* New York: Harper, 1927.

———. *The Medea and Some Poems.* New York: Harper, 1935.

———. *My Soul's High Song: The Collected Writings of Countee Cullen.* Edited by Gerald Early. New York: Anchor, 1991.

———. *On These I Stand: Selected and New Poems.* New York: Harper, 1947.

Cullen, Countee, ed. *Caroling Dusk.* New York: Harper, 1927.

Cunard, Nancy, ed. *Negro.* London: Wishart, 1934.

Cuney, Waring. "Hard Time Blues." In *The Negro Caravan*, edited by Sterling Brown, Arthur P. Davis and Ulysses Lee (375-377). New York: Dryden Press, 1941.

———. *Puzzles.* Utrecht: De Roos, 1960.

———. *Storefront Church.* London: P. Breman, 1973.

Cuney, Waring, Langston Hughes, and Bruce M. Wright, eds. *Lincoln University Poets: Centennial Anthology.* New York: Fine Editions Press, 1954.

Cuthbert, Marion. *April Grasses.* New York: The Woman's Press, 1936.

Davidman, Joy. *Letters to a Comrade.* New Haven: Yale University Press, 1938.

Davidman, Joy, ed. *War Poems of the United Nations.* New York: Dial Press, 1943.

Davis, Benjamin J. *The Path of Negro Liberation.* New York: New Century Publishers, 1947.

Davis, Arthur P. *From the Dark Tower: Afro-American Writers, 1900–1960.* Washington, D.C.: Howard University Press, 1974.

Davis, Frank Marshall. *Black Man's Verse.* Chicago: Black Cat, 1935.

———. *47th Street Poems.* Prairie City, Ill.: Decker, 1948.

———. *I Am the American Negro.* Chicago: Black Cat, 1937.

———. *Livin' the Blues: Memoirs of a Black Journalist and Poet.* Madison: University of Wisconsin Press, 1992.

———. "Snapshots of the Cotton South." *New Challenge* 2,2 (Fall 1937): 40–46.

———. *Through Sepia Eyes.* Chicago: Black Cat Press, 1938.

De Jongh, James. *Vicious Modernism: Black Harlem and the Literary Imagination.* Cambridge: Cambridge University Press, 1990.

DeKoven, Marianne. "The Politics of Modernist Form." *New Literary History* 23 (1992): 675–690.

Denisoff, R. Serge. *Great Day Coming: Folk Music and the American Left.* Baltimore: Penguin, 1973.

———. *Sing a Song of Social Significance.* Bowling Green, Ohio: Bowling Green State University Popular Press, 1983.

Denning, Michael. *The Cultural Front: The Laboring of American Culture in the Twentieth Century.* New York: Verso, 1996

———."The End of Mass Culture." *International Labor and Working-Class History* 37 (Spring 1990): 5–18.

Deutsch, Babette. Review of *Montage of a Dream Deferred*. 1951. In *Langston Hughes: Critical Perspectives Past and Present*, (32). New York: Amistad, 1993.

Dickstein, Morris. *The Gates of Eden: American Culture in the Sixties*. New York: Basic Books, 1977.

Diedrich, Maria. *Kommunismus im Afroamerikanischen Roman*. Stuttgart: Metzler, 1979.

Dixon, Robert M. W., and John Godrich. *Blues and Gospel Records, 1902–1943*. Chigwell, Essex: Storyville Publications, 1982.

Dodson, Owen. "Divine Comedy." In *Black Theater USA*, edited by James V. Hatch and Ted Shine, (322–349). New York: Free Press, 1974.

———. "Negro History: A Sonnet Sequence." *New Masses* 19,3 (April 14, 1936): 21.

———. *Powerful Long Ladder*. New York: Farrar, Straus, 1947.

Douglas, Ann. *Terrible Honesty: Mongrel Manhattan in the 1920s*. New York: Farrar, Straus and Giroux, 1995.

Draper, Theodore. *American Communism and Soviet Russia*. New York: Viking, 1960.

———. *The Roots of American Communism*. New York: Viking, 1957.

Du Bois, W. E. B. *The Souls of Black Folk*. 1903. New York: Signet, 1969.

Dudziak, Mary L. "Josephine Baker, Racial Protest, and the Cold War." *Journal of American History* 81,2 (September 1994): 543–570.

Dunbar, Paul Laurence. *The Collected Poetry of Paul Laurence Dunbar*. Edited by Joanne Braxton. Charlottesville: University of Virginia Press, 1993.

———. *Sport of the Gods*. 1902. New York: Dodd, Mead, 1981.

Eastman, Max. *Artists in Uniform: A Study of Literature and Bureaucratism*. New York: Knopf, 1934.

Edwards, Brent. "Wandering Forms: The Culture and Politics of Black Modernism in France, 1921–1935." Colloquim paper, W. E. B. Du Bois Institute, Harvard University (March 5, 1997).

Eleaszer, Robert B. *Singers in the Dawn: A Brief Anthology of American Negro Poetry*. Atlanta: Conference on Education and Race Relations, 1934.

Eliot, T. S. *Selected Essays*. New York: Harcourt, Brace, 1950.

Ellison, Ralph. *Going to the Territory*. New York: Random House, 1986.

———. *Invisible Man*. New York: Random House: 1952.

———. *Shadow and Act*. New York: Random House, 1964.

Emanuel, James A. *Langston Hughes*. Boston: Twayne, 1967.

———. "Renaissance Sonneteers." *Black World* 24,11 (September 1975): 32–45.

Engdahl, Louis. "A Negro Mother Fights." *Daily Worker* (June 4, 1932): 4.

Evans, Walker. *Walker Evans at Work*. New York: Harper and Row, 1982.

Fabio, Sarah Webster. "Who Speaks Negro." *Negro Digest* 16,2 (December 1966): 54–58.

Fabre, Michel. "The Poetry of Richard Wright." In *Critical Essays on Richard Wright*, edited by Yoshinobu Hakutani, (252–272). Boston: G.K. Hall, 1982.

———. *The Unfinished Quest of Richard Wright*. New York: Morrow, 1973.

———. *The World of Richard Wright*. Jackson: University of Mississippi Press, 1985.

Fairclough, Adam. *Race and Democracy: The Civil Rights Struggle in Louisiana, 1915–1972*. Athens: University of Georgia Press, 1995.

Farnsworth, Robert M. *Melvin B. Tolson, 1898–1966: Plain Talk and Poetic Prophecy*. Columbia: University of Missouri Press. 1984.

Fearing, Kenneth. *New and Selected Poems*. Bloomington: Indiana University Press, 1956.

———. "Limiting Devices" (Review of *Fine Clothes to the Jew*). *New Masses* 3 (September 1927): 29.

Federal Writers Project. *American Stuff: An Anthology of Prose and Verse by Members of the Federal Writers Project.* New York: Viking, 1937.

———. *New York City Guide: A Comprehensive Guide to the Five Boroughs of New York.* New York: Random House, 1939.

Ferruggia, Gabriella. "Organizing the 'Ivory Tower': The Communist Party and the United Front of Intellectuals During the Late Thirties." *Storia Nordamericana* 6,1–2 (1989): 141–159.

Fetrow, Fred M. *Robert Hayden.* Boston: Twayne, 1984.

Fields, Maurice C. *The Collected Poems of Maurice C. Fields.* New York: Exposition Press, 1940.

Filatova, Lydia. "Langston Hughes: American Writer." *International Literature* 1 (January 1933): 99–107.

Filreis, Alan. *Modernism from Right to Left: Wallace Stevens, the Thirties, and Literary Radicalism.* Cambridge: Cambridge University Press, 1994.

Fishbein, Leslie. *Rebels in Bohemia: The Radicals of The Masses 1911–1917.* Chapel Hill: University of North Carolina Press, 1982.

Fisher, Dexter, and Robert B. Stepto, eds. *Afro-American Literature: The Reconstruction of Instruction.* New York: Modern Language Association, 1979.

Flasch, Joy. *Melvin B. Tolson.* New York: Twayne, 1972.

Fleischauer, Carl, and Beverly W. Brannan. *Documenting America, 1935–1943.* Berkeley: University of California Press, 1988.

Foley, Barbara. *Radical Representations: Politics and Form in U.S. Proletarian Fiction, 1929–1941.* Durham: Duke University Press, 1993.

Folsom, Franklin. *Days of Anger, Days of Hope: A Memoir of the League of American Writers, 1937–1942.* Niwot: University Press of Colorado, 1994.

Foner, Philip S. *American Socialism and Black Americans: From the Age of Jackson to World War II.* Westport: Greenwood Press, 1977.

Foner, Philip S., and James A. Allen, eds. *American Communism and Black Americans: A Documentary History: 1919–1929.* Philadelphia: Temple University Press, 1987.

Foner, Philip S., and Herbert Shapiro, eds. *American Communism and Black Americans: A Documentary History, 1930–1934.* Philadelphia: Temple University Press, 1991.

Ford, James W. *The Negro and the Democratic Front.* New York: International, 1938.

Ford, James W., and William Patterson. "On the Question of the Work of the American Communist Party Among Negroes." In *American Communism and Black Americans: A Documentary History: 1919–1929,* edited by Philip S. Foner and Herbert Shapiro, (166–172). Philadelphia: Temple University Press, 1987.

Ford, Nick Aaron. *Songs from the Dark.* Boston: Meador, 1940.

Foster, William Z. *History of the Communist Party of the United States.* New York: International, 1952.

———. "On Self-Determination for the Negro People." *Political Affairs* 35 (October 1956): 549–554.

———. *Toward Soviet America.* New York: Coward-McCann, 1932.

Fraden, Rena. *Blueprints for a Black Federal Theatre, 1935–1939.* Cambridge: Cambridge University Press, 1994.

Funaroff, Sol. *The Spider and the Clock.* New York: International, 1938.

Gabbin, Joanne V. *Sterling A. Brown: Building the Black Aesthetic Tradition.* Westport, Conn.: Greenwood, 1985.

Gardner, Benjamin Franklin. *Black.* Caldwell, Idaho: Caxton, 1933.

Gates, Henry Louis, Jr. *Figures in Black.* New York: Oxford University Press, 1987.

———. *Loose Canons: Notes on the Culture Wars.* New York: Oxford University Press, 1992.

————. *The Signifying Monkey: A Theory of Afro-American Literary Criticism*. New York: Oxford, 1988.

————. "The Trope of a New Negro and the Reconstruction of the Image of the Black." *Representations* 24 (Fall 1988): 129–155.

Gates, Henry Louis, Jr., and K. A. Appiah, eds. *Langston Hughes*. New York: Amistad, 1993.

Gayle, Addison, Jr., ed. *The Black Aestetic*. New York: Doubleday, 1971.

Gellert, Lawrence. *Me and My Captain: Chain Gang Negro Songs of Protest*. New York: Hours Press, 1935.

————. *Negro Songs of Protest*. New York: American Music League, 1936.

Gettleman, Marvin E. "The New York Workers School, 1923–1944: Communist Education in American Society." In *New Studies in the Politics and Culture of U.S. Communism*, edited by Michael E. Brown, Randy Martin, Frank Rosengarten, and George Snedeker, (261–280). New York: Monthly Review Press, 1993.

Gilbert, James B. *Writers and Partisans: A History of Literary Radicalism in America*. New York: Wiley, 1968.

Gilbert, Sandra M., and Susan Gubar. *No Man's Land: The Place of the Woman Writer in the Twentieth Century, Volume 1: War of the Words*. New Haven: Yale University Press, 1988.

Giovanni, Nikki, and Margaret Walker. *A Poetic Equation: Conversations Between Nikki Giovanni and Margaret Walker*. Washington, D.C.: Howard University Press, 1974.

Glazer, Nathan. *The Social Basis of American Communism*. Cambridge: Harvard University Press, 1961.

Gold, Mike. "Proletarian Realism." *New Masses* 6 (September 1930): 5.

————. "Where the Battle Is Fought." *The Nation* 123 (July 14, 1926): 37.

————. "Wilder: Prophet of the Genteel Christ." *The New Republic* 64 (October 22, 1930): 263–264.

Gold, Mike, Fred Ellis, William Gropper, Joshua Kunitz, A. B. Magill, and Harry Alan Potamkin. "The Charkov Conference of Revolutionary Writers." *New Masses* 6 (February 1931): 6–8.

Gomez, Manuel, ed. *Poems for Workers*. Chicago: Daily Worker Publishing, 1927.

Gooch, Brad. *City Poet: The Life and Times of Frank O'Hara*. New York: Knopf, 1993.

Gordon, Eugene. "Social and Political Problems of the Negro Writer." In *American Writers' Congress*, edited by Henry Hart, (141–145). New York: International, 1935.

Gorky, Maxim. *Articles and Pamphlets*. Moscow: Foreign Languages Publishing House, 1951.

Gorman, Paul R. *Left Intellectuals and Popular Culture in Twentieth-Century America*. Chapel Hill: University of North Carolina Press, 1996.

Gosse, Van. "'To Organize in Every Neighborhood, In Every Home:' The Gender Politics of American Communists Between the Wars." *Radical History Review* 50 (1991) 108–141.

Govan, Sandra Y. "Gwendolyn Bennett: Dramatic Tension in Her Life and Art." *Langston Hughes Review* 6,2 (Fall 1987): 29–35.

Graham, Marcus, ed. *An Anthology of Revolutionary Poetry*. New York: Active Press, 1929.

Graham, Maryemma. "The Practice of a Social Art." In *Langston Hughes*, edited by Henry Louis Gates Jr. and K. A. Appiah, (213–235). New York: Amistad, 1993.

Graziano, John. "Black Musical Theater and the Harlem Renaissance Movement." In *Black Music in the Harlem Renaissance*, edited by Samuel A. Floyd Jr., (87–110). Knoxville: University of Tennessee Press, 1990.

Greenberg, Cheryl. *Or Does It Explode: Black Harlem in the Great Depression*. New York: Oxford University Press, 1991.

Greenberg, Clement. "Avant-Garde and Kitch." *Partisan Review* 6,5 (Fall 1939): 34–49.

Greene, Roland. *Post-Petrarchanism: Origin and Innovations of the Western Lyric Sequence*. Princeton: Princeton University Press, 1991.

Guilbaut, Serge. *How New York Stole the Idea of Modern Art: Abstract Expressionism, Freedom and the Cold War*. Chicago: University of Chicago Press, 1983.

Guinn, Bishop I. E. "Arise Ye Garvey Nation." (Broadside) Cincinnati: n.p., 1921.

———. "Our Home in Africa." (Broadside) Cincinnati: n.p., 1921.

Guttman, Allen. "The Brief Embattled Course of Proletarian Poetry." In *Proletarian Writers of the Thirties*, edited by David Madden, (252–269). Carbondale: Southern Illinois University Press, 1968.

Hall, Stuart. "Notes on Deconstructing the 'Popular.'" In *People's History and Socialist Theory*, edited by Raphael Samuel, (227–241). London: Routledge and Kegan Paul, 1981.

Harper, Frances E. W. *Iola Leroy*. 1893. Boston: Beacon Press, 1987.

Harper, Phillip Brian. *Framing the Margins: The Social Logic of Postmodern Culture*. New York: Oxford University Press, 1994.

Harris, Helen C., Lucia Mae Pitts, and Tomi Carolyn Tinsley. *Triad*. Washington D.C.: Plymouth Press, 1945.

Hart, Henry, ed. *The American Writers' Congress*. New York: International Publishers, 1935.

———. *The Writer in the Changing World*. New York: Equinox Cooperative, 1937.

Hatch, James V. *Sorrow Is the Only Faithful One: The Life of Owen Dodson*. Urbana: University of Illinois Press, 1993.

Hatch, James V., Douglas A. M. Ward, and Joe Weixlmann. "The Rungs of a Powerful Long Ladder: An Owen Dodson Bibliography." *Black American Literature Forum* 14,2 (Summer 1980): 60–68.

Hawkins, Walter Everette. *Chords and Discords*. Boston: Gorham Press, 1920.

Hayden, Robert. *Collected Poems*. New York: Liveright, 1985.

———. *Heart-Shape in the Dust*. Detroit: Falcon, 1940.

Hayden, Robert, and Myles O'Higgins. *The Lion and the Archer*. Nashville: Counterpoise, 1948.

Haynes, Jack. "Scottsboro Mass Chant." *The Rebel Poet* 1,10–11–12 (October-November-December 1931): 4.

Haywood, Harry. "Against Bourgeois-Liberal Distortions of Leninism on the Negro Question in the United States." *The Communist* 9 (August 1930): 694–712.

———. *Black Bolshevik: Autobiography of an Afro-American Communist*. Chicago: Liberator, 1978.

———. *Negro Liberation*. New York: International Publishers, 1948.

———. *The Road to Negro Liberation*. New York: Workers' Library Publishers, 1934.

Healey, Dorothy, and Maurice Isserman. *Dorothy Healey Remembers: A Life in the American Communist Party*. New York: Oxford University Press, 1990.

Henderson, Stephen. *Understanding the New Black Poetry: Black Speech and Black Music as Poetic References*. New York: Morrow, 1973.

Hicks, Granville. *The Great Tradition*. New York: MacMillan, 1933.

———. *Part of the Truth*. New York: Harcourt Brace and World, 1965.

———. "Problems of American Fellow Travellers." *International Literature* 3 (July 1933): 106–108.

Hicks, Granville, Michael Gold, Isidor Schneider, Joseph North, Paul Peters, and Alan Calmer, eds. *Proletarian Literature in the United States: An Anthology*. New York: International Publishers, 1935.

Hill, Julious C. *A Song of Magnolia*. Boston: Meador, 1937.

Hill, Robert A., ed. *The FBI's Racon: Racial Conditions in the United States During World War II*. Boston: Northeastern University Press, 1995.

Hoffman, Erwin D. "The Genesis of the Modern Movement for Equal Rights in South Carolina, 1930–1939." In *The Negro in Depression and War: Prelude to Revolution, 1930–1945*, edited by Bernard Sternsher, (193–214). Chicago: Quadrangle, 1969.

Homberger, Eric. *American Writers and Radical Politics, 1900–1939*. New York: St. Martin's, 1986.

Honey, Maureen, ed. *Shadowed Dreams: Women's Poetry of the Harlem Renaissance*. New Brunswick: Rutgers University Press, 1989.

Honey, Michael. "Labor, the Left, and Civil Rights in the South: Memphis during the CIO Era." In *Anti-Communism: The Politics of Manipulation*, edited by Gerald Erickson and Judith Joel, (57–85). Minneapolis: MEP Publications, 1987.

———. *Southern Labor and Black Civil Rights*. Urbana: University of Illinois Press, 1993.

Horne, Frank. *Haverstraw*. London: P. Breman, 1963.

Horne, Gerald. *Black and Red: W. E. B. Du Bois and the Afro-American Response to the Cold War 1944–1963*. Albany: State University of New York Press, 1986.

———. *Black Liberation / Red Scare: Ben Davis and the Communist Party*. Newark: Univeristy of Delaware Press, 1994.

———. *Communist Front?: The Civil Rights Congress, 1946–1956*. Teaneck: Fairleigh Dickinson Univeristy Press, 1988.

———. "The Red and the Black: The Communist Party and African Americans in Historical Perspective." In *New Studies in the Politics and Culture of U.S. Communism*, edited by Michael E. Brown, Randy Martin, Frank Rosengarten, and George Snedeker, (199–238). New York: Monthly Review Press, 1993.

Howe, Irving, and Lewis Coser. *The American Communist Party: A Critical History*. Boston: Beacon, 1957.

Huggins, Nathan I. *Harlem Renaissance*. New York: Oxford University Press, 1971.

Huggins, Nathan I., ed. *Voices from the Harlem Renaissance*. New York: Oxford University Press, 1976.

Hughes, Langston. *A New Song*. New York: International Workers Order, 1938.

———. "Attention Christians" (Broadside containing "Goodbye Christ") Pasadena: n.p., 1940.

———. "August 19th: A Poem for Clarence Norris." (Broadside) Birmingham: Communist Party of Alabama, 1934.

———. *The Best of Simple*. New York: Hill and Wang, 1961.

———. *The Big Sea: an Autobiography*. New York: Knopf, 1940.

———. *The Collected Poems of Langston Hughes*. Edited by Arnold Rampersad and David Roessel. New York: Knopf, 1994.

———. *Dear Lovely Death*. Amenia: Troutbeck Press, 1931.

———. "Don't You Want to Be Free." *One Act Play Magazine* 2 (October 1938): 359–393.

———. *The Dream Keeper and Other Poems*. New York: Knopf, 1932.

———. *Fields of Wonder*. New York: Knopf, 1947.

———. *Fine Clothes to the Jew*. New York: Knopf, 1927.

———. *Freedom's Plow*. New York: Musette Publishers, 1943.

———. *Good Morning Revolution*. Edited by Faith Berry. New York: Citadel Press, 1992.

———. *I Wonder as I Wander*. New York: Rinehart, 1956.

———. *Jim Crow's Last Stand*. Atlanta: Negro Publication Society of America, 1943.

———. *Lament for Dark Peoples and Other Poems*. Amsterdam: H. van Krimpen, 1944.

———. *Langston Hughes and the Chicago Defender: Essays on Race, Politics and Culture, 1942–1962*, edited by Christopher C. De Santis. Urbana: University of Illinois Press, 1995.

———. *Langston Hughes: "I, Too, Am America," an Anthology*. Moscow: Raduga, 1986.

———. *The Langston Hughes Reader: The Selected Writings of Langston Hughes*. New York: George Braziller, 1958.

———. *Montage of a Dream Deferred*. New York: Holt, 1951.

———. *The Negro Mother and other Dramatic Recitations*. New York: Golden Stair, 1931.

———. "The Negro Artist and the Racial Mountain." 1926. In *Voices from the Harlem Renaissance*, edited by Nathan I. Huggins, (305–309). New York: Oxford University Press, 1976.

———. *One Way Ticket*. New York: Knopf, 1949.

———. "Scottsboro Limited." *New Masses* 7 (November 1931): 18–21.

———. *Scottsboro Limited*. New York: Golden Stair, 1932.

———. *Selected Poems of Langston Hughes*. New York: Knopf, 1959.

———. *Shakespeare in Harlem*. New York: Knopf, 1942.

———. "To Negro Writers." In *American Writers' Congress*, edited by Henry Hart, (139–141). New York: International, 1935.

———. *The Ways of White Folks*. New York: Knopf, 1934.

———. *The Weary Blues*. New York: Knopf, 1926.

Hughes, Langston, and Arna Bontemps, eds. *The Poetry of the Negro, 1760–1949*. Garden City, N.Y.: Doubleday, 1949.

Hughes, Langston, and Federico Garcia Lorca. "Deux Poemes par Federico Garcia Lorca and Langston Hughes." *Les Poétes du Monde Défendent le Peuple Espagnol* 3 (n.d.)

Hull, Gloria. *Color, Sex, and Poetry: Three Women Writers of the Harlem Renaissance*. Bloomington: Indiana University Press, 1987.

Hurston, Zora Neale. *Mules and Men*. 1935. Bloomington: Indiana University Press, 1978.

———. *The Sanctified Church*. Berkeley: Turtle Island, 1983.

———. *Their Eyes Were Watching God*. 1937. Champaign: Illinois University Press, 1978.

Hutchinson, Earl Ofari. *Blacks and Reds: Race and Class in Conflict 1919–1990*. East Lansing: Michigan State University Press, 1995.

Hutchinson, George B. *The Harlem Renaissance in Black and White*. Cambridge: Harvard University Press, 1995.

———. "Jean Toomer and the 'New Negroes' of Washington." *American Literature* 63,4 (December 1991): 683–692.

———. "Mediating 'Race' and 'Nation': The Cultural Politics of *The Messenger*." *African American Review* 28,4 (Winter 1994): 531–548.

Huyssen, Andreas. *After the Great Divide: Modernism, Mass Culture, Postmodernism*. Bloomington: Indiana University Press, 1986.

Ickringill, Steve, ed. *Looking Inward, Looking Outward: From the 1930s through the 1940s*. Amsterdam: VU University Press, 1990.

Ickstadt, Heinz, Rob Kroes and Brian Lee, eds. *The Thirties: Politics and Culture in a Time of Broken Dreams*. Amsterdam: Free University Press, 1987.

Irving, Katrina. "Displacing Homosexuality: The Use of Ethnicity in Willa Cather's *My Antonia*." *Modern Fiction Studies* 36,1 (Spring 1990): 91–102.

Iser, Wolfgang. *The Implied Reader: Patterns in Communication in Prose Fiction from Bunyan to Beckett*. Baltimore: Johns Hopkins University Press, 1974.

Isserman, Maurice. *Which Side Are You On?: The American Communist Party during the Second World War*. Middletown, Conn.: Weslyan University Press, 1982

Jackson, Blyden, and Louis Rubin Jr. *Black Poetry in America: Two Essays in Historical Interpretation*. Baton Rouge: Louisiana State University Press, 1974.

James, C. L. R., George Breitman, Edgar Keemer, et al. *Fighting Racism in World War II*. New York: Monad, 1980.

Jameson, Fredric. "Reification and Utopia in Mass Culture." *Social Text* 1 (Winter 1979): 130–148.

Jauss, Hans Robert. "Literary History as a Challenge to Literary Theory." *New Literary History* 2 (Autumn 1970): 7–37.

Jemie, Onwuchekwa. *Langston Hughes: An Introduction to the Poetry*. New York: Columbia University Press, 1976.

Jerome, V. J. "A Negro Mother to Her Child." *The Rebel Poet* 1 (August 1932): 4.

Johanningsmeier, Edward P. *Forging American Communism: The Life of William Z. Foster*. Princeton: Princeton University Press, 1994.

Johnson, Abby Arthur, and Ronald Maberry Johnson. *Propaganda and Aesthetics: The Literary Politics of African-American Magazines in the Twentieth Century*. Amherst: University of Massachusetts Press, 1979.

Johnson, Charles S., ed. *Ebony and Topaz: A Collecteana*. New York: National Urban League, 1927.

Johnson, Daniel M., and Rex R. Campbell. *Black Migration in America: A Social and Demographic History*. Durham: Duke University Press, 1981.

Johnson, Helene. "A Southern Roud." *Fire* 1.1 (November 1926): 17.

Johnson, James Weldon, ed. *The Book of American Negro Poetry*. New York: Harcourt, Brace, 1922, 1931.

———. *God's Trombones*. New York: Viking, 1927.

Jones, Ernest. "Letters from Freckles to Bricktop." *Bronzeman* 3.8 (July 1932): 26.

Jones, Gayl. *Liberating Voices: Oral Tradition in African American Literature*. Cambridge: Harvard University Press, 1991.

Jones, Jacqueline. *Labor of Love, Labor of Sorrow: Black Women, Work, and the Family from Slavery to the Present*. New York: Random House, 1985.

Jones, Kirkland C. *Renaissance Man from Louisiana: A Biography of Arna Wendell Bontemps*. Westport: Greenwood Press, 1992.

Kalaidjian, Walter. *American Culture Between the Wars: Revisionary Modernism and Postmodern Critique*. New York: Columbia University Press, 1993.

———. *Languages of Liberation: The Social Text in Contemporary American Poetry*. New York: Columbia University Press, 1989.

Kanet, Roger E. "The Comintern and the 'Negro Question': Communist Policy in the U.S. and Africa, 1921–1941." *Survey* 19,4 (Autumn 1973): 986–122.

Kaufman, Bob. *Solitudes Crowded with Loneliness*. New York: New Directions, 1965.

Kaye, H. E. "The Negroes and Religion." *Daily Worker* (February 18, 1929): 3.

Kazin, Alfred. *On Native Grounds*. New York: Harcourt, Brace, 1942.

Keeran, Roger. "The Communist Influence on American Labor." In *New Studies in the Politics and Culture of U.S. Communism*, edited by Michael E. Brown, Randy Martin, Frank Rosengarten, and George Snedeker, (163–198). New York: Monthly Review Press, 1993.

———. "National Groups and the Popular Front: The Case of the International Workers Order." *Journal of American Ethnic History* 14,3 (Spring 1995): 23–29.

Keizs, Marcia Veronica. "The Development of a Dialectic: Private and Public Patterns in the Work of Margaret Walker and Gwendolyn Brooks." D.E. diss., Teachers College, Columbia University, 1984.

Kelley, Robin D. G. "'Afric's Sons with Banner Red': African-American Communists and the Politics of Culture, 1919–1934." In *Imagining Home: Class, Culture and Nationalism in the African Diaspora*, edited by Sidney J. Lemelle and Robin D. G. Kelley, (35–54). New York: Verso, 1994.

———. "'Comrades, Praise Gawd for Lenin and Them:' Ideology and Culture Among Black Communists in Alabama 1930–1935." *Science and Society* 52 (Spring 1988): 59–82.

———. *Hammer and Hoe: Alabama Communists During the Great Depression*. Chapel Hill: University of North Carolina Press, 1990.

———. *Race Rebels: Culture, Politics and the Black Working Class*. New York: Macmillan, 1994.

Kenkeleba House. *Charles Alston, Artist and Teacher*. New York: Kenkeleba House, 1990.

Kennedy, William J. *Authorizing Petrarch*. Ithaca: Cornell University Press, 1994.

Kent, George E. *A Life of Gwendolyn Brooks*. Lexington: University of Kentucky Press, 1990.

———. *Blackness and the Adventure of Western Civilization*. Chicago: Third World, 1972.

Kerlin, Robert T., ed. *Negro Poets and Their Poems*. Washington, D.C.: Associated Publishers, 1923.

Kinnemon, Keneth. *The Emergence of Richard Wright*. Urbana: University of Illinois Press, 1972.

———. "Richard Wright, Proletarian Poet." In *Critical Essays on Richard Wright*, edited by Yoshinobu Hakutani, (243–251). Boston: G.K. Hall, 1982.

Kirschke, Amy Helene. *Aaron Douglas: Art, Race and the Harlem Renaissance*. Jackson: University Press of Mississippi, 1995.

Klehr, Harvey. *Communist Cadre*. Stanford: Hoover Institution Press, 1979.

———. *The Heyday of American Communism*. New York: Basic Books, 1984.

Klehr, Harvey, and William Tompson. "Self-Determination in the Black Belt: The Beginning of a Communist Policy." *Labor History* 30 (Summer 1989): 354–366.

Klein, Herbert. "John Henry—'Bad Nigger.'" *Left Front* 1,4 (May-June 1934): 7–9.

Klein, Marcus. *Foreigners: The Making of American Literature 1900–1940*. Chicago: University of Chicago Press, 1981.

Knox, Jean Lindsay. *A Key to Brotherhood*. New York: Paebar, 1932.

Kornbluth, Joyce L. *Rebel Voices: An IWW Anthology*. Ann Arbor: University of Michigan Press, 1968.

Kornweibel, Theodore, Jr. *No Crystal Stair: Black Life and the Messenger 1917–1928*. Westport: Greenwood Press, 1975.

Korstad, Robert, and Nelson Lichtenstein. "Opportunities Found and Lost: Labor, Radicals, and the Early Civil Rights Movement." *Journal of American History* 75,3 (December 1988): 786–812.

Kramer, Aaron. "Remembering Owen Dodson." *Freedomways* 23,4 (Fourth Quarter 1983): 258–269.

Kramer, Victor A., ed. *The Harlem Renaissance Re-Examined*. New York: AMS, 1987.

Kreymborg, Alfred, Lewis Mumford, and Paul Rosenfeld, eds. *The New Caravan*. New York: Macaulay, 1936.

Kruse, William F. "'Prayers at Negro Meetings' in the United States." *Daily Worker* (February 18, 1929): 3.

Kutulas, Judy. "Becoming 'More Liberal': League of American Writers." *Journal of American Culture* 13 (Spring 1990): 71–80.

———. *Long War: The Intellectual People's Front and Anti-Stalinism, 1930–1940*. Durham: Duke University Press, 1995.

Kutzinski, Vera. *Against the American Grain: Myth and History in William Carlos Williams, Jay Wright and Nicolas Guillen*. Baltimore: Johns Hopkins University Press, 1987.

———. "The Distant Closeness of Dancing Doubles: Sterling Brown and William Carlos Williams." *Black American Literature Forum* 16,1 (Spring 1982): 19–25.

Lacey, Candida Ann. "Striking Fictions: Women Writers and the Making of Proletarian Realism." *Women Studies International Forum* 9,4 (1986): 373–384.

Larsen, Nella. *Quicksand and Passing*. New Brunswick: Rutgers University Press, 1986.

Lauter, Paul. "Race and Gender in the Shaping of the American Literary Canon: A Case Study from the Twenties." *Feminist Studies* 9,3 (Fall 1983): 435–463.

Lawrence, Will. "Johnson's Death a Loss to Nation." Crusader News Agency (Week of July 28, 1938): 6.

League of American Writers, the American Artists Congress and the United American Artists, C.I.O. *In Defense of Culture: Official Program of the Fourth American Writers Congress and the Congress of American Artists*. New York: New Union Press, 1941.

League of Professional Groups for Foster and Ford. *Culture and the Crisis*. New York: Workers Library Publishers, 1932.

Lee, Don L. "On *Kaleidoscope* and Robert Hayden." *Negro Digest* 17,3 (January 1968): 51–52, 90–94.

Lenin, V. I. *Selected Works, Volume I.* Moscow: Progress Publishers, 1970.

Le Sueur, Meridel. "Proletarian Literature and the Middle West." In *American Writers Congress*, edited by Henry Hart, (135–138). New York: International, 1935.

Levine, Ira. *Left-Wing Dramatic Theory in the American Theatre.* Ann Arbor: University of Michigan Press, 1985.

Levine, Lawrence W. *Black Culture and Black Consciousness.* New York: Oxford University Press, 1977.

Lewis, David Levering. *When Harlem Was in Vogue.* New York: Knopf, 1981.

Lewis, John. *The Left Book Club: An Historical Record.* London: Victor Gollancz, 1970.

Lieberman, Robbie. *My Song Is My Weapon: People's Songs, American Communism and the Politics of Culture, 1930–1950.* Urbana: University of Illinois Press, 1989.

Lindberg, Kathryne V. "Whose Canon? Gwendolyn Brooks: Founder at the Center of the 'Margins.'" In *Gendered Modernisms: American Women Poets and Their Readers*, edited by Margaret Dickie and Thomas Travisano, (283–311). Philadelphia: University of Pennsylvania Press, 1996.

Lipsitz, George. *Rainbow at Midnight: Labor and Culture in the 1940s.* Urbana: University of Illinois Press, 1994.

Lively, Adam. "Continuity and Radicalism in American Black Nationalist Thought, 1914–1929." *Journal of American Studies* 18,2 (1984): 207–235.

Locke, Alain. "The Eleventh Hour of Nordicism." *Opportunity* 13,1 (January 1935): 8–12.

———. "Sterling Brown: The New Negro Folk Poet." In *Negro*, edited by Nancy Cunard (111–115). London: Wishart and Co, 1934.

———. "We Turn to Prose: A Retrospective of the Literature of the Negro for 1931." *Opportunity* 10,2 (February 1932): 40–44.

Locke, Alain, ed. *Four Negro Poets.* New York: Simon and Schuster. 1927.

———. *The New Negro: An Interpretation.* New York: Boni, 1925.

Lott, Eric. "Double V, Double Time: Bebop's Politics of Style." *Callaloo* 11,3 (Summer 1988): 597–605.

———. *Love and Theft: Blackface Minstrelsy and the American Working Class.* New York: Oxford University Press, 1993.

Lyons, Paul. *Philadelphia Communists, 1936–1956.* Philadelphia: Temple University Press, 1982.

Madden, David. *Proletarian Writers of the 1930s.* Carbondale: Southern Illinois University Press, 1968.

Magidov, R. *Negry Poïyt, Antologija Negritjanskoi Poezii.* New York: Izdanie Soîuza Russkikh Revoljutsionykh Rabotnikov Iskusstva im. Maksima Gorkovo, 1934.

Mangione, Jerre. *The Dream and the Deal: the Federal Writers Project 1935–1943.* Boston: Little, Brown, 1972.

Mariani, Paul. *William Carols Williams: A New World Naked.* New York: McGraw, Hill 1981.

Martin, Charles H. *The Angelo Herndon Case and Southern Justice.* Baton Rouge: Louisiana State University Press, 1976.

Martin, Louis. "Blood, Sweat, and Ink." *Common Ground* 4,2 (Winter 1944): 37–42.

Martin, Tony. *Literary Garveyism: Garvey, Black Arts, and the Harlem Renaissance.* Dover, Mass.: Majority, 1983.

Marx, Karl. *The 18th Brumaire of Louis Bonaparte.* 1852. New York: International, 1963.

Marx, Karl, and Frederick Engels. *The German Ideology.* New York: International, 1970.

Maxwell, William J. "Dialectical Engagements: The 'New Negro' and the Old Left, 1918–1940." Ph.D. diss., Duke University, 1993.

———. "The Proletarian as New Negro: Mike Gold's Harlem Renaissance." In *Radical Revisions: Rereading 1930s Culture*, edited by Bill Mullen and Sherry Linkon, (91–117). Urbana: University of Illinois Press, 1996.

McKay, Claude. *A Long Way from Home*. New York: Lee Furman, 1937.

———. *The Dialect Poetry of Claude McKay*. Plainview: Books for Libraries Press, 1972.

———. *Harlem: Negro Metropolis*. New York: E.P. Dutton, 1940.

———. *Harlem Shadows*. New York: Harcourt, Brace, 1922.

———. *The Negoes in America*. Translated by Robert J. Winter. Edited by Alan L. McLeod. Port Washington: Kennikat, 1979.

McKay, Nellie K. *Jean Toomer, Artist, A Study of his Literary Life and Work, 1894–1936*. Chapel Hill: University of North Carolina Press, 1984.

Meier, August, and Elliott Rudwick. *Black Detroit and the Rise of the UAW*. New York: Oxford University Press, 1979.

Melhem, D. H. *Gwendolyn Brooks: Poetry and the Heroic Voice*. Lexington: University of Kentucky Press, 1987.

Merriweather, Claybron W. *Goober Peas*. Boston: Christopher, 1932.

Michaels, Walter Benn. "American Modernism and the Poetics of Identity." *Modernism/Modernity* 1,1 (January 1994): 38–56.

Miller, James A. "African American Writing of the 1930s: A Prologue." In *Radical Revisions: Rereading 1930s Culture*, edited by Bill Mullen and Sherry Linkon, (78–90). Urbana: University of Illinois Press, 1996.

Miller, R. Baxter, ed. *The Art and Imagination of Langston Hughes*. Lexington: University of Kentucky Press, 1989.

———. *Black Poets Between Worlds, 1940–1960*. Knoxville: University of Tennessee Press, 1986.

Mitford, Jessica. *A Fine Old Conflict*. New York: Knopf, 1977.

Monroe, Harriet. "Poetry of the Left." *Poetry* 48,4 (July 1936): 212–216.

Moore, Richard B. *Richard Moore, Caribbean Militant in Harlem: Collected Writings 1920–1972*. Edited by Joyce Moore Turner and W. Burghardt Turner. Bloomington: Indiana University Press, 1988.

Moorty, Maria, and Gary Smith, eds. *A Life Distilled: Gwendolyn Brooks, Her Poetry and Fiction*. Urbana: University of Illinois Press, 1987.

Mullen, Bill. "Popular Fronts: *Negro Story* Magazine and the Literary Resistance to World War II." *African American Review* 30,1 (Spring 1996): 5–15.

Mullen, Bill, and Sherry Linkon, eds. *Radical Revisions: Rereading 1930s Culture*. Urbana: University of Illinois Press, 1996.

Mullen, Edward J., ed. *Critical Essays on Langston Hughes*. Boston: G.K. Hall, 1986.

Murphy, Beatrice, ed. *Ebony Rhythm: An Anthology of Contemporary Negro Verse*. New York: Exposition, 1949.

———. *Negro Voices*. New York: Henry Harrison, 1938.

Murphy, James F. *The Proletarian Moment: The Controversy Over Leftism in Literature*. Urbana: University of Illinois Press, 1991.

Murray, Albert. *The Omni-Americans*. New York: Outerbridge & Dienstfrey, 1970.

———. *Stomping the Blues*. New York: Da Capo, 1976.

Myers, Constance Ashton. *The Prophet's Army: Trotskyists in American, 1928–1941*. Westport: Greenwood Press, 1977.

Naison, Mark. "Communism and Harlem Intellectuals in the Popular Front: Anti-Fascism and the Politics of Black Culture." *Journal of Ethnic Studies* 9,1 (Spring 1981): 1–25.

———. *Communists in Harlem During the Depression*. Urbana: University of Illinois Press, 1983.

National Negro Congress. "Fight for Negro Rights" (Official Program of the First NNC Convention). Chicago: Stern Printing, 1936.

Nekola, Charlotte, and Paula Rabinowitz, eds. *Writing Red: An Anthology of Women Writers, 1930–1940*. New York: Feminist Press, 1987.

Nelson, Cary. "Poetry Chorus: Dialogic Politics in 1930s Poetry." In *Radical Revisions: Rereading*

1930s Culture, edited by Bill Mullen and Sherry Linkon, (29–59). Urbana: University of Illinois Press, 1996.

———. *Repression and Recovery: Modern American Poetry and the Politics of Cultural Memory.* Madison: University of Wisconsin Press, 1989.

———. "What Happens When We Put the Left at the Center." *American Literature* 66,4 (December 1994): 771–779.

Nelson, Cary, and Jefferson Hendricks. *Edwin Rolfe.* Urbana, University of Illinois Press, 1990.

Nichols, Charles H., ed. *Arna Bontemps-Langston Hughes Letters 1925–1967.* New York: Dodd, 1980.

Nielsen, Aldon Lynn. *Reading Race: White American Poets and the Racial Discourse in the Twentieth Century.* Athens: University of Georgia Press, 1988.

———. *Writing Between the Lines: Race and Intertextuality.* Athens: University of Georgia Press, 1994.

North, Joseph. *No Men Are Strangers.* New York: International Publishers, 1958.

———. "Reportage." In *American Writers' Congress,* edited by Henry Hart, (120–122). New York: International, 1935.

North, Joseph, ed. *New Masses: An Anthology of the Rebel Thirties.* New York: International Publishers, 1969.

North, Michael. *The Dialect of Modernism: Race, Language and Twentieth-Century Literature.* New York: Oxford University Press, 1994.

O'Daniel, Therman B., ed. *Langston Hughes: Black Genius: A Critical Evaluation.* New York: Morrow, 1971.

Oktenberg, Adrian. "From the Bottom Up: Three Radicals of the Thirties." In *A Gift of Tongues: Critical Challenges in Contemporary American Poetry,* edited by Marie Harris and Kathleen Aguero, (83–111). Athens: University of Georgia Press, 1987.

Oliver, Paul. "'Sales Tax On It:' Race Records in the New Deal Years." In *Nothing Else to Fear: New Perspectives on America in the Thirties,* edited by Stephen W. Baskerville and Ralph Willet, (194–213). Manchester: Manchester Univeristy Press, 1985.

———. *The Story of the Blues.* London: Chilton, 1969.

O'Meally, Robert. Review of *The Letters of Carl Van Vechten. Times Literary Supplement* 4461 (September 30, 1988): 1066.

Orens, Michel. "A 'Sixties Saga: The Life and Death of Umbra (Part I)." *Freedomways* 24,3 (Third Quarter, 1984): 167–181.

———. "A 'Sixties Saga: The Life and Death of Umbra (Part II)." *Freedomways* 24,4 (Fourth Quarter, 1984): 237–254.

Ottanelli, Fraser. *Communist Party of the United States: from the Depression to World War II.* New Brunswick: Rutgers University Press, 1991.

Ottley, Roi. *'New World A-Coming.'* 1943. New York: Arno, 1969.

Painter, Nell. *The Narrative of Hosea Hudson, His Life as a Negro Communist in the South.* Cambridge: Harvard University Press, 1979.

Palmer, Robert. *Deep Blues.* New York: Viking, 1981.

Parry, William T. "In the Beginning." *Science and Society* 50,3 (Fall 1986): 321–323.

Patterson, William L. "Awake Negro Poets." *New Masses* 4 (October 1928): 10.

———. *The Man Who Cried Genocide.* New York: International, 1971.

Pearson, Nathan W. *Goin' to Kansas City.* Urbana: University of Illinois Press, 1987.

Peck, David. "'The Tradition of American Revolutionary Literature': The Monthly *New Masses,* 1926–1933." *Science & Society* 42,4 (Winter 1978–1979): 385–409.

Pells, Richard H. *Radical Visions and American Dreams: Culture and Social Thought in the Depression Years.* New York: Harper, 1974.

Penkower, Monty Noam. *The Federal Writers' Project: A Study in Government Patronage of the Arts.* Urbana: University of Illinois Press, 1977.

Perkins, David. *A History of Modern Poetry: From the 1890s to the High Modernist Mode.* Cambridge: Harvard University Press, 1976.

———. *A History of Modern Poetry: Modernism and After.* Cambridge: Harvard University Press, 1987.

———. *Is Literary History Possible?* Baltimore: Johns Hopkins University Press, 1992.

Petry, Ann. "Just Browsing" (Review of *Shakespeare in Harlem*). *People's Voice* 1,9 (April 11, 1942): 25.

Phillips, William. *A Partisan View.* Briarcliff Manor, N.Y.: Stein and Day, 1983.

———. "The New Black Intellectuals." *Partisan Review* 62,3 (1995): 349–350.

Pinsky, Robert. *Poetry and the World.* New York: Ecco Press, 1988.

Platt, Leon. "Smash the Ugly Head of White Chauvinism." *Daily Worker* (May 18, 1932): 4.

Pound, Ezra. "Address to the John Reed Club of Philadelphia." *Left Review* 1,3 (March 1934): 4–5.

———. *Selected Poems of Ezra Pound.* New York: New Directions, 1957.

Rabinowitz, Paula. *Labor and Desire: Women's Revolutionary Fiction in Depression America.* Chapel Hill: University of North Carolina Press, 1991.

———. *They Must Be Represented: The Politics of Documentary.* New York: Verso, 1994.

Rachleff, Melissa. "Photojournalism in Harlem: Morgan and Marvin Smith and the Construction of Power, 1934–1943." In *Visual Journal: Harlem and D.C. in the Thirties and Forties,* edited by Deborah Willis and James Lusaka, (15–33). Washington, D.C.: Smithsonian Institution Press, 1996.

Rampersad, Arnold. "Langston Hughes and his Critics on the Left." *Langston Hughes Review* 5,2 (Fall 1986): 34–40.

———. *The Life of Langston Hughes, Volume I: 1902–1941, I, Too, Sing America.* Oxford: Oxford University Press, 1986.

———. *The Life of Langston Hughes, Volume II: 1941–1967, I Dream a World.* Oxford: Oxford University Press, 1988.

Randall, Dudley. "The Black Aesthetic in the Thirties, Forties and Fifties." In *The Black Aesthetic,* edited by Addison Gayle Jr. 1971. (315–326). New York: Anchor, 1972.

Record, Wilson. *The Negro and the Communist Party.* Chapel Hill: University of North Carolina Press, 1951.

Redding, J. Saunders. "Old Forms, Old Rhythms, Old Words" (Review of *One-Way Ticket*). *Saturday Review of Literature* 32 (January 22, 1949): 24.

———. *To Make a Poet Black.* Chapel Hill: University of North Carolina Press, 1939.

Redmond, Eugene B. *Drumvoices: The Mission of Afro-American Poetry: A Critical History.* Garden City: Anchor, 1976.

Reilly, Charlie. *Conversations with Amiri Baraka.* Jackson: University of Mississippi Press, 1994.

Reilly, John M., ed. *Richard Wright: The Critical Reception.* New York: Burt, Franklin, 1978.

Rolfe, Edwin. *Collected Poems.* Edited by Cary Nelson and Jefferson Hendricks. Urbana: University of Illinois Press, 1993.

Rowell, Charles H. "'Let Me Be with Old Jazzbo:' An Interview with Sterling Brown." *Callaloo* 14,4 (Fall 1991): 795–815.

Rubin, Rachel Lee. "Reading, Writing and the Rackets: Jewish Gangsters in Interwar Russian and American Narrative." Ph.D. diss., Yale University, 1995.

Rubinstein, Annette T. "The Cultural World of the Communist Party: An Historical Overview." In *New Studies in the Politics and Culture of U.S. Communism,* edited by Michael E. Brown, Randy Martin, Frank Rosengarten, and George Snedeker (139–260). New York: Monthly Review Press, 1993.

Rukeyser, Muriel. *U.S. 1*. New York: Covici-Friede, 1938.

Russell, Mariann. *Melvin B. Tolson's Harlem Gallery: A Literary Analysis*. Columbia: University of Missouri Press, 1980.

Russell, Tony. *Blacks, Whites and Blues*. New York: Stein and Day, 1970.

Salzman, Jack, ed. *Years of Protest: A Collection of American Writings of the 1930's*. Indianapolis: Pegasus, 1967.

S. B. "The Movies As a Weapon Against the Working Class." *Daily Worker* (May 20, 1930): 4.

Schucard, Alan R. *Countee Cullen*. Boston: Twayne, 1984.

Schuyler, George S. "The Negro-Art Hokum." *The Nation* 122,3180 (June 16, 1926): 662–663.

Schwartz, Lawrence. *Marxism and Culture: The CPUSA and Aesthetics in the 1930's*. Port Washington: Kennikat, 1980.

Seaver, Edwin, ed. *Cross Section 1944: A Collection of New American Writing*. New York: L. B. Fischer, 1944.

————. *Cross Section 1945: A Collection of New American Writing*. New York: L. B. Fischer, 1945.

Seward, Adrienne Lanier. "Early Black Film and Folk Tradition." Ph.D. diss., Indiana University, 1985.

Shaw, Harry B. *Gwendolyn Brooks*. Boston: Twayne Publishers, 1980.

Sillen, Samuel. "Negro Caravan" (Review). *New Masses* 44,2 (July 14, 1942): 23–24.

Simana, Jabari Onaje. "Black Writers Experience Communism: An Interdisciplinary Study of Imaginative Writers, their Critics and the CPUSA." Ph.D. diss., Emory University, 1978.

Simon. Rita J., ed. *As We Saw the Thirties: Essays on Social and Political Movements of a Decade*. Urbana: University of Illinois Press, 1967.

Singh, Amrijit, William S. Shiver, and Stanley Brodwin, eds. *The Harlem Renaissance: Revaluations*. New York: Garland, 1989.

Sitkoff, Harvard. *A New Deal for Blacks: The Emergence of Civil Rights as a National Issue, Volume I: The Depression Decade*. New York: Oxford University Press, 1978.

Smith, Bernard. *A World Remembered: 1925–1950*. Atlantic Highlands, N.J.: Humanities Press, 1994.

————. Review of *Anthology of Negro Literature* (V. F. Calverton). *New Masses* 5,9 (February 1930): 18.

Smith, Bernard, ed. *The Democratic Spirit: A Collection of American Writings from the Earliest Times to the Present*. New York: Knopf, 1941.

Solbrig, Ingeborg. "Herder and the Harlem Renaissance of Black Culture in America: The Case of the Neger-Idyllen." In *Herder Today: Contributions from the International Herder Conference*, edited by Kurt Mueller-Vollmer (402-414). New York: Walter de Gruyter, 1990.

Sollors, Werner. "A Critique of Pure Pluralism." In *Reconstructing American Literary History*, edited by Sacvan Bercovitch, (250–279). Cambridge: Harvard University Press, 1986.

————. *Beyond Ethnicity: Consent and Descent in American Culture*. Oxford: Oxford University Press, 1986.

Solomon, Mark I. *Red and Black: Communism and Afro-Americans, 1929–1935*. New York: Garland, 1988.

Southern, Eileen. *The Music of Black Americans*. New York: W.W. Norton, 1983.

Sporn, Paul. *Against Itself: The Federal Theater and Writers' Projects in the Midwest*. Detroit: Wayne State University Press, 1995.

Spellman, A. B. *Black Music: Four Lives*. 1966. New York: Schocken, 1970.

Stalin, J. V. *Marxism and the National Question*. 1914. Tirana, Albania: The "8 Nëntori" Publishing House, 1979.

Stanford, Ann Folwell. "Dialectics of Desire: War and the Resistive Voice in Gwendolyn

Brooks's 'Negro Hero' and 'Gay Chaps at the Bar.'" *African-American Review* 26,2 (Summer 1992): 197–211.

Stephanson, Anders. "Interview with Gil Green." In *New Studies in the Politics and Culture of U.S. Communism,* edited by Michael E. Brown, Randy Martin, Frank Rosengarten, and George Snedeker, (307–326). New York: Monthly Review Press, 1993.

———."The CPUSA Conception of the Rooseveltian State, 1933–1939." *Radical History Review* 24 (Fall 1980): 160–176.

Staub, Michael E. *Voices of Persuasion: Politics of Representation in 1930s America.* Cambridge: Cambridge University Press, 1994.

Stepto, Robert B. "I Thought I Knew These People: Richard Wright and the Afro-American Literary Tradition." In *Chant of Saints,* edited by Michael S. Harper and Robert B. Stepto, (195–211). Urbana: University of Illinois Press, 1979.

———. "Sterling A. Brown: Outsider in the Harlem Renaissance." *The Harlem Renaissance: Revolutions,* edited by Amrijit Singh, William S. Shiver, and Stanley Brodwin, (73–81). New York: Garland, 1989.

———. "Teaching Afro-American Literature: Survey or Tradition." In *Afro-American Literature: The Reconstruction of Instruction,* edited by Dexter Miller and Robert B. Stepto, (8–24). New York: Modern Language Association of America, 1979.

Stewart, Donald. *Fighting Words.* New York: Harcourt and Brace, 1940.

Stone, Albert E. *The Return of Nat Turner: History, Literature, and Cultural Politics in Sixties America.* Athens: University of Georgia Press, 1992.

Stott, William. *Documentary Expression and Thirties America.* New York: Oxford University Press, 1973.

Stowe, David. *Swing Change: Big-Band Jazz in New Deal America.* Cambridge: Harvard University Press, 1994.

Streitmatter, Rodger, and Barbara Diggs-Brown. "Marvel Cooke: An African-American Woman Journalist Who Agitated for Racial Reform." *Afro-Americans in New York Life and History* 16,2 (1992): 47–68.

Sullivan, Patricia. *Days of Hope: Race and Democracy in the New Deal Era.* Chapel Hill: University of North Carolina Press, 1996.

Sundquist, Eric J. *To Wake the Nations: Race in the Making of American Literature.* Cambridge: Harvard University Press, 1993.

Susman, Warren I. *Culture as History: The Transformation of American Society in the Twentieth Century.* New York: Pantheon. 1973.

———. "The Thirties." In *The Development of American Culture,* edited by Stanley Cohen and Lorman Ratner, (179–218). Englewood Cliffs, N.J.: Prentice-Hall, 1970.

Susman, Warren I., ed. *Culture and Commitment: 1929–1945.* New York: George Braziller, 1973.

Sylvers, Malcolm. "American Communists in the Popular Front Period: Reorganization or Disorganization?" *Journal of American Studies* 23,3 (1989): 375–393.

Taggard, Genevieve. *May Days: An Anthology of Verse from Masses-Liberator.* New York: Boni and Liveright, 1925.

Talley, Thomas. *Negro Folk Rhymes.* 1922. Knoxville: University of Tennessee Press, 1991.

Taylor, Brennen. "UNIA and American Communism in Conflict, 1917–1928: A Historical Analysis in Negro Social Welfare." Ph.D. diss., University of Pittsburgh, 1983.

Taylor, Clyde. "The Human Image in Sterling Brown's Poetry." *The Black Scholar* 12,2 (March-April 1981): 13–20.

Teres, Harvey. "Remaking Marxist Criticism: *Partisan Review*'s Eliotic Leftism, 1934–1936." *American Literature* 64,4 (March 1992): 127–153.

————. *Renewing the Left: Politics, Imagination, and the New York Intellectuals.* New York: Oxford University Press, 1996.

Thomas, Richard W. *Life for Us Is What We Make It: Building Black Community in Detroit, 1915–1945.* Bloomington: Indiana University Press, 1992

Thurman, Wallace. *Infants of the Spring.* New York: Macauley, 1932.

Tolson, Melvin B. *A Gallery of Harlem Portraits.* Edited by Robert Farnsworth. Columbia: University of Missouri Press, 1979.

————. *Caviar and Cabbage: Selected Columns by Melvin B. Tolson from the "Washington Tribune," 1937–1944.* Columbia: University of Missouri Press, 1982.

————. *Harlem Gallery: Book I, The Curator.* New York: Twayne, 1965.

————. *Libretto for the Republic of Liberia.* New York: Twayne, 1953.

————. *Rendezvous With America.* New York: Dodd, Mead, 1944.

Toomer, Jean. *Cane.* New York: Liveright, 1923.

————. *The Wayward and the Seeking,* edited by Darwin T. Turner. Washington, D.C.: Howard University Press, 1980.

Tracy, Steven. *Langston Hughes and the Blues.* Urbana: University of Illinois Press, 1988.

Trent, Lucia, and Ralph Cheney, eds. *Justice Arraigned.* New York: Dean and Co., 1928.

Trotman, C. James. "The Measured Steps of a Powerful Long Ladder: The Poetry of Owen Dodson." *Obsidian II* 1,1–2 (Spring-Summer 1986): 96–107.

Turner, Lucy Mae. ' *Bout Cullud Folkses.* New York: Henry Harrison, 1938.

Tygiel, Jules. *Baseball's Great Experiment: Jackie Robinson and his Legacy.* New York: Oxford University Press, 1983.

Umbra Poets. "The Umbra Poets." *Mainstream* 16,7 (July 1963): 7–14.

Vendler, Helen. "The Unweary Blues" (Review of *The Collected Poems of Langston Hughes*). *The New Republic* 212,10 (March 6, 1995): 37–42.

Vertov, Dziga. "The Writings of Dziga Vertov." In *Film Culture Reader*, edited by P. Adams Sitney, (353–375). New York: Praeger, 1970.

Wagner, Jean. *Black Poets of the United States: From Paul Laurence Dunbar to Langston Hughes.* Urbana: University of Illinois Press, 1973.

Wald, Alan M. "Culture and Commitment: U.S. Communist Writers Reconsidered." In *New Studies in the Politics and Culture of U.S. Communism,* edited by Michael E. Brown, Randy Martin, Frank Rosengarten, and George Snedeker, (281–306). New York: Monthly Review Press, 1993.

————. "Literary Leftism Reconsidered." *Science and Society* 57,2 (Summer 1993): 214–222.

————. *The New York Intellectuals: The Rise and Fall of the Anti-Stalinist Left from the 1930s to the 1980s.* Chapel Hill: University of North Carolina Press, 1987.

————. *Writing from the Left: New Essays on Radical Culture and Politics.* New York: Verso, 1994.

Walker, Margaret A. *For My People.* New Haven: Yale University Press, 1942.

————. *How I Wrote Jubilee and Other Essays on Life and Literature.* New York: Feminist Press, 1990.

————. "New Poets." *Phylon* 11 (Fall 1950): 345–354.

————. *Richard Wright, Daemonic Genius.* New York: Warner Books, 1988.

————. *This Is My Century: New and Collected Poems.* Athens: University of Georgia Press, 1989.

Walton, Eda Lou. "Nothing New Under the Sun" (Review of *Shakespeare in Harlem*). *New Masses* 43,11 (June 16, 1942): 23.

Warshow, Robert. *The Immediate Experience: Movies, Comics, Theatre and Other Aspects of Popular Culture.* New York: Doubleday, 1962.

Weinstone, William. "Formative Period of CPUSA." *Political Affairs* 48,9–10 (September-October 1969): 7–19.

Werner, Craig. *Playing the Changes: From Afro-Modernism to the Jazz Impulse*. Urbana: University of Illinois Press, 1994.

West, Don. *In a Land of Plenty: A Don West Reader*. Minneapolis: West End Press, 1982.

White, Newman, and Walter Jackson, eds. *An Anthology of Verse by American Negroes*. Durham, N.C.: Trinity College Press, 1924.

Wilcox, Leonard. *V. F. Calverton: Radical in the American Grain*. Philadelphia: Temple University Press, 1992.

Williams, Pontheolla T. *Robert Hayden: A Critical Analysis of His Poetry*. Urbana: University of Illinois Press. 1987.

Williams, Raymond. *Marxism and Literature*. Oxford: Oxford University Press, 1977.

Williams, William Carlos. *The Collected Poems of William Carlos Williams: Volume I, 1909–1939*. New York: New Directions, 1986.

Wilson, Edmund. *The Shores of Light: A Literary Chronicle of the 1920s and 1930s*. New York: Farrar, Strauss, 1952.

Wintz, Cary D. *Black Culture and the Harlem Renaissance*. Houston: Rice University Press, 1988.

Wixson, Douglass. *Worker-Writer in America: Jack Conroy and the Tradition of Midwestern Literary Radicalism, 1898–1990*. Urbana: University of Illinois Press, 1994.

Wolfe, Charles, and Kip Lornell. *The Life and Legend of Leadbelly*. New York: HarperCollins, 1992.

Woods, Gregory. "Gay Re-Readings of the Harlem Renaissance Poets." *Journal of Homosexuality* 25,2–3 (August-September 1993): 127–142.

Wormley, Beatrice F., and Charles W. Carter, eds. *An Anthology of Negro Poetry by Negroes and Others*. Trenton: Works Progress Administration New Jersey, 1930.

Wright, Richard. "Blueprint for Negro Writing." *New Challenge* (Fall 1937): 53–64.

———. *Early Works*. New York: Library of America, 1991.

———. "I Am a Red Slogan." In *The World of Richard Wright*, by Michel Fabré, (236). Jackson: University of Mississippi Press, 1985.

———. "Joe Louis Uncovers Dynamite." In *New Masses: An Anthology of the Rebel Thirties*, edited by Joseph North, (175–179). New York: International.

———. "King Joe." *New Letters* 38,2 (December 1971): 42–45.

———. *Later Works*. New York: Library of America, 1991.

Yoseloff, Thomas, ed. *Seven Poets in Search of an Answer*. New York: Bernard Ackerman, 1944.

Young, James O. *Black Writers of the Thirties*. Baton Rouge: Louisiana State University Press, 1973.

Index